Cw Potter

D0414703

COLONISATION
AND
VETERAN
SETTLEMENT
IN ITALY

COLONISATION
AND
VETERAN
SETTLEMENT
IN ITALY

47–14 B.C.

LAWRENCE KEPPIE

BRITISH SCHOOL AT ROME
1983

Published by
The British School at Rome,
1, Lowther Gardens,
Exhibition Road,
London
SW7 2AA

ISBN 0 904152 06 5

Printed in England by
Stephen Austin and Sons Ltd, Hertford

CONTENTS

MAPS AND PLANS

LIST OF PLATES

INTRODUCTION

Between 47 and 14 B.C., at least 130,000 time-served veterans of the Roman army received land grants in Italy at the hands of Caesar, the Triumvirs or Augustus. The rôle played by veterans in the politics of the times is widely recognised, if differently assessed. However, precise data on the various settlement programmes prove to be elusive, and any account must be pieced together from a combination of random literary, epigraphic and archaeological sources. In the past, the literary record alone has been subjected to close scrutiny. Here, special attention will also be paid to the epigraphic record of settlement, in particular to epitaphs of individual veteran soldiers. In addition, archaeological evidence, both of building work in the colonies and of land measurement in their territories, will be adduced. With careful handling, these ever-expanding bodies of material should serve to deepen our understanding of the impact of veteran settlement on town and countryside alike.

Almost a century has now elapsed since the appearance in the journal *Hermes* for 1883 of Theodor Mommsen's masterly analysis *Die italischen Bürgercolonien von Sulla bis Vespasian*. Very shortly afterwards Ettore Pais published a thoughtful study of colonisation in Italy under the Triumvirs and Augustus in the first volume of the periodical *Museo italiano di Antichità classica*. These two papers (together with Pais' later publications) remain basic reading. Among more recent work, it will be evident how much I owe to the scholarship of Emilio Gabba and Peter Brunt. The latter's *Italian Manpower* (Oxford, 1971) has been a constant companion to my studies. A monograph by Hans-Christian Schneider, *Das Problem der Veteranenversorgung in der späteren römischen Republik* (Bonn, 1977), deals mainly with the legal framework and political background to the settlement programmes of the Late Republic, with little space devoted to the colonies which resulted, or the veterans themselves.

The present book had its origins in a dissertation *Veterans in Italian Society under the Early Principate* submitted in 1971, in part satisfaction of the requirements for the degree of Bachelor of Philosophy in Ancient History at the University of Oxford, under the supervision of Mr. A. N. Sherwin-White. That dissertation served above all as an apprenticeship for a D.Phil. thesis submitted in 1979, on which the following pages are substantially based, except that several chapters, which continued the story of colonisation and official settlement down to the Flavian dynasty and Nerva, have been hived off for separate publication. The thesis was begun during tenure of a Scholarship in Classical Studies in the British School at Rome, from October 1971 until December 1972. I must express my thanks to its Faculty of Archaeology, History and Letters for electing me to the Scholarship. During this lengthy sojourn in Italy, and in the course of several subsequent visits, I was able to travel to all but a handful of the fifty or more towns where veteran settlement took place on a substantial scale in this period, and to see most of the inscriptions which fall to be discussed here. The late John Ward-Perkins, then Director of the School, Anna Fazzari and Tony Luttrell offered advice and practical help, and laboured to secure me admittance to archaeological sites, museums and libraries all over Italy.

A particular word of thanks is due to the directors and staffs of the following institutions: the Museo Campano (Capua), the Museo Nazionale Atestino (Este), the Museo Fiorelli (Lucera), the Museo 'Ala Ponzone' (Cremona), the Museo Civico (Vicenza), the Museo Capitolare (Atri), the Museo del Sannio (Benevento), the Biblioteca Comunale (Tortona) and the Biblioteca Comunale Federiciana (Fano). The local offices of the various Soprintendenze alle Antichità many times proved a fruitful source of information and assistance. My gratitude must go also to the many Italians of all ages, whose genuine interest enlivened long hours of travel, and whose kindness and concern often unbolted doors when all seemed lost, leaving me with a permanent love of their race and country. My own recent participation in joint Italian-British excavations at the Latin colony of Fregellae has extended my awareness of Italian topography and countryside, always to advantage.

Throughout the following pages, Latin forms of town names are employed except that (to obviate confusion) the colonies at Aosta and Turin are referred to by their modern names. In both cases the Latin names *Augusta Praetoria* and *Augusta Taurinorum* constitute the Roman titulature of the town. However, modern geographical names for rivers, mountains, etc. are normally preferred, where these will be more familiar to readers. It is hoped that such inconsistency will not prove too distracting. All dates here are B.C. except where specified to the contrary. The use of Greek in the footnotes and text is deliberately avoided, except where the original wording seems crucial to the understanding of an author's meaning; in such cases, an English translation, or paraphrase, normally accompanies the Greek. The phrases 'post-Philippi colony' and 'post-Actium colony' serve to indicate that the colony was established, or reinforced, in the settlement programmes following immediately upon those battles.

The photographs grouped at the end of the book were taken, or made available by, the Museo Campano, the Museo Nazionale Atestino (through the kindness of Dr. Chieco Bianchi), the Biblioteca Apostolica Vaticana, the Hunter Coin Cabinet, University of Glasgow (through the kindness of Dr. J. D. Bateson), the Ministry of Defence, and the author. Full acknowledgements will be found below each photograph. The maps were prepared by Mr. Dennis Gallagher, and the final draft of the manuscript typed by Mrs. Betty Gardiner.

Among scholars whom I pestered for advice, and whose valuable time I consumed with my pleas, I am glad here to thank Mr. Michael Crawford, Professor Oswald Dilke, the late Mr. Martin Frederiksen, Professor G. D. B. Jones, and Professor John Mann. The examiners of my D.Phil. thesis, Mr. Frank Lepper and Miss Joyce Reynolds, offered many helpful comments. The British School's editor, Professor T. P. Wiseman, and Mr. Michael Crawford, made other valuable suggestions during the preparatory stage for publication, which are gladly incorporated. The task of proof-reading was shared by Professor Anne Robertson and Mr. M. J. Hopkinson.

Above all, however, I owe a special debt to my supervisor, Professor P. A. Brunt, who guided my studies over a period of seven years, and showed kindness and understanding at my often ineffectual progress. His inspiration and example have made no small contribution towards whatever merit the following pages may be found to possess.

LAWRENCE KEPPIE
Hunterian Museum
University of Glasgow

September 1981

ABBREVIATIONS

The abbreviations employed subscribe for the most part to the system offered by *l'Année Philologique*, or are otherwise familiar. The following list comprises some significant variations (mostly where a less terse abbreviation of some Italian periodicals is here preferred) and additions.

ACeSDIR	*Atti del Centro Studi e Documentazione sull'Italia Romana* (Milano-Varese)
ANRW	*Aufstieg und Niedergang der römischen Welt* (Berlin-New York)
Arch.Stor.Parm.	*Archivio Storico per le Provincie Parmensi*
Arch.Stor.Pug.	*Archivio Storico Pugliese*
Ath.Ann.Arch.	*Athens Annals of Archaeology*
Atl.Aereofotografico	*Atlante Aereofotografico delle sedi umane in Italia: parte seconda, le sedi antiche scomparse* (Firenze, 1970)
Att.Ist.Ven.	*Atti dell'Istituto Veneto*
Att.Mem.Soc.Istr.	*Atti e Memorie della Società Istriana*
Boll.Soc.Piem.Arch.	*Bollettino della Società Piemontese di Archeologia*
Boll.Stor.Crem.	*Bollettino Storico Cremonese*
Boll.Stor.Piac.	*Bollettino Storico Piacentino*
EAA	*Enciclopedia dell'Arte Antica classica e orientale*
Epigr.Stud.	*Epigraphische Studien*
Fasti Arch.	*Fasti Archaeologici*
Giorn.It.Fil.	*Giornale Italiano di Filologia*
Mem.Acc.Linc.	*Memorie della classe di scienze morali e storiche dell'Accademia dei Lincei*
Mem.Pont.Acc.	*Memorie della Pontificia Accademia romana di Archeologia*
Quad.Ist.Top.Ant.	*Quaderni dell'Istituto di Topografia Antica dell'Università di Roma*
Rend.Ist.Lomb.	*Rendiconti dell'Istituto Lombardo*
Rend.Acc.Linc.	*Rendiconti della classe di scienze morali, storiche e filologiche dell'Accademia dei Lincei*
Rend.Acc.Nap.	*Rendiconti dell'Accademia di Archeologia, Lettere e Belle Arti di Napoli*
Rend.Pont.Acc.	*Rendiconti della Pontificia Accademia romana di Archeologia*
Riv.Ist.Arch.	*Rivista dell'Istituto nazionale di Archeologia e Storia dell'Arte*
Riv.Stor.Ant.	*Rivista Storica dell'Antichità*

Epigraphic publications and *corpora* have been abbreviated as follows:

AE	*l'Année Épigraphique*

CIL	*Corpus Inscriptionum Latinarum*. Reference to inscriptions published in *CIL* is normally by volume and number only (e.g. X 4866)
EE	*Ephemeris Epigraphica*
EJ²	*Documents illustrating the Reigns of Augustus and Tiberius*, ed. V. Ehrenberg and A.H.M.Jones, revised by D.M.Stockton (Oxford, 1976)
IIt	*Inscriptiones Italiae*
ILLRP	*Inscriptiones Latinae Liberae Rei Publicae*, ed. A.Degrassi (Firenze, 1957 and 1963)
ILP	*Iscrizioni Latine di Paestum*, ed. M.Mello and G.Voza (Napoli, 1968)
ILS	*Inscriptiones Latinae Selectae*, ed. H.Dessau (Berlin, 1892–1916)
MW	*Select Documents of the Principates of the Flavian Emperors*, ed. M.McCrum and A.G.Woodhead (Cambridge, 1961)

SELECT BIBLIOGRAPHY

of works cited by author's name or in a shortened form

Beloch, *It.Bund* — K.J.Beloch, *Der italische Bund unter Roms Hegemonie* (Leipzig, 1880)

Beloch, *RG* — K.J.Beloch, *Römische Geschichte bis zum Beginn der punischen Kriege* (Berlin-Leipzig, 1926)

Blake — M.E.Blake, *Ancient Roman Construction in Italy from the prehistoric Period to Augustus,* vol.i (Washington, 1947)

Blume, *Feldmesser* — F.Blume, K.Lachmann and A.Rudorff, *Die Schriften der römischen Feldmesser* (Berlin, 1848-52), 2 vols.

Botermann — H.Botermann, *Die Soldaten und die römische Politik in der Zeit von Caesars Tod bis zur Begründung des Zweiten Triumvirats* (München, 1968) = *Zetemata* xlvi

Broughton, *MRR* — T.R.S.Broughton, *The Magistrates of the Roman Republic* (New York, 1951-52), 2 vols.

Bruns, *FIRA*[7] — C.Bruns, *Fontes Iuris Romani Antiqui* (Tübingen, 1909)

Brunt, *AL* — P.A.Brunt, 'The Army and the Land in the Roman Revolution', *JRS* lii (1962), 69–86

Brunt, *IM* — P.A.Brunt, *Italian Manpower, 225 B.C.—A.D. 14* (Oxford, 1971)

Castagnoli, *Ricerche* — F.Castagnoli, *Le ricerche sui resti della centuriazione* (Roma, 1958)

Degrassi, *SVA* — E.Degrassi, *Scritti vari di antichità* (Roma-Venezia-Trieste, 1962–71), 4 vols.

Duncan-Jones — R.P.Duncan-Jones, *The Economy of the Roman Empire: Quantitative Studies* (Cambridge, 1974)

Frank, *ESAR* — T.Frank, *An Economic Survey of Ancient Rome,* vol.i (Baltimore, 1933), vol.v (Baltimore, 1940)

Gabba, *Ricerche* — E.Gabba, 'Ricerche sull'esercito professionale romana da Mario ad Augusto', *Athenaeum* xxix (1951), 171–272. Reprinted with corrections and additions, in *Esercito e società nella tarda Repubblica romana* (Firenze, 1973), 47–174 = *Republican Rome: The Army and the Allies* (Oxford, 1976), 20–69

Gabba, *Colonie triumvirali* — E.Gabba, 'Sulle colonie triumvirali di Antonio in Italia', *PdP* viii (1953), 101–110.

Gabba, *Appiani V* — E.Gabba, *Appiani Bellorum Civilium Liber Quintus* (Firenze, 1970)

Galsterer-Kröll, *Beinamen* — B.Galsterer-Kröll, 'Untersuchungen zu den Beinamen der Städte des Imperium Romanum', *Epigr.Stud.* 9 (1972), 44–145

Grant, *FITA* — M.Grant, *From Imperium to Auctoritas* (Cambridge, 1946)

xiii

Harmand   J.Harmand, *L'armée et le soldat à Rome de 107 à 50 avant notre ère* (Paris, 1967).

Harris   W.V.Harris, *Rome in Etruria and Umbria* (Oxford, 1971)

Kornemann   E.Kornemann, art.*Coloniae,* in *RE* IV (1901), cols. 511–88

Levick   B.M.Levick, *Roman Colonies in Southern Asia Minor* (Oxford, 1967)

Mommsen, *Bürgercolonien*   Th.Mommsen, 'Die italischen Bürgercolonien von Sulla bis Vespasian', *Hermes* xviii (1883), 161–213 = *Gesammelte Schriften* (Berlin, 1905–13), V 203–53

Mommsen, *GS*   Th.Mommsen, *Gesammelte Schriften* (Berlin, 1905–13), 8 vols.

Mommsen, *RGDA*   Th.Mommsen, *Res Gestae Divi Augusti,* ed. 2 (Berlin, 1883)

Nissen, *IL*   H.Nissen, *Italische Landeskunde* (Berlin, 1883–1902), 2 vols.

Pais, *Colonie militari*   E.Pais, 'Le colonie militari dedotte in Italia dai Triumviri e da Augusto', *Museo italiano di Antichità classica* i (1884), 33–65

Pais, *Colonizzazione*   E.Pais, *Storia della colonizzazione di Roma antica,* vol.i (Roma, 1923)

Pais, *Serie cronologica*   E.Pais, 'Serie cronologica delle colonie romane e latine dall' età regia fino all'impero', parte seconda, *Rend.Acc.Linc.* ser.6, i (1925), 345–412

Pontiroli, *Catalogo*   G.Pontiroli, *Catalogo della sezione archeologica del museo civico 'Ala Ponzone' di Cremona* (Milano, 1974)

Ritterling, *Legio*   E.Ritterling, art. *Legio,* in *RE* XII.i (1924), ii (1925), cols. 1211–1829

Rostovtzeff, *SEHRE*   M.Rostovtzeff, *The Social and Economic History of the Roman Empire,* 2nd ed., revised by P.M.Fraser (Oxford, 1957), 2 vols.

Salmon   E.T.Salmon, *Roman Colonization under the Republic* (London, 1969)

Schmitthenner   W.C.G.Schmitthenner, *The Armies of the Triumviral Period: a Study of the Origins of the Roman Imperial Legions* (D.Phil. thesis, Oxford, 1958, unpub.)

Schneider, *Veteranenversorgung*   H.-C. Schneider, *Das Problem der Veteranenversorgung in der späteren römischen Republik* (Bonn, 1977)

Schulze, *Eigennamen*   W.Schulze, *Zur Geschichte lateinischer Eigennamen* (Berlin, 1933)

Syme, *RR*   R.Syme, *The Roman Revolution* (Oxford, 1952)

Taylor, *VDRR*   L.R.Taylor, *The Voting Districts of the Roman Republic* (Rome, 1960)

Thomsen, *It.Regions*   R.Thomsen, *The Italic Regions from Augustus to the Lombard Invasion* (København, 1947) = *Classica et Mediaevalia, Dissertationes* no.IV

Toynbee   A.H.Toynbee, *Hannibal's Legacy* (London, 1965),
                           2 vols.
Tozzi   P.Tozzi, *Storia padana antica* (Milano, 1972)
Vittinghoff   F.Vittinghoff, *Römische Kolonisation und Bürger-
                           rechtspolitik unter Caesar und Augustus* (Mainz, 1951)
Wiseman   T.P.Wiseman, *New Men in the Roman Senate,
                           139 B.C.–A.D. 14* (Oxford, 1971)

CHAPTER ONE

THE IDENTIFICATION AND DATING OF COLONIES

1. *The nature of settlement*

For the most part, the time-served veterans of the Roman army discharged between 47 B.C. and 14 B.C. were settled in colonies, that is, they were despatched in often substantial numbers to towns which subsequently bore the title and prefix *colonia*. As will become apparent, in Italy the majority of these colonies were already established townships, some of them *coloniae civium Romanorum*, the rest mostly *municipia*. Only a few were 'new towns' in the modern sense, where the township was itself created from scratch at the moment of settlement. Indeed after Philippi it was the proven prosperity of the towns and the fertility of their territories which led to selection as colonies.

The colony was among the most venerable institutions of the Roman state by which its power in Italy had been extended and consolidated.[1] It also contributed substantially to satisfying the land-hunger of a growing population. By the mid second century B.C., this aspect, and with it the need to resettle the depressed urban and rural poor, had become pre-eminent. It was a natural extension to find in colonisation a convenient vehicle for the settlement of discharged soldiery.

The terms veteran settlement and colonisation were not synonymous in the Late Republic. Caesar's settlement programmes benefited both civilians and military personnel. A small number of colonies founded after Actium received non-military settlers, but none of them (it will be argued here) was in Italy. Conversely, veterans might be sent in groups to *municipia* without altering the title or constitution of the town, forming enclaves or identifiable groupings to which the name *colonia* and its Greek equivalents are sometimes found applied. It will be seen below that the majority of settlements in Italy for Caesar's veterans in 47–44 took this form. So far as can be determined, most (if not all) of the veteran settlements which followed the campaigns of Philippi and of Actium resulted in the formal establishment of colonies, or the refoundation and reinforcement of towns which already possessed that status. It is probable that Augustus later in his reign reverted to the Caesarian practice of despatching veterans in groups to *municipia* without granting colonial charters. The decision on whether to proceed to the formal creation of a colony might not be taken merely, or principally, on the grounds of the number of veterans being despatched, but with an eye to prevailing political circumstances.

The identification of towns which can be counted as colonies of the Caesarian, Triumviral and Augustan ages in Italy does not by itself present a particular problem. Lists drawn up long ago by Mommsen, Pais, Kornemann and Beloch

---

[1] Of the extensive modern literature, mention may be made here of the essays by E. de Ruggiero, *Diz. Epig.* II (1900), *s.v. colonia*, 415–58; E. Kornemann, *RE* IV (1901), *s.v. colonia*, 511–87; also E. T. Salmon, *Roman Colonization under the Republic* (London, 1969).

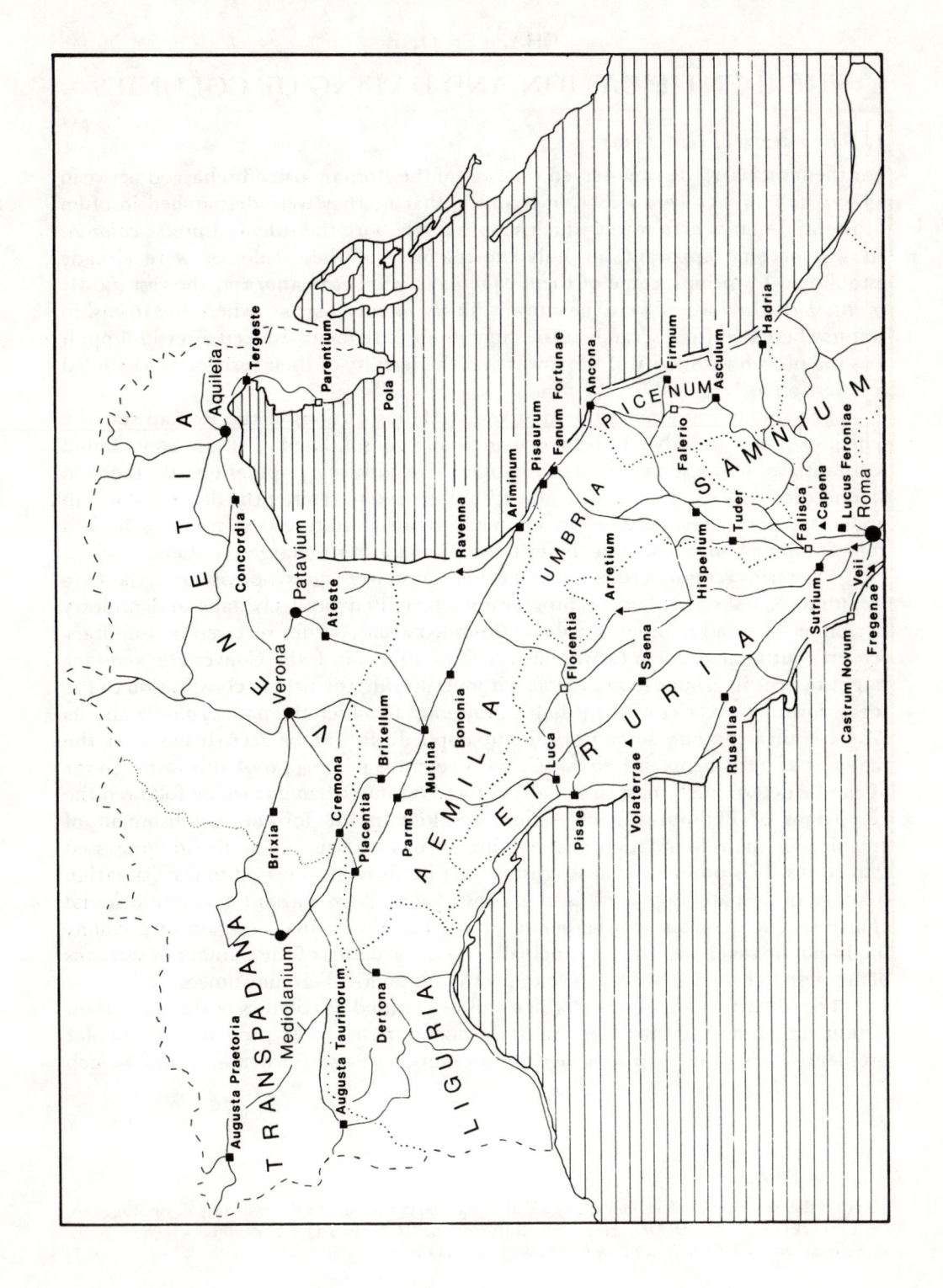

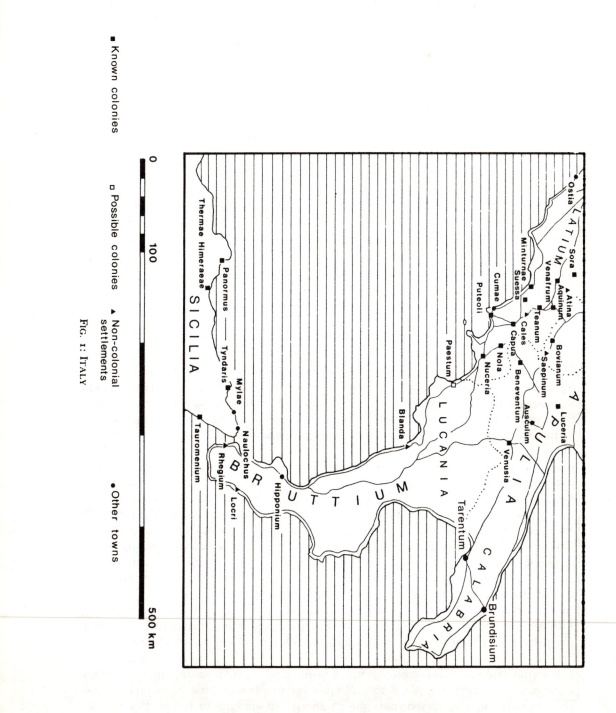

FIG. 1: ITALY

■ Known colonies

□ Possible colonies

▲ Non-colonial settlements

● Other towns

require only slight modification,[2] though some doubts can now be removed and others reinforced with the aid of the enlarged epigraphic corpus now available. More difficult, however, is the allocation of these colonies to particular settlement programmes.

About 50 towns out of a total of over 400 in Italy acquired or reacquired colonial status during the period under review (Fig. 1), and under the Empire they formed an identifiable group which may be distinguished from earlier or later foundations. The most valuable form of attestation is specific reference in one of the mainstream historical writers. The disruption and discontent which followed the settlements after Philippi and is reflected in the pages of the historians, allows the secure identification of many of the post-Philippi foundations. About colonies founded or reinforced in the aftermath of Actium we are less well informed. Epigraphic or literary reference may reveal the title *colonia* borne under the Empire by a town which was previously a *municipium* or *praefectura* or *vicus*. Much less certainly a change in the titles of the chief magistrates at just this time from *IIIIviri* to *IIviri* may be indicative of a foundation, though the mere appearance of *IIviri* at a town can be no guarantee of colonial status.[3]

There are, however, a number of sources, literary and epigraphic, which offer (or seem to offer) a particular guide to the foundations or refoundations of this time, and a proper appreciation of their value is a necessary prelude to an assessment of the various settlement programmes. It is to these that we must first turn. To aid the reader, a check-list of the known or likely colonies established in Italy between 47 and 14 B.C. is appended to this chapter (below, pp. 20-22).

2. *The Elder Pliny*

A major source for the identification of the colonies of the later first century B.C. in Italy has always been the admittedly brief account of the peninsula given by the Elder Pliny in the Third Book of his *Historia Naturalis*.[4] The paragraph with which he introduces the account is of prime importance, in that it describes the procedure he intends to follow:

> *Nunc ambitum eius (sc. Italiae) urbesque enumerabimus, qua in re praefari necessarium est auctorem nos divum Augustum secuturos discriptionemque ab eo factam Italiae totius in regiones XI, sed ordine eo qui litorum tractu fiet; urbium quidem vicinitates oratione utique praepropera servari non posse, itaque interiore in parte digestionem in litteras eiusdem nos secuturos, coloniarum mentione signata quas ille in eo prodidit numero.*

---

[2] Th. Mommsen, *Bürgercolonien* 161-213; E. Pais, *Colonie militari* 33-65; idem, *Serie cronologica* 345-412; Kornemann 524 ff.; K. J. Beloch, *It. Bund* 10; idem, *RG* 510. Note also the list provided by A. Degrassi, in *Guido allo studio della civiltà romana antica* I[2] (Napoli, 1959), 321-27 = *SVA* IV, 87-95.

[3] A. Degrassi, 'Quattuorviri in colonie romane e in municipi retti da duoviri', *Mem.Acc.Linc.* ser. 8, ii (1949), 281-344 = *SVA* I, 99-177.

[4] iii.46. Discussed by Mommsen, *Bürgercolonien* 190; O. Cuntz, *De Augusto Plinii Geographicorum Auctore* (Bonn, 1888); D. Detlefsen, *Die Beschreibung Italiens in der Naturalis Historia des Plinius und ihre Quellen* (Leipzig, 1901); R. Thomsen, *It. Regions* 17; Harris 303-5.

Here Pliny states, in rather compressed fashion, that his source or inspiration will be the deified emperor Augustus, and in his ordering of the material Pliny will follow Augustus' own 'division' (or 'distribution') of Italy into eleven *regiones*. The regions will be described in a sequence determined by their position along the coast. In such a concentrated account, precise geographical interrelationships could not be preserved. Accordingly, the inland communities would be ranged alphabetically within each region; colonies which Augustus 'reported in that total' would receive special mention.

From the listings which follow, it becomes clear that Pliny is amalgamating two principal sources: a 'periplus' account of the coastline which cited many geographical features, and the Augustan work to which he alludes. The account of the coastal features was drawn from Artemidorus or less probably Varro.[5] Professor Rudi Thomsen has shown reason to suppose, in a detailed and exhaustive study, that Pliny's Augustan source was a set of alphabetical lists of Italian communities arranged according to tribes, and that the composition of these lists antedated the 'regionalisation' of Italy.[6] For parts of northern Italy, where Pliny breaks away from the alphabetical sequence, it seems that he drew upon the historian Cornelius Nepos.

Pliny proclaims an intention to name as colonies those towns which Augustus had designated as such in his listing. It quickly becomes apparent that Augustus' choice of colonies was neither a complete catalogue of foundations up to his time nor a disinterested selection. All but a very few of the old colonies of the Republic, and the foundations of the Gracchi and of Sulla, are described as *oppida*, or included in the alphabetical lists without any special designation; the *coloniae* of Pliny's list are those which achieved that status, or had it renewed, from Caesar onwards.

It is not clear from his account how or where Pliny found these colonies designated. Beloch and others believed, almost certainly correctly, that the colonies were included in the alphabetical lists of communities, but were distinguished in some way, perhaps by the employment of a different coloured ink or (if the lists were inscribed on stone or bronze) paint, or by placing the designation C or COL in the margin next to the relevant town.[7]

The towns to which the prefix *colonia* is applied in Pliny's account of Italy are listed below, in the order in which they appear:

---

[5] Detlefsen, op.cit., 4 ff., 30 ff.; K. G. Sallmann, *Die Geographie des älteren Plinius in ihrem Verhältnis zu Varro* (Berlin, 1971), 236.

[6] *It. Regions* 17 ff., 55 ff.

[7] Thomsen, *It. Regions* 43. Note that the use of the abbreviation *C* for *colonia* could account for *Calagna* (= *C Anagnia*) and *Casentium* (repeated from the unidentified *Asetium*) in the *Liber Coloniarum*, 230. 13, 231. 14-15.

	Region	Coastal List	Inland List
IX	Liguria		Dertona
VII	Etruria	Luca	Falisca
		Pisae	Lucus Feroniae
			Rusellae
			Saena
			Sutrium
I	Latium et Campania	Ostia	Capua
		Antium	Aquinum
		Minturnae	Suessa
		Puteoli	Venafrum
			Sora
			Teanum
			Nola
III	Lucania et Bruttii	—	—
II	Apulia et Calabria	—	Luceria
			Venusia
			Beneventum
IV	Samnium	—	Bovianum Vetus et alterum cognomine Undecumanorum
V	Picenum	Hadria	—
		Firmum	
		Asculum	
		Ancona	
VI	Umbria	Fanum Fortunae	Hispellum
		Pisaurum	Tuder
VIII	Aemilia	Ariminum	Bononia
			Brixellum
			Mutina
			Parma
			Placentia
XI	Transpadana	—	Augusta Taurinorum
			Augusta Praetoria
X	Venetia et Histria	Concordia	Cremona
		Aquileia	Brixia
		Tergeste	Ateste
		Pola	

There are surprises both of inclusion and omission in this list, though close inspection of the text and allowance for inexactness of expression have removed some anomalies. Pisae and Firmum can now be seen to have been among Pliny's designated *coloniae*;[8] it will be suggested below (p. 162) that the apparent double reference to towns with the name Bovianum derives from the inclusion in the Augustan alphabetical lists of *Bovianenses Veteres* and *Bovianenses Undecumani*, two categories of citizen members of a single town, Bovianum.

[8] Mommsen, *Bürgercolonien* 191 n. 1, 192 n. 1.

It is likely that the 'periplus' source made mention of at least some of the Republican colonies of Roman or Latin status. Pliny himself, we must suppose, had the task of inserting the colony designation for towns which were described as such in the Augustan source, while removing it from those Republican foundations which had not been reinforced later or had ceased to be colonies after the Social War.[9] The colony prefix was thus, it would seem, added to Ancona, Asculum, Concordia, Fanum, Pisae, Pola and Tergeste. In excising references to Republican colonies, he appears on present evidence to have overlooked three towns: Aquileia, one of the most important and prosperous of the Latin Colonies, and Ostia and Antium, the two most ancient of the *coloniae maritimae*. It was suggested by Beloch that their inclusion here must be proof of refoundation under Augustus, but solid evidence is lacking in all three cases.[10] It may be that Pliny deliberately allowed these conspicuous examples of Republican colonisation to remain in his account. As indicated above, many of the coastal Augustan colonies are correctly designated, but some omissions remain. Nuceria, which we should have expected to find designated as a colony in the Augustan source, is not so described by Pliny, and less certainly he has failed to apply the same designation to Parentium or to retain it for Paestum or Castrum Novum in Etruria.

There are some surprises also in the inland lists, where we should have supposed Pliny's task to be much simpler. In particular he attributes colony rank to Falerii in Etruria (*colonia Falisca*), and to Brixellum, but denies it to Falerio in Picenum, and to Florentia. Mommsen argued that the appearance of Falisca and the absence of Falerio were interrelated; the double error as he saw it could only be explained by the existence of a separate list of colonies on which Pliny misread the unfamiliar Picene Falerio for Etruscan Falerii. However, the entry for *colonia Falisca* is precise and detailed, and heads a list of inland Etruscan colonies, all of which are likely to be genuine foundations of the Augustan age (below, p. 170).

Mommsen suggested that Pliny did not find the colonies marked in Augustus' lists, but had at his disposal what was in fact a separate chronological list of colonies from Augustus' day down to his own time;[11] he noted the appearance among Italian *coloniae* of Teanum (which he believed to be a Claudian colony) and of Bovianum and Luceria (both in his day considered Flavian). However, all three colonies can now be assigned to the later first century B.C. No separate list is required, and its existence seems all but precluded by Pliny's own description of his source.

In his town-lists for the provinces Pliny included *coloniae* of later date down to Vespasian; individual foundations are often ascribed to particular emperors. We might wonder that he did not update his avowedly Augustan list for Italy. The presence of later colonies cannot be wholly discounted: of towns unexpectedly present in Pliny's list, Antium was reinforced by Nero, and Aquileia is sometimes,

[9] From his description of Cosa, it can be deduced that the periplus source referred to the town as *colonia* (iii. 51). Pliny takes care to indicate that the colony at Tarentum no longer existed (iii. 99); Eporedia, a *colonia* of 100 B.C., is described as *oppidum a populo Romano conditum* (iii. 123).

[10] *It. Bund* 5. The description of Ostia as *colonia a Romano rege deducta* (iii. 56) implies knowledge that it was not an Augustan foundation. On Aquileia, A. Degrassi, *Il confine nord-orientale dell'Italia romana* (Bern, 1954), 19.

[11] *Bürgercolonien* 200. For some later reservations, idem, *GS* V(1908), 275.

without much probability, considered a Claudian or Flavian colony. However, given the specific acknowledgment of Augustus as his source for Italian colonies, we might expect any later foundations or reinforcements to be assigned to particular emperors.

A total of 46 towns are given the title *colonia* by Pliny in his account of Italy. The great majority can be confirmed as colonies of the Triumviral or Augustan ages from epigraphic or literary sources. Out of the 46 towns named, at least 41 (perhaps 43) were correctly transferred from his Augustan source. The only clear exceptions seem to be Ostia, Antium and Aquileia. Colonies established as part of the post-Philippi and post-Actium settlement programmes appear, together with Aosta which we know to have been founded in 25 B.C., but there is no clear reference to Caesar's work, either in 59 or in 47–44, when at least two other towns, Calatia and Casilinum, acquired colonial status. Pliny makes no mention of Calatia (unless Mommsen's emendation of Caiatiae for Calatiae is rejected at iii.63); Casilinum is named among towns of Latium and Campania 'which used to exist'.[12] By the time of the compilation of the Augustan lists, it is likely that both towns had in any case ceased to enjoy independent status (below, p. 144). No attempt is made by Pliny to allocate colonies to particular settlement programmes, and it may be that no differentiation was offered in the Augustan source.

Commentators have been concerned to isolate and highlight inaccuracies and omissions in Pliny's choice of colonies. Its fundamental value should not be forgotten. The list must form a starting point in any attempt to identify those towns which acquired or reacquired colonial status in Italy from Caesar onwards. How this group of colonies should be related to the 28 towns which Augustus was later to claim in the *Res Gestae* as particularly his own creations is a question reserved for a later chapter (below, p. 80).

3. *The* Liber Coloniarum

The fragmentary compilation which has come to be somewhat misleadingly entitled the *Liber Coloniarum* probably reached the form in which it survives today in the first half of the fourth century A.D.; the arrangement of entries as reconstructed from the various manuscript sources has been shown to correspond in most sections to the regional division of Italy prevailing at that time. Later in the same century, a number of sections were rewritten and regrouped (the so-called *Liber Coloniarum* II), partly for clearer and fuller presentation, and partly to bring them into line with the revised boundaries of the later fourth century regions.[13]

The *Liber* consists of a lengthy series of entries giving often profuse details of the survey and reallocation of land in central and southern Italy between the age of the Gracchi and the end of the second century A.D. References to assignments made between 47 B.C. and the death of Augustus predominate, but not to the exclusion of earlier or later work.

---

[12] Mommsen, *CIL* X, p. 444; Pliny *NH* iii. 70 (Casilinum).

[13] The texts were assembled by C. Lachmann, in Blume, *Feldmesser* I, 209–62. The fundamental study of its content was by Mommsen, in Blume, *Feldmesser* II, 145–214 = *GS* V 146–99. For a commentary on individual entries, see Pais, *Colonizzazione* 145 ff. Thomsen, *It.Regions* 261 ff. provides a useful if somewhat laboured survey. References throughout are to the edition of Lachmann.

It would appear that this *Liber Coloniarum* had its genesis in a *liber* or *commentarius* drawn up under the direction of Augustus, giving details of land allocation in the *territoria* of Italian towns up to his own time; precisely how the material was arranged is far from clear. The initial heading of the *Liber* as preserved in the *Arcerianus A*, the most reliable manuscript, is *Liber Augusti Caesaris et Neronis;* elsewhere the material is said to have been derived *ex libris Augusti et Neronis Caesarum,* and (twice) *ex commentario Claudi Caesaris.*[14] The first two personages were easily identified by Pais as the emperors Augustus and Nero, who is otherwise known to have been prominent as a coloniser in Italy (below, p. 210).[15] However, Rudi Thomsen has argued forcibly that the Nero of these passages, and of five individual entries in the *Liber* itself, should be identified with Tiberius, Ti. Claudius Nero prior to his adoption by Augustus in A.D. 4. The Drusus Caesar mentioned elsewhere as the instigator of settlement he plausibly identified as Tiberius' brother, despite the difficulties of nomenclature.[16] As Thomsen's conjecture on the identity of Nero (and of Drusus) has important implications for our appreciation of land settlement in Italy in the middle and later years of Augustus, it must be considered in some detail. Five entries in the *Liber* (on the towns of Aesernia, Atina, Beneventum, Castrimoenium, and Saepinum) refer to work carried out by *Nero, Nero Claudius, Nero Claudius Caesar, Nero Caesar* or *imp. Nero Caesar.*[17] This list accords ill with what we know of the emperor Nero's colonising activities in Italy (below, p. 210).

One entry in the *Liber* where activity by *Nero Claudius* is noted is that on Saepinum, which we know to have been a *municipium* under the Empire. Inscriptions reveal that Tiberius and Drusus jointly undertook the construction of a wall-circuit there; the work was completed in A.D. 4/5, but must have been initiated much earlier. Archaeological evidence confirms that a new town-site was laid out at Saepinum during Augustus' reign.[18] Some resurvey of the *ager Saepinas* may well have accompanied this activity. Similarly, it may be possible to link another of the 'Nero' entries (on Atina) with veteran settlement in the middle years of Augustus (below, p. 85).

There could therefore be some reason to think that the *Liber* which we have today is based on a compilation dating to the middle part of Augustus' reign, perhaps drawn up after the settlement programme of 14 B.C., or the conclusion of other schemes in which both Tiberius and Drusus took part.[19] Less certainly the

---

[14] 209. 2–3, 211. 23, 229. 12, 239. 15.

[15] *Colonizzazione* 145.

[16] *It. Regions* 271 ff. (developing a hint by Mommsen, in Blume, *Feldmesser* II, 187. As the elder Drusus was never adopted into the Julian House, he did not acquire the name Caesar. It is much less likely that Tiberius' son, Drusus Julius Caesar, is meant here.

[17] *LC* 260. 7, 230. 4, 231. 6, 233. 5, 237. 15. Drusus Caesar is mentioned in entries on Anagnia (230. 15, repeated at 231. 16), Ulubrae (239. 2) and Cereatae Marianae (233. 8). Work at Cumae and Velitrae (232. 12, 238. 20) is ascribed to 'Claudius Caesar'.

[18] *ILS* 147 = *EJ*[2] 79; P. Braconi et al., *Sepino: archeologia e continuità* (Campobasso, 1979). For an inscription from the forum at Sepino, honouring Drusus, cf. M. G. Malatesta, 'Dedica a Druso Germanico e all' imperatore Nerone', *Arch. Class.* xii (1960), 222–3.

[19] Below, pp. 82 ff. In a list of emperors responsible for land settlement (*Demonstratio Artis Geometricae*, in Blume, *Feldmesser* I, 404), Nero and Nero Caesar are separately listed.

references to *Claudius Caesar* may likewise conceal mention of the young Tiberius.[20]

The material was worked over, and updated, by Balbus, an *agrimensor* in imperial service under Trajan, as part of the growing body of literature on land survey (below, p. 12). That the Augustan *liber* or *commentarius* should have remained a valuable reference work over several centuries should not cause surprise. A number of epitomes or extracts were evidently made of it, varying considerably in comprehensiveness and in fullness of entries, and departing to varying degrees from the format of the original. The fourth century compiler of the *Liber Coloniarum* had before him several epitomes, some very incomplete, from which he endeavoured to produce a single edition, without however any noticeable attempt to recreate the uniformity of presentation which may be presumed in the original.

Modern commentators are wont to extract details from the *Liber* without adequate consideration of the overall layout of the work. The format of individual sections of the *Liber* varies considerably and it seems worthwhile here to indicate briefly the methods of presentation employed. In the short opening section, *provincia Lucania,* all the towns mentioned are described as *pr(a)efecturae,* while in the following *provincia Brittiorum* and *provincia Apulia* each entry is introduced by the word *ager* followed by the adjectival form of the town-name, e.g. *ager Buxentinus.* This formula is employed also in *pars Piceni* and in *provincia Piceni.* Meanwhile, in *provincia Calabria* and *provincia Sicilia,* the entries are introduced by the word *territorium* together with the town-name in its adjectival or substantive form. In *provincia Tuscia* two methods of presentation are employed: in the first part of that section all the towns mentioned are described as *coloniae,* in the second the *ager* formula is used. *Provincia Valeria* likewise combines these two methods of presentation. The employment of such terms as *ager* and *territorium* reflects a preoccupation with what was the basic purpose of the *Liber,* to provide details of resurvey and land assignment within the territory of each town. The most detailed section, that entitled *civitates Campaniae,* consists of a roughly alphabetical list of some 70 entries, most of which begin with the town concerned being expressly described as either *colonia* or *oppidum.* In the list of towns in central Italy which closes the earlier edition of the *Liber,* and in those sections revised in the later fourth century, the *ager* formula is most common, but use is made also of town-names in substantive form, occasionally with the added designation as *colonia, oppidum* or *municipium.*

It need not be doubted that the Augustan *liber* covered the entire peninsula of Italy to the northern frontier; there may have been other lists detailing land assignments in the provinces. However, the *Liber Coloniarum,* as preserved for us in a combination of manuscript sources, deals only with the more southerly of the two Vicarates into which Italy was divided under Diocletian, i.e. *Italia Suburbicaria,* and was thus probably drawn up for particular use within that area.[21]

The value of the *Liber Colonarium* as an independent source for the identification of colonies of any date is thus seriously limited geographically.

[20]Mommsen, followed by Pais, *Colonnizazione* 165, emended *Claudi Caesaris* (211. 23, 229. 10) to *C. Iuli Caesaris,* without good reason. For activity of the emperor Claudius at Cumae, see below, p. 210.

[21]Thomsen, *It. Regions* 291 ff.

Moreover, the compiler frequently chose to work from (or was forced back upon) epitomes employing the designations *ager, territorium,* or (in one section) *praefectura,* [22] whatever the status of the town so described. Equally a section in which all the towns are indiscriminately designated as *coloniae* offers no sure evidence on the status of these towns; thus in *provincia Tuscia,* where the entries themselves are unusually lengthy and apparently authoritative, several colonies, e.g. Tuder and Sutrium, are correctly described, but the same designation is applied to Volaterrae, Capena, Tarquinii and other towns which never possessed that status. Other known colonies within the same geographical area are not mentioned at all. In the section *civitates Campaniae,* all but three genuine colonies of the later first century B.C., for which entries appear, are correctly designated, [23] but a further 15 towns, where a change to colonial status at that time is either unsuspected or directly refutable by literary or epigraphic evidence, are described as *coloniae,* thus undercutting any confidence in the value of the section, as regards the status of individual towns.

Many of the entries, particularly among the *civitates Campaniae,* offer precise details about the author of settlement or its legal framework (e.g. *lege Iulia,* by which Caesarian settlements either in 59–58 or in 47–44 B.C. seem implied), *lege triumvirale* (the post-Philippi settlements), or *lege Augustea* (which in this context probably means settlement from 30 B.C. onwards). This information, where we can check it, is often correct. On the other hand, post-Philippi settlements can be classed as Augustan and *vice versa;* Caesar is credited with colonies we might reasonably regard as post-Philippi or post-Actium. The establishment of the colony at Nola is ascribed to Vespasian, that at Minturnae at first sight to Caligula, with earlier settlement at both towns ignored. The entry on Capua alludes to Caesarian work there in 59 B.C., and includes a title (*Iulia*) which the colony perhaps obtained after Philippi, but there is no reference to the known later work of Octavian, Nero and (as it now appears) Vespasian. Many entries have obviously been abbreviated; others have probably disappeared altogether.

The information collected under Augustus and revised under Trajan suffered such vicissitudes of fortune between its initial assembly and the fourth century that the greatest care must be taken in the use of it. Mommsen's approach was admirably cautious, but his handling of the *Liber's* statements was gently but firmly criticised by his pupil Ettore Pais. [24] The latter appreciated correctly that the *Liber* contained much valuable information for scholars concerned with land settlement in Italy, and tried hard to make sense of individual entries. On several occasions, however, Pais was at fault in his interpretation of the epigraphic evidence adduced in support. In general, Mommsen's careful handling of the data has stood the test of time, and his warning on their inexpert use remains true today. [25]

---

[22] The term *praefectura,* normally applied under the Republic to a partially self-governing community of Roman citizens, seems employed here as a synonym for *ager,* and to lack constitutional overtones. For another, separate, meaning, see below, p. 91.

[23] Exceptions are Venafrum (*oppidum,* 239. 7), Bovianum (*oppidum,* 231. 8) and Suessa (*muro ducta,* 237. 11).

[24] Mommsen, in Blume, *Feldmesser* II, 145 ff.; Pais, *Colonizzazione,* i–vii.

[25] *Bürgercolonien* 174.

For several epitomators, and probably for the fourth century editor, the correct identification of a town as *colonia* was probably of little import, any meaningful distinction between *coloniae* and *municipia* having long since been eroded. It would not be surprising if the epitomators, finding details of land re-allocation in the Augustan or other periods, were happy to assume that promotion to *colonia* was an automatic result of such activity. As we shall see, there are several instances under Caesar, and possibly during Augustus' middle years, where the despatch of *coloni* did not result in the appellation *colonia* being attached to a town, and it could be argued that, when the *Liber* specifies settlement at towns which we know remained *municipia* under the Empire, it is alluding to precisely this form of settlement.

Yet, while we must exercise extreme care in accepting statements in the *Liber* on the status of particular towns, there is much subsidiary information which can be shown to be substantially correct. The technical data (details of the type of centuriation, the shape and placing of terminal stones, the orientation of *cardines* and *decumani*) were essential constituents of each entry, and information of this kind begins to assume greater authority as more and more Roman field-systems are identified on the ground (below, p. 88).

4. *The* Gromatici Veteres

The Liber Coloniarum must not, however, be viewed in isolation, but is best studied in conjunction with a series of fragmentary treatises on land survey, whose authors are known collectively as the *Gromatici Veteres,* from their principal surveying instrument, the *groma*. The earliest and most coherent essays are ascribed to Julius Frontinus (possibly, but not certainly, the Flavian consular and governor of Britain), Balbus, Hyginus, Siculus Flaccus and Hyginus Gromaticus. The aim of each author was to help future *agrimensores* understand and in turn elucidate the intricacies of the land-settlement process. As each author was obliged to discuss and explain a number of set topics, such as *subseciva, limites* and *termini,* and often drew heavily on his predecessors, there is an initial impression of repetitiveness, which the fragmentary condition of the surviving treatises does nothing to dispel.[26]

For the various writers the period down to Augustus' death was the era of colonisation *par excellence,* and it was to his settlement programmes in particular that the *Gromatici* looked for models and inspiration for their work. Almost no distinction was made, or remembered, between settlements of 47–44, 41, 36, 30 B.C. or later. The fact that most of the veteran settlement of the period was complete before Octavian assumed the title Augustus was long forgotten.[27] The extensive alterations in landholding which took place at this time necessitated, it is clear, a full overhaul of existing records. Augustan reorganisation formed the basis for the training of *agrimensores* in future generations.[28]

[26] The treatises were edited, together with the *Liber Coloniarum,* in Blume, *Feldmesser* I; references are to this edition. C. Thulin, *Corpus Agrimensorum Romanorum* I.i (Teubner ed., 1913) has texts of Frontinus and the commentator Agennius, Hyginus, Siculus Flaccus and Hyginus Gromaticus.

[27] For Siculus Flaccus, the *tempora Augusti* might begin in 44 B.C. (162. 10).

[28] Two of the gromatic writers, Balbus and Hyginus Gromaticus, were later believed (wrongly) to have worked in the Augustan period; *LC* 239. 14 with Mommsen, in Blume, *Feldmesser* II, 146; Diehl, *RE* X (1917), 628 ff.

The debt to archival material of the Augustan age is apparent from the treatises themselves. Whenever a name is required for an individual colonist, he is (as might be expected) a Titius or a Seius, but the colony itself is almost invariably a *colonia Iulia* or *colonia Augusta;* occasionally reference is made to a *colonia Augusta Concordia* or *colonia Iulia Constantia,*[29] but even where such specific titulature is employed, there may be no need to assume that a particular colony is envisaged. If the body of settlers requires a collective description, they are designated *Iulienses* or *Augustini,* and at one point where it seemed useful to mention a legion by name, Hyginus Gromaticus selects V *Alaudae,* Caesar's *legio vernacula,* which had ceased to exist when he wrote.[30]

The pages of the *Gromatici* are frequently enlivened by reference to particular colonies. It is noticeable that the great majority were those founded or reinforced after Philippi or Actium. The difficulties in laying out a grid are exemplified by Hispellum, the expropriation of the land of neighbouring towns by Asculum, the naming of *limites* from convenient geographical features by Fanum, and an unusual orientation of *cardo* and *decumanus* by Capua.[31] The exceptional size of some *centuriae* prompts a mention of Cremona, allowance for the changing course of rivers, a reference to Pisaurum, and benefactions of the colony's founder, a mention of Tuder.[32] The appearance among such *exempla* of Republican or provincial colonies is rare.[33] These colonies are cited by the *Gromatici* as convenient stock examples of particular irregularities. There was no need to note those colonies where the laying out of the *centuriae,* or the orientation of the *cardo* and *decumanus,* had presented no problems. We may imagine that every surveyor was acquainted with the unusual orientation of the grid in the *ager Campanus* and the extra-large size of *centuriae* at Cremona (below, p. 90). These towns are well known as colonies and cannot be added to our list.

The illustrations which appear sporadically in the texts of the *Gromatici* were studied by Schulten and Castagnoli, and more recently have been brought back into prominence by Dilke.[34] Those derived from the *Palatinus* are the most valuable (Pl. V, VI). The illustrations may take the form of black and white or coloured representations of towns and their territories, or can be merely line-diagrams. Their independent value must not be exaggerated; most take their information directly

---

[29] 54. 22, 85. 29; Figs. 186–7.

[30] 200. 6.

[31] 179. 10, 18. 11, 30. 2, 29. 5, 170. 16.

[32] 30. 19, 170. 19, 159. 22, 52. 11, 157. 21, 158. 5, 52. 22. Note also references to Suessa (3. 2, 48. 17), Lucus Feroniae (46. 17, 47. 19), Nola (162. 3), and Minturnae (178. 5).

[33] Emerita (22. 8, 51. 21, 171. 6), Ammaedara (180. 2), Terracina (179. 13).

[34] A. Schulten, 'Römische Flurkarten', *Hermes* xxxiii (1898), 534–65; F. Castagnoli, 'Le 'formae' delle colonie romane e le miniature dei codici dei gromatici', *Mem. Acc. Linc.* ser. 7, iv (1943), 83–118; O. A. W. Dilke, 'Maps in the Treatises of Roman Land Surveyors', *Geog. J.* cxxvii (1961), 417–26; idem, 'Illustrations from Roman Surveyors' Manuals', *Imago Mundi* xxi (1967), 9–29. The coloured illustrations in MS *Arcerianus A* can be studied to advantage in H. Butzmann (ed.), *Corpus Agrimensorum Romanorum: Codex Arcerianus A* (Leiden, 1970). The collection of illustrations at the end of Blume, *Feldmesser* I was edited by Rudorff. Thulin (*op. cit.,* n.26) has some additional drawings, from MS P(*alatinus*).

from the accompanying text. Even where a colony is mentioned by name in these illustrations, it is possible in only a few cases to recognise a specific locality.[35] Similarly, walled towns may be called *colonia Iulia* or *colonia Augusta,* but it is rash to see here the abbreviated titulature of a particular town.[36]

The difficulties inherent in attempting to link any illustration too closely with a precise locality are exemplified by two 'maps' which accompany a passage in Hyginus Gromaticus on the importance of accurate and complete records of land allocation. The first shows a wide tract of countryside, with several place-names, and a road network radiating from a *colonia Iulia Augusta.* Castagnoli, following Schulten, showed good reason to identify the colony with Turin, though several of the place-names and geographical features have no factual basis.[37] The second map is broadly similar. Here roads (one a *via consularis*) link a *colonia Augusta* to adjoining towns. Though Castagnoli dismissed this illustration as totally worthless, it may once have depicted an area of the *ager Campanus* around Capua.[38] Nevertheless many inappropriate and imaginary elements have been imported to enhance its value and appearance. Almost certainly many of the illustrations have been distorted in the copying, with non-essential details discarded and precise local allusions diluted, so that they now appear featureless and derivative.

5. *The titles of the colonies*

The giving of fresh names or titles to newly-established or reconstituted townships in Italy and the provinces is a familiar feature of Roman expansion in the Republic. The names might derive from the *nomina* or *cognomina* of supervising magistrates. More frequently the establishment of a town, particularly of a *colonia,* brought about a change to a more auspicious name-form. A large number of the colonies established under Caesar, the Triumvirs and Augustus, in Italy and the provinces, bore honorific titles, at the very least the names *Iulia* or *Augusta,* or both, frequently supplemented by one or more auspicious epithets (see list at p. 20). If the epigraphic corpus had been fuller, we should doubtless have found that almost every colony carried a title which linked it to the *gens Iulia,* and emphasised the continuing bond of *clientela.* A study of the occurrence and use of such titles allows a valuable check on the colony-list culled from the Elder Pliny, provides a rather limited guide to the foundation dates of individual colonies, and permits some appreciation of the continuing pride of the towns over succeeding generations in their acquisition of a new status at this time.[39] Under the Empire there developed,

[35] For Minturnae, see Rudorff Fig. 150 and below, p. 141 (Pl. VI); for Terracina, see Fig. 153 with O. A. W. and M. S. Dilke, 'Terracina and the Pomptine Marshes', *G&R* xxx (1961), 172–8; for Hispellum, see Fig. 152 and below, p. 171 (Pl. V).

[36] As often by Schulten, loc.cit.

[37] Fig. 196b; Castagnoli, loc.cit. (n. 34), 112, no. viii; Dilke, loc.cit. in *Geog. J.* (n. 34), 421, no. 6.

[38] Fig. 197a; Castagnoli, loc.cit., no. ix; Dilke, loc.cit., no. 7. Nearby is a town named Atella, and a *mons sacer* (= Tifata?). The road from Capua to Puteoli was known as *via consularis* (Pliny *NH* xviii. 111), but the term could be applied more generally to any major road of Republican date.

[39] The evidence for titles in Italy was ably discussed by Mommsen, *Bürgercolonien* 180–6. The earlier study by B. Borghesi, under the heading 'Sulla iscrizione perugina della Porta Marzia', in his *Oeuvres Complètes* (Paris, 1869), V, 257–83 retains some value. Titles attached to every kind of provincial township have been assembled in an authoritative study by B. Galsterer-Kröll, 'Untersuchungen zu den Beinamen der Städte des Imperium Romanum', *Epigr. Stud.* 9 (1972), 44–145.

especially in the provinces, an obsession with the acquisition and display of a whole string of splendid titles acquired from successive emperors, often on the flimsiest of pretexts.[40] As will be seen, colonies in Italy were more reticent in the accumulation and use of titles, perhaps through a less pressing need to emphasise their links with Rome.

In the provinces the half century from Caesar's dictatorship was marked by the award of titles to a vast number of newly established or reconstituted townships, whatever the rank of the town or the legal status of its population. Colonies and *municipia* of Roman or Latin status, and peregrine towns, might acquire titles drawn from the nomenclature of the *gens Iulia*. In Italy, however, the occurrence of titles derived from any ruling house is confined almost exclusively to colonies and provides a valuable indicator of status.[41]

Of known or likely Caesarian, Triumviral or Augustan colonies in Italy, at least 21 bore the title Iulia;[42] of these, 8 possessed in addition the title *Augusta*. There are also 5 *coloniae Augustae*, whose titulature cannot yet be shown to include *Iulia*, and a further 25 or more towns for which no such titles are as yet attested. Those known are listed below:

coloniae Iuliae	coloniae Iuliae Augustae	coloniae Augustae
Castrum Novum	Beneventum	Aosta
Concordia	Capua	Ariminum
Fanum	Dertona	Brixia
Hispellum	Parma	Nola
Lucus Feroniae	Puteoli	Placentia
Parentium	Sutrium	
Pisae	Turin	
Pisaurum	Venafrum	
Pola		
Saena		
Sora		
Suessa		
Tuder		

Scholars have sometimes used the terms 'Julian' and 'Augustan' colonies as synonyms for the foundations of the post-Philippi and post-Actium programmes respectively. More judiciously it can be claimed that, while the title *colonia Iulia*

[40] See Dio liv. 23. 8 for a scathing comment on the practices of his own day; F. G. B. Millar, *The Emperor in the Roman World* (London, 1977), 394 ff.

[41] Italian *municipia* for which some titles are attested are (1) Veii, *municipium Augustum Veiens* by A.D. 1; (2) Perusia, which became *Augusta Perusia*, perhaps after rebuilding under Augustus; (3) Rhegium Iulium, so-named probably after settlement there by veterans in 36 B.C. (below, p. 71); (4) Blanda Iulia, possibly so-named for the same reason; (5) Augusta Bagiennorum, a fresh creation after 27 B.C.; (6) Iulium Carnicum and (7) Forum Iulium, both probably so-named by Caesar.

[42] The title *Iulia* has also been claimed for three other colonies, but in each case the (epigraphic) evidence is suspect. For Firmum, VI 1471; for Rusellae, *AE* 1960, 329; for Luca, *AE* 1965, 244, following *Mainzer Zeitschrift* lix (1964), 58. Fig. 190 of the gromatic corpus shows a stretch of ground bounded on one side by *fines Iuliensium* and on the other by *fines Mantuanorum*; the *Iulienses* may thus be colonists at Cremona, which would be identified as *colonia Iulia*, but the evidence should not be pressed.

could have been granted to a town during the lifetime of Caesar, or during the ascendancy of Octavian up to 27 B.C., likely colonies of the age whose titulature includes the name *Augusta* must have received some additional attention or reinforcement from Augustus between 27 B.C. and A.D. 14. This distinction provides a useful starting point for discussion. It will thus be apparent that colonies founded or planned by Caesar (or named in his honour), and those established in the aftermath of Philippi, Naulochus and Actium, i.e. the vast majority of those created within the period under discussion, would be eligible to bear the title *Iulia*. By itself this title provides little assistance on the dating of colonies. It was again in use by Tiberius after A.D. 14[43]; likewise after A.D. 14 the title *Augusta* became common property of the emperors and was awarded to many towns throughout the following three centuries.

In addition to names derived from members of the *gens Iulia*, many colonies founded by the Triumvirs and Augustus in Italy acquired auspicious epithets, in adjectival or less frequently substantive form. *Felix, Firma, Fida, Opsequens, Concordia,* and *Constantia* are epithets found attached to Italian colonies, and reference to the large corpus of provincial evidence on titles borne by communities of all kinds shows a vast array of concepts, personifications and catchwords called into use in this period, to express the hopes, loyalties, aspirations or antecedents of the colonists. Most offer little guidance towards the dating of individual colonies.[44]

The titles were attached to existing town-names. As has already been stated, only a few of the colonies established between 47 and 14 B.C. were 'new towns' on virgin sites, for which a completely new name was necessary or desirable. It is likely that at most four towns in Italy fell into this category: Aosta, Turin, Concordia, and (if the initial foundation was not much earlier) Florentia. In each case the original site name has been suppressed. Pliny's reference to *Pola quae nunc Pietas Iulia* implies an expectation or belief that the old site-name would be (or had been) superseded. In the event the old name survived.[45]

Caesar made use of *Iulia* in the naming of provincial colonies (and other newly constituted communities), but it is not clear that any Italian towns were awarded this title during his lifetime. Several known post-Philippi colonies bore the title *Iulia* under the Empire (Pisaurum, Hispellum, Capua, Beneventum); another (Ariminum) is known later as *colonia Augusta*. It is often assumed that all the post-Philippi colonies acquired the title *Iulia* at once, but we lack contemporary literary or epigraphic evidence. The settlements after Philippi were put into effect by Octavian on behalf of the Triumvirs, but a majority of legionaries owed particular loyalty to Antony (below, p. 62), and their colonies were established by Antony's

[43] Below, p. 209 n. 15. The possible award of *Iulia* at a much later date, to reflect honour on imperial ladies of the Flavian or Severan houses, or on emperors whose names included Iulius (i.e. Maximinus and Philippus) has to be kept in mind.

[44] *Concordia* became part of the titulature of the post-Philippi colonies at Capua and Beneventum, and forms the name of *colonia Iulia Concordia* in Venetia. The concept has been thought particularly relevant for the Triumvirs, but it was important for Caesar also, as S. Weinstock, *Divus Julius* (Oxford, 1971), 260 shows. The ubiquitous title *Felix* offers no sure guide to dating.

[45] *NH* iii. 129. Otherwise Pliny has no mention of the titles awarded to Italian colonies.

nominees and lieutenants. Not every provincial colony of these years acquired the title *Iulia* immediately.[46]

From time to time it has been suggested that the title *Antonia* was attached to or adopted by those colonies in Italy whose members had served under Antony.[47] The whole question of the existence of a category of 'Antonian' legionaries is discussed elsewhere (below, p. 66). It is evident that some veterans retained an affection for Antony up to the Actium campaign. Not unexpectedly, no epigraphic evidence for *coloniae Antoniae* can be adduced, but the adoption of the title *Antonia* in the decade after Philippi, however unofficially and however briefly, cannot be ruled out. In the later 30s B.C. Octavian took pains to win over the 'Antonian' colonies. It would not be surprising if some titles were adjusted or added at this time, with any vestige of Antonian origins or sympathies being suppressed. Later, Augustus could be hailed as the *parens* of Bononia, testimony to his eventual success in winning over that most recalcitrant of Antonian strongholds (below, p. 114).

Colonies founded after Actium may be credited with an immediate award of *Iulia* in honour of Octavian. At a date unknown, but necessarily after 27 B.C., several towns which were already colonies acquired the additional title *Augusta*. At least two of these, Beneventum and Capua, were post-Philippi colonies. Others, which could well belong immediately after Actium, likewise became *Iulia Augusta;* they are Dertona, Parma, Puteoli, Sutrium, Turin and Venafrum.

In addition there are a number of colonies of the post-Philippi and post-Actium schemes which bear the title *Augusta* alone, without *Iulia*. These are Ariminum, Brixia, Nola and (as now attested) Placentia. It is possible that in every case these were *coloniae Iuliae Augustae*, of which the full titles are not yet available. Provincial colonies of Augustus' reign founded after 27 B.C. regularly bear the single title *Augusta*, less frequently *Iulia* and *Augusta* combined.[48] The colony of Aosta, *Augusta Praetoria Salassorum,* is the sole example of a foundation in Italy which we know belongs after 27 B.C., but the possibility that some others of the colonies belong likewise to the middle years of Augustus' reign cannot be ruled out. It is not known why or when the title *Augusta* was awarded to some of the post-Philippi or post-Actium colonies. Some towns may have acquired it to celebrate an Augustan benefaction, yet others might enjoy Augustus' munificence (Fanum is an example), or possess an edifice or public building apparently named in his honour (as Lucus Feroniae) without change in titulature. There must be some suspicion that the title *Augusta* reflects additional veteran settlement between 27 B.C. and 14 A.D.; on the other hand, Augustus may have wished later to link more closely to

[46]Lugdunum was at first *Copia Munatia* (after its founder, Plancus), Celsa had the title *Lepida* (after Lepidus, the Triumvir), and Norba Caesarina acquired part of its name from the proconsul Norbanus Flaccus; Galsterer-Kröll, *Beinamen* nos. 259, 180, 157.

[47]E. Gabba, *Colonie triumvirali* 101 ff. Colonies established or reinforced in the East by Antony in the decade after Philippi may well have had the title *Antonia,* but specific examples are hard to find. The coin legends adduced by Grant, *FITA* 264, 274 f are of uncertain relevance.

[48]Augusta Emerita was founded in 25 B.C., Caesarea Augusta in 19 B.C., Aroe Augusta Patrae perhaps in 16 B.C. Other Spanish colonies with *Augusta* alone (Astigi and Tucci) could date from 14 B.C. However, several of the Pisidian colonies, which seem likely to date after 25 B.C., have *Iulia* as well as *Augusta* in their titulature.

his name certain colonies, perhaps the 28 which he was to claim in the *Res Gestae* as his own foundations (below, p. 80).

At several provincial colonies the numeral of the legion in which the colonists had served before final discharge was included in the titulature.[49] This legionary number can appear in adjectival form (e.g. *Sextanorum, Decumanorum*) or as a sequence of numerals. For the colonists, military service was a unifying factor which they might wish to perpetuate in the colony's titulature. There are no epigraphically attested examples of the use of legionary numerals in Italian colonies where (it could be argued) the colonists felt less need or desire to stress their military origins. The Elder Pliny has a reference to *colonia Bovianum Vetus et alterum cognomine Undecumanorum*. It can hardly be doubted that members of a legion XI were settled at Bovianum, so that they formed a separate and identifiable group in the population of the town (below, p. 163).

Though it might appear that the parading of legionary numerals was eschewed in Italy, some reminiscence might appear of the antecedents and joint experiences of the colonists. The clearest example of this is Aosta (*Augusta Praetoria*) where the latter title must reflect the drawing of the colonists from the ranks of the *cohortes praetoriae*. This same title *Praetoria* (if correctly restored) is attached to the colony of *Iulia Sora* in Latium on an inscription of the mid-third century A.D. The titulature of Suessa and (less certainly) Teanum includes the title *Classica*, which should reflect the military service of legionary colonists at sea with a naval squadron. It may be that titles were transferred from the military unit to the town, but specific links are hard to document.[50] No titles can be adduced which make direct reference to the battles at either Philippi or Actium.

It would be rash to claim that the precise meaning of every title is perfectly understood. Sutrium is described as *colonia Coniuncta Iulia* on an inscription of early imperial (probably Augustan) date, but the nature of the 'union' being commemorated is not known. Similar uncertainty surrounds the title *Civica* attached on two inscriptions to the colony at Brixia. The title has frequently been interpreted as denoting a civilian, i.e. non-military, colony, but it is doubtful if Latin usage would permit this meaning (p. 194).

An interesting sidelight on the use of titles is provided by the practice in some colonies with regard to the naming of freed *servi publici*. In most towns such freedmen were named Publicius, but at Beneventum they received the *nomen* Concordius, at Pisae they received Obsequentius, at Pola they received Pollentius, and at Sullan Pompeii they received Venerius.[51] These *nomina* derive from the known titulature of the colonies. An examination of the names of such *liberti* at

---

[49] Galsterer-Kröll, *Beinamen* 68.

[50] Titles common to legions and to colonies in this period are *Classica, Equestris, Felix, Firma, Gemella/Gemina, Martia* and *Victrix*. It must be very likely that *colonia Iulia Equestris* at Nyon derived its title from the legion X *Equestris*, though it is hard to determine when some of its members could have been settled there, J. G. P. Best, 'Colonia Iulia Equestris and Legio Decima Equestris', *Talanta* iii (1971), 1–10; R. Frei-Stolba, 'Colonia Iulia Equestris', *Historia* xxiii (1974), 439–62. But note p. 40, n. 84 below.

[51] For Concordii at Beneventum, A. Varone, 'Due Umbrii decurioni beneventani', *Rend.Acc. Linc.* ser. 8, xxxi (1976), 103–8; Pollentius, *ILS* 6677; Venerius, X 1013; Obsequentius, *ILS* 6600. For Concordii at Brixellum, below, p. 189.

other colonies could provide evidence for titulature not epigraphically attested. A *libertus* at Hadria is named Venerius, suggesting that the town may have been *colonia Veneria;* at Nuceria, a *libertus* is called Constantius, which should help to confirm *Constantia* as part of the titulature of that town.[52] There may, however, on occasion be some suspicion that such names merely attest the existence of local cults of which the *liberti* had once been temple-slaves.[53]

The evidence of colony-titles provides no small confirmation for the list obtainable from the Elder Pliny. There is, however, a small group of towns whose titles might seem to reflect colonisation at this time, but which are not accorded colony rank by Pliny. These include Parentium in Histria and Castrum Novum in Etruria, both undoubted *coloniae Iuliae;* both towns could have acquired the title much later (below, pp. 202, 172). Cumae has on occasion been considered a *colonia Iulia* on the basis of inscriptions which seem to call it *c(olonia) I(ulia)*. It will, however, be argued (below, p. 149) that these inscriptions are not applicable to Cumae.[54]

In any study of colony titles it must be remembered that the evidence (principally epigraphic) is uneven in distribution, and spread in time over three centuries. The sequence of titles employed may vary from generation to generation, according to the personal whim of the dedicator, the space available on the stone, and the political sensitivities of the day. We can never claim to know the full titulature of a town when only one inscription testifies to any. Less illustrious elements may be omitted, *Iulia* for example in preference for *Augusta,* both in favour of later (and so more recent) awards. Within a single town, habits will vary. By no means every inscription to call a town a *colonia* will give details of the titulature we know it possessed.[55] The record of titles remains disappointingly incomplete.

---

[52] Venerius, IX 5020; Constantius, X 1092 and below, p. 151.

[53] Schulze, *Eigennamen* 482 ff.; L. Halkin, *Les esclaves publics chez les Romains* (Bruxelles, 1897), 146 ff. Colony titles could on occasion have derived from such cults, in accordance with earlier practice.

[54] Abellinum in southern Campania is entitled *colonia Veneria Livia Augusta Alexandriana* on an inscription of A.D. 240 (X 1117). The title *Livia* (if correctly read) might seem a clear reference to the wife of Augusta, named Iulia Augusta after her husband's death. No parallel is available for a colony named in her honour, though the town of Betharamphtha was renamed *Livias* and later *Iulias* by Herodes Antipas; A. H. M. Jones, *The Herods of Judaea* (Oxford, 1938), 177. Caesar employed the names of his relations to eke out the choice of titles for newly established peregrine communities in Spain, and later empresses were so honoured. Livia's prestige was considerable, but no link can be established between her and Abellinum, which on other evidence has been thought to owe its foundation as a colony to Sulla or to the Gracchi; Mommsen, *CIL* X, p. 127; Pais, *Colonizzazione* 203-4. The title *Livia* could indicate a link with the Elder—or Younger—Livius Drusus.

[55] At Beneventum, only three inscriptions out of a total of 13, on which the town is described as *colonia,* give details of titulature. A single Pompeian wax tablet describes Puteoli as *Iulia Augusta* (below, p. 147); a further 20 or more give the place of issue simply as *Puteoli.*

LIST OF KNOWN OR LIKELY COLONIES IN ITALY (47–14 B.C.)

The names of towns which possessed colonial status before 47 B.C. are prefixed by *

town	record of foundation	status in LC	appearance in Pliny's List (P)	titles under the Empire
ANCONA	App. *BC* v.23 (41 B.C.)	—	P	—
AQUINUM	—	colonia	P	—
ARIMINUM	App. *BC* iv.3 (41 B.C.)	—	P	Augusta XI 408, 411 = *ILS* 6656, XII 1529
ASCULUM	—	—	P	—
ATESTE	Sylloge 6 (30 B.C.)	—	P	—
AUGUSTA PRAETORIA	Strabo iv.6.7. Dio liii.25.5 (25 B.C.)	—	—	Praetoria Augusta Pliny *NH* iii.43 Augusta Praetoria Salassorum Pliny *NH* iii.123 Augusta *AE* 1951, 135 etc.
AUGUSTA TAURINORUM	—	—	P	Iulia Augusta V 7047, ?6954, ?7629 Augusta V 6480, 6991 etc. Pliny *NH* iii.123
BENEVENTUM	App. *BC* iv.3 (41 B.C.)	colonia	P	Iulia Concordia *AE* 1969/1970, 167 (A.D. 126) Iulia Concordia Augusta Felix IX 2165, *AE* 1969/1970, 168 (A.D. 197–8) Felix IX 2043, 1645 Concordia *LC* 231.5
BONONIA	—	—	P	—
BOVIANUM	—	oppidum	P	Undecumanorum Pliny *NH* iii.107
BRIXELLUM	—	—	P	—
BRIXIA	—	—	P	Civica Augusta V Sup. 1265 = *ILS* 4190, V 4212 = *ILS* 6714
?*CALATIA	Nic. Dam. F130.136 (45? B.C.)	—	—	—
*CAPUA	App. *BC* iv.3 (41 B.C.)	colonia	P	Iulia Felix Augusta X 3832 = *ILS* 6309 (Antoninus) Concordia Iulia Valeria Felix X 3867 = *ILS* 6310 (Diocletian/Constantine) Felix Augusta …d(?) *EE* VIII 481 Iulia Felix *LC* 231.19

town	record of foundation	status in LC	appearance in Pliny's List (P)	titles under the Empire
?*CASILINUM	Cic. Phil. ii. 102 (44 B.C.)	—	—	—
CASTRUM NOVUM	—	—	—	Iulia XI 3576–8 (Gallienus)
CONCORDIA	—	—	P	Iulia V 1884 = ILS 6689, V 1901, VI 414 = ILS 4315b
CREMONA	Virg. Ecl. ix 28; Hyg. Grom. 170.19 (41 B.C.)	—	P	
*DERTONA	—	—	P	[?Iulia]Augusta V 7376 (22 B.C.) Iulia V 1636 = ILS 1361
FALERIO	—	—	—	—
FALISCA	—	colonia	P	Iunonia LC 217.5
FANUM	—	—	P	Iulia Vitr. de Arch. v.1.6; XI 6232, 6238 = ILS 6651
FIRMUM	—	—	P	(Iulia?) VI 1471
*FLORENTIA	—	colonia	—	—
HADRIA	—	—	P	(Veneria?) IX 5020
HISPELLUM	—	—	P	Iulia XI 5269a, 5278 = ILS 6624 Flavia Constans XI 5283 = ILS 6623
LUCA	—	—	P	(Iulia?) AE 1965, 244
LUCERIA	—	—	P	—
LUCUS FERONIAE	—	—	P	Iulia Felix IX 3938 = ILS 6589, AE 1954, 162; 1962, 86–7
*MINTURNAE	—	colonia	P	—
*MUTINA	—	—	P	—
*NOLA	—	colonia	P	Felix Augusta X 1244 (Diocletian) Augusta LC 236.3
NUCERIA	App. BC iv.3 (41 B.C.)	colonia	P	Constantia IV 3882 = ILS 5146, AE 1926, 122, LC 235.20
PAESTUM	—	—	—	Flavia Prima ILP 86

town	record of foundation	status in LC	appearance in Pliny's List (P)	titles under the Empire
PARENTIUM	—	—	—	Iulia V 335 = ILS 6678
*PARMA	—	—	P	Iulia Augusta XI 1059
PISAE	—	—	P	Opsequens Iulia ILS 139 ;
*PISAURUM	Plut. Ant. 60 (41 B.C.)	—	P	Iulia Felix XI 6335 = ILS 7218 (A.D. 256), XI 6377
PLACENTIA	—	—	P	Augusta AE 1959, 36
POLA	—	—	P	Pietas Iulia Pliny NH iii.129 Iulia Pollentia Herculanea V 8139 = ILS 6676
*PUTEOLI	—	colonia	P	Iulia Augusta (below, p. 147) Claudia Neronensis IV 2152 = ILS 6326, Neronensis Claudia Augusta X 5369 = ILS 6327 Flavia Augusta AE 1941, 72 (A.D. 95); X 1641 (A.D. 139), X 1650–1 (A.D. 196), X 1653 = ILS 480 (A.D. 226), etc. Augusta VIII 7959; LC 236.11
RUSELLAE	—	—	P	(Iulia?) AE 1960, 329
SAENA	—	—	P	Iulia Tab. Peut. III.3
SORA	—	colonia	P	Iulia Pra . . . X 5711 (mid 3rd century)
SUESSA	—	—	P	Iulia Felix Classica X 4832
SUTRIUM	—	colonia	P	Coniunc(ta) Iulia XI 3254 Augusta Iulia XI 3322
TEANUM	—	colonia	P	Cl(assica), or Cl(audia), Firma X 4781, 4799
TERGESTE	—	—	P	—
TUDER	—	colonia	P	Iulia Fida XI 4646 (Trajan) Fida LC 214.3
VENAFRUM	—	oppidum	P	Iulia X 4875 (Augustus) Augusta Iulia X 4894
?*VENUSIA	App. BC iv.3 (41 B.C.)	—	P	—

CHAPTER TWO

SOLDIERS AND VETERANS

1. *The legions from Caesar to Augustus*

There is no need here to describe in detail the composition and disposition of the Roman Army in the last years of the Republic.[1] Nevertheless some appreciation of the history of individual legions may be desirable if any attempt is to be made to establish the date and circumstances of their disbandment and subsequent settlement. However, it must be emphasised at the outset that much remains indistinct and uncertain; many of the legions whose presence is suspected by virtue of the numerical sequence are not attested at all in the literary or epigraphic sources. Other legions, for example those raised by D. Brutus, L. Antonius and Sextus Pompeius, had an ephemeral existence, and have left no sure record.

When Caesar quitted the province of Cisalpina in January 49 B.C., he had at his disposal 10 legions including his own *legio vernacula,* now numbered V, the *Alaudae.* In the following months he built up his forces with startling rapidity, by the enlistment of fresh troops and by the incorporation of deserters from the Pompeian cause. By the eve of Pharsalus it can be estimated that Caesar had under his command over 30 legions, their numbers running in near perfect sequence from I to about XXXIV;[2] this total was further augmented after the battle by the creation of three or four legions out of the survivors of Pompey's forces. In 47, with Pompeian resistance all but crushed, Caesar set in motion the machinery for the disbandment of his veteran Gallic legions (V-XIV), but he did not permit the total number of legions in service to decline; fresh units were created and, if the total under arms at his death has been correctly estimated at 37, we may conclude that the numerical sequence now extended to XXXXVII; the highest numeral attested is XXXXI.[3]

Any attempt to establish the total number of veterans to whom allotments were made after Philippi must be grounded in a study of the legions in existence by Caesar's death. For as our sources clearly state, and recent studies have emphasised, the allotments promised at the Bononia conference were intended for, and distributed to, those men who could claim to have served their full *stipendia,* at this time almost certainly a minimum of six years (below, p. 36). Thus, at the time when

[1] W. C. G. Schmitthenner, *The Armies of the Triumviral Period* (D.Phil. thesis, Oxford, 1958); P. A. Brunt, *Italian Manpower, 225 B.C.–A.D. 14* (Oxford, 1971), 473 ff. Other valuable surveys by A. Von Domaszewski, 'Die Heere der Bürgerkriege in den Jahre 49 bis 42 vor Christus', *NHJ* iv (1894), 157–88; W. Kubitschek, 'Legio', *RE* XII (1924), 1205 ff.; E. Ritterling, ibid. 1211 ff.; H. M. D. Parker, *The Roman Legions* (Oxford, 1928), 47 ff.; A. Passerini, 'Legio', *Diz.Epig.* IV (1949), 549 ff. For sound discussion of detailed points, H. Botermann, *Die Soldaten und die römische Politik in der Zeit von Caesars Tod bis zur Begründung des Zweiten Triumvirats* (Munchen, 1968); I. Hahn, 'Die Legionsorganisation des Zweiten Triumvirats', *Acta Antiqua* xvii (1969), 199–222.

[2] Von Domaszewski, loc.cit.; Schmitthenner 21. By August 49 legion XXX was already in being; *B.Alex.* 53. 5.

[3] Schmitthenner 8 ff.; Brunt, *IM* 474–8. The sequence would go higher if numerals of legions destroyed with Curio in Africa (Caes. *BC* ii. 23, 42), surrendered by C. Antonius in Macedonia (Dio xli. 40; Caes. *BC* iii. 10. 5) or annihilated under C. Calvisius (App. *BC* ii. 60) had not been re-used.

the Triumvirs made public announcement of the rewards which victory would bring
to their time-served soldiers, it may be concluded that these promises were aimed at
those who had entered the ranks not later than the massive expansion of Caesarian
forces in 49; conceivably the offer included all those who had joined the service of
the Dictator before Pharsalus. The rewards were not intended for all those in service
in 43, even if they were to participate in the campaign against the Liberators.

Some 37 legions were under arms in March 44 B.C. Of these, about 28 could lay
claim to an origin in or before 48 B.C. From this number it can be estimated that 18
or 19 were stationed at the time of Philippi in Italy or in provinces controlled by the
Triumvirs (see Table below). The remaining 9 or 10, through the accident of having
been placed by Caesar as garrisons of provinces east of the Adriatic, were necessarily
excluded from the settlement schemes. The identification of legions settled in Italy
after Philippi is thus partly a problem of elimination.

In addition we must not fail to take account of the 'evocate' units, those
Caesarian legions re-formed by Octavian, Lepidus, Ventidius and Antony in 44–43.
The Gallic legions of the Dictator would have faded from the historical record but
for the shortness of life remaining to their former commander; while their vigour
and memories remained fresh, they were natural recipients of attention in the
confusion after his death. Octavian succeeded in re-forming VII and VIII from
colonies at Calatia and Casilinum, Antony re-formed V *Alaudae*, Lepidus benefited
from his proximity to Caesarian colonies in Narbonensis to re-form at least two such
units and perhaps a third,[4] and Ventidius managed to find sufficient veterans of
VII and VIII to form rival legions probably in Campania, and possibly to
reconstitute Caesar's IX somewhere in Picenum (below, p. 54). All these legions
probably survived until Philippi and most (perhaps all) fought in the battle. There is
no sure evidence for the re-forming of the other Caesarian legions (but see below,
p. 57).[5] The actual number of Caesarian veterans in each evocate legion must have
varied and need never have been large. There would be no shortage of recruits to fill
out such illustrious formations; their prestige was enormous and their proclivities a
matter of anxious concern.

The following list comprises those legions thought to be in existence at the time
of Philippi, and which contained a component of men who by 41 B.C. could be
considered veterans. Evocate legions are marked *.

[4] By May 44, Lepidus had been able to increase his forces from four to seven legions. Two of the
new formations were the veteran legions VI and X, recalled from Arelate and Narbo. The third could
have been a fresh levy, but that it too was an evocate legion has been proposed on the basic of Cic. *Fam.*
x. 11. 2 and Suet. *Tib.* 4. 1; neither text is conclusive. Brunt identified the third legion as VII recalled
from Baeterrae (see his *IM* 589), but a more likely candidate, if one is required, would be legion XII.
Antony possessed a XII *Antiqua*, and a veteran of XII *Paterna* is known at Parma (below, p. 189).

[5] Cic. *Ad Brut.* xiv. 3 reports a legion XIV in the army of Brutus, probably in Illyricum. It could
have been a fresh formation rather than Caesar's old legion of that numeral.

Legion	Year of formation	Under control of
I	48	Not known
II	48	Antony
III	48	Antony
IIII *Macedonica*	48	Octavian
V *Alaudae**	51	Antony
VI*	53/52	Lepidus/Antony
VII*	before 58	Octavian
VIII*	before 58	Octavian
VII*	before 58	Ventidius/Antony
VIII*	before 58	Ventidius/Antony
IX*	before 58	Ventidius/Antony
X*	before 58	Lepidus/Antony
XII*?	58	Lepidus/Antony?
XV	49	Not known
XVI	49	Not known
XVII	49	Not known
XVIII	49	Not known
XIX	49	Not known
XX	49	Not known
XXI	49	Not known
XXII	49	Not known
XXIII	49	Not known
XXIV	49	Not known
XXV	49	Not known
XXVI	49	Octavian
XXVII	49	Liberators
XXVIII	49	Pollio/Antony
XXIX	49	Octavian
XXX	49	Pollio/Antony
XXXI	49	Liberators?
XXXII	49	Not known
XXXIII	49	Not known
XXXIV	48?	Not known
XXXV	48?	Antony
XXXVI	48	Liberators
XXXVII	48	Liberators
XXXVIII	48?	Liberators?
legio Martia	49/48?	Octavian

With Octavian	With Antony	With Liberators
IIII *Macedonica*	II	XXVII
Martia	III	XXXI?
VII*	V *Alaudae**	XXXVI
VIII*	VI*	XXXVII
XXVI	VII*	XXXVIII?
XXIX	VIII*	
	IX*	
	X*	
	XII*?	*Unassigned*
	XXVIII	*but probably with Triumvirs*[6]
	XXX	XIX
	XXXV	XXI

[6] Legion XXI was in Spain in 49 B.C., so could have passed from Pollio to Antony. A veteran of XIX is likely to have been settled after Philippi at Nuceria (Sylloge 86); hence it should have belonged to the Triumvirs earlier. Veterans of legions found away from colonies, e.g. XXXIII at (?)Terventum (below, p. 163), could have fought for the Liberators; they would not qualify for land settlement in colonies.

Unassigned

I
XV
XVI
XVII
XVIII
XX
XXII
XXIII
XXIV
XXV
XXXII
XXXIII
XXXIV

The months succeeding Philippi witnessed the dissolution of the majority of legions which had been in service under Caesar. After the battle, those survivors not entitled to discharge, together with some 14,000 men from the defeated army, were placed together into 11 legions, several if not all of which were formed round the most senior and loyal of the existing Triumviral formations. Of these eleven Octavian carried back to Italy only three, which we may easily identify as those most closely allied to him from 44 onwards: IIII *Macedonica*, and the evocate VII and VIII.[7] The process was not so much one of disbandment as of amalgamation, and doubtless it was as fiercely resisted by the legions as it has been by our own armed forces in recent years. The formations which Octavian found remaining in the west—upwards of 20 legions in all—were in the main recruit legions of 45–44 and 44–43.

Schmitthenner has argued with plausibility that the foundations of the imperial numbering system were laid in the months following Octavian's return to Italy, and that the numerical sequence established by 40 was to endure for three centuries.[8] Continuing imperfections in our knowledge preclude certain judgement, but it may be imagined that Octavian took the opportunity to proceed to the creation of a unified numerical sequence. The five legions of Pansa's consular group, raised to fight Antony in 43, would (if still existing) provide a convenient foundation on which to build.[9] The evident grafting on of Antonian legions after Actium to an already complete, or all but complete, numerical sequence supports Schmitthenner's interpretation; the low numerals of Octavian's legions at Perusia in 41 suggest that a new sequence was already in being.[10] Some anomalies remained, largely due to the deliberate retention of existing numerals by legions which had formed part of Octavian's army group before Philippi. For example, two legions with the numeral IIII (*Macedonica* and another at one time called *Sorana*) evidently

[7] Among legions retained by Antony we can securely identify III *Gallica*, V *Alaudae*, VI *Ferrata*, X *Equestris* (see list at p. 28).

[8] Schmitthenner 65 ff.

[9] As members of this group we can tentatively identify II *Sabina*, IV *Sorana*, and V *Urbana*. A legion I established at Luceria, probably after Actium (below, p. 165), may belong to this group.

[10] Legions IV, VI, VII, XI and XII were in his forces at that time; *ILLRP* 1114–1117a; XI 6721[21-22]

retained their identities, and to these we must add XXXXI, raised about 45 B.C., which seems likely to have survived until 36 B.C., and perhaps until Actium.

In general, the period between Perusia and Actium, so far as legionary movements and dispositions are concerned, is one of almost total obscurity. Passing references in Appian provide the information that a legion XIII participated in the military build-up against Sextus Pompeius, and that in 36 B.C. a legion I was temporarily based on Puteoli. An inference from a title later attached to a legion X indicates its involvement in naval exploits of the same year.[11] A list of legions which provided veterans for a single post-Actium colony, Ateste, is the most valuable indicator we have of the composition of Octavian's army in the years immediately before 31 (below, p. 195).

About Antony's legions in the decade up to Actium we are potentially better informed, thanks to a coin issue (whose longevity in circulation he can hardly have foreseen) which commemorated or alleged the existence of 30 legions under Antony's command, numbered in neat and uninterrupted sequence from I to XXX.[12] A separate issue, not necessarily so extensive or complete, commemorated the titles borne by some legions: three are known—XII *Antiqua* (Pl. VIIB), XVII *Classica* and XVIII *Lybica*. It has been doubted whether Antony could have controlled as many as 30 legions, at least concurrently, and indeed the genuineness of the rarely found coins above XXIII is not now accepted.[13] Plutarch states that Antony had 100,000 legionaries at the time of Actium, and later that the land army which surrendered after the battle consisted of 19 legions.[14] Another 20,000 were embarked on his ships, perhaps 4 legions in all.[15] It may have been to the personnel of these 23 legions that he distributed the well-known coin issue. After the battle we are expressly told that he could muster 4 legions in Cyrenaica, of which we can identify one, with the numeral VIII, recorded on what may have been a matching coin series issued by Antony's legate, Pinarius Scarpus.[16]

Octavian's strength at Actium is given by Plutarch as 80,000 men, which (as Brunt has suggested) may represent the paper strength of 16 legions.[17] Eight, *navibus impositae* according to Orosius, participated in the sea-battle.[18] Schmitt-henner and Brunt have argued that the legions which fought on shipboard were drawn from the force enumerated by Plutarch, but it is more likely, given our knowledge of the size of Antony's land army, that they should be added to the total

---

[11] App. *BC* v. 87, v. 112; below, p. 31 (X *Fretensis*).

[12] H. A. Grueber, BMC *Roman Republic* II (London, 1910), 526 ff.; W. W. Tarn, 'Antony's Legions', *CQ* xxvi (1932), 75–81; Brunt, *IM* 505 ff.

[13] M. H. Crawford, *Roman Republican Coinage* (Cambridge, 1974), 539, 552.

[14] *Ant.* 61. 1, 68. 2.

[15] Plut. *Ant.* 64. 1; Dio l. 23.

[16] Oros. vi. 19. 15; E. A. Sydenham, *Roman Republican Coinage* (London, 1952), 200, no. 1279. A coin, having on its obverse what is alleged to be the head of the young Octavian, and on its reverse a lion running right, with the legend LEG XVI, may reflect a matching series issued by Octavian himself. See J. Friedlaender, 'Eine Legionsmünze des Augustus', *Zeitschrift für Numismatik* ii (1875), 117–9; Ritterling 1761; Grant, *FITA* 60 n. 7, 206–10; Grueber, op.cit. (n. 12), 417. But the issue may belong much later, perhaps in A.D. 68–69 (M. H. Crawford, pers.comm.)

[17] Plut. *Ant.* 61; Brunt, *IM* 501.

[18] vi. 19. 8.

supplied by Plutarch.[19] We have no information on the number of legions remaining in the west, but it must be improbable that Octavian's total forces on the eve of Actium amounted to less than 30 legions. All would contain a component of time-served men eligible for discharge. The following table lists those legions thought to be in existence at this time:

with Octavian	with Antony numismatic evidence	other evidence
I	I	
II Sabina	II	
III?	III	III Gallica
IIII Macedonica	IV	III Cyrenaica
IV Sorana	V	IV (Scythica)?
V Urbana	VI	V Alaudae
VI	VII	VI Ferrata
VII Paterna?	VIII	
VIII	IX	
IX	X	X Equestris
X Fretensis	XI	
XI	XII Antiqua	
XII Paterna	XIII	
XIII	XIV	
XIV	XV	
XV	XVI	
XVI?	XVII Classica	
XVII?	XVIII Lybica	
XVIII	XIX	
XIX	XX	
and other numerals up to XXV?	XXI	
	XXII	
XXXXI (if still existing, and others of this group, if any)	XXIII	

After the battle, a week of hard bargaining ensured the incorporation into the victorious army of at least 5 or 6 Antonian legions, with their original numerals, traditions and (in some cases) titles. These were the 'Gallic' legions V *Alaudae*, VI *Ferrata*, and X *Equestris* (hereafter *Gemina*), together with III *Gallica*, III *Cyrenaica*, and perhaps IV (later *Scythica*). There may be other legions (e.g. XII *Fulminata*) which we cannot now recognise as Antonian, and it can be assumed that Antonian soldiers were received individually or in small groups into Octavian's own legions.[20] The legion XXII *Deiotariana* was probably formed now, from remnants of Antony's legions in Cyrenaica, which had once formed part of the private army of King Deiotarus of Galatia.

When faced with epigraphic evidence for individual legions, the scholar's chief problem is to establish to which numerical sequence the legion should be assigned.

---

[19] Schmitthenner 121 ff.; Brunt, *IM* 501.
[20] The title *Gemina* is likely to reflect amalgamation at this time (below, p. 32).

Resplendent titles may be available to assist — or mislead (see below). On the other hand, knowledge of the place of settlement may be helpful towards establishing the legion's likely antecedents. Legions with numerals up to about XXX could belong to Caesar's recruitment programme of 49–48 B.C., to Octavian's reconstituted armies after Philippi, or to Antony. A legion whose numeral is above XXX may be considered a creation of Caesar. In fact, when we are dealing with settlement in Italy, most legions with numerals above XXV seem likely to be his. This conclusion is of some significance: colonies in which veterans of high numbered legions are found should belong after Philippi. A single known exception is legion XXXXI which cannot have reached its colony at Tuder before 36, and perhaps not before Actium, and there may be others in this group.

The legions which emerged from the reorganisation following Actium formed the army of the early Empire. They were quickly embroiled in foreign wars, in Macedonia, Gaul and Spain. The former Antonian legions were in part retained in the east (III *Gallica*, III *Cyrenaica*, VI *Ferrata*, XXII *Deiotariana* and IV *Scythica* — if Antonian), but two (V *Alaudae* and X, now *Gemina*) were transferred to Spain where they were shortly to provide the manpower of a joint colony at *Augusta Emerita* in 25 B.C.[21] The reorganisation of the legions need not have been completed on the very morrow of Actium; it may have taken several years before the size of the permanent standing force of the Empire was calculated and implemented.

2. *The titles of the legions*

The study of the legions in the later first century B.C. is consistently enriched by the developing practice of adoption by the legions of honorific titles. One factor which encouraged their use at this time was undoubtedly the co-existence of legions bearing the same numeral in the armies of Caesar and Pompey, and later in those of Octavian, Antony and Lepidus. Legions raised by Pollio, Sextus Pompeius, Plancus, D. Brutus and L. Antonius necessarily added to the potential confusion.[22]

Titles are found attached to legions in the Triumviral period which fade completely from sight in the generation after Actium. We must not be led necessarily to the conclusion that the legion bearing the title in question had been disbanded. Examination of the titles would suggest that some were not the result of any official awards by Octavian, Antony or other commanders, but arose from spontaneous assumption by the soldiers themselves, in the desire to commemorate some especially notable exploit in which they had recently been involved, or some experience uppermost in the mind of perhaps just one member of the legion when a particular inscription was set up. Several titles can be found attached within a brief space of time to what seems from other evidence to be the same legion.[23]

Caesar pays frequent and sustained tribute to the valour and resolution of his

[21] R. Wiegels, 'Zum Territorium der augusteischen Kolonie Emerita', *Madrider Mitt.* xvii (1974), 258–84.

[22] *Glandes* of the Social War from Asculum may make mention of a *l(egio) Gal(lica)* and a *l(egio) Ibe(rica)*, but the readings are not beyond dispute; IX 6086 [xvii–xviii]; *RE* XII (1925), 1205. The paper by I. Bersanetti, 'Sui sopranomi imperiali variabili delle legioni', *Athenaeum* xxi (1943), 79–91 deals only with the Empire.

[23] For example, II *Sabina* may be the same legion as II *Gallica,* and both identifiable with the later II *Augusta*; V *Urbana* may be identified with V *Gallica,* and both with the imperial V *Macedonica.*

legions but gives no hint that they had been granted or had adopted any titles to commemorate exploits under his command during the Gallic or Civil Wars, though suitable incidents are not hard to find. The title *Equestris,* attested epigraphically for legion X, seems likely to commemorate an incident in 58 B.C., when Caesar, preparing for a parley with Ariovistus, put some legionaries on horseback to act as a bodyguard.[24] Ironically, the earliest literary references concern irregularly constituted units, the *legio Pontica* of D. Calvinus, and the better known *Alaudae,* which, initially lacking numerals by the unusual circumstances of their creation, required special description for ease of identification.[25] During the winter months of 44/43 Cicero makes frequent mention of the *Alaudae,*[26] the most junior of the Dictator's Gallic legions, which perhaps acquired the title on formation in about 51 B.C.[27] Alone of the imperial legions, the V *Alaudae* does not possess as its distinguishing epithet an adjective, but a plural and normally indeclinable noun. Almost contemporary reference is made by Cicero to the *legio Martia* which emerged in 43 as the core of the allegedly pro-senatorial army.[28] In Cicero's preoccupation with the latter title we may see in part an attempt to build up the reputation of one of Octavian's legions to serve as the senatorial counterpart to the *Alaudae,* now the mainstay of Antony's army. If credence can be given to an anecdote in Valerius Maximus, the *legio Martia* already had this title in 46 B.C.; it may then have been acquired at Pharsalus.[29]

A number of imperial legions continued under the Empire to carry titles already attested in the Triumviral period. In other cases the appeal of the title was evidently insufficient to guarantee its survival; the glamour of later achievements supervened. Titles were by no means regularised by Actium. At some date after 27 B.C. the title *Augusta* was awarded to three legions, II, III, and VIII, effectively

---

[24] Caes. *BG* i. 42 and below, p. 32; J. G. P. Best, 'Colonia Iulia Equestris and Legio Decima Equestris', *Talanta* iii (1971), 1–10.

[25] *B.Alex.* 34. 5, 39. 2; Suet. *Caes.* 24. 2. Pompey in 49 gave the title *Gemella* to a legion formed out of two formerly in Cilicia (Caes. *BC* iii. 4. 1).

[26] Cic.*Phil.* i. 20, v. 12, xiii. 3, 37; *Att.* xvi. 8. 2.

[27] The title derives from the Gallic name for a crested lark (Pliny *NH* xi. 121) and should commemorate a bird-crested helmet worn by its founder members. Attaching a bird-crest to a military helmet was familar Celtic practice; O. Klindt-Jensen, *Gundestrupkedelen* (København, 1961), Figs. 10, 40. Compare the story of M. Valerius Corvus (Liv. vii. 26).

[28] Cic.*Phil.* iii. 6, iii. 39, iv. 5, v. 53, xii. 8, xiv. 32; *Fam.* x. 30, x. 33. Cf. App. *BC* iii. 45, 66–7, 93; iv. 115. Ritterling considered the lack of numeral indicative of a *legio vernacula,* but Appian specifically describes its members as Italians; *Legio* 1792 n; App. *BC* iii. 69.

[29] Valerius reports (iii. 2. 19) that during the African campaign, Caesar halted a rout of *legio Martia* by confronting and shaming its *aquilifer* (cf. App. *BC* ii. 95; Plut. *Caes.* 52). Caesar had with him (in addition to his veteran formations) five of the younger legions, of which we can identify four as XXVI, XXVIII, XXIX and XXX (see O.C.T. at *B.Afr.* 60. 2). *Martia* may be one of these, but all are attested epigraphically at colonies without the appearance of this title; in any case *legio Martia* was destroyed at sea in 42, so that none (or very few) of its members would require settlement. *Martia* may then have been the fifth of the younger legions, whose number is not yet known. Schmitthenner suggested that *legio Martia* bore the numeral III, but III *Gallica* (which has the Caesarian bull-emblem) preserves this numeral into the Empire, and fought in these years for Antony. (Schmitthenner 16). If *Martia* was a creation of 49 B.C. (and this must be very likely), it would possess a high numeral, awkward for Cicero to enunciate in its adjectival form alongside legion IIII (*quarta*), hence perhaps a preference for the laudatory epithet.

suppressing whatever inevitably less prestigious titles they had borne before the award. It should not be assumed that these were fresh creations of Augustus' principate.[30]

The title *Classica* attached to a legion indicates that its members served, not necessarily in a purely temporary capacity, as marines aboard one of the squadrons whose activities are frequently alluded to in the pages of Appian and Dio.[31] It would not be surprising if by Actium a substantial number of legions in the armies of Antony and Octavian had seen some service at sea. Antony's army included a legion XVII *Classica,* and a centurion of legion XXX *Classica* was settled at Locri on the toe of Italy (Sylloge 76). A veteran settled at Tuder is described as having served as *centurio legionis XXXXI et centurio classicus* (Sylloge 94). In my view legion XXXXI had at one time acted as a *legio classica,* which service the centurion desired to commemorate (below, p. 176). There is no particular need to see in this title a desire to commemorate participation in a sea battle, whether Mylae, Naulochus or Actium itself.[32] The most famous *legio classica* of the period is X *Fretensis* whose title should emanate from a successful action fought at sea in the *Fretum Siculum,* the Roman 'Channel', presumably during operations against Sextus Pompeius.[33] In Italy the title *Classica* is found attached to the colonies of Suessa and perhaps Teanum (below, p. 139). It seems reasonable to see in this title evidence for settlement of *legiones classicae,* rather than of peregrine sailors as Pais supposed.[34]

A veteran at Parma is described as having served in legion XII *Paterna* (Sylloge 88). It would be natural to interpret this title as indicative of service under the elder Caesar, coupled with loyalty towards his adopted son, Octavian. We lack evidence that Octavian re-formed a legion with this numeral, and the make-up of his forces before Philippi seems well documented. It may be that XII *Paterna* was a 'shadow legion' raised by Octavian after 41 B.C., to match the genuinely Caesarian XII *Antiqua* in Antony's army.[35] Caesar's legions could be thought of as part of

---

[30] If Dio liv. 11. 5 is believed, a *legio Augusta* had gained that title early in Augustus' Principate, only to lose it in 19 B.C.

[31] App. *BC* iv. 65, 86, 99, v. 2, 25, 26, 55–6; Dio xlix. 1. 2; J. Kromayer, 'Die Entwicklung der römischen Flotte . . .', *Philologus* lvi (1897), 426–91. A galley-type was used by Antony on his legionary coin series and other issues.

[32] From the numismatic evidence we know that Antony possessed a XVII *Classica* prior to Actium, but he had (so far as is known) fought no sea battle.

[33] Ritterling, *Legio* 1671; for its naval emblems under the Empire, D. Barag, 'Brick Stamp-Impressions of the Legio X Fretensis', *BJ* clxvii (1967), 244–67.

[34] *Colonizzazione* 268. The title belonged also to the colony of Forum Iulii in Narbonensis, and perhaps to Rusguniae in Mauretania (*AE* 1956, 60). A citizen L. Trebius, described as *miles classicus* and commemorated at Aquileia (V 938), who had served for 17 years *ad latus Augusti,* was perhaps a member of a *legio classica*. Notice also the marine Gabienus whose death is reported by Pliny, *NH* vii. 178.

[35] XII *Paterna* could then be identified with Octavian's XII *Victrix* at Perusia, where Scaeva, probably Caesar's famous centurion, is found serving as its *primus pilus* (*ILLRP* 1116a). Several of Octavian's legions with bull-emblems cannot derive directly from the Dictator's formations (V *Macedonica,* VI *Victrix,* X *Fretensis*). They are best seen as 'shadow legions' raised to match the genuinely Caesarian V *Alaudae,* VI *Ferrata* and X *Equestris,* then serving with Antony. A small core of *evocati* would be sufficient to allege continuity with Caesar.

Octavian's inheritance—they were his father's friends (πατρικοί φίλοι).[36] Appian refers to the efforts of two legions settled at Ancona to effect a reconciliation between the rival leaders of the Caesarian cause: the legions were Καίσαρί τε ὄντα πατρῷα καὶ ἐστρατευμένα Ἀντωνίῳ.[37] Having served both under Octavian's father and under Antony, they were ideally suited to mediate. The Greek πατρικός and πατρῷος translate naturally into the Latin *paternus*. Octavian's legion VII, re-formed in 44, seems also to have borne the title *Paterna,* and the same title was later adopted by two Caesarian colonies in Narbonensis, both perhaps eager to assert their loyalty to Octavian.[38]

Under the Early Empire, three legions, X, XIII and XIV, bore the title *Gemina,* an epithet which, like the epithet *Gemella* attested several times in the Triumviral Age,[39] should indicate that they were formed by the amalgamation of pre-existing units. Nothing is known directly about the antecedents of either XIII *Gemina* or XIV *Gemina,* though Octavian had legions with these numerals already before Actium. However, X *Gemina* appears to be the imperial successor of Caesar's old Tenth. The latter appears as *Veneria* on an epitaph from Cremona (Sylloge 66), and as *Equestris* on two epitaphs from the colony of Patrae, and on a recently published tomb monument at Pompeii.[40] The title *Veneria* commemorates Caesar's alleged descent from Venus, and *Equestris* may derive from an incident involving legion X during the Gallic War (above, p. 30). That X *Equestris* is to be identified with X *Gemina* rather than with the imperial X *Fretensis* seems clear from a partially preserved dedication in the Forum of Augustus at Rome, set up by centurions and other ranks of the legion X *Gemina Equestris,* at a date presumably after 2 B.C.[41] Suetonius records that Augustus disbanded a tenth legion after a mutiny, an event which, if not duplicating the well-known incident of 47 B.C., should belong after Naulochus or Actium, more probably the latter.[42] In the decade after Philippi, the old Tenth Legion served with Antony in the East, and was presumably present in the land army at Actium. After the battle we could imagine some discontent among its members at being excluded (along with other Antonian troops) from settlement in Italy. It may have been now that Octavian substantially recast the legion, with an influx of recruits, or legionaries loyal to himself, so producing the title *Gemina.*[43] The appearance of two titles on the dedication in the Forum of Augustus may indicate a transitional phase, with the old title surviving, but secondary, and soon to fall into oblivion.[44] The process of amalgamation,

[36] Nic.Dam. F130. 115; App. *BC* iii. 42; cf. Cic.*Phil.* iv. 3.

[37] App. *BC* v. 23.

[38] Sylloge 60 (legion VII *Paterna*); Arelate (*Iulia Paterna Sextanorum*), Narbo (*Iulia Paterna Decumanorum*). Legions re-formed from both colonies fought during these years with Antony.

[39] Caes. *BC* iii. 4. 1; XI 7495 (*legio Gemella*); *ILS* 2228 (VI *Gemella*), *AE* 1956, 160 (VIIII *Gemella?*).

[40] III 508; Ph. Petsas, 'A new Latin Inscription from Patras', *Ath.Ann.Arch.* iv (1971), 112–5; P. Castrén, 'About the *legio X Equestris*', *Arctos* viii (1974), 5–7.

[41] *NS* 1933, 463 = *AE* 1934, 152. The wording of the inscription is curious, and may not yet have been correctly interpreted in all its aspects.

[42] *Aug.* 24. R. Syme, 'Some Notes on the Legions under Augustus', *JRS* xxiii (1933), 14–33.

[43] For an excellent survey of the evidence for X *Equestris* and an attempt to reconstruct its history, R. Frei-Stolba, 'Legio X Equestris', *Talanta* x–xi (1978–79), 44–61.

[44] It is the only legion of the Civil War period to bear two titles on the same inscription.

producing legions called *Gemina*, is specifically ascribed to Octavian by Dio Cassius.[45]

Yet no legion of the Empire is known to have adopted as its permanent epithet a title which commemorates specifically the battles of the Civil Wars. Perhaps there remained a reluctance to parade such victories. There survives from the Triumviral period one inscription of a legion VIII *Mutinensis* (Sylloge 92), most easily identifiable as the Caesarian evocate unit which fought for Octavian at Mutina in 43.[46] The title was not necessarily long-lived. Several veterans of a legion XI, settled after Actium at Ateste in north-east Italy, assumed the surname *Actiacus* (below, p. 111), but there is no indication that any legion was ever styled *Actiaca* from its participation in the battle.[47] Nor is any celebration of Philippi evident, unless the title *Macedonica*, found attached to several imperial legions, refers to service at that battle, which was fought on the eastern border of the Macedonian province.[48] Even granted that a somewhat indirect commemoration of the battle was perhaps the most acceptable politically, the legions which bore the title *Macedonica* can almost all be shown to have served more permanently in Macedonia at other times.[49]

The use of honorific epithets in the Triumviral period was by no means universal. There are many legions for which no title is as yet attested. A glance at the memorials of veterans who died at the colonies of Ateste and Beneventum indicates how arbitrary might be the employment of such titles, and how varied was their use from legion to legion (below, pp. 200, 160). It was indeed not until the Flavian period that legions came to employ titles as a matter of course.

3. *The* cohortes praetoriae.

One element of the army of the later first century B.C. remains to be considered here: the *cohortes praetoriae*, élite units of citizen troops, whose members were drawn from the ranks of the legions themselves. In earlier generations it had become customary for a magistrate on campaign to have at his disposal a *cohors praetoria* of picked men. Caesar, at least in Gaul, did not inherit or create a special force of this type, but a well-timed remark that his favourite Tenth Legion might serve as his *cohors praetoria* suggests that its function and duties were well known.[50]

---

[45] lv. 23. On the amalgamations following the Civil Wars of A.D. 68–9, E. B. Birley, 'A Note on the Title Gemina', *JRS* xviii (1928), 56–60; supplemented by A. Garzetti, 'Legio VII Hisp(ana)', in *Legio VII Gemina* (Leon, 1970), 331–6.

[46] It is less easy to suppose that the title is a geographical epithet, like II *Sabina* and IIII *Sorana*, reflecting an area of recruitment.

[47] As Schmitthenner 152 supposes. Also G. Webster, *The Roman Imperial* Army (London, 1969), 112 n. 1. Under the Empire the legion had Neptune as one of its emblems.

[48] Mommsen, *RGDA* 69 n. 4. Legion IIII *Macedonica* took part in the battle (App. BC iv. 117).

[49] Legions VII and XI formed part of the garrison of the Balkans from Augustus onwards. VI *Macedonica* is known only from the epitaph of a tribune at Ephesus, and may be an Antonian legion, identifiable with VI *Ferrata* (*AE* 1899, 73 = *ILS* 8862). Two inscriptions from Corinth erected in honour of a proconsul of Achaea refer to his earlier service as senatorial tribune of VIIII *Macedonica* (*ILS* 928; *AE* 1919, 1: *PIR*[2] A 993). But his military service probably postdates Augustus, and the legion can be identified with IX *Hispana*, which served in the Balkans until A.D. 43.

[50] Caes. *BG* i. 42. On the history of the *cohortes* before the Empire, Harmand 455–62; A. Passerini, *Le coorti pretorie* (Roma, 1939), 3–40.

Cohortes praetoriae are attested in number and strength only after Caesar's death. In May 44 Antony assembled a force of up to 6000 veterans, drawn in part at least from colonists established at Calatia and Casilinum. Tribunes were appointed to command subdivisions of this force, suggesting a legionary framework, but it may be suspected that the subdivision had a ceremonial rather than a military function (below, p. 53). Octavian drew veterans from the same two towns to bolster his march on Rome. His troops, some 3000 men in all, were ranged by centuries, and formed the basis of the evocate legions VII and VIII. Neither force can be reckoned a formal *cohors praetoria,* but both showed the way for future developments.

Antony, on landing at Brundisium in 44, was quick to form a *cohors praetoria* of 1000 men, its members distinguished by their physical prowess and military bearing.[51] By the time of Forum Gallorum, Octavian and Hirtius had likewise formed special cohorts, doubtless from the two evocate and two Macedonian legions under their control. The contest between the *cohortes praetoriae* of both sides formed the centrepiece of the battle, and casualties were heavy. However, the *cohortes praetoriae* of the main protagonists must have been quickly filled out again, since, when in November 43 Octavian, Antony and Lepidus entered Rome, each marched at the head of a Praetorian cohort and a single legion.[52]

The *cohors praetoria* of Octavian (Appian gives it a strength of close on 2000 men) was not in the van of his forces transported to Macedonia. Rather it was among the supplementary troops which were intercepted and largely destroyed by Murcus and Ahenobarbus during the crossing of the Adriatic on the very day of the battle.[53] After Philippi 8000 time-served men, who had turned down the proffered discharge and *praemia,* were formed into *cohortes praetoriae,* and 4000 men each assigned to Octavian and Antony. Now if not earlier we may assume that members of this *corps d'élite* were divided into a plurality of cohorts, perhaps 1000 men, less probably 500 men, strong. Octavian's cohorts accompanied his army against Perusia, but thereafter they fade from sight until Actium, when according to Orosius Octavian placed 5 such *cohortes* aboard his warships.[54]

Of Antony's parallel formations we hear rather more. In 40 B.C. they accompanied him to Brundisium. In the spring of 37, during the visit of Antony and Octavia to Tarentum, Octavian offered to his sister a bodyguard of 1000 men to be selected by Antony; we may suppose that these troops went in due course to reinforce his *cohortes praetoriae.* At least three cohorts took part in the Parthian campaign of the following year. Their casualties will not have been negligible, and in 35 Antony was able to obtain 2000 picked men to make good some of his losses, from a force brought to Greece by Octavia. Numismatic evidence testifies to the

[51] App. *BC* iii. 45.

[52] App. *BC* iv. 7.

[53] Almost certainly Octavian's *cohors* had been with him at Rhegium (App. *BC* iv. 86), and when Octavian travelled by sea to Brundisium in response to a sudden summons from Antony, it was left to follow by land. Passerini is surely wrong (op.cit., 31 n. 1) to suppose that the 2,000 men represented the combined cohorts of Octavian and Antony.

[54] App. *BC* v. 3, 34; Orosius vi. 19. 8.

existence of at least two *cohortes praetoriae* and a single *cohors speculatorum* in his army on the eve of Actium. [55]

It may be assumed that from the outset members of *cohortes praetoriae* were paid at a higher rate than the legionaries from whose ranks they were drawn. In the Late Republic they probably received one and a half times the legionary's *stipendium;* Dio states that in 27 B.C. Augustus ordained that they should thenceforward receive double the legionary pay: in fact it seems more likely that Augustus *doubled* the existing rate, so that they were paid from this time onwards three times as much as the legionaries. [56] In the settlement programmes of these years the Praetorians (if we may use that term) should have received land allocations appropriate to their status. Octavian's own *cohors* was almost entirely lost at sea in 42, but those of Antony, and Lepidus, and of other proconsuls (if existing) would require settlement; perhaps in that year Praetorians were settled at the town of Philippi itself, along with the veterans of at least one legion. [57] After Naulochus Octavian's *cohortes* (all of them re-enlisted men) would be eligible for settlement, unless they again chose to continue in service. After Actium it would appear that two, perhaps three, cohorts were sent to Ateste with other legionaries, and similarly at Sora it is possible that a legion was combined with a detachment of Praetorians (below, p. 136). The time-served members of a single cohort were established at Gunugu in Mauretania, perhaps at this time or a few years later, and in 25 B.C. the *cohortes praetoriae*, now 9 in number, provided the manpower for a new colony at Aosta (below, p. 205). The total number of veterans, if correctly given by Strabo as 3000, would represent a large-scale clearance of time-served personnel, paving the way for the peacetime imperial guard so familiar from the pages of Tacitus and Suetonius.

4. *Military service in the Late Republic*

The time-expired soldiery of the legions and the *cohortes praetoriae* will in the following chapters be consistently referred to as veterans, but this term should not in the Late Republic be thought necessarily to imply advanced age, decrepitude or long service. [58] The duration of army service required of recruits in the first century B.C. has been variously computed. Polybius in an emended passage seems to state that in his time the legal requirement was 16 years for the foot soldier and 10 years

---

[55] App. *BC* v. 59, 95; Plut. *Ant.* 39, 53; Dio xlix. 33. 4. For the numismatic evidence, above, n. 12. A grade of *speculator* is attested already under the Republic, attached to the legions, but no separate cohorts are otherwise known. Under the Empire, *speculatores* formed an élite group within the *cohortes praetoriae* and the legions, with special security duties; *RE* IIIA (1929), 1583–6.

[56] P. A. Brunt, 'Pay and Superannuation in the Roman Army', *PBSR* xviii (1950), 50–71, esp. at 55.

[57] *RE* XIX (1938), 2233; *EJ*[2] 259 (legion XXVIII). Some civilian colonists were placed there after Actium (Dio li. 4. 6).

[58] To describe time-served veterans, Appian regularly uses the term ἐστρατευμένος,. A soldier already established in a colony is a κληροῦχος or ἀπῳκισμένος. On literary and epigraphic use of the term *veteranus* at this time, below, p. 44. On the advanced age of veterans, App. *BC* iii. 46 (where they are described as γηρῶντες); Plut.*Caes.* 37. 3; Dio xlv. 38. 4, xlv. 39, xlvi. 26. 5. Cf. App. *BC* ii. 75, 79.

for the *eques*.[59] On the other hand, emphasis has recently been put on evidence which seems sufficient to indicate that, in the second century and in the first, no more than six years of continuous service might be demanded of recruits, and that a man who had completed six *stipendia* could be deemed to have done his full service, and was entitled to share in whatever *praemia* were being made available.[60] Men retained by their generals beyond this limit felt they had a legitimate grievance. This evidence does not weaken Polybius' testimony. Rather, we may conclude that 16 years of service was the maximum that could be legally demanded of a citizen between the ages of 17 and 46, but in practice six years was the regular term. Nevertheless a man could be called out again as an *evocatus* in times of need to the maximum of 16 years.[61]

Caesar's veterans had served well over six years by the time of their release in 47–44; the nucleus of his army in Gaul was already in being before Caesar's appointment, and must have contained soldiers already well through their six year minimum. There was doubtless a continual drain of men incapacitated by age, ill-health and war wounds, and Caesar's own account indicates that the strength of the legions was kept up, at least during the years in Gaul, by the normal method of annual supplementation. Lacking, however, is any hint of a deliberate policy of renewal by the release of those who had completed the six year period. The conclusion could be that all those who were fit for further service were retained. Already in 50 Caesar's troops could be portrayed as war-weary and ready for discharge; he had to face insubordination and near mutiny at Placentia in 49, and at Rome in 47, from men who could claim that they were no longer legally required to serve.[62] By 46 there were men who had seen 12 years of service under Caesar alone. Only the prospect of booty, and the expected fulfilment of lavish promises — together with personal loyalty — induced them to remain with him so long.

The veterans released after Philippi were, as Schmitthenner and Brunt have ably demonstrated, mainly recruits of 49–48, who were enlisted during the massive build-up of forces which accompanied Caesar's southwards advance into the peninsula and his preparations for Pharsalus.[63] At the time of Naulochus Octavian acceded under duress to requests for release (a) by men who had fought at Mutina and Philippi, and (b), in Dio's version, men who had served for more than 10 years (below, p. 70). We might be led to think that 10 years was now the legal minimum, and that Octavian was granting a special concession to those who had been longest under his command and had contributed most visibly to his victories. More

---

[59] vi. 19. 2, with F. W. Walbank, *A Historical Commentary on Polybius*, I(Oxford, 1957), 698. The MSS state that infantry served six years and the cavalry 10, but as the period required of the latter was normally the shorter of the two, some emendation seems inevitable.

[60] Brunt, *AL* 80; idem, *IM* 333–5, 399–401. For earlier discussions favouring a short term of service, T. Steinwender, 'Altersklassen und reguläre Dienstzeit des Legionars', *Philologus* xlviii (1889), 285–305; E. Cavaignac, 'Les six Ans de Service et la Guerre d'Espagne', *Rev. de Phil.* xxv (1951), 169–77. The evidence is reviewed sensibly by Schneider, *Veteranenversorgung* 17–19.

[61] Thus when the Senate offered *vacatio militiae* to soldiers who would fight on its behalf in 43, the exemption consisted in their non-liability for call-out as *evocati*; Cic.*Phil.* v. 53; Dio xlvi. 29. 3.

[62] App. *BC* ii. 92.

[63] Schmitthenner 62–64; Brunt, *IM* 466–7. Such men could be described as having served the 'complete period' of their service; App. *BC* v. 3.

probably, indeed almost certainly, all those who had been under arms since 43 B.C. were now entitled to release.

The veterans discharged after Actium were, we may imagine, largely the recruits of 42–40, with the residue of earlier levies. Therefore veterans settled in 31–30 B.C. must have served for about 10 to 12 years. The groups of colonies established in or about 25 and 21 B.C. might then be thought to have accommodated the recruits of 39–31 B.C., and the shadowy but probably very important settlement programme of 14 B.C. (below, p. 83) those who had enlisted in the immediate aftermath of Actium to fill the gaps caused by large-scale discharges at that time. Such men will have served about 16 years.[64]

The agitation by the soldiery for release receives an unsympathetic hearing from the historians who ascribe the unrest to insatiable greed and a predilection for blackmail.[65] This largely ignores the justice of their pleas for discharge, which both Caesar and Octavian, mindful of the tasks ahead and dependent on the skills of their experienced troops, sought to divert or ignore. The historians, who had only known the long-service professional army of the Empire, could not fail to be surprised at repeated requests for release after a relatively short period of service.

It will be clear that the Civil Wars which followed Caesar's death witnessed a lengthening out of legionary service, well beyond the six-year limit postulated above. A figure of 16 years was prescribed formally as the regular requirement by the Augustan ordinances of 13 B.C.[66] The long-service professional army was now finally established.

We cannot know what proportion of the soldiery were willing recruits, impelled to service by genuine hopes and fears, or by a basic love of excitement and adventure. Brunt has emphasised the continuing importance of conscription in providing men for the legions, particularly in the special circumstances of civil war.[67] Many, if not most, of those enlisted in 49 B.C. or later, when under the sudden pressure of events the army was massively expanded, presumably had no wish to extend their service beyond the minimum.

Of those released after Philippi some 8000 volunteered to remain in service, about one-sixth of the total eligible for discharge at that time (below, p. 60). Here we must be in the presence of the army's professional core, men who were prepared to forego the allotments to which they were now entitled, in a preference for continued service. A group of *evocati* found with Octavian's forces in the Sicilian War were evidently colonised veterans who found the lure of military life too

---

[64] For a suggestion of rather longer periods served under arms in these years, Brunt, *IM* 332 ff.

[65] App. *BC* ii. 47, Dio xli. 26 (Placentia, 49 B.C.). App. *BC* ii. 93, Dio xlii. 53, Suet. *Caes.* 70 (Rome, 47 B.C.). App. *BC* v. 128, Dio xlix. 13 (Messana, 36 B.C.). Dio can adduce as proof of the soldiers' lack of sincerity in their request for release in 36 B.C. the fact that the majority were still in their prime (xlix. 13).

[66] This had been the upper limit under the Republic, as Polybius' evidence (above, p. 35) indicates. Augustus also ordained a period of four years in the reserves. There was a Republican precedent here also, as Polybius (vi. 19. 2) reports a higher figure of 20 years to be demanded of men in especially critical situations.

[67] *AL* 75; idem, *IM* 391 ff.

strong.[68] Appian's narrative of the mutiny at Messana implies that some men entitled to discharge did not wish to be released, and later we know that several thousand veterans discharged at that time resumed service later, in somewhat confused circumstances (below, p. 71). Such men must always have been a minority. For the rest, military service was at best a brief but potentially very profitable interlude.

On enlistment the recruit to the long-service imperial army was aged on average between 17 and 23;[69] we have no comparable figures for the Late Republic, but if we imagine that a recruit was aged 20 when he began his service, the veteran of Caesar's army who had been under arms from 58 until 46 would have been in his early thirties on discharge; some men, more particularly the centurions, would be much older.[70] The exigencies of the times brought back to the legions many experienced soldiers in middle age, who had seen service many years before, and whose expertise was particularly valuable in the training of new formations.[71] A soldier, Q. Canuleius, is known to have enlisted in Caesar's VIIth legion at the age of either 17 (the minimum age for a recruit) or 18 (his age at death); his younger brother C. Canuleius, who also served in legion VII, died at the age of 35 after discharge (presumably by Caesar) and after a further period of service as *evocatus* (Sylloge 61; Pl. IA).

Many of the recruits of 49–48 can only have been in their later twenties on discharge after Philippi. Similarly, veterans released after Naulochus and Actium need not have been much over thirty. One section of the Table of Heraclea, which is Caesarian in date (at the latest), allowed men who had served six years in the ranks of the legions to stand for municipal office before the normal minimum age of 30, evidently envisaging that soldiers could have returned home before reaching that age.[72]

5. *The rewards of service*

Military service in the Roman Republic was the duty of every citizen and not felt to require any special rewards on completion of the statutory period. Pay had been introduced at an early date, but, in so far as its purchasing power can be established, it was barely sufficient to cover living expenses. It was doubled by Caesar at a

---

[68] App. *BC* v. 110.

[69] G. Forni, *Il reclutamento delle legioni da Augusto a Diocleziano* (Milano-Roma, 1953), 27, 135 ff.

[70] *B. Afr.* 45 notes a man with 36 years service, but the text is disputed.

[71] Granonius of Luceria, who had served under Lentulus Spinther in the mid 50s, either in Spain or Cicilia, joined Pompey in 49/48 (*ILLRP* 502), probably while the latter was based at Luceria early in 49 (Caes. *BC* iii. 24). T. Flavius Petro at Reate, *centurio an evocatus* (Suet. *Vesp.* 1. 2), was presumably called out now. C. Nasennius of Suessa, who had been a centurion under Q. Metellus in Crete in 69–67, sought Cicero's help to obtain *aliquid auctoritatis* in Brutus' army in Macedonia, perhaps as centurion or (better) tribune (Cic. *Ad Brut.* xv. 1. 2). Old soldiers of Pompey released in 62 were encouraged to join his forces in 49 *spe praemiorum atque ordinum*, i.e. the rank of centurion (Caes. *BC* i. 3).

[72] *ILS* 6085. 91; Brunt, *IM* 519–23; M. W. Frederiksen, 'The Republican Municipal Laws: Errors and Drafts', *JRS* lv (1965), 183–98.

date unknown, but probably by 49 B.C.[73] Pay might be supplemented by booty, and
by donatives on the occasion of a triumph. In the immediate aftermath of the
Hannibalic War time-served veterans received land grants in Italy as part of the
consolidation of Roman power in the peninsula, the amount of land being rigidly
determined by the number of years spent with the standards.[74] In the Latin
Colonies of the early second century B.C., soldiers received land grants according to
their military rank.[75]

It is, however, only from the time of Marius that the problem of veterans and
the *praemia* they might receive on discharge began to loom large in Roman political
life.[76] Marius may well have held out some promise of land in Africa to those who
would serve with him against Jugurtha; hence in part the *tanta lubido cum Mario
eundi*. Land grants were made available under the *Lex Appuleia* of 103. The
veterans of his northern campaigns were to be rewarded with land, likewise on the
proposal of Saturninus, in Cisalpina, and (less predictably) in Macedonia, Achaea,
Corsica and Sicily.[77] Despite the lack of any direct record and despite the annul-
ment of Saturninus' legislation, there is reason to suppose that some veterans did
receive land.[78]

Sulla established his victorious army (not merely his time-expired men, but all
those serving with him, if we are really to believe the figures in Appian) on the
territories of towns which had espoused the Marian or Italic causes with excessive
zeal.[79] In 59 B.C. Pompey was able to secure land for veterans of his eastern
campaigns, but only in the teeth of senatorial opposition and with Caesar's aid. He
had already experienced a rebuff in an attempt to secure similar rewards for
veterans of his Spanish campaigns ten years before.[80]

It must be emphasised, however, that the great mass of time-served veterans
had little expectation that any pressure would be exerted on their behalf, and the
temptation to see in the land grants of the last century B.C. a recognised right or
pension must be firmly resisted. The 'problem' of veteran settlement forms a far
from coherent theme in the politics of the Late Republic. There is nothing to show
that the provision of land grants to veterans on completion of military service was
felt as a necessary concomitant or consequence of any of Marius' reforms. For the

---

[73] Suet. *Caes.* 26. 3; Harmand 262-8; Brunt, loc.cit. (n. 56).

[74] Liv. xxxi. 49. 5.

[75] Liv. xxxv. 9. 7, xxxvii. 57. 7, xl. 34. 2.

[76] Gabba, *Ricerche* 171 ff. remains basic reading for a rounded appreciation of the phenomenon.
Brunt, *IM* 294 ff. cites the literary evidence. See also F. T. Hinrichs, 'Das legale Landversprechen im
Bellum Civile', *Historia* xviii (1969), 521-44; Schneider, *Veteranenversorgung* 99 ff. for a discussion
along traditional lines of many familiar topics.

[77] E. Gabba, 'Mario e Silla', in *ANRW* I.i (Berlin-New York, 1972), 764-805, esp. 778. For the
resulting 'colonies', the status of which is disputed, cf. Brunt, *IM* 577-80; E. Gabba, 'Ricerche su
alcuni punti di storia Mariana', *Athenaeum* xxix (1951), 12-24.

[78] *De Vir. Ill.* 73. 5; App. *BC* i. 29; Pliny *NH* iii. 80 for *colonia Mariana* on Corsica; M. H.
Crawford, *Roman Republican Coinage* (Cambridge, 1974), 629. The colony at Eporedia, founded in
100 B.C., apparently on a senatorial initiative, could have served to accommodate Marian veterans.

[79] App. *BC* i. 100; Brunt, *IM* 300-12.

[80] R. E. Smith, 'The Lex Plotia Agraria and Pompey's Spanish Veterans', *CQ* li (1957), 82-85;
Brunt, *IM* 312 ff.

most part, soldiers whose service was complete and who had been released from the military oath returned to their homes in the peninsula or remained in the province of their service with whatever booty and donatives they had been able to amass. Nevertheless, by Caesar's time it could almost be taken for granted that, if a general cared to press for additional benefits for his men, these would take the form of land grants, sometimes as part of more general schemes for the resettlement of the landless population and the regeneration of Italy. But the initiative remained in the hands of the general or of politicians at Rome.

It is not clear whether Caesar made any specific promises regarding land to his veterans, either in Gaul or at any time during the Civil War, but already in 47 preparations for land settlement were in hand.[81] The prospect of land grants, which Caesar had made a reality for his own men in 47–44, proved an allurement too strong to resist in the years after his murder. The Senate promised land in advance to those who would fight in its interest in the spring of 43, and Antony made a counter-claim to similar benefits on behalf of soldiers loyal to him.[82] A direct equation between military service and land settlement had been established. The territories of 18 prosperous Italian towns were held out in advance to spur on the armies of the Triumvirate, not as an inducement to enlist (although this may not have been quite clear at the time), but as a reinforcement of loyalties in a civil war. We need not doubt, however, that recruits began to look forward to such rewards as the natural conclusion to their service, and the prospect of a land grant, with the substantial improvement in social status which might result, in return for as little as six years continuous service, was an obvious inducement to military service. By the Pact of Misenum, time-served men in the army of Sextus Pompeius were in due course to be rewarded on a par with those of the Triumvirs, and the mutineers of the army in Sicily specifically asked for the same rewards as already given to those of their comrades released after Philippi.[83] We may imagine that the prospect of land was very much in the minds of Octavian's time-served men on the eve of Actium, whether or not any specific promise had been made. Our sources give no hint. By Actium a grant of land on discharge had become an accepted condition of military service, one which was to subsist until 13 B.C. when Octavian substituted a cash gratuity.[84]

For the soldiers of the Civil War armies, land was not the only reward in prospect. They looked for and received cash bounties (see list below, p. 42, with full references). After Naulochus the demand was for land and money (χωρία καὶ χρήματα);[85] they had been led to expect both.

[81] Later he could be portrayed as already anxious at Pharsalus that his soldiers receive their proper rewards; Lucan *Phars.* vii. 257.

[82] Cic.*Phil.* v. 53, viii. 25; Dio xlvi. 29. 3.

[83] App. *BC* v. 73, 128.

[84] Below, p. 208. Land was the reward for citizens. There is no clear evidence that auxiliaries received any, though almost certainly they qualified on occasion for cash bounties. For the suggestion that auxiliary cavalry formed the manpower of *colonia Iulia Equestris* at Noviodunum, see Vittinghoff 23 n. 6. For a discussion of the identity of settlers at Rhegium in 36 B.C., below, p. 71.

[85] App. *BC* v. 128.

In 49 B.C. Caesar could claim to have made his soldiers rich men by the plunder of Gaul,[86] and we may imagine that individuals had profited greatly by the plunder of such towns as Avaricum and Cenabum, and by the general opportunities of the campaigns. During the Civil War he made generous promises, the prospect of whose fulfilment went far to assuage the grievances of his troops at their protracted service. At the time of the mutiny in 47 B.C., he offered a further 1000 *denarii* over and above the sums already promised. The promises were finally made good at his triumph in September 46, when a lump sum of 5000 or (according to Suetonius) 6000 *denarii* was paid out to legionaries. Centurions received twice, and tribunes four times, the basic figure. Particular legions might chance by the accident of service to receive additional rewards; individuals could be rewarded for their valour.[87]

In the confused events of 44 the Caesarian veterans were able to profit by the need that Antony and especially Octavian had of their services. Octavian offered 5000 *denarii* to his soldiers on the eve of the campaign against Antony, and the Senate made similar promises in an attempt to divert their loyalty to the state. Its motives fell some way short of sincerity, as subsequent events were to show. Octavian did in fact pay the sum of 2500 *denarii* to the legions which accompanied him to Rome in July 43, with a promise of the remainder.

Those soldiers fortunate enough to be in Rome during the proscriptions stood, it seems, to gain substantially from the head-money offered by the Triumvirs. Centurions, each with a squad of men, drawn largely (we may imagine) from the *cohors praetoria* and the single legion each Triumvir brought to Rome in November 43, led the search for fugitives; the sum of 25,000 *denarii* was payable for each man tracked down. The tribune who killed Cicero received ten times this sum from a delighted Antony. A centurion's uniform was the best disguise for the proscribed themselves, if they wished to avoid detection.[88]

At the time of Philippi, the sum of 5000 *denarii* was offered as an incentive to victory by the Triumvirs. All those who participated in the battle were to benefit. After the battle one of Antony's urgent tasks was to collect the enormous sums required. Work began towards this end, but there is no clear evidence that the bounty was ever paid. In 41 Octavian sought to put Antony in a bad light by trying to make good the deficit from temple funds, and in October of the following year both he and Antony were faced by an angry deputation of colonised veterans seeking the promised money.[89]

After Naulochus Octavian distributed a donative of 500 *denarii*. Appian states that this went only to those who had agreed to remain in service, but Dio seems to indicate that the whole army, including veterans, received it. In the run-up to Actium, Octavian made a distribution to serving troops, and although we are not told specifically of any cash donative promised before or after the battle, Dio's statement that upon the capture of Alexandria Octavian paid all his soldiers 'what

---

[86] App. *BC* ii. 47.

[87] Caes. *BC* iii. 53; *B. Alex.* 19, 77; App. *BC* iv. 101.

[88] App. *BC* iv passim, with esp. iv. 11 (rewards of 25,000 denarii), iv. 12 (centurions in charge of search parties), iv. 20 (the tribune who killed Cicero), iv. 35 (looting by soldiers), iv. 46 (disguise).

[89] App. *BC* v. 13; Dio xlviii. 30. 2.

was still owing' may serve as evidence of the fulfilment of such a promise. At the time of his triumph in 29 Octavian paid out a *triumphale congiarium* of 250 *denarii* to colonised veterans; we are told that 120,000 men benefited. It was possible therefore for individual veterans to amass substantial sums in the course of the Civil Wars,[90] but once peace had returned, no further donatives were paid out to serving troops, except to the Praetorians and other units in the capital, before the general distribution effected in accordance with Augustus' will in A.D. 14.[91]

Cash donatives to soldiers 59–29 B.C.

		amount in denarii		
date	circumstances and recipients	basic rate	centurions	ref.
1. Caesar				
51	to the whole army *praedae nomine*	50	500	Caes.*BG* viii.4
50	to legion I, on release to join Pompey	250	—	App.*BC*.ii.29
49	to whole army before Ilerda campaign	500	—	Suet.*Caes*.38 cf.Caes.*BC* i.39
47	in response to a mutiny	1000 (promise)	—	App.*BC* ii.92; cf.Plut.*Caes*.52.2
46	to the veteran legions after Thapsus	—	—	B.*Afr.* 86
46	to the veteran Gallic legions, at his triumph	5000 or 6000	10,000 (20,000 to tribunes & prefects) —	App.*BC* ii.102 Dio xliii.21 Suet.*Caes*.38
2. Octavian and Antony (44–42 B.C.)				
	Octavian			
44	to VII and VIII in Campania	500	—	App.*BC* iii.40 Dio xlv.12
44	Antony at Brundisium to II, IIII, *Martia*, XXXV, and presumably to *coh.pr.* and *V Alaudae*	100	—	App.*BC* iii.44
44	Antony at Rome to II, XXXV, *coh.pr.*, V *Alaudae*	500	—	App.*BC* iii.45
44	Octavian at Alba Fucens to VII, VIII, IIII, *Martia*	500 with a promise of 5000	—	App.*BC* iii.48 Dio xlv.13.4
43	Octavian on return to Rome, to his legions including I, II, III, IV, VII, VIII, IIII, *Martia*, XXVI, XXIX, and to *coh.pr.*	2500	—	App.*BC* iii.94 Dio xlvi.46
42	Antony and Octavian at Philippi, to all those present	5000 (promise)	25,000 (50,000 to tribunes)	App.*BC* iv.120 Plut.*Ant*.23

[90] For property and movables owned or acquired by soldiers of their families, Caes. *BG* v. 31; App. *BC* ii. 46, 53; Brunt, *AL* 69 ff.

[91] Dio lv. 6. 4.

| date | circumstances and recipients | amount in denarii | | ref. |
		basic rate	centurions	
Notice also:				
42	the Liberators, to their army on the eve of Philippi	1500	7500 (more to tribunes)	App.*BC* iv.100
42	Brutus, after First Philippi	1000	more	App.*BC* iv.118
41	L.Antonius, to two legions at Alba	—	—	App.*BC* v.30
3. *Octavian* (41–29 B.C.)				
41	in lieu of promised bounty?	—	—	App.*BC* v.22
36	after Naulochus to the whole army (Dio); to those who remained in service (Appian)	500	—	Dio xlix.14 App.*BC* v.129
32	to serving soldiers	—	—	Dio l.7
30	to veterans at Brundisium	—	—	Dio li.4
30	to legions present at capture of Alexandria (at the same time Octavian paid out to all his soldiers 'what was still owing')	250	—	Dio li.17
29	to colonists, on the occasion of his triumph	250	—	RG 15.5 Dio li.21.3
4. *Antony* (41–30 B.C.)				
	at the end of the Parthian campaign	100	—	Dio xlix 31.4
	on eve of Actium	—	—	above, p. 27

6. *The epigraphic evidence for veteran colonists*

It is time now to turn to the veterans themselves. Individual epitaphs are discussed below (Chapters 6–9) in the context of particular colonies, but it may be helpful to prefix that account with an assessment of the criteria employed in the identification and dating of relevant inscriptions amid the ever growing body of material from Italian towns. It is from an identification of individual veterans that a picture of the destinations of discharged legions can be built up.

Several approaches are available. Firstly, epitaphs may be datable to the later first century B.C. by the details of military service and the name of the legion in which the veteran served; secondly the layout of the inscriptions or the formulae employed may have chronological implications; so thirdly may the scale or style of the monument itself. Lastly, an examination of the lettering may allow the inscription to be placed at this time. As will emerge, only the first and second can have decisive value. Scrutiny of an epigraphic text alone, as published in the *Corpus Inscriptionum Latinarum* or in *l'Année Épigraphique* (or in other journals), may give little hint of the dimensions of the monument or gravestone, or of the type or standard of the decoration or execution. There can be no substitute for autopsy. A Sylloge of inscriptions of known or likely veteran colonists is presented below as an appendix (pp. 212 ff).

The majority of epigraphic records of veterans take the form of grave monuments, on which the name of the soldier and brief details of his military service are inscribed. It is therefore only after death that they come before us. The veterans being discussed were settled at known times, by Caesar, the Triumvirs and Augustus, but they would die indiscriminately throughout or even after the latter's long reign, with the epitaph prepared either during the lifetime of the veteran (often under his personal supervision) or immediately after his death by a member of his family or heir.

It is evident that any examination must start with a scrutiny of inscriptions which are dated to the period by the information they contain. The epitaph of M. Billienus at Ateste (Sylloge 6; Pl. IB) specifies settlement after a naval battle; he and four (perhaps five) other veterans settled there identify that battle as Actium by their adoption of the surname *Actiacus* (below, p. 111). Equally helpful towards close dating may be specification of military service in legions which are believed not to have survived the reorganisation of forces after Philippi or Actium. Very high numerals may identify such formations, or the use of a title that recalls events or aspirations of these years but is not found in use later.

The groups of veteran-inscriptions recovered at Beneventum and Ateste form an obvious basis for discussion. Beneventum was established after Philippi by Munatius Plancus; Ateste became a colony after Actium (below, pp. 155, 195). In the use of particular formulae and in the layout of basic information there is a notable consistency within and between the two groups. We can note at once the terseness of many of the inscriptions, which can be confined to a statement of the personal name, filiation, tribe, and name (and perhaps title) of the legion in which service was done. The majority of men lack *cognomina,* and the voting tribe given is that of the town of settlement, adopted at the moment of *deductio* or at the first local census thereafter.[92] The failure in most cases to specify the town of origin restricts any attempt to establish recruitment areas. The description of military service is brief, normally abbreviated to the letters L or LEG (i.e. *legione* or *legionis*), together with numeral (and title) of the legion. The veteran's name, filiation and tribe are often placed together to form the first line of the epitaph, with the number (and title) of the legion placed separately in the second. Where the veteran has attained some rank within the legion, this is specified, but the title *veteranus* appears rarely. The number of years served under arms, and the age at death, are generally left unspecified, in contrast to the effusive epitaphs of later generations. Military decorations, (e.g. crowns, bangles, torques and medals) can be carved on the stone; they are seldom mentioned in the inscription (see Pl. IC).[93] Brief details of the man's family, heirs, and household may follow.

The word *veteranus* is first used by writers of the Ciceronian age, to describe a time-served and so discharged soldier, or (more frequently) as an adjective in apposition to *miles,* of a long-serving and experienced soldier, in contrast to the

[92] G. Forni, '"Doppia tribù" di cittadini e cambiamenti di tribù romane', in *Tetraonyma: miscellanea graeco-romana* (Genova, 1966), 139–56.

[93] Sylloge 24 (Ateste) and perhaps 52 (Beneventum) have *dona* carved on the stone, but no mention occurs on the inscription. For a comprehensive study of *dona*, see now V. A. Maxfield, *The Military Decorations of the Roman Army* (London, 1981).

newly enlisted and untried recruit. The evocate legionaries of Caesar, actively engaged on opposite sides in 44–3, are frequently described by Cicero as *veterani*.[94] Epigraphically too the word is not attested before this time. Its very absence from an epitaph may be a useful chronological guide. For the majority of veterans of the Caesarian, Triumviral and early Augustan ages, the designation *legione* (or *legionis*) was felt sufficient. On occasion other combinations of titulature might be employed to express the developing concept of the retired soldier: he is termed *miles missicius veteranus,* or *miles veteranus,* or will employ just *miles*.[95] Standardisation, with the phrase *veteranus legionis,* was not achieved until the end of Augustus' reign.

The absence of the title *veteranus* from these epitaphs poses a particular problem, that is of distinguishing discharged soldiers from those still serving. The identification of epitaphs of soldiers who died on service in the Civil Wars is not easy.[96] It is possible that men dying on active service were often not commemorated, at least on stone; in later ages the existence of communal burial clubs secured the erection of a suitable memorial in most circumstances. A suspicion could remain that some of the men considered in these pages died on service and are commemorated in their home towns. Nevertheless the concentration of inscriptions of the type outlined above in known or likely colonies and their *territoria* must form an argument for their inclusion here.

Care must be taken to exclude veterans of earlier and later generations. The epitaphs of ordinary soldiers, which can with certainty be assigned a date much before the death of Caesar, are not numerous,[97] and it is a lack of such records that hinders a proper appreciation of (for example) the scope of Sullan settlement in Italy. The relative paucity of inscriptions of Republican date may be the explanation here, or the financial incapacity of the veterans at death. On the other hand it may be that military service, as a duty incumbent on every citizen and as the common experience of a large sector of the male community, was not felt to require separate mention. Veterans of succeeding generations must likewise be excluded. It is possible that some of the inscriptions which seem to fall on the edges of the type described in the foregoing pages relate to veterans of the settlement programme of 14 B.C., or are recipients of cash gratuities in the later decades of Augustus' reign (below, pp. 82, 208). Certainty is unattainable, given the degree of variation in the traditions and habits of craftsmen and workshops throughout the peninsula. Though it is evident that there was no sudden alteration in the formulae used to describe military service, a gradual change in fashion can be observed in datable inscriptions, in particular (for the present purpose) on epitaphs of veterans settled at

---

[94] Caes. *BG* i. 24, *BC* i. 25, iii. 28, etc.; Sall. *Cat.* 59. 5, 60. 3; H. Merguet, *Lexikon zu den Reden des Cicero,* IV (Jena, 1884), 881.

[95] Sylloge 5 (Ateste), 59 (Cales), 71 (Fanum); *ILS* 2249 (Thuburnica).

[96] App. *BC* ii. 82 for burial of the dead after Pharsalus, and the tomb of Crastinus; *ILLRP* 502 for Granonius who died at Athens in 49/48; Sylloge 61 for the soldier Q. Canuleius who died on active service under Caesar in Gaul, (Pl. IA).

[97] Perhaps IX 4123, V 2114, *ILLRP* 501.

Antiochia Pisidiae in or soon after 25 B.C., at Patrae perhaps in 16 B.C., at Emona in A.D. 14 and in Dalmatia and Pannonia in the early years of Tiberius' reign.[98]

Attempts to date military inscriptions solely from the type or style of funerary monument are unremunerative. For the most part the style of the monument or grave-marker, and of the decoration employed to enhance it, conforms to local sculptural and funerary traditions. On a few slabs the military service of the deceased is confirmed by the appearance of *dona militaria* or a display of arms. The appearance of weaponry sometimes establishes the military antecedents of the deceased where the inscription itself is fragmentary or lost, but military insignia *can* appear on tombstones where army service is unlikely or impossible.[99] There is now at Boston a fine marble slab recording P. Gessius P.f.Rom., his freedwoman wife and a son by her (Pl. IIB). The inscription is accompanied by busts of the three carved in relief; on artistic grounds the slab has been dated to about 50 B.C. Gessius himself appears in a leather cuirass, with a cloak over his left shoulder; he may have been holding a *gladius*.[100] It seems a reasonable conclusion that Gessius was a soldier or veteran of the first century B.C., though the inscription gives no hint of military service. The slab was erected after Gessius' death by the freedwoman, in accordance with the wishes of the son, who predeceased her. The portrayal of Gessius in uniform may have seemed a sufficient indicator of his military antecedents. His rank cannot be established, but Gessius' features, which reveal a rather sour, hard-bitten and weary man of mature years, suggest prolonged service in the ranks, as do the details of his family circle and the very absence of specification of his achievements or position. The tribe *Romilia* may be thought to identify Gessius as a man born in, or settled at, either Ateste or Sora (the only towns known to have been in *Romilia*, and both colonies of this time), but a findspot near modern Viterbo is reported[101] so that he could have been settled in a small non-colonial settlement in southern Etruria. Alternatively, he may have returned to his home town from either Ateste or Sora; Ernst Badian has postulated a family of P.Gessii at Forum Clodii near Viterbo under the Republic.[102] One fragment of a tomb monument preserved at Saepinum, possibly the scene of a small-scale settlement in 14 B.C. (above, p. 9), shows a figure in military dress, whom the accompanying inscription identifies as

[98]Antiochia: *ILS* 2237-8; III 6827-8; *JRS* vi (1916), 90; *TAPA* lvii (1926), 227 no. 56; Levick 56 ff. Patrae: III 503-4, 507-9; *Ath.Ann.Arch.* iv (1971), 122. Tiberius: III 3845 = *ILS* 2264; III 3847 = 10757; III 3848; J. J. Wilkes, 'A Note on the Mutiny of the Pannonian Legions in A.D. 14', *CQ* lvii (1963), 268-71; idem, *Dalmatia* (London, 1969), 110 ff.

[99]For a tombstone at Ateste, decorated with military insignia including a centurion's *vitis*, *NS* 1906, 419 no. 8 and below, p. 201. Other stones from Ateste show representations of weapons but are of freedmen, V 2604; *NS* 1922, 15.

[100]L. D. Caskey, 'Recent Acquisitions of the Museum of Fine Arts, Boston', *AJA* xli (1937), 525-31; Degrassi, *ILLRP* 503 with *Imagines* no. 219; M. Rostovtzeff, *Social and Economic History of the Hellenistic World* (Oxford, 1941), 992 with pl. cvi; M. B. Comstock and C. C. Vermeule, *Sculpture in Stone* (Boston, 1976), 200-1 no. 319 with fig.

[101]I am grateful to Dr. Cornelius Vermeule, of the Museum of Fine Arts, Boston, for information on its findspot. For this type of funerary monument, see now D. E. E. Kleiner, *Roman Group Portraiture* (New York and London, 1977), nos. 39, 49, 55, 88.

[102]Wiseman no. 196; E. Badian, 'Notes on Roman Senators of the Republic', *Historia* xii (1963), 129-43.

C.Raius Perulla.[103] The inscription makes no reference to military service, but it may be wondered whether he is a colonist of the time.

A number of veterans settled at Ateste had their ashes placed in cylindrical *cippi* topped by a detachable lid, on which may be carved in very high relief the figures of two lions devouring a lamb or calf (Pl. IIA). The imagery has, however, no military connotation, and this type of *cippus* is not confined to veterans; the imagery symbolises the continuing cycle of life and death.[104] At Beneventum some veterans were commemorated by monuments whose decoration includes a frieze of metopes showing spears, shields and other military items. The style is a familiar one, and especially popular in the Augustan age; it is not confined to the grave-monuments of soldiers.[105]

The size and standard of the monument can be a useful gauge of the wealth or social status of the veteran, his family or his heirs. Elaborate tomb monuments from southern and central Italy, erected in the Augustan age by centurions and *primipilares,* have recently been studied by Filippo Coarelli.[106] Decorated with military emblems, and the paraphernalia of later civic success, the monuments testify to the pride of the centurions and long-remembered military achievements.

The very fact that any epitaph was set up may indicate a minimum level of prosperity.[107] Nevertheless the smallest limestone or marble plaque may be set into a tomb façade of great size and pretensions. Many of the smaller epitaphs were designed to form part of family grave-plots, so that the absence from an inscription of reference to a wife or family is not in such cases conclusive. Wives, children, and members of a *familia* could have separate stones, the placing of which within a demarcated plot would make clear any such relationships.[108] The epitaphs were erected beside the roads leading away from the town concerned, or more frequently (as will be argued later) on the land belonging to the veteran and his family in the *territorium.*

The dating of epitaphs to the last century B.C. by an examination of lettering alone is a hazardous endeavour. It is well known that the heavy squat lettering of the Republic was giving way (at least in Rome itself) during Augustus' reign to the familiar shaded capitals of the Empire.[109] Many of the veteran-epitaphs exhibit

---

[103] IX 2532; P. Braconi et al., *Sepino: archeologia e continuità* (Campobasso, 1979), 25. Notice also the epitaph of C. Vibius Macer from Villa Vallelunga near the Fucine Lake; *AE* 1891, 15 (with sketch) = *EE* VIII 172. An array of *dona militaria,* suggestive of service in the ranks followed by the centurionate, is depicted, but no military service is noted on the accompanying inscription.

[104] Sylloge 3, 14, 15, 20, ?25. For the style, G. B. Montanari, 'Monumenti funerari atestini', *Riv.Ist.Arch.* n.s. viii (1959), 111–45; H. Gabelmann, 'Oberitalische Rundaltäre', *Röm.Mitt.* lxxv (1968), 87–105.

[105] Sylloge 31, 41; cf. IX 1615. Note also M. Torelli, 'Monumenti funerari romani con fregio dorico', *D.Arch.* ii (1968), 32–54.

[106] F. Coarelli, 'Su un monumento funerario romano nell'abbazia di San Gulielmo al Goleto', *D.Arch.* i (1967), 46–71. Cf. S. Diebner, *Aesernia-Venafrum: Untersuchungen zu den römischen Steindenkmälern zweier Städte Mittelitaliens* (Roma, 1979).

[107] Duncan-Jones 79, 127.

[108] *NS* 1893, 57 ff. (= Sylloge 24) for a group of epitaphs commemorating a veteran and his family on a single plot at Monselice; below, p. 198.

[109] J. S. and A. E. Gordon, *Contributions to the Palaeography of Latin Inscriptions* (Berkeley, 1957), with the review by R. P. Oliver, *AJP* lxxxi (1960), 189–97.

lettering that fits easily into the last generation of the Republic, which helps to
confirm their date, but others are less easily categorised. Allowance must once again
be made for the traditions and practices of individual craftsmen and workshops.[110]
The so-called Republican letter-forms can persist well into the Empire, even in
important cities. A recently published epitaph of a military man from Telesia
(Sylloge 54) would, on palaeographic grounds alone, be most easily assigned to the
earlier half of the first century B.C., but a reference in the inscription to military
service in a legion known to have been settled at nearby Beneventum must, it seems,
determine the date (below, p. 155).

Dating of veteran epitaphs to the period under review rests therefore principally on specification in the inscription of military service, which can by various
means be confined to the later first century B.C. Without doubt the civilian inscriptions from any colony must include the names of families and descendants of
military colonists, and it could be argued that the sifting of the *nomina* found in a
particular colony would isolate non-local name forms, which might have been
introduced by veterans. The ultimate origins of a great many Italian names have
been pinpointed by the careful researches of Schulten, Schulze and others, and it is
often possible to establish the likely origin of known veteran settlers by this
method.[111] But such a line of investigation is fraught with difficulty: the arrival of
non-local names in a particular locality could have resulted from earlier colonisation, from viritane grants of *ager publicus*, from population movement before
(and after) the Late Republic, from individual grants of citizenship, and the
gradual adoption of Latin name-forms by the population.[112] Given the increasing
importance of Cisalpina as a recruiting ground, many veterans settled (for example)
at Ateste, Brixia or Cremona, may themselves have been local men and not immi-
grants from the south. For the most part, an attempt to identify likely veterans from
nomenclature alone is eschewed in this study, except where it may be judged to have
some greater probability of success.[113]

In all some 90 veterans can be identified as settlers in Italy under the
Caesarian, Triumviral and Augustan schemes down to 14 B.C. The sample is
minute, certainly less than 0.1 per cent of all those settled in this period.[114] The
evidence is far from evenly spread. Large concentrations have survived at Ateste and
Beneventum, but many colonies can show only one stone, or none. We know that
3000 Praetorians were sent to Aosta in 25 B.C. Not a single epitaph of a colonist has
come to light from that town or its territory.

[110]Notice here the comments of A. Degrassi, 'L'epigrafia latina in Italia nell'ultimo ventennio e i
criteri del nuovo insegnamento', *SVA* I, 651–61; G. C. Susini, *The Roman Stonecutter* (Oxford, 1973),
59 ff.

[111]A. Schulten, 'Italische Namen und Stämme', *Klio* ii (1902), 167–93, 440–65; ibid. iii (1903),
235–67; W. Schulze, *Zur Geschichte lateinischer Eigennamen* (Berlin, 1933); A. Holder, *Alt-Celtischer
Sprachschatz* (Leipzig, 1896–1913).

[112]For migration and population movement in Italy, G. E. F. Chilver, *Cisalpine Gaul* (Oxford,
1941), 71 ff.; E. T. Salmon, *Samnium and the Samnites* (Cambridge, 1967), 310, 388; Brunt, *IM* 190,
and many other works.

[113]Below, pp. 159, 207. For the names of veterans reflected in modern place- and farm-names,
below, pp. 159, 179, 203.

[114]Another 20 or more epitaphs have survived from provincial colonies. On the calculation of
likely survival rates for inscriptions, an endeavour hindered by so many variables, Duncan-Jones 360–2.

CHAPTER THREE

THE SETTLEMENT PROGRAMMES[1]

1. *Caesar's veterans, 47–44 B.C.*

When Caesar returned to Rome in September 47, he had been away from the city for more than 20 months; over a year had passed since the crushing defeat of the Pompeian forces at Pharsalus. The veteran legions among Caesar's forces had mostly been ferried back to Italy soon after the battle, and billeted on Italian towns to await further assignments.[2] Not surprisingly, with the war seemingly over, and Caesar himself far away, their tempers reached boiling point, and when the Dictator finally returned, a deputation travelled northwards from Campania to confront him with their common grievances.

Caesar quelled the discontent by appealing to their loyalty, by nourishing an expectation of imminent enrichment, and by making a specific statement of intent on the provision of land. Rather than dispossess owners on a large scale, he would make use of whatever *ager publicus* was available, and his own estates, and buy more land where necessary. Mass settlement in the Sullan manner, however, he would avoid; according to Dio, the veterans were to be settled individually and far apart, to minimise disruption and backlash.[3] Some were discharged at once (those with at least a modicum of farming experience) in the autumn of 47, and were given land, as a guarantee of Caesar's good faith, and as a foretaste of the rewards all would receive in due course.[4] Members of VI *Ferrata*, sent back to Italy after sterling service in Egypt and Asia, were probably released now,[5] but it was some considerable time before land became available for them. Caesar could not afford to disperse the main strength of his veteran legions with an African campaign in the offing. At first he may have hoped to restrict their participation, and to use only V *Alaudae*, together with selected cohorts from the rest, but by February 46 four

---

[1] Among previous works concerned with, or alluding to, the settlement programmes from Caesar onwards, mention may be made of the following: A. W. Zumpt, 'De Coloniis Romanorum Militaribus' in his *Commentationes Epigraphicae* (Berlin, 1850), 195–502; B. Borghesi, *Oeuvres Complètes* V (Paris, 1869), 258–76; K. J. Beloch, *It. Bund* (Leipzig, 1880), 10–13; Th. Mommsen, *Bürgercolonien* 161–213; E. Pais, *Colonie militari* 37–58; idem, *Serie cronologica* 345–412; L. Hollaender, *De militum coloniis ab Augusto in Italia deductis* (Halle, 1880); E. Gabba, *Colonie triumvirali* 101–10; P. A. Brunt, *IM* 319 ff.; H.-C. Schneider, *Veteranenversorgung*, 161–263. Notice may also be taken of two dissertations: F. T. Hinrichs, *Die Ansiedlungsgesetze und Landanweisungen im letzten Jahrhundert der römischen Republik* (Heidelberg, 1957), which deals primarily with technical and legal aspects, especially relating to the 'Lex Mamilia Roscia'; H. Chocholle, *Die Veteranenversorgung im römischen Heeres von den Anfängen bis auf Augustus (14 n.)* (Wien, 1952), which provides a useful, though uncritical, compilation, and extensive citation, of the literary sources and some epigraphic material, relating to veteran settlement in Italy and the provinces.

[2] Cic. *Phil.* ii. 59, 62; Dio xlii. 30.

[3] App. *BC* ii. 94; Dio xlii. 52–55; Suet. *Caes.* 38; Vittinghoff 49–95; M. Gelzer, *Caesar* (Eng. trans., Oxford, 1968), 283–4; Brunt, *IM* 255, 319–26.

[4] Dio xlii. 55; Plut. *Caes.* 51. 1.

[5] *B. Alex.* 77.

more veteran legions had been transported. After the battle of Thapsus some men were discharged on the spot and evidently settled in Africa.[6]

Discharges began in earnest after Caesar's return to Italy in July 46, more probably after his triumphs in late September, though preparations for land settlement could well have been in hand from the previous autumn. The work of survey, allocation and settlement continued until March 44, and remained unfinished at Caesar's death, though he did not feel obliged himself to remain in Italy for its completion. Most if not all the veterans were presumably discharged in the autumn of 46. Only V *Alaudae*, VI and X are known to have participated in the Spanish campaign of 45.[7] By late in the previous year it was probably known that VI and X were destined for settlement in Transalpina, and Caesar perhaps diverted them while all but on the march to their new homes. Certainly on his return journey from Spain in the summer of 45, he stopped at Narbo, perhaps briefly to initiate or observe settlement work under Ti. Claudius Nero; Antony joined him there in August of that year.[8] Caesar's visit to Campania in December 45 could have included an inspection of veterans of legion VII at Calatia. In all probability V *Alaudae* was retained in service at least until late 45. At his death veterans of at least one legion (which can be identified as VIII) remained in the city, on the point of departure for Casilinum. Members of V *Alaudae* may also have been in Rome, or were more likely brigaded somewhere in southern Italy until their formal release.[9]

The men released by Caesar in 47–44 were the time-served members of his Gallic legions (V—XIV). These ten legions had on paper a strength of perhaps 50,000 men, but several, doubtless all, had fallen well below strength during the Civil War. By 47 we know that VI was down to under 1000 men actually with the standards; service in Spain in 45 must have reduced it further. The ranks of legion X were noticeably thin in the same campaign.[10] It is difficult to suppose that more than 20,000 men in all were released by Caesar; of these perhaps 15,000 at most were accommodated in Italy.

It has sometimes been asserted that the settlement programmes were carried

----

[6] Dio (xliii. 14. 1) states that 'the older men' were released, to guard against the repetition of a mutiny. Rather it may be suspected that soldiers who had expressed a desire to settle there were given the opportunity. Note App. *BC* v. 26 (presence of discharged veterans in Africa in 41 B.C.); *ILS* 6784 (a veteran of legion XIII at Uthina); *ILS* 2249 (a veteran of V *Alaudae* at Thuburnica).

[7] *B. Hisp.* 12. 5, 30. 7.

[8] Cic. *Phil.* ii. 76–8; Suet. *Tib.* 4. 1; J. Kromayer, 'Die Militaercolonien Octavians und Caesars in Gallia Narbonensis', *Hermes* xxxi (1896), 1–18.

[9] It has sometimes been claimed that V *Alaudae*, probably the most junior of the dictator's Gallic legions, remained under arms at his death, and was then in Italy, at or near Brundisium, to be the core of his army for the Parthian campaign; see Schmitthenner 170 n. 14, and more recently Botermann 181–5. Both argue strongly that Caesar would not have found room in Italy for V *Alaudae* while excluding most (or all) of VI and X from settlement there. Nevertheless I incline to the view that Brunt (*IM* 477–78) is correct in his belief that the legion had been disbanded by Caesar's death, and was subsequently re-formed in the autumn of 44. To the arguments he adduces I would add Cic. *Phil.* xiii. 3, where Cicero couples members of V *Alaudae* with *ceteri veterani*, all of whom had already devoured *praemia* received from Caesar. Appian's ἐξεστρατευμένων δὲ ἐν ⟨τέλος⟩ can only be the *Alaudae* (*BC* iii. 46), as no other veteran legion is reported among his forces in northern Italy.

[10] *B. Alex.* 69. 1; *B. Hisp.* 31. 4. Already in August 48, VI and XXVII together amounted temporarily to only 3,200 men; Caes. *BC* iii. 106, cf. Brunt *IM* 690–93.

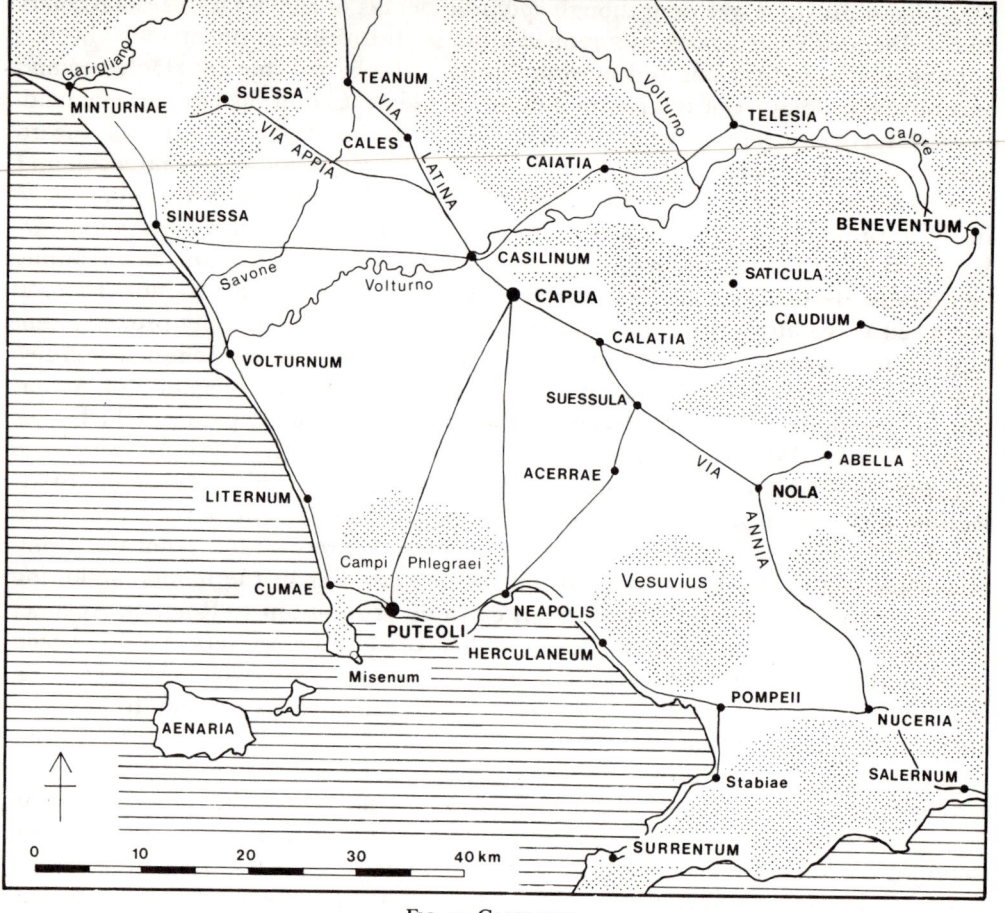

FIG. 2: CAMPANIA

out by virtue of Caesar's dictatorial powers,[11] but scattered references appear to identify a *lex Iulia* specifically authorising the programme and detailing its purpose.[12] To supervise the work Caesar selected senators (often, so far as we are aware, of no particular renown) to be personal representatives of himself as sole *deductor*. Most probably these substitutes had the title *praefectus*.[13] There has been some discussion on their jurisdiction, but full juridical competence seems essential for the speedy completion of the difficult tasks confronting them.[14]

[11] Kornemann 569.

[12] Cic. *Phil.* v. 53; Suet. *Caes.* 81; App. *BC* iii. 3; *LC* 220. 9. In the view of the present writer, the 'Lex Mamilia' belongs to the 50s B.C., and provided legal backing for a general programme of 'municipalisation' of Italian communities, or modernisation of their institutions. Thus it has no direct bearing on veteran settlement under Caesar. Other scholars, however, prefer to date it to 49 B.C., or even 45 B.C.: F. T. Hinrichs, 'Das legale Landversprechen im Bellum Civile', *Historia* xviii (1969), 520-44; Schneider, *Veteranenversorgung* 171 ff.

[13] Kornemann 570; Grant, *FITA* 10. Q. Hortensius settled proletarians at Cassandreia and Dium in 44-42 as *praefectus*. For L. Memmius, *praefectus* for Octavian at Luca after Philippi, below, p. 174.

[14] Cic. *Fam.* xiii. 7 indicates knowledge that the correspondent Cluvius was not a *deductor*, and suggests some uncertainty over the precise powers delegated to him.

Cicero provides welcome though sporadic details of the areas of responsibility of the Dictator's agents. In common doubtless with other eminent men, he was approached by individuals and by communities who hoped that his eloquence and arguments could avert or reduce their losses. We learn that in the late summer of 46 Caesar's surveyors were active in the adjoining territories of Veii and Capena. Cicero feared for his own estate at Tusculum; it remained intact, though we may wonder at his legal right of title, or if the proximity of *ager publicus* occasioned his concern.[15] In the autumn of 45 he addressed vain pleas to a former proconsul of Sardinia, Q. Valerius Orca, to desist from expropriations in the *ager Volaterranus* made public by Sulla; a particular cause for his concern was that one of his friends, recently advanced to senatorial status by Caesar, lost at a stroke the family property that supported this new rank.[16] A certain Cluvius was entreated by the great man to spare public land in Cisalpina rented by the Campanian municipality of Atella; Cluvius had already exempted the public land of Regium Lepidum, which thus escaped being distributed to veterans. These are the only direct references to settlement in Cisalpina at this time.[17] Cicero also wrote to an otherwise unknown M. Rutilius who was engaged in similar but unlocalised settlement work.[18]

Further details on the location of settlements are recoverable from the movements and activities of Octavian, Antony and Ventidius in the months following Caesar's murder (Fig. 2).[19] On his journey from Brundisium to Rome in April 44 Octavian was greeted *en route* by large numbers of his father's veterans, who flocked in from all sides.[20] His itinerary must have included Calatia where VII had been recently established, but we may wonder whether other groups met him from settlements in Apulia, Samnium, Campania or Latium.

In late April 44 Antony moved southwards into Campania to superintend the settlement of legion VIII at Casilinum, personally ploughing the sacred furrow to define its limits. He took the opportunity of visiting other groups of veterans, sounding out their feelings at recent events, and advising them to keep up a regular arms drill in case of future need.[21] He spent less than two weeks at Casilinum, and went on into Samnium;[22] he may have remained there about a week. The aim of this latter visit was doubtless to meet other veterans, perhaps members of legion XI (see below) or of V *Alaudae*, soon to be the backbone of his support. At the beginning of May he returned to Rome at the head of a large body of colonists, numbered by his enemies at 6,000. We are told that the 6,000 (quickly subdivided into cohorts, with officers drawn from their own ranks) were to serve as Antony's

---

[15] Cic. *Fam.* ix. 17.

[16] Cic. *Fam.* xiii. 4, 5.

[17] Cic. *Fam.* xiii. 7. Grant (*FITA* 8–11) identified him with C. Clovius, who issued coins as a *praefectus* in northern Italy in 45; cf. Broughton, *MRR* II, 313, with *Suppl.*, 17. M. H. Crawford, *Roman Republican Coinage* (Cambridge, 1974), 94 n. 1 demurs.

[18] Cic. *Fam.* xiii. 8.

[19] For an excellent analysis of the fast-moving events of these months, see Botermann 14–25.

[20] App. *BC* iii. 12.

[21] Cic. *Phil.* ii. 100; *Att.* xiv. 21. 2. Their equipment was to be inspected monthly by the *IIviri* of the settlements, some of them doubtless their former tribunes or centurions.

[22] Cic. *Att.* xiv. 20.

bodyguard. Appian, whose account telescopes the events of March to May 44, even says that the Senate authorised and approved its formation.[23] But the assembly and convoying of veterans to Rome that spring was related to a more immediate goal: the passing through the *comitia* in June of a series of bills, the most important of which brought about a reallocation of provincial commands in Antony's favour.[24] Other measures of direct benefit to the veterans follows: a *lex Antonia agraria* continued Caesar's work in the resettlement of civilians and veterans.[25] Members of its commission were later found at work in Campania and on or close to the line of the Via Cassia.[26] It is hard to think that any veterans remained to be settled in June 44, except possibly V *Alaudae*, the most junior of the dictator's legions, perhaps not catered for in existing legislation. Most of the intended recipients under the bill must have been civilians. Also at the beginning of June Antony saw to the tabling of a *lex iudiciaria*, one of its provisions particularly favourable to veterans, with the establishment of a third decury of jurymen, on which time-served veterans, especially centurions, could serve (below, p. 108).

To raise 6000 men (or fewer if Appian's figure is exaggerated) must have entailed stripping the settlements at Calatia and Casilinum, and others, and the drawing together of men still in Rome, and of members of V *Alaudae*. A majority would surely wish to return to their allotments without delay, and we may imagine that the strength of the 'bodyguard' was quickly reduced.[27]

No sooner had Antony departed in October of the same year to make contact with his Macedonian legions at Brundisium than Octavian descended on Campania with his closest adherents and a convoy of wagons piled high with cash. He passed through (or round) Casilinum and Capua, and went first to Calatia where legion VII was already established before Caesar's death.[28] Nicolaus alleges that Octavian gave his first attentions to legion VII because of its greater reputation. More importantly, in the current context, legion VIII at Casilinum had recently been settled by Antony.[29] Octavian was less certain of his likely reception there.

After some initial hesitancy on the part of the veterans—some must recently have been to Rome in Antony's interest—he received substantial support from members of both legions whom he persuaded to escort him to the other 'colonies'.[30] He received an ecstatic reception at Cales and Teanum (where settlements, perhaps also of VII, or VIII, can be postulated), and like Antony proceeded into Samnium, presumably to make trial of veterans established there. The sequence of halts could

[23] Cic. *Phil.* ii. 108; App. *BC* iii. 5.

[24] Cic. *Att.* xiv. 22; *Fam.* xi. 2, with Botermann 21.

[25] For its scope and purpose, W. Sternkopf, 'Lex Antonia Agraria', *Hermes* xlvii (1912), 146–51; Broughton, *MRR* II 332–3. A land commission with seven members, including Antony and L. Antonius, was established. A likely colleague is Decidius Saxa, who had professional expertise as a surveyor and land measurer; see R. Syme, 'Who was Decidius Saxa?', *JRS* xxvii (1937), 127–37. That some veterans were settled under the June legislation seems clear from Cic. *Phil.* vi. 14; *Att.* xv. 5; *Fam.* xi. 2.

[26] Cic. *Phil.* x. 22, xii. 23.

[27] It continued to exist in some form until his departure for Brundisium; App. *BC* iii. 32, 39.

[28] Nic. Dam. F130. 132 ff.; Dio xlv. 12; App. *BC* iii. 40; Vell. ii. 61. 1; Botermann 36–45.

[29] Nic. Dam. F130. 136; Cic. *Phil.* v. 3.

[30] Nic. Dam. F130. 138; Cic. *Att.* xvi. 8.

suggest a route through Venafrum towards Bovianum. Capua itself served as a convenient base for his activities.[31] In all he raised some 3,000 men round cadres of VII and VIII, and marched northwards to the city.

His later activities too should provide clues to the location of Caesarian settlements. After the failure of the coup in November 44 he retired into Etruria, visiting (we may assume) the known groups at Veii and Capena, Volaterrae and perhaps others.[32] His precise route is not attested, but he travelled on to the vicinity of Ravenna—Strabo has an unsupported reference to Roman colonists there—where veterans settled in the eastern parts of Cisalpina could join him.[33] The chief assembly point for his forces was the strategically placed town of Arretium on the Via Cassia. Almost certainly this was the site of another settlement, peopled by the *Arretini Iulienses* reported by the Elder Pliny.[34] These accretions to his strength helped to fill out VII and VIII and to provide the core for a new legion.

In the meantime Antony had returned to Rome from the south bringing with him V *Alaudae* and a Praetorian cohort. The remainder of his forces took the coastal route to the north, a journey which not all were destined to complete.[35] It is evident that he must have re-formed legion V from settlements in Apulia or Samnium or both, unless the legion was still marking time in southern Italy awaiting the formal allocation of land.[36] As the senatorial forces gathered to oppose Antony, Ventidius Bassus made a similar foray to centres of Caesarian veterans, and began re-forming legions in Antony's interest. Two were re-formed in colonies south of Rome (as Appian's rather perplexing narrative may imply), and a third perhaps in Picenum; his itinerary included Ancona.[37] Pollio, in a letter to Cicero, gives their numerals as VII, VIII, and IX, from which we may suspect that Ventidius' itinerary had included Campania, where those veterans of VII and VIII remaining, perhaps a majority, might have been enlisted, and (less certainly) that a part of legion IX was distributed in Picenum.[38]

There is some evidence that, as averred by Dio and Appian, Caesar attempted to refrain from confiscation, at least on any large scale, but concentrated on the use of public lands, or the public territory of individual towns, and any land to which the legal title was unsound. The availability of such land must have determined the choice of sites. If we are correct to assume that the state could repossess the abandoned allotments of earlier settlement schemes (below, p. 95), some comparisons in location might be made between Caesar's settlements and the colonies of Sulla, or

---

[31] Cic. *Att.* xvi. 9, 11.

[32] Dio xlv. 13. For a discussion of his activities in Etruria and the support he acquired, see M. Sordi, 'Ottaviano e l'Etruria nel 44 a.C.', *SE* xl (1972), 3–18.

[33] App. *BC* iii. 42; Strabo v. 1. 11.

[34] The *Iulienses* are best seen as settlers of 47–44 B.C., rather than after Philippi (Brunt, *IM* 306), or later in Augustus' reign (Brunt, *IM* 337 n. 1). Arretium was also the home town of his friend C. Maecenas.

[35] On his return journey to Rome, he halted at Casilinum (Cic. Att. xvi. 10), perhaps to observe and if necessary counteract the results of Octavian's visit.

[36] For the ingenious but impossible theory that V *Alaudae* was settled in 45–44 by Plancus at Lugdunum, see M. Rambaud, 'L'origine militaire de la colonie de *Lugdunum*', *CRAI* 1964, 252–77.

[37] App. *BC* iii. 66; Cic. *Phil.* xii. 23.

[38] Cic. *Fam.* x. 33. 4; Botermann 196–7; *RE* VIIIA (1955), 801.

the areas proposed for settlement by Rullus and actually distributed in 59–58, but direct links are hard to document.[39] Sulla had confiscated the entire territories of Arretium and Volaterrae, without in the end distributing much to veterans, and the legal title of the remaining inhabitants was a matter for doubt and debate over the next three decades.[40] In 59, under the first *lex agraria,* Caesar had specifically exempted the *ager Volaterranus* and presumably that part of the *ager Arretinus* which remained in the hands of the old inhabitants, but increased pressure to find land caused both towns to be included in the scheme of 47–44.[41] Caesar added his own estates, and doubtless purchased, or exchanged, much more land, to make up viable blocks of territory. Purchase was for him, as for Rullus, an important means of securing land. Much land would be available through confiscation of the estates of Pompey and his supporters, and this could be utilised where conveniently situated. Entries in the *Liber Coloniarum* ascribe to Caesar work at a number of towns, but we cannot distinguish Caesarian activity of 59–58 from that in 47–44.[42] There is some confirmation for the *Liber*'s testimony on one town, Bovianum, if the epithet *Undecumanorum* can be given a Caesarian origin (below, p. 163). The presence of part of Caesar's legion XI at Bovianum could account for the interest of both Antony and Octavian in central Samnium in 44 B.C. After Caesar's death, Brutus was to tax him with widespread confiscation from innocent owners, and promised compensation to the dispossessed;[43] it may have been former holders of public land whom Brutus proposed to conciliate in this way. Yet we cannot know that Caesar's activities were entirely commendable, or that pressure was not put on landowners to sell, with vague promises of compensation, not always fulfilled on his death.

Each of the legions contained a mixture of Italians and Cisalpines, in varying proportions. Legions VII–X formed the garrison of the Gallic provinces on Caesar's arrival, and were presumably constituted mainly from Italians. Legions VI and XI–XIV had been raised in Caesar's province, both north and south of the Po, and all the legions obtained periodic supplementation from the same source, though we may imagine a constant trickle of men from the peninsula travelling north in the hope of enlistment. Legion V *Alaudae* was raised beyond the Alps, from native Transalpines, as Suetonius' account makes clear.[44] By 49 Caesar's army possessed a substantial coherence in outlook and background, which was an additional factor in its support of his cause. Before Pharsalus, Labienus could encourage Pompey by

[39] For lists of towns where settlement was proposed by Rullus, Cic. *Leg. Agr.* ii. 66, 71, 86, Frag. 2; these included Casilinum, Teanum and Cales. In 60 the tribune Flavius had envisaged that land could be obtained in the *ager Campanus,* from estates in the possession of *Sullani homines,* from the territories of Arretium and Volaterrae, and by purchase (Cic. *Att.* i. 19. 4). Similarly in 43 B.C., D. Brutus imagined that allotments for veterans supporting the Senate could be obtained *ex agris Sullanis et agro Campano* (Cic. *Fam.* xi. 20).

[40] Cic. *Att.* i. 19.

[41] Cic. *Fam.* xiii. 4. 2.

[42] Settlements under a *lex Iulia* which seems likely to be Caesarian are reported at Aesernia, Ancona, Aufidena, Ausculum, Bovianum, Capitulum, Florentia, Herdoniae, Larinum, Luna, Tuder and Veii; work is ascribed to Caesar by name at Capua, Cures Sabini, Minturnae and Volturnum.

[43] App. *BC* iii. 139–41.

[44] *Caes.* 24. 2.

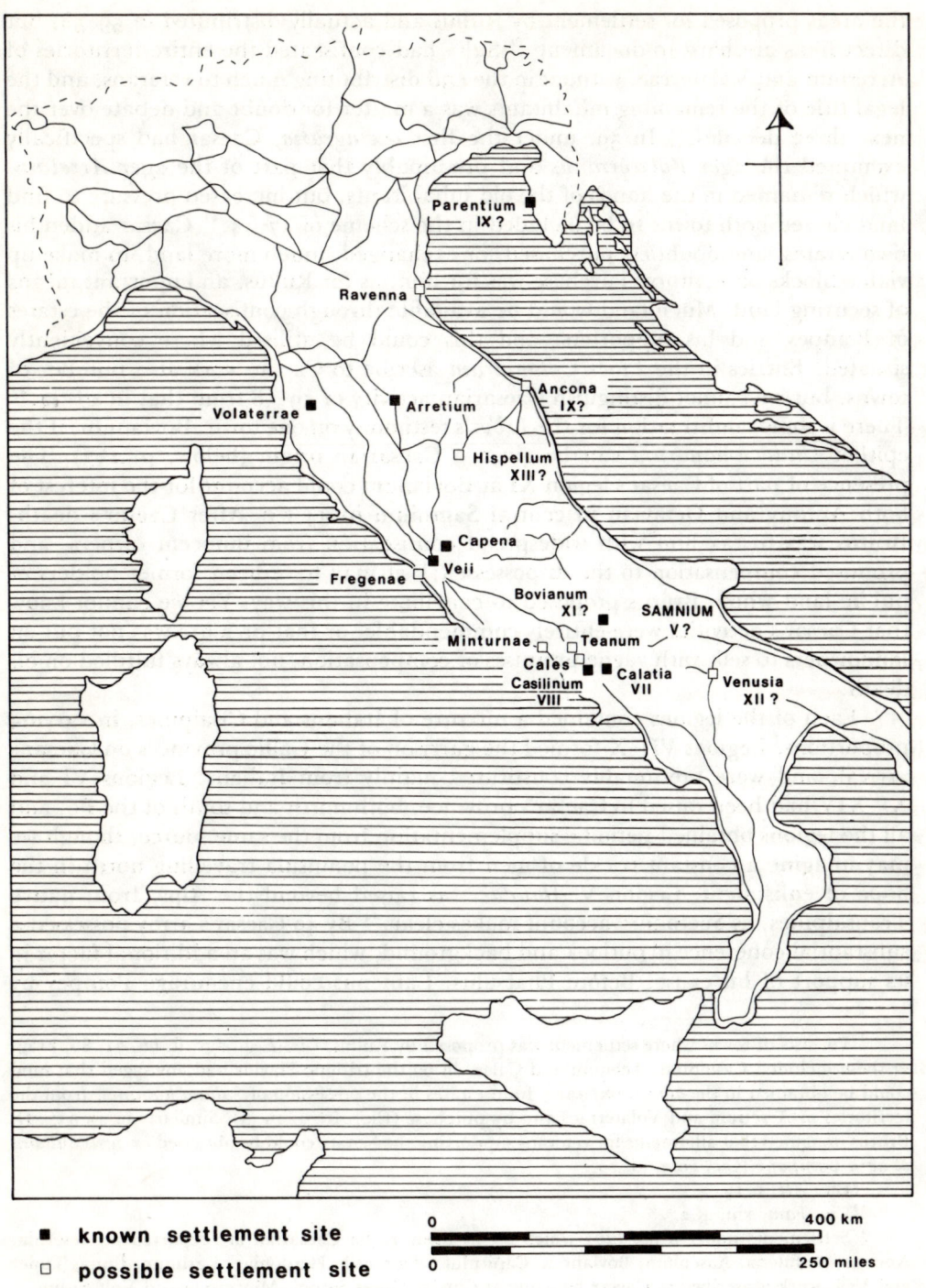

- ■ **known settlement site**
- □ **possible settlement site**

0   400 km

0   250 miles

FIG. 3: CAESAR'S SETTLEMENTS, 47–44 B.C.

emphasising that the genuinely Italian element in Caesar's army was now so diluted that it should prove no match for Pompey's own forces. The claim was an exaggeration, and his estimate of their fighting qualities at variance with reality, as he must have known full well.[45] We should expect that both Transalpina and Cisalpina played an important part in Caesar's plans for the demobilisation and settlement of his veteran legions.

Something can now be said on the location of individual legions after settlement (Fig. 3). Legions VI and X were drafted to Transalpina, though we cannot be sure that some members of both legions did not receive land in Italy. A third legionary group is perhaps to be looked for in the same general area, if Lepidus did indeed succeed in re-forming three evocate formations there in the summer of 44. Substantial numbers from legion VII were established at Calatia and from VIII at Casilinum. Teanum and Cales, and other towns, including perhaps Minturnae, (below, p. 142) could have received small groups also from VII and VIII. Octavian enlisted 3,000 men from among the veterans of these two legions in the autumn of 44, which should imply that all or nearly all their personnel were settled in Campania.[46] There is no secure evidence for settlement at Capua itself, though the contrary is frequently averred.[47] Much less certainly, part of IX was accommodated in Picenum; others of its members perhaps received land in Histria, if an inscription from Parentium is a true commemoration of settlement there at this time.[48] Finally, to complete the scanty record, a section of XI may have received land at Bovianum.

Appian notes several times that Caesar held together his legions in their military framework ἀθρόους ὑπὸ σημείοις καὶ συντάξει στρατιωτικῇ.[49] We have already seen evidence of concentrations of men from VII and VIII in Campania, and for VI and X in Transalpina. Caesar had, in Dio's version, promised to distribute his men ἄλλους ἄλλῃ, by which he may have meant in small groups rather than individually. Perhaps cohortal organisation at most was maintained among settlers from IX in Picenum, or in Etruria, where Veii and Capena, and perhaps Volaterrae and Arretium, might all have received settlers from the same legion. Many more small settlements doubtless remain to be identified.[50] Of legions as yet unallocated to districts in Italy it is reasonable to assign the groups settled in Etruria to one, and to think that the others may have been accommodated in Cisalpina. It may be noted that epitaphs of veterans of legions XII and XIII have

---

[45] Caes. *BC* iii. 87.

[46] I find no evidence to support the view that VII was divided between Calatia and Narbonensian Baeterrae at this time, as Brunt *IM* 258.

[47] Mommsen, *Bürgercolonien* 168; Botermann 1. The comments of Suet. *Caes.* 81 and Dio xlv. 12. 2 should refer to assignments within the territory of Calatia, later incorporated into that of Capua.

[48] Below, p. 202; Sylloge 87. The theory that legion IX was settled by Plancus at Raurica in 44–43 lacks supporting evidence; see B. H. Isaac, 'Colonia Munatia Triumphalis and Legio Nona Triumphalis?', *Talanta* iii (1971), 11–43.

[49] *BC* ii. 139–41; cf. ii. 133, iii. 81.

[50] In November 44 Tibur served as a convenient rallying point for veterans (App. *BC* iii. 45–6). A fragmentary inscription from Fregenae in southern Etruria was erected in 46/45 by unspecified *coloni* to Caesar as *dictator tertium* (XI 3727). This may testify to another small settlement, but Fregenae was already a maritime Roman colony of 245 B.C. Other towns in Etruria where some settlement at this time may be suspected are Castrum Novum (below, p. 172) and perhaps Florentia (below, p. 175).

come to light at or near the post-Philippi colonies at Venusia and Hispellum (Sylloge 74–5, 97), which could serve as evidence for small-scale Caesarian settlement at both towns in 47–44. Alternatively, the men could be *evocati* established after Philippi (below, p. 67).

Caesar's veterans: suggested location of settlements, 47–44 B.C.

legion	Italy			provinces
V *Alaudae*	?			Thuburnica?
VI	?			Arelate
VII	Calatia	}	? Cales	?
			? Teanum	
VIII	Casilinum	}	? Minturnae	?
IX	Picenum?			Parentium?
X	?			Narbo
XI	Bovianum (and elsewhere in Samnium?)			?
XII	Venusia?			Gaul?
XIII	Hispellum?			Uthina?
XIV	?			?

   The settlement of time-served veterans formed but a part of Caesar's wider schemes for the regeneration of Italy and the development of the provinces, which continued and expanded the work of his consulship. Up to 80,000 civilians, many of them freedmen and their families, were drained away from the city of Rome, and were accommodated in colonies in Spain, Africa, Illyricum, Macedonia and the East. Only one colonist in four or five was a veteran, but most of the latter, unlike the civilians, received land within Italy itself. Occasionally it seems that, at least in the provinces, civilian and military colonists were settled side by side.[51]
   The veteran settlements of Caesar in Italy did not lead for the most part, or at all, to the formal establishment of new *coloniae,* though several existing colonies were reinforced.[52] The constitutions of the towns in whose *territoria* the veterans were established apparently remained unchanged. Plutarch, Appian, Nicolaus and Cicero all refer to Caesar's settlements as *coloniae,* or the Greek equivalents, but it seems that the veterans merely formed enclaves within existing *municipia.*[53] This too suggests that Caesar took pains to minimise disturbance, and to cut down the likelihood of future troubles, displaying thereby a degree of tact which his successors in this sphere, the Triumvirs, did not always care to exhibit.

2. *After Philippi*

By the end of November 42 the fighting at Philippi was over and those time-served men entitled to discharge were separated and despatched to Italy to await settle-

---

   [51] At Carthage (Strabo xvii. 3. 15); Corinth (Plut. *Caes.* 57 with Strabo viii. 6. 23). A veteran of legion XXX served as *IIvir* in proletarian Urso (*ILS* 2233). Civilian and military colonists were evidently combined at Capua in 59 B.C.
   [52] So Calatia and Casilinum (if, as seems likely, they had become *coloniae* in 59 B.C.), Arretium (Sullan) and Minturnae (295 B.C.).
   [53] App. *BC* iii. 12, 31, 87; Cic. *Phil* v. 53; *Att.* xvi. 8; Plut. *Caes.* 57, *Ant.* 16; Nic. Dam. F130. 56, 131.

ment. Octavian reached Brundisium soon after, but, detained there by illness, did not arrive in Rome before January 41.[54]

That the principal reward for the legionaries was to be land had been decided upon at Bononia in October 43, and the settlement programme was apparently carried out by virtue of the *lex Titia,* by which legal backing had been accorded to the various provisions of the Bononia agreement.[55] By a pact finalised at Philippi itself, Octavian and Antony had agreed that the former should be given a free hand to organise the settlements, and this Octavian proceeded to do, to the total exclusion of Antony's supporters. According to Dio, commissioners for the individual colonies had already been designated at Bononia; it was perhaps these men that Octavian early in 41 replaced by his own nominees. But, after vigorous representations by L. Antonius and Fulvia, he was forced to concede, and Antonian partisans were selected (or reappointed) to supervise the settlement of veterans of the absent Triumvir.[56] The Antonians appointed to continue the work—we may imagine that Octavian's men had already got the survey under way—allowed extra licence to the veterans, in a bid to counteract his influence.

A few of these supervisors—the οἰκισταί of the historians—can be identified, and others tentatively named from among known sympathisers of Antony and Octavian. At Luca an otherwise unknown L. Memmius acted on Octavian's behalf as *praefectus legionum* XXVI *et* VII (Pl. IIIA; below, p. 174). Elsewhere in his interest we may identify less securely the aged Calpurnius Piso Caesoninus at Pola (below, p. 204; but his work could belong earlier). Octavian himself is credited by Appian with participating in the settlement of at least one group (perhaps at Teanum, see below, p. 140) in the summer of 41. No activity by Agrippa is reported; more probably he remained in command of Octavian's main military strength at Capua. Of the Antonian commissioners, the most distinguished was L. Munatius Plancus, consul throughout 42, and so on hand in Italy. Plancus took over the settlement at Beneventum, perhaps also with the designation *praefectus* (a title which his commemorative epitaph at Gaieta does not report).[57] The jurist Alfenus Varus is a possible commissioner at Cremona.[58] Other prominent Antonians—Ventidius, Pollio, and Calenus—were distracted by provincial commands, though Pollio was perhaps allotted, or assumed, a general supervisory role in colonies within his own province of Cisalpina. Other, lesser, figures would also be involved.[59] L. Antonius himself, with experience gained three years earlier, need not have been debarred by consular office from participation in the work. Equally, Ti. Claudius Nero, later to

---

[54] Dio xlviii. 5. 1.

[55] Dio xlvii. 2. 1 with App. *BC* iv. 7. Part of a joint edict by the Triumvirs on particulars of land survey is preserved at *LC* 212-3. See F. T. Hinrichs, 'Das legale Landversprechen im Bellum Civile', *Historia* xviii (1969), 521-44.

[56] Dio xlvii. 14. 4; App. *BC* v. 14.

[57] *ILS* 886; Broughton, *MRR* II 374 considers that Plancus acted as *proconsul*.

[58] The old view that Pollio, Varus and the equestrian Cornelius Gallus acted jointly as commissioners at Cremona has been adequately exploded by Broughton, *MRR* II 377.

[59] R. Syme, 'Pollio, Saloninus and Salonae', *CQ* xxxi (1937), 39-48; H. Bennett, 'Vergil and Pollio', *AJP* li (1930), 325-42; A. B. Bosworth, 'Asinius Pollio and Augustus', *Historia* xxi (1972), 441-73. For other prominent friends of Antony, see R. Syme, *RR* 210.

join L. Antonius at Perusia and thereafter to stir Campania in his interest, may have participated; Nero had already served Caesar himself in a similar capacity.[60]

The task of expropriating land began early in 41, and representatives of the dispossessed flocked to Rome to put their cases before Octavian, the consul L. Antonius, their patrons and their friends, largely we may imagine to no avail. By the time of the outbreak of the Perusine War in the summer of 41, the work of settlement was well advanced; the 'residue of the colonies' were already in hand before hostilities erupted in earnest.[61] The briefness of the time-span serves as testimony to the insistence of the veterans and the ruthlessness of the exactions. Some reminiscence of the settlement work may appear in the coinage of the moneyer Ti. Sempronius Gracchus, on the reverse of whose issues (datable to about 40 B.C.) appear military standards, together with a plough and a surveyor's rod.[62]

According to Appian, in a speech placed in the mouth of Antony at Ephesus, the total number of veterans requiring land and money was 170,000.[63] It can be estimated that about 100,000 men fought for the Triumvirs at Philippi. After the battle, in which casualties on the side of the Triumvirs can be estimated at 20,000, the time-served were identified and segregated, and the remainder, together with some 14,000 from the defeated armies of the Liberators, reorganised into 11 legions, for which a total strength about 50,000-55,000 can be assumed; the lower figure is perhaps more likely. It follows that about 44,000 were offered discharge at this time, and, of these, 8000 elected to continue under arms (above, p. 37). Thus the total sent back to Italy should have numbered about 36,000. Evocate Caesarian legionaries must be included in the above figure; we may judge the number of *evocati* from up to 9 legions, who survived the battle, at not more than 10,000. It will shortly become clear that not all returned to allotments given by Caesar; some gained a fresh allocation of land in a post-Philippi colony. If it is imagined that half had to be provided for in addition to those whose *stipendia* were now for the first time complete, allotments would be required for some 31,000 men; to these must be added the time-served men of legions which had remained in Italy, the western provinces, and Africa. About six legions fell into this category, from which perhaps 15,000 can be added, making for a total of about 46,000; all but a few were accommodated in Italy. The only known overseas colony of this time was at Philippi itself.[64] The computation of 170,000 men is either Appian's own, or if genuinely from the mouth of Antony, then a deliberate over-estimate. Later the Antonian agent Manius was to claim that 34 legions, and not the 28 which had hitherto been deemed eligible, were being given land by Octavian. These six additional legions cannot be securely identified: they were not evocate units or the garrison legions of the west, both categories being included in the 28 already catered for. We may wonder if Octavian was endeavouring to find land for time-served men who formed

[60] Suet. *Tib.* 4. 2; Vell. ii. 75. 1.

[61] App. *BC* v. 12, 19.

[62] M. H. Crawford, *Roman Republican Coinage* (Cambridge, 1974), no. 525. The allusion may also be to the land-settlement activities of Gracchus' forebears in 133–122 B.C.

[63] *BC* v. 5. For discussion of the numbers released, see Schmitthenner 144; Brunt, *IM* 488–93.

[64] Philippi received veterans from a legion XXVIII (*EJ*[2] 259) and of the Praetorian cohorts (above, p. 35).

the core of newer legions.[65] Brunt has suggested that the figure of 170,000 represents Appian's estimate of the total paper strength of the 28 legions requiring settlement, but the figure could as easily be linked to the 34 legions if each of the latter was estimated to contain 5,000 men.[66]

In all 18 cities were to lose their land by the Bononia agreement for the benefit of the veterans. The method of acquiring land was simple and callous: wholesale confiscation from owners mostly innocent of any disaffection or disloyalty. With good reason could the dispossessed complain of the injustice of their plight. Sulla had in the main selected as colonies towns most persistent in their opposition to his cause, but now the institution of colonisation was being turned with a vengeance against the very people who had perfected it.

The 18 cities were selected at Bononia in October 43, and their identity quickly became known. It is possible that legions were already allocated to specific towns at this time. The criteria for selection were known prosperity and proven fertility of their lands; the 18 were towns καὶ περιουσίᾳ καὶ ἐδάφεσι καὶ οἴκοις εἰς κάλλος διαφέρουσαι.[67] Appian names seven which he says were particularly prosperous: Capua, Rhegium, Venusia, Beneventum, Nuceria, Ariminum and Vibo. The 18 are described by Appian as Ἰταλικαὶ πόλεις, and the seven named all lie south of the Rubicon. However, several of the towns, where we know or suspect that settlement took place after Philippi, lay in Cisalpina, and we should ask whether these (e.g. Cremona, Concordia, Luca and Bononia) must be computed in addition. It is, however, more probable that Cisalpina played from the start a significant part in the settlement plans of the Triumvirs, and that colonies there formed part of the original group. One of the towns selected (Bononia) was the scene of their conference, and the attractions of its *territorium* would have been visible on all sides.[68]

The decision to make the total 18 may have been random, based on a rough calculation of likely capacity, or represent a compromise figure reached only after protracted negotiation. However, it would be attractive to suppose that the figure had a particular and immediate relevance, in that the Triumvirs judged their combined forces at Bononia to consist of just 18 legions which, after the successful conclusion of the forthcoming struggle, would be eligible for land settlement.[69] Just such a list of 18 legions can be compiled from formations then directly under the control of Octavian, Lepidus, Pollio, Plancus, Ventidius and Antony at this time. Of these Octavian had four (IIII, *Martia*, XXVI, and XXIX), Lepidus four (none identifiable), Plancus three (none identifiable), Pollio two or three (XXVIII, XXX

[65] App. *BC* v. 22. Alternatively, Appian may have erred by adding twice over the number of 'western' legions to the 22 which fought at Philippi.

[66] *IM* 490.

[67] App. *BC* iv. 3.

[68] Cisalpina was still a province at the time of the Bononia conference, and was then assigned to Pollio for the period 42–41 or 42–40. Octavian returned from Philippi with the agreement of Antony that it should be added to Italy forthwith, but his claim to this effect was disputed, and Pollio proved reluctant to surrender the command.

[69] For suggestions of a link with the number of legions to be settled, see A. Von Domaszewski, 'Die Heere der Bürgerkriege in den Jahre 49 bis 42 vor Christus', *NHJ* iv (1894), 157–88, at 183; Botermann 166–7, 204.

and ?XXI), and Antony three (II, XXXV, and one formerly belonging to D. Brutus), a total of 16 or 17. To these could be added either the remaining legion in Africa, or one probably now in Sardinia, or both if Pollio had only two legions.[70] The 18 should be legions with a component of time-served men on whose loyalty the Triumvirs could rely, or sought, in October 43. It may be concluded that their intention was to distribute legions singly among the colonies.

One factor, however, disturbed this neat distribution — the evocate legions. Of these there were in the Triumvirs' armies about nine: VII and VIII with Octavian, V *Alaudae* with Antony, VI, X and perhaps another (XII?) with Lepidus, and VII, VIII, and IX with Ventidius. At Bononia it may have been assumed that *evocati* would return after the coming campaign to the allotments received from Caesar. Cicero imagined that *evocati* from VII and VIII, who had (as he thought) rallied to the side of the Senate, could be allocated enlarged holdings in their old colonies, and we might assume from an authoritative passage of Siculus Flaccus that all *evocati* went home after Philippi.[71]

Yet it seems clear that many *evocati* sought and received fresh allotments after Philippi. Antony's figure of 28 legions for whom land and money had to be provided represents a combination of the younger legions (those recruited in 49–48) and the evocate formations. The number of legions to be accommodated thus grew unexpectedly, but it is not clear that the basic list of 18 prospective colonies was correspondingly enlarged. Already before Philippi Octavian had made a show of exempting Vibo (Hipponium) and Rhegium,[72] to prevent these important harbour towns from welcoming the ships of Sextus, but, while substitutes were perhaps found in north-east Italy (see below), the total probably remained stable. The earnest representations of the dispossessed that the burden should be shared more equitably may imply that the number of towns affected was not greatly altered, though Lucius Antonius was later to claim that all Italy was being handed over to veterans.[73] The proscription of more cities was politically unacceptable, and, where the land of a particular town proved insufficient, the balance was acquired at the expense of its neighbours, until all the colonists had received their allotted portion (below, p. 89).

Some small-scale work may be evidenced by the *Liber Coloniarum*. Numerous entries report work carried out *a Triumviris* or *lege triumvirale* at towns which remained *municipia* under the Empire; some of the towns in this category, which lie close to known colonies, may have suffered by their expansion, and other references may testify to detached *praefecturae* of individual colonies.[74] In most cases we lack the means of verifying this information. Small groups of veterans, perhaps from

---

[70] Botermann achieves the figure of 18 by including V *Alaudae* and the younger of the two legions under the control of D. Brutus. Despite her careful assessment (loc.cit. n. 69), the case for neither can be maintained. For V *Alaudae*, see above, p. 50. Brutus' younger legion was raised about 45 B.C., and would not have veterans eligible for settlement in any number after Philippi.

[71] Cic. *Phil.* v. 53; Sic. Flacc. 162. 9.

[72] App. *BC* iv. 86.

[73] App. *BC* v. 22.

[74] The towns mentioned are Allifae, Asetium, Falerii, Formiae, Interamna Lirenas, Ligures Baebiani et Corneliani, Nepet, Pausulum, Potentia, Ricina, Sena Gallica, Setia, Signia, Telesia, Tolentinum, Ulubrae, and Volaterrae.

those additional legions of whose inclusion in the programme Manius complains, may have been accommodated in this way.

However, while the number of legions requiring settlement grew, it does not follow that the total number of veterans for whom land had to be found in 41 was much higher than that envisaged at the time of Bononia. With casualties in the battle itself, and the decision of a substantial number to continue in service (the latter eventuality at least could not have been confidently anticipated), together with the almost total loss of the *legio Martia* during the crossing of the Adriatic, the numbers to be provided for need not have exceeded the original estimates.[75]

Frequent attempts have been made to select the 18 cities of the Triumvirs, sometimes on the flimsiest of evidence.[76] More recently scholars have been reticent over the conclusive allocation of colonies among the various schemes of the period.[77] Nevertheless a provisional list of colonies where land was assigned to veterans in the aftermath of Philippi can be drawn up, by specific attestation in the literary sources, or by observation of the movements of Octavian and others during the Perusine War, or by the identification of epitaphs of veterans likely to have been settled at this time. Appian names Capua, Ariminum, Beneventum, Nuceria and Venusia; from other literary references we may add Ancona, Bononia, Cremona, Hispellum, Pisaurum, and perhaps Teanum and Asculum. The epigraphic evidence allows the inclusion of Luca, Firmum, probably Aquinum, Concordia and Tergeste and (less certainly) Hadria. A provisional list is tabulated below:

	town	attestation	legions	titulature
1.	Ancona	App.*BC* v.23	(2 legions)	—
2.	Aquinum?	—	III	—
3.	Ariminum	App.*BC* iv.3	—	*Augusta*
4.	Asculum?	—	—	—
5.	Beneventum	App.*BC* iv.3	VI, XXX	*Iulia Concordia*
		ILS 886		*Augusta Felix*
6.	Bononia	Suet.*Aug.* 17.2	—	—
		Dio l.6.3		
7.	Capua	App.*BC* iv.3	VII/VIII?	*Concordia Iulia*
				Felix Augusta
8.	Concordia	—	—	*Iulia Concordia*
9.	Cremona	Verg.*Ecl.*ix.28	X, XV or II?	—
10.	Firmum	—	IIII *Mac.*	(*Iulia?*)
11.	Hadria?	—	XXIX?	(*Veneria?*)
12.	Hispellum	Prop.*El.*iv.1.130	XIII?	*Iulia*
13.	Luca	*ILS* 887	VII, XXVI	—
14.	Nuceria	App.*BC* iv.3	XIX	*Constantia*
15.	Pisaurum	Plut.*Ant.*60.2	—	*Iulia Felix*
16.	Teanum?	App.*BC* v.19–20	VIII	*Cl(assica?) Firma*
17.	Tergeste?	(below, p. 201)	—	—
18.	Venusia	App.*BC* iv.3	XII?	—

[75] But *evocati* requiring resettlement would receive allotments at above the basic rate.

[76] A. W. Zumpt, in *Commentationes Epigraphicae* (Berlin, 1850), 332; B. Borghesi, *Oeuvres Complètes* V (Paris, 1869), 258–76; K. J. Beloch, *It. Bund* 10–13; L. Hollaender, *De militum coloniis ab Augusto in Italia deductis* (Halle, 1880), passim; Mommsen, *Bürgercolonien* 169; Pais, *Colonie militari* 37–9; idem, *Serie cronologica* 366; Gabba, *Colonie triumvirali* 101–10; M. Volponi, *Lo sfondo italico della lotta triumvirale* (Genova, 1975), 85 ff.; Schneider, *Veteranenversorgung* 222–5.

[77] Brunt, *IM* 329, 608–10; Harris 299.

It is assumed here that, where Appian states that a town was marked out at Bononia for settlement after the victory, and where we know it was a colony under the Empire from other evidence, it did receive settlers after Philippi. Future discoveries of epigraphic evidence will determine whether Aquinum, Hadria, Teanum, Tergeste, or Asculum are correctly included. Other towns (e.g. Florentia) may need to be substituted, but I consider it unlikely that the list will require significant alteration. Neither Tergeste nor Concordia can be easily thought of as among the most flourishing cities of Italy; Concordia is likely to have been a fresh creation of the later first century (below, p. 201). I conjecture that these towns were introduced as substitutes for the now exempted Vibo (Hipponium) and Rhegium. Pola, often included by scholars in lists of post-Philippi colonies, could as easily be a civilian colony of 47–44, one of Caesar's foundations on the coast of Illyricum (below, p. 204).

It is evident that legions were frequently sent to the post-Philippi colonies in pairs. Such a course could hardly be avoided if 28 legions were to be accommodated in 16 or 18 towns. The doubling up of legions in colonies is frequently attested throughout this period.[78] In the post-Philippi settlement, Appian reports that two legions with Antonian sympathies had been placed together at Ancona, and epigraphic evidence provides confirmation for Luca, almost certainly for Beneventum, less securely for Cremona. It seems that one of the younger group of legions (i.e. those raised in 49–48) might share a colony with an evocate formation: at Luca we find XXVI, one of these younger legions, coupled with VII (not XXVII, see below, p. 174). At Beneventum inscriptions identify settlers belonging to XXX and VI (here identified as the evocate Caesarian unit, previously settled at Arelate). Less certainly, at Cremona, the evocate legion X may have shared the colony with a legion XV or a legion II, the last mentioned perhaps formerly of the Macedonian garrison.

Some Caesarian *evocati*, it would seem, did not return after Philippi to the allotments laboriously prepared in 47–44, but received land elsewhere. Members of VI, otherwise known to have been established at Arelate, are now found at Beneventum, and at least one former member of X, whose colony was Narbo, is attested at Cremona. Perhaps resettlement in Italy was an agreed price for the adhesion of those who had been excluded from it by the Dictator. Their numbers cannot have been high. The perplexing order of legions on L. Memmius' memorial (XXVI *et* VII), which transgresses both seniority and numerical sequence, is best explained if XXVI provided a considerable majority of men actually settled at Luca. Veterans of Caesar's VII and VIII were placed at Calatia and Casilinum in 45–44. Those *evocati* who did return could expect to receive enlarged holdings, which might have resulted in an overflow, so that some were moved elsewhere. Hence perhaps the appearance of what is manifestly Octavian's VII at Luca, and his VIII at Teanum (below, pp. 175, 140). Enlarged allotments at Capua itself could have been reserved for members of the pro-Antonian VII and VIII re-enlisted by Ventidius.

---

[78] So at Berytus, Patrae, Acci (*colonia Gemella*), Antiochia Pisidiae, Caesarea Augusta (three legions), and Augusta Emerita.

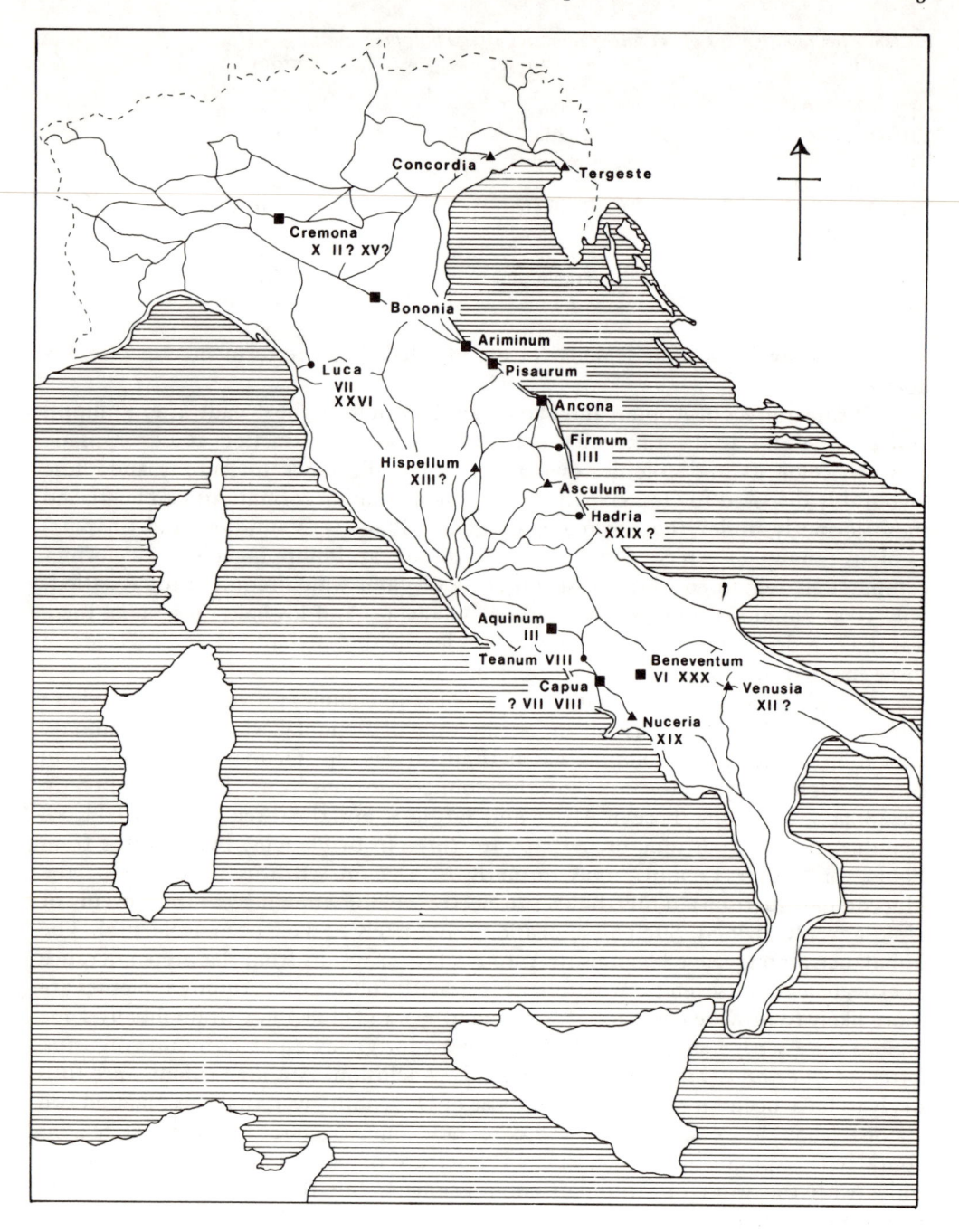

- colony of Octavian
- colony of Antony
- colony of uncertain loyalty

FIG. 4: SETTLEMENTS AFTER PHILIPPI

Evidence for resettlement of evocate legionaries after Philippi

legion	moved from	settled at
V	?	?
VI	Arelate	Beneventum
VII (Octavian)	Calatia	Luca
VIII (Octavian)	Casilinum	Teanum
VII (Ventidius)	Calatia	Capua?
VIII (Ventidius)	Casilinum	Capua?
IX (Ventidius)	Picenum?	?
X	Narbo	Cremona
XII	Transalpina?	Venusia?
XIII	?	Hispellum?

There is no evidence that legions XI or XIV had been re-formed after Caesar's death.

The narratives of Appian and Dio make clear that, in the decade after Philippi, and particularly at the time of the Perusine War, a distinction could be made between colonists and colonies owing particular allegiance to Antony and those favourably disposed to Octavian.[79] Among the Antonian formations can be placed those formerly under the command of Pollio, Plancus, Ventidius, and (in part) Lepidus, many of which fought under Antony at Philippi while their former commanders remained in the west. Of the 28 legions which required to be settled, only 11 at the most can be considered pro-Octavian, and his hold on some of these was shaky indeed. The total includes legions left behind in Sardinia and Africa, and three handed over by Lepidus to strengthen his forces.

It might seem therefore that only a minority of colonies provided for Octavian's soldiers. This, however, was not so. At the time of Bononia, when the preliminary allocation of legions to colonies was perhaps drawn up, Octavian could claim to control eight or perhaps nine of the younger legions (i.e. those recruited in 49–48 B.C.), including those in Africa and Sardinia, and the three just received from Lepidus; Antony had nine or perhaps 10 (three from Plancus, two or three from Pollio, one from Lepidus, one formerly of Decimus Brutus, and two of the Macedonian garrison). Thus the 18 prospective colonies might seem to be evenly or almost evenly divided. Such an allocation is not likely to have been accidental. The imbalance among the 28 legions in Antony's favour results from the preponderance of evocate legions (seven to two) under his sway. It follows that Antony's colonies are more likely to provide evidence of settlement by pairs of legions. Undoubtedly some legions were settled singly, as III *Macedonica* for Octavian at Firmum; Augustus' letter *ad quartanos suos* surely requires this conclusion. Antony's colonies are thus likely to have been larger in size than those of Octavian, given that most housed two legions (though we can never estimate how many veterans individual legions contained). Appian in fact associates the seizure of land from adjoining communities with the work of Antonian commissioners, but this may be the result of Octavian's propaganda.[80]

Literary evidence suggests that Pisaurum, Ancona, Bononia, and less certainly

[79] Pais, *Colonie militari* 41; Gabba, *Colonie triumvirali* 101 develops this point.
[80] *BC* v. 14.

Ariminum received settlers from legions which had been associated before or during the Philippi campaign with Antony.[81] A division between colonies owing allegiance to Octavian and to Antony is apparent also from the epigraphic corpus: Luca received settlers from XXVI and VII, both of which can confidently be placed in Octavian's sphere of influence (XXVI he had acquired from Africa, VII in Campania). At Beneventum, Munatius Plancus (whose sympathies at this time were with Antony) settled the evocate legion VI of Lepidus along with Pollio's XXX; both surely passed to Antony at Bononia. At Cremona, Lepidus' evocate legion X may be tentatively linked with XV, or Antony's legion II. If Aquinum is indeed a post-Philippi colony (below, p. 137), the legion III attested there must be Antony's III *Gallica,* which helps to establish the proclivities of colonists there. Firmum received settlers from Octavian's IIII *Macedonica.* Likewise Hadria (or it and Pola, if legion XXIX was divided between the two) can be ascribed to Octavian; legion XXIX had been among his forces since July 43. Teanum, scene of a projected meeting between Octavian and Lucius, has a veteran of VIII *Mutinensis* (below, p. 140); this is clearly Octavian's formation (that of Ventidius did not fight at Mutina and could not claim the title). The sequence of Appian's narrative in any case suggests that Octavian was then temporarily based on Teanum, supervising the settlement of veterans there.[82]

Thus the following table of loyalties can be tentatively advanced:

Octavian:		Antony:	
	Firmum		Ancona
	Hadria?		Aquinum
	Luca		Ariminum?
	Teanum		Beneventum
			Bononia
			Capua?
			Cremona
			Pisaurum

Venusia too could be considered Antonian, if a former member of legion XII is a genuine settler there. This legion was possibly re-formed by Lepidus (above, p. 24), and passed to Antony. The remaining colonies (Nuceria with XIX, Hispellum perhaps with *evocati* from XIII, Concordia, Tergeste and Asculum) cannot be assigned to either party.

Appian states that the 18 colonies were selected for settlement because of their outstanding general prosperity, which should provide a useful criterion in the identification of those not named. Colonies might on these grounds be looked for in Campania, in Cisalpina, the Arno valley, the Pianura Umbra and elsewhere. Of the seven towns named by Appian, five (Capua, Beneventum, Nuceria, Ariminum, and Venusia) would probably merit inclusion in any list of prosperous Italian towns, but the other two (Vibo and Rhegium) are less obvious candidates. It is tempting to think that only their exemption by Octavian brought them to the notice of Appian. Of others known or suspected to belong to the 18, most (e.g. Bononia, Hispellum, Aquinum, Luca, Teanum, and Concordia) were major centres lying amid extensive

---

[81] Plut. *Ant.* 60. 2; App. *BC* v. 23; Dio l. 6. 3; App. *BC* v. 33.
[82] *BC* v. 19.

flat (and mostly fertile) land, easily accommodating large numbers of veterans. However, others (Ancona, Firmum, Tergeste and Pisaurum) seem less easily admissible into this category, but all had some fertile land at their disposal. It is wise not to press Appian's words too far, or think that we can accurately determine the prosperity of any town at this particular time. Hillsides suitable for vineyards or olive groves could provide a higher return than cornfields in the plains. But other factors were not ignored in the selection of sites: many lay at important road junctions, the control of which could monitor and restrict the movement of hostile forces into and within Italy. At first sight it might seem that a body of veterans scattered in the *territorium,* and preoccupied (as I shall argue) with agriculture, could exert little influence on events, but public opinion was quick to see, and hostile politicians to claim, that colonies of this and other schemes were designed to provide garrisons and strongpoints, to dominate Italy.[83] We may instance Capua and Beneventum, controlling approaches to Rome from the south, and (in the north) Cremona, Ariminum, Bononia and Luca well placed to monitor access from Cisalpina into the peninsula. In any list of towns, the control of which would give mastery over Italy, the above mentioned would scarcely be absent. It is noticeable that many of the most strategically placed were occupied by Antonian troops. Meanwhile some but not all of Octavian's troops were relegated to isolated backwaters, e.g. Firmum and Hadria.[84] If the above distinction is more than illusory, the selection of colonies for individual legions must go back to Bononia. It would be unthinkable for Octavian to assign such strategic points to Antonian troops in the early months of 41.

The outbreak of the Perusine War found most probably all, or nearly all, the veterans already at their colonies, putting their steadings in order. The onset of hostilities caught several of the chief partisans of both protagonists preoccupied with the settlement of the veterans, on whose expertise and support they were shortly to rely. It is evident that not all the partisans of Antonius relished the rôle which the march of events, or deliberate timing by Lucius, had enjoined.[85]

In the south, Plancus assumed command of forces regrouped by the energetic Fulvia. Later he had two legions, easily identifiable as VI and XXX, upon whose settlement at Beneventum he was currently engaged. With their help he intercepted and cut up a legion of Octavian, probably one *en route* to Rome from Brundisium;

---

[83] App. *BC* ii. 140, v. 2; Cic. *Leg. Agr.* i. 16, ii. 75, 98.

[84] Perhaps we should also assign Vibo and Rhegium to Octavian on this account. Luca on the other hand was a road centre of some note. Personal animosities cannot be shown to have played more than a minor role in site-selection; see Cic. *Phil.* vii. 23 for Firmum, Servius on *Ecl.* ix. 28 for Cremona. Servius (who confuses the campaigns of Philippi and Actium) states that the *Cremonenses* were punished for their support of Antony (*Proem.* p. 2 Thilo), but it seems likely that the town received colonists from one or more Antonian legions (below, p. 190). Teanum had Brutus and Cassius as patrons (Cic. *Phil.* ii. 107).

[85] For a narrative of events, M. Reinhold, 'The Perusine War', *CW* xxvi (1932–33), 180–3; E. Gabba, *Appiani V* p. xlvii–iv; idem, 'The Perusine War and Triumviral Italy', *HSCP* lxxv (1971), 139–60; P. Wallmann, 'Untersuchungen zu militarischen Problemen der Perusinischen Krieges,' *Talanta* vi (1975), 58–91. Macrobius has the story that Asinius Pollio used force against the people of Patavium to obtain money and arms (*Sat.* i. 11. 22). The story, if genuine, could belong to the period of the Perusine War, or its aftermath, rather than be linked to the exactions following Philippi. Patavium had supported the senatorial cause in 43 B.C. (Cic. *Phil.* xii. 10).

at Beneventum he was ideally placed to entrap it.[86] The Antonian commanders in the north were slow to react, and, even though they had substantial regular forces at their command, did not penetrate into Italy until October or November 41. That veterans of the Antonian colonies in the north were included in their augmented forces, is highly likely, but nowhere specified. Lucius Antonius, having collected those Antonian veterans he could muster in central Italy and Etruria, and raising additional levies, retired into the hilltop fortress of Perusia, where he could count on some local support from the population of the Pianura Umbra, in part dispossessed in favour of the colony at Hispellum.[87]

With the fall of Perusia Octavian allowed the colonists in Lucius' camp to disperse to their allotments. Plancus' two legions, on a southwards trek towards safety and their homes, and abandoned by Plancus, surrendered to Agrippa at Camerinum; doubtless they then returned, or were convoyed, to Beneventum.[88] The greater part of the *ager Perusinus* was now confiscated, though whether it was now distributed to veterans, or later, is not clear (cf. below, p. 179).

Later in the year, when Antony came to Brundisium to parley with Octavian, Agrippa was despatched with a military force to oppose him. He called out veterans in colonies along his route. Among those whom he sought to persuade should be Antonian veterans at Beneventum, recently returned from Camerinum. Their lack of enthusiasm is hardly surprising and they soon dispersed. Somewhat later, Octavian, presumably travelling on the same route, make a further attempt to harness their support, again without success, though he did persuade men whom he had settled personally to follow him to Brundisium.[89] He may have prevailed on men at Teanum, though not at Venusia which did not lie directly on his known line of march. Antony's Praetorian cohorts, composed of time-served men who had turned down land-settlement, soon entered into discussion with the colonists, some their former comrades in arms, which prepared the way for the Pact of Brundisium. With its conclusion the veterans could return to their colonies, and give more serious attention to the management of their new estates.

3. *After Naulochus*

In September 36, by the victory of Naulochus, Octavian brought to a welcome conclusion the long drawn out struggle against Sextus Pompeius. With the latter's subsequent capture and death Appian draws to a close his *Civil Wars,* and it seems clear that the victory was widely seen, or presented, as marking the end of civil strife and the return of peace within Italy and beyond.[90]

The battle itself was fought at sea, but substantial numbers of Octavian's troops had been embarked, and their experience helped to secure the victory. His army probably contained 21 legions in all.[91] After the battle, when the forces of

---

[86] App. *BC* v. 33, 50.

[87] He may have enlisted colonists from Hispellum (but the allegiance of the colonists is not known), or Florentia (if the latter was a colony of this time).

[88] App. *BC* v. 50.

[89] Dio xlviii. 28. 2; App. *BC* v. 57.

[90] Syme, *RR* 233; *ILS* 8893.

[91] Schmitthenner 85–89; Brunt, *IM* 498–500.

Lepidus and Pompeius, together with his own, were marshalled at Messana, Octavian incorporated an unknown but possibly quite substantial number of his opponents' citizen troops into his legions, and agreed under duress (after a near mutiny led by his own legions) to discharge some 20,000 time-served men.[92] In the long-term he could probably afford a slimming down of his forces, but at the time he acceded to the demands of the soldiery only, if our sources are correct, with very bad grace. According to Appian, the beneficiaries fell into two categories: (a) men who had served with him in the Mutina campaign, and so had supported him from the earliest days, and (b) men who had fought at Philippi. We may imagine that the latter had been particularly irked at exclusion from settlement in 41, and had waited a further seven years for a suitable opportunity to air their grievances with some hope of success. In the first category can be identified members of IIII *Macedonica,* of VII and VIII, and any of the four consular legions of Pansa (if still existing) which had participated in the fighting around Mutina, though not technically the fifth legion (V *Urbana*), which had remained behind in central Italy to screen the capital.[93] Under the second category, many other members of IIII, VII and VIII, as reconstituted after Philippi, became eligible. To these we can add Octavian's *cohortes praetoriae,* formed from time-served men after the battle in 42. How many of these legions were in fact present with Octavian in Sicily cannot be determined, but as the most experienced and reliable of his forces few can have been absent.[94]

Dio has a somewhat different account.[95] Those who had fought at Mutina were again deemed the most deserving category, but eligibility was extended to men who had been under arms for at least 10 years, i.e. since about September 46. Many of those who had fought at Philippi would again merit inclusion in this category, which also sufficed to include the younger members of those legions which had chanced not to participate in the Philippi campaign itself. On Dio's version we should perhaps have to include here founder members of legion XXXXI, and any others of that class (above, p. 29).

The total number who qualified for release out of Octavian's army in Sicily was computed by Appian at 20,000, a not unlikely figure. The men were transported to the mainland forthwith, though there was some considerable delay before allotments were ready. Dio reports that Octavian made use of public land where available, and bought more. We may think that abandoned allotments of earlier schemes were utilised. Both Dio and Velleius have the information that Capua was reinforced at this time — according to Dio it stood in need of many more colonists. Public land belonging to the town was used up, and Capua compensated by the award or promise of land in Crete giving an annual revenue of 1,200,000 sesterces, and an aqueduct.[96] Recently Panciera has argued persuasively that the Cretan

---

[92] App. *BC* v. 129; Oros. vi. 18. 33; Dio xlix. 14.
[93] As its title surely implies; below, p. 196.
[94] Legions I, XIII and X *Fretensis* can be added (above, p. 27).
[95] xlix. 14.
[96] xlix. 14. 5; Vell. ii. 81. 2. Below, p. 145.

land, and the aqueduct, were compensation for the permanent loss of territory in favour of a colony at Puteoli established at this time.[97] Later in his narrative, under the following year, Dio notes that some men were sent to colonies in Gaul.

On the location of settlement in Italy (apart from the *ager Campanus*) no direct evidence is available (Fig. 5). We may think that veterans of VII and VIII, who had enlisted in Octavian's interest to fill out the evocate formations in Campania in 44, would have received land at Capua. Epigraphic evidence allows some confirmation and could suggest that they shared the colony with some members of X *Fretensis* (below, p. 146). Other foundations of the time can only be tentatively identified — perhaps Tuder, which received veterans of legion XXXXI at an unspecified date; on Dio's testimony its founder members could well have qualified for release after Naulochus. One centurion of the legion had served as *centurio classicus,* perhaps at that battle (below, p. 176).

More certainly the population of Rhegium was strengthened by the addition of 'some men from the naval expeditionary force'. These may have been peregrine sailors from Octavian's fleet, granted *civitas* on discharge; alternatively they could have been members of one or more *legiones classicae.*[98] Thus Rhegium, one of the original 18 colonies of the Bononia agreement, did in the end receive settlers, and a title (*Iulium*) from Octavian, but not the rank and status of *colonia.*[99] Aticius, a centurion of Cisalpine origin, from Mutina, who had served in legion XXX *Classica,* and who died at Locri on the toe of Italy, was conceivably released at this time (Sylloge 76). Legion XXX was, it is generally thought, disbanded after Philippi, and settled at Beneventum. Aticius may simply be a 'stray' from Beneventum, or he could have been one of the *evocati* who accompanied Octavian (despite earlier Antonian proclivities) in the campaign against Sextus Pompeius. The title could reflect additional service, not shared by other members of the legion.[100]

Diodorus reports that in Sicily itself Augustus expelled the population of Tauromenium and installed colonists. If the foundation followed close upon Naulochus, as has been averred,[101] perhaps other sailors were despatched, for Appian reports that all the time-served legionaries were 'released forthwith and sent out of the island'.[102] But the colony could date from much later in Augustus' reign.

In the following year, some of the veterans released after Naulochus, perhaps

[97] S. Panciera, 'Appunti su Pozzuoli romana', in *I campi flegrei nell' archeologia e nella storia* (Roma, 1977), 191–211. Below, p. 148.

[98] Strabo vi. 1. 6. For a document conferring benefits on Seleucus, a Syrian navarch in Octavian's fleet at Naulochus, P. Roussel, 'Un Surien au service de Rome et d'Octave', *Syria* xv (1934), 33–74; *EJ²* 301. Cf. *EJ²* 302, for an edict published while Octavian was still *triumvir reipublicae constituendae,* conferring citizenship and exemption from taxation and compulsory military service on veterans and their families, apparently in a provincial context.

[99] *CIL* X, p. 3. The town of Blanda, on the Lucanian coastline, also bore the title *Iulia* under the Empire, perhaps as a result of similar settlement.

[100] No title is given to the legion on the dozen or more epitaphs of its veterans settled at Beneventum (below, p. 160).

[101] Diodorus xvi. 7. 1; Brunt, *IM* 331, 597. Some of Lepidus' men could have been sent there, see Hyg. Grom. 177. 9.

[102] App. *BC* v. 129.

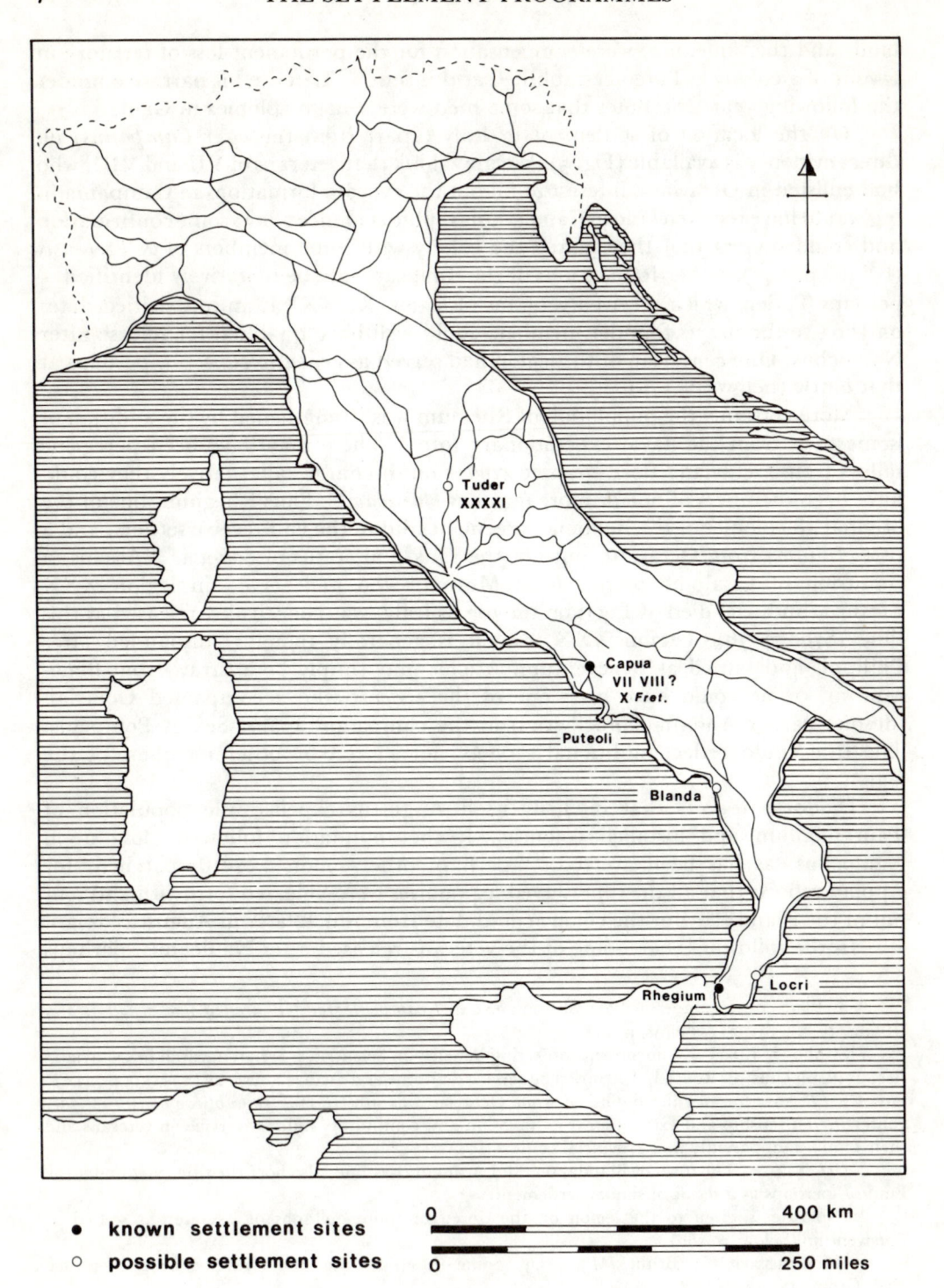

known settlement sites
possible settlement sites

0   400 km

0   250 miles

Fig. 5: Settlements after Naulochus

in exasperation at the slowness of the settlement process (or short of cash), volunteered to resume military service, and were formed into a separate 'legion' (more probably a corps of *evocati*). When land was finally ready, some obtained release, and were in fact settled in Gaul. Others who genuinely wished to remain in service continued under arms, probably until Actium. These events as reported by Dio have been taken as evidence for a second major mutiny,[103] but should in my view represent a minor local disturbance, probably in Italy, perhaps at Rome itself, occasioned by delays in receiving the promised allotments.[104]

The scope of settlement in Gaul is difficult to assess. Dio states that 'a few of the oldest men' were sent there, but it is possible that others, perhaps large numbers, were despatched.[105] We could imagine that the colonies of Narbo and Arelate (weakened by the permanent departure of *evocati* who had joined Lepidus in the summer of 44) received a supplement at this time. Other colonies could have been established from scratch, perhaps Arausio whose settlers came from a legion II *Gallica*, Baeterrae (legion VII), and Forum Iulii (legion VIII). All three numerals were borne by legions in Octavian's army, which (on Appian's criteria) would qualify for release at this time.[106] The titles *Pacensis* and *Classica* used by Forum Iulii have sometimes been thought to commemorate Actium, but both could reflect victorious participation by its colonists in the battle of Naulochus.

The numbers for whom land had to be found in Italy cannot be determined. They may have numbered 10,000-15,000 in all. The total, well below that of the Philippi settlement, is far from negligible, and sufficient to reinforce many of the existing colonies. Antony was to complain that Octavian had distributed almost the whole of Italy to his own soldiers, leaving nothing for Antony's men who would expect similar rewards before too long.[107]

4. *After Actium*

It was another sea-battle, at Actium, which left Octavian the undisputed master of the Roman world in September 31 B.C.; the victory ushered in a fresh programme of land settlement.[108] For the post-Philippi settlement, Appian's detailed narrative of the subsequent confiscations and uproar, and the participation of veterans in events of the Perusine War, together with the experiences of prominent poets, allow a fairly complete list of colonies to be drawn up. For the details of the post-Actium schemes on the other hand, the now curtailed sources are almost completely silent.[109] A list of colonies established after Actium has to be brought together by elimination and default. The epigraphic data too are less helpful: Ateste is the only

[103] Schmitthenner 104-5; Syme, *RR* 255.

[104] So W. Drumann—P. Groebe, *Geschichte Roms* IV (Leipzig, 1908), 280.

[105] xlix. 34.

[106] J. Kromayer, 'Die Militaercolonien Octavians und Caesars in Gallia Narbonensis', *Hermes* xxxi (1896), 1-18. On legion II *Gallica*, A. Piganiol, 'Nouvelles Inscriptions d'Orange', *CRAI* 1951, 366-74.

[107] Plut. *Ant.* 55.

[108] For the legal background, Schneider, *Veteranenversorgung* 229 ff.; Grant, *FITA* 293. The *Liber Coloniarum* contains frequent references to a *lex Augustea* which could belong now, but may be later.

[109] But see Hor. *Od.* iii. 4. 37-8; *Sat.* ii. 6. 55.

colony which can be shown clearly to belong to the post-Actium settlement (below, p. 196), though careful sifting of the evidence may allow the inclusion of Sora, Venafrum and others. Though Augustus in his later years was prone to gloss over or ignore events of his youth, the circumstances surrounding the post-Philippi foundations are the better known today.

The discharge of time-served men after Actium followed the now familiar sequence. The capitulation of Antonian forces was followed by an amalgamation of the two armies. Next, those citizens among the united forces, who were 'over age', were separated from the mass and sent on to Italy, presumably in the first instance to Brundisium.[110] The rest were dispersed. Once again some discontent welled up among veterans awaiting formal settlement. Octavian at first despatched Agrippa to quell the unrest, but soon after was compelled himself to return from his winter base at Samos. After a stormy voyage he landed at Brundisium early in 30. Some of the veterans were summoned thither, and a preliminary assignment took place during a short visit of 27 days.[111]

According to Dio (our only source for the following events), Octavian then assigned land 'to those who had campaigned with him throughout', and presented a lump sum in cash to the rest.[112] We might conclude that the only soldiers to benefit were men who had served with Octavian since Mutina, or since the reorganisation after Philippi, but we must imagine that all time-served men who had earlier campaigned under Sextus Pompeius or Lepidus received land; many must have participated in the Illyrian War and had fought on Octavian's side at Actium. This was no occasion for discrimination among his own forces, and the groups released now had probably been serving under one or more commanders since about 40 B.C., if not earlier (above, p. 37). It was surely the Antonians whose reward was confined to the cash bounty.

In any attempt to establish the numbers who benefited in 30 B.C., we might seem to possess a unique and authoritative statement, from the pen of Augustus himself. In the *Res Gestae,* Augustus states that, on the occasion of his triple triumph of August 29, he paid out to those of his soldiers who were *coloni* (i.e. colonised veterans) a *congiarium triumphale* of 250 *denarii,* and that the recipients numbered 120,000. This figure is naturally taken to represent the total released after Actium and given land at that time.[113] But the figure seems impossibly large. Octavian's entire legionary force hardly amounted to that total. He had to provide for the time-served men from at least 25 or, at most, 30 legions from his own army, most of which had been recruited or at least reconstituted in 41–40. All would contain some

---

[110]Suet. *Aug.* 17; Dio li. 3. 1 (καὶ ἔπειτα τοὺς μὲν πολίτας τοὺς ἔξω τῆς ἡλικίας ἀπ' ἀμφοτέρων, μηδὲν μηδενὶ δούς, ἐς τὴν Ἰταλίαν ἀπέπεμψε, τοὺς δὲ δὴ λοιποὺς διέσπειρεν). The distinction here is not between time-served and the younger men, but between the 'citizens' and the 'rest'. The latter should include all younger men who were retained under arms, and sent away to new stations, and non-citizens who were dispersed.

[111]Plut. *Ant.* 73; Dio li. 4; Tac. *Ann.* i. 42; Suet. *Aug.* 17. 3; Oros. vi. 19. 14.

[112] καὶ αὐτῶν ὁ Καῖσαρ τοῖς μὲν ἄλλοις χρήματα ἔδωκε, τοῖς δὲ διὰ παντὸς συστρατεύσασι καὶ γῆν προσκατένειμε (Dio li. 4. 5). It would be easiest to suppose that Octavian gave his own veterans land, 'in addition' to money, so that they received both, though the structure of the sentence does not strictly speaking require this.

[113]*RG* 15. 3. E. G. Hardy, 'Augustus and his Legionaries', *CQ* xiv (1920), 187–94.

proportion of time-served men. Some had seen fighting in Sicily and Illyricum, though battle casualties at Actium should have been confined to the eight legions which fought on shipboard. Some 20,000 men from his legions had already been released in 36–35. On the other hand, many men taken over from the armies of Lepidus and Sextus Pompeius would now be eligible for release. Nevertheless it would be difficult to imagine that the number of time-served men among Octavian's forces at this juncture could exceed 40,000-50,000, and even this estimate may be too high.

In a search to complete the total given by the *Res Gestae,* we might think first of Antony's veterans. It is difficult to estimate their number, but not easy to imagine that the residue of *citizens* in the ranks of his legions could amount to the required 70,000-80,000 men. With casualties over the previous decade, particularly in the Parthian War, a figure of 30,000-35,000 is much more probable.[114] By no means all would be Italians normally domiciled in Italy itself. Augustus states that the *congiarium* was paid to *coloni,* i.e. to men settled on land which he had provided. We cannot be certain that all the citizens among the Antonians in fact received land (below, p. 79).

In order to make up the total to 120,000, Brunt has argued that colonists of Philippi and Naulochus were included in the donative.[115] The totals of those discharged in 41 and 36 (including those settled in the Antonian foundations of 41, whom he could hardly exclude) would amount, with allowance for deaths, abandonment of land, and unwillingness to accept the money, to fewer than 50,000 in all by 29 B.C. However, it would be strange if the *congiarium* marking a triumph was paid out to men who had taken no part in the fighting and indeed had ceased to be soldiers up to 12 years before. Traditionally a *congiarium* went on these occasions to soldiers who had accompanied the general home from his province for his triumph and been released into civilian life. The veterans of Actium had of course already been released before the Egyptian campaign and the completion of the war. The money was distributed not at the triumph but in *coloni(i)s.* The *congiarium* is often seen as a reward for those who fought at Actium, but the basic amount (250 *denarii*) is low (above, p. 41), and Dio's narrative of Octavian's Egyptian campaign could suggest that he used the spoils of Alexandria to pay his armies their due reward already in 30.[116] Financial hand-outs at the time of the triumph were not confined to the soldiery; at the same time Octavian rewarded the city *plebs.* This was a distribution to loyal subjects to mark the successful conclusion of civil strife. It would be highly appropriate to make a cash payment in 29 to all those who had persevered, if not succeeded, on the land over the previous decade. I calculate that the numbers settled in Italy in the post-Actium settlement scheme as not more than 50,000.

---

[114] The 'Roman' element in his army for the Parthian campaign totalled 60,000 (Plut. *Ant.* 37). Infantry losses in that campaign were over 20,000, but not all would be citizen troops. See W. W. Tarn, 'Antony's Legions', *CQ* xxvi (1932), 75–81; Brunt, *IM* 502–7.

[115] *IM* 338. For similar calculations, Pais, *Colonie militari* 42.

[116] πάντες μὲν οἱ στρατιῶται τὰ ἐποφειλόμενά σφισιν ἐκομίσαντο. Those who took part in the Egyptian campaign received an additional 250 *denarii* in place of booty, which could suggest that payments to the victorious army were somewhat higher (Dio li. 17. 7).

Dio states that communities which had sided with Antony were uprooted and transported to new homes in the provinces, to Philippi, Dyrrachium and other places.[117] It has been suggested that Antonian veterans from the post-Philippi colonies would be among the first to be dispossessed of their allotments.[118] However, it would be strange if Octavian's efforts to win them over in the decade up to Actium were followed by wholesale transportation after the campaign had been won. Epigraphic evidence from known Antonian colonies suggests that they remained on their estates.[119]

We cannot tell how widespread was emigration at this time to the provinces. It may have been substantial and not restricted to groups with known Antonian sympathies. Dio may simply be reporting a story invented later to explain Octavian's actions at this time.[120] He states that the majority were offered compensation in the form of land, and that only a minority received cash payments. Not all the land offered need have been in the provinces, though I do not find in the title *Civica*, later attached to the colony of Brixia, any secure evidence for the settlement there of civilian colonists at this or any other time (below, p. 194).

Augustus records in the *Res Gestae* that, in the two years 30 and 14 B.C. combined, he paid 600,000,000 sesterces for Italian land and 260,000,000 sesterces for provincial land, on which to settle the veterans of his army.[121] Most of the cost for Italian land was probably incurred in the former year. How much land was acquired by purchase at that time we cannot accurately determine, but a rough calculation could suggest that the full figure of 600,000,000 sesterces might provide allotments for some 24,000 veterans, at most.[122] This is under half the total number which it is suggested were rewarded in the post-Actium settlement.

The list below comprises those colonies which have not yet been mentioned in the present chapter, and which for that reason may be tentatively proposed as belonging to the post-Actium settlement programme (Fig. 6):[123]

---

[117]Dio li. 4. 6. For Philippi as a colony of 41 B.C., above, p. 35. Dyrrachium is likely to have been one of Caesar's proletarian colonies.

[118]Pais, *Colonie militari* 43; Gabba, *Ricerche* 243; Brunt, *IM* 333, 338.

[119]At Beneventum (below, p. 155); Cremona (below, p. 190).

[120]Unless the selection of Parma was linked to the sympathies of Cassius Parmensis, one of Caesar's assassins, executed after Actium (Val. Max. i. 7. 7).

[121]*RG* 16. 1.

[122]A total based on the twin assumptions: (a) that land would cost about 500 sesterces per *iugerum*, and (b) that every soldier received 50 *iugera* (cf. below, p. 93). But the land may have cost much more, up to 1,000 sesterces (Columella iii. 3. 8), and the soldiers have been given considerably smaller allotments. See Duncan-Jones 48 on the difficulties in the use of Columella's figure.

[123]For attempts to list post-Actium colonies, see Zumpt, op. cit. (n. 76) 347; Borghesi, op. cit. 259; Pais, *Colonie militari* 34 and passim; idem, *Serie cronologica* 384–98; Mommsen, *Bürgercolonien* 172; Kornemann 535; Brunt, *IM* 608–10; Schneider, *Veteranenversorgung* 245 ff. For Augusta Praetoria, founded in 25 B.C., below, p. 205.

town	attestation	legion(s)	titulature
1. Ateste	Sylloge 6	V, XI, with contingents from IV, IX, XII, XIV, XV, XIIX, coh. I pr., coh. II pr., coh. V pr.?	—
2. Augusta Taurinorum	—	—	Iulia Augusta
3. Bovianum	—	—	—
4. Brixellum	—	—	—
5. Brixia	—	II?, X?	Civica Augusta
6. Castrum Novum	—	—	Iulia
7. Dertona	—	—	Iulia Augusta
8. Falerio?	—	—	—
9. Falisca?	—	—	Iunonia
10. Fanum	—	VIII	Iulia
11. Luceria	—	I, VI	—
12. Lucus Feroniae	—	—	Iulia Felix
13. Minturnae	—	—	—
14. Mutina	—	—	—
15. Nola	—	—	Augusta Felix
16. Paestum?	—	—	(Flavia Prima)
17. Parentium?	—	—	Iulia
18. Parma	—	XII Paterna	Iulia Augusta
19. Pisae	—	XIX	Opsequens Iulia
20. Placentia	—	—	Augusta
21. Puteoli?	—	—	Iulia Augusta
22. Rusellae	—	—	(Iulia?)
23. Saena	—	—	Iulia
24. Sora	—	IIII, coh.pr.?	Iulia Pra . . .
25. Suessa	—	leg.classica?	Iulia Felix Classica
26. Sutrium	—	—	Coniuncta Iulia Augusta
27. Tuder?	—	XXXXI	Fida Iulia
28. Venafrum	—	II Sabina?	Augusta Iulia

The above list has the names of 28 towns to which colonists were perhaps sent at this time. Some are doubtful, and perhaps should be set aside (Falisca, Castrum Novum, Parentium, Falerio, Paestum). It was suggested above (p. 71) that Tuder and Puteoli might have been established as colonies in 36 B.C. We are left with perhaps 21 towns as a minimum number of colonies of the immediately post-Actium settlement. Only Ateste can be dated to this time on positive evidence (Sylloge 6), but Sora probably received settlers from legion IIII *Sorana,* and Venafrum from a legion II *Sabina,* both of which seem unlikely (if their histories have been correctly reconstructed) to have had time-served men available after Philippi (above, p. 26). Fanum and Pisae can plausibly be added, as the colonies which probably received members of like numbered legions (VIII, XIX) after Philippi are already known. Parma too could be dated to 30 B.C., if the legion attested there (XII *Paterna*) has been correctly identified as a shadow formation of Octavian, matching a unit of Antony's army (above, p. 31).

We might think that once again the number of colonies founded was directly related to the total of legions requiring settlement. It was suggested that Octavian should have possessed at least 25 legions, or as many as 30, at this time (above,

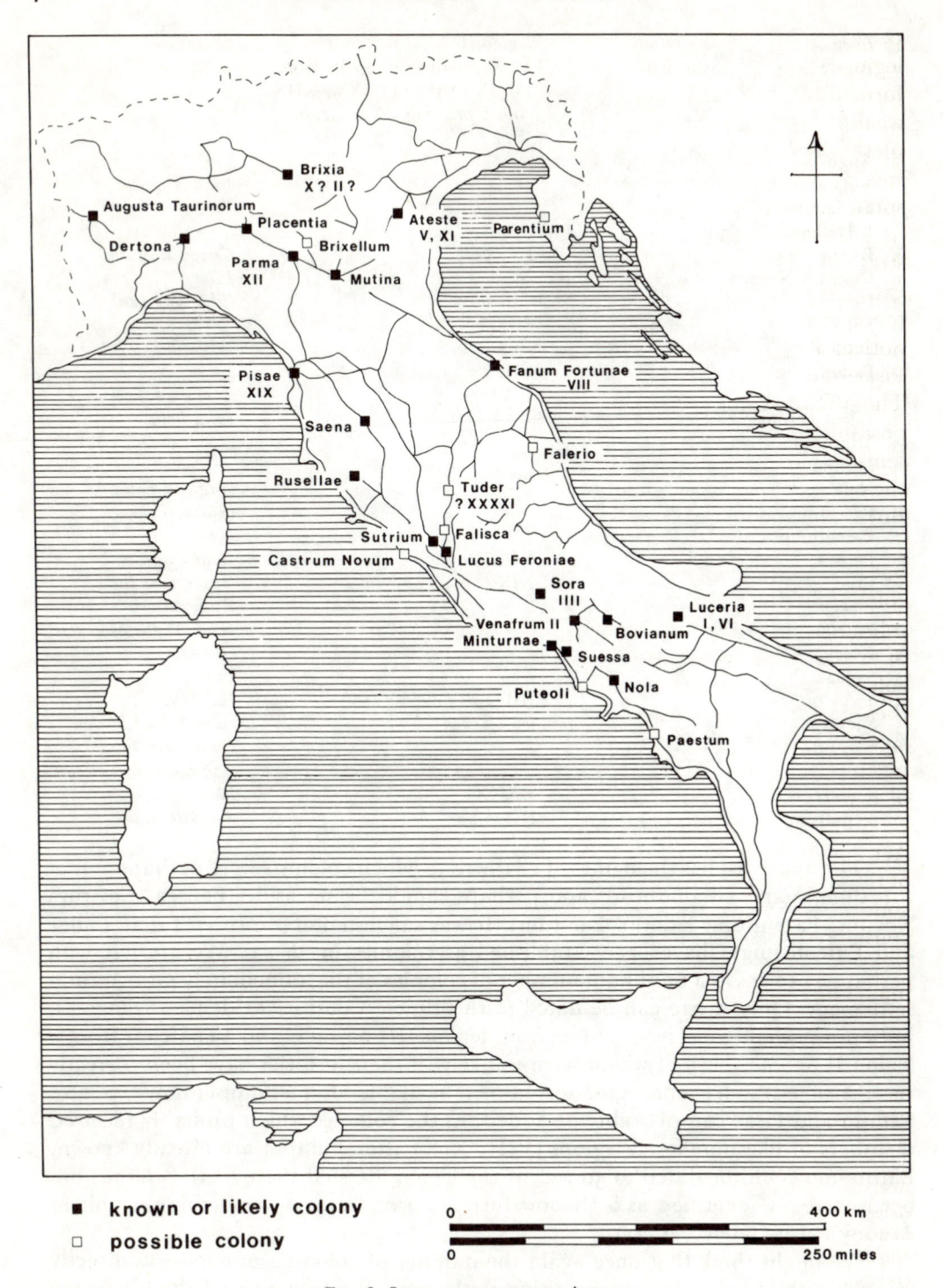

Fig. 6: Settlements after Actium

p. 27). But it seems that legions were again doubled up on occasion: we know of two legions (I and VI) at Luceria, and no fewer than eight at Ateste round a nucleus formed by V *Urbana* and XI. Unless many of the units at Ateste were exceptionally weak, this colony must have been one of the largest established at this time. The plethora of legions at Ateste could be the result of successive reinforcements, but special circumstances may apply (below, p. 197). Other colonies may have been small, perhaps very small, with a legion split between two towns.

There is no evidence that colonies after Actium were selected particularly on strategic grounds; there is an even spread throughout the peninsula (except in the extreme south), with the wide plains of Cisalpina, both north and south of the Po, more extensively utilised now than after Philippi. Some of the new colonies stand in noticeable juxtaposition to those of the post-Philippi settlement, e.g. Fanum to Pisaurum, Brixia to Cremona, Pisae to Luca, and Falerio (if a colony) to Firmum. The juxtaposition is probably accidental, though it could be tempting to see in the positioning of some an endeavour to swamp and stifle any surviving Antonian sentiments.[124] A Caesarian veteran-enclave in the *ager Capenas* was expanded into the colony of Lucus Feroniae probably at this time, and other such settlements (e.g. Bovianum) could have been upgraded now.

It would not be surprising if many of the post-Philippi colonies were reinforced, but very little evidence can be adduced.[125] The title *Augusta* later attached to colonies of the post-Philippi scheme has been taken as sufficient proof of such a refoundation or reinforcement, but the title was first introduced in 27, and evidence of any retrospective award is not to hand. The title *Iulia* is borne by a number of colonies of the same programme with known or suspected Antonian sympathies, but these may have acquired it at Octavian's gift or insistence before rather than after Actium (above, p. 17). Entries in the *Liber Coloniarum* which report work carried out by *Augustus* may once again serve as evidence for small-scale settlement, some of it perhaps after Actium.[126]

The sources differ on the rewards given to Antony's time-served men after Actium. Velleius reports that life and pardon were the sole reward for the surrender of those serving on shipboard; he does not say whether the land army exacted better conditions. Dio's account implies that only the citizens among Antony's men were considered for reward, and when *praemia* came to be allocated, these may have received cash but not land. However, Hyginus Gromaticus notes that Octavian made no distinction between his own troops and those of Antony or Lepidus in the

---

[124] Firmum and Luca probably housed veterans of legions owing allegiance to Octavian. It is possible, even probable, that after Actium Octavian reversed losses of territory sustained by some towns in 41 B.C. This seems likely at Cremona (below, p. 195), where Brixia recovered some land, and perhaps at Firmum (below, p. 183).

[125] For Beneventum, see below, p. 159.

[126] Work is ascribed to *Augustus,* or was carried out *limitibus Augusteis* or *terminis Augusteis* at Acerrae, Aesernia, Ameria, Ancona, Atella, Arretium, Aternum, Castrum Novum (in Picenum), Cales, Carseoli, Caudium, Consentia, Cupra, Corfinium, Cumae, ?Divinos, Falerio, Forum Popilii, Fundi, Gravisca, Hadria, Liternum, Ligures Baebiani et Corneliani, Marsi Marruvium, Nuceria, Nursia, Pinna, Puteoli, Sora, Surrentum, Teanum, Teate, Telesia, Trebula, Truentum, and Velitrae. Only a handful of these towns became colonies. Notice also T. R. S. Broughton, 'Some Non-colonial Coloni of Augustus', *TAPA* lxvi (1935), 18–24.

distribution of land grants: *pariter et suarum legionum milites colonos fecit, alios in Italia, alios in provinciis*[127]. We might expect that, when Antony's land army negotiated with Octavian after the battle, suitable recompense, on a par with the victorious troops, was uppermost in their minds. There is a little evidence for the presence of Antonians in Italy after Actium, not certainly testifying to official settlement — a veteran of V *Alaudae* is attested near Beneventum; he bears the *cognomen* Arsaces which could denote participation in Antony's Parthian War (below, p. 159). A veteran of the same campaign entertained Augustus on gold plate at Bononia, the proceeds of the war (below, p. 113). Both Beneventum and Bononia were Antonian colonies after Philippi, and perhaps received additional, Antonian, settlers at this time. Alternatively both men could have been *evocati*, returning to their estates after further service with their former commander.

Rather we should expect that any of the Antonians who did get land were rewarded in the provinces, and a number of foundations can be placed at this time: a rash of colonies, all probably quite small, on the coast of Mauretania, and others in the African province itself.[128] In the east we may suspect Patrae, Berytus (and Heliopolis?) and perhaps Alexandria Troas, but the evidence is insecure.[129] Some existing colonies in Macedonia were reinforced, partly if not wholly by civilians from Italy.[130] Yet it is difficult to imagine that the numbers benefiting were very large, and Dio is perhaps right to allege that only citizen members of Antony's forces got any reward for their service. These were the men transferred to Italy after the battle, and perhaps sent on to the provinces as soon as land was found.

In the *Res Gestae* Augustus was later to claim that he had founded 28 colonies in Italy, all of them prosperous and flourishing when he wrote. The total is repeated by Suetonius.[131] At first reading we should conclude that these 28 colonies housed the 120,000 colonists whom he proudly reports as receiving his donative *in coloni(i)s*. This total of 28 cannot have included all those Italian colonies founded or re-inforced between 41 B.C. and his death. Augustus is making a deliberate selection from among the 50 or so colonies established after Philippi, Naulochus, Actium and later.

Two avenues of approach are available, by which this higher figure can be reduced to the 28 claimed by Augustus. Long ago Beloch claimed that the 46 colonies named in Pliny's lists (above, p. 4) represented a simple addition of the 18 post-Philippi colonies to which Appian testifies and the 28 admitted by Augustus. The latter were therefore in his view the post-Actium foundations. This view was endorsed by Cuntz, and has recently been taken up (in a modified form) by Gabba.[132] The colonies of 41 B.C. were all put into effect by virtue of the *lex Titia* or

[127] Vell. ii. 85. 2; Dio li. 4. 6; Hyg. Grom. 177. 11.

[128] Vittinghoff 116–8; Brunt, *IM* 593–7.

[129] Vittinghoff 126–35. A veteran of legion XVI is attested at Alexandria Troas (*AE* 1914, 204).

[130] Dio li. 4. 6; Brunt, *IM* 598.

[131] *RG* 28. 2: *Italia autem XXVIII* [*colo*]*nias quae vivo me celeberrimae et frequentissimae fuerunt me*[*a auctoritate*] *deductas habet.* Ἰταλία δὲ εἴκοσι ὀκτὼ ἀποικίας ἔχει ἐπ' ἐμοῦ καταχθείσας ἃι ἐμοῦ περιόντος πληθύουσαι ἐτύγχανον. Cf. Suet. *Aug.* 46.

[132] Beloch, *It. Bund* 6; O. Cuntz, *De Augusto Plinii Geographicorum Auctore* (Bonn, 1888), 25; Gabba, *Colonie triumvirali* 106–110.

under the joint authority of the Triumvirs; it is not clear that Augustus could legally claim that any had been established under his *auctoritas*.[133] We have seen that the post-Actium colonies could have numbered about 28.

On the other hand, Mommsen, Pais, and more recently Brunt have argued that the 28 colonies of the *Res Gestae* cannot be totally separated from the 18 of Appian, and that at least some of the latter must be included in the former calculation.[134] Brunt argued that Augustus reached the reduced total by excluding (a) those towns already possessing colonial status before his time, and which he merely reinforced, and (b) those colonies of the post-Philippi settlement which he did not personally superintend, i.e. colonies housing Antony's veterans and established by the latter's nominees. The fact that Octavian refounded Bononia in 32 B.C. 'in order that (the colonists) should appear to have been settled by *him*' must indicate that Octavian did not regard any of the 'Antonian' group as his own.[135] The specific mention of Bononia may suggest that his treatment of it was unique; the others remained 'Antonian'. It has often in the past been claimed that any colony bearing the titles *Iulia* or *Augusta,* or both, must have been included in Augustus' selection of 28.[136] Such an approach is unsound, inspiring false confidence, and subject to revision and dislocation, as more epigraphic evidence becomes available. Almost certainly all but a very few of the colonies established from 41 B.C. onwards carried a name derived from the *gens Iulia,* and the appearance of such titles offers no guarantee of a special position in Augustus' calculations.

From a passage in Cicero's *Philippics* it seems clear that a colony, *dum esset incolumis,* could not be refounded, though it was in order (and indeed had always been common) for additional groups of settlers to be sent out later, to bolster the population, or occupy land available in its territory. This constituted an *adscriptio colonorum,* not a *deductio.*[137] It must be asked whether the Triumvirs or Octavian were troubled by this distinction. In 44 B.C. Antony had been sufficiently in doubt over his work at Casilinum as to consult Cicero, whose reply in the circumstances was bound to be negative. Dio notes that Octavian refounded Carthage, a refoundation only made possible because Lepidus had allegedly depopulated it, so annulling the original Caesarian charter.[138] Dio's phrasing suggests that some difficulty was felt or confessed, but that an excuse for refoundation was easily to hand, if desired. Octavian could have claimed the same for any colony in Italy needing extra colonists, and Hyginus Gromaticus avers that Augustus refounded many old colonies *dato iterum coloniae nomine*; his example is Minturnae, a *colonia maritima* of 295 B.C.[139] The reason for refoundation (exhaustion from the

---

[133] The word *auctoritas* is restored. The Greek version has the rather colourless ἐπ' ἐμοῦ καταχθείσας.

[134] Mommsen, *RGDA* 122; idem, *Bürgercolonien* 186-9; Pais, *Colonie militari* 41; Brunt, *IM* 608-9.

[135] Dio l. 6. 3.

[136] Mommsen, *Bürgercolonien* 188; Gabba, *Colonie triumvirali* 109.

[137] Cic. *Phil.* ii. 102. For the phraseology of reinforcement, Cic. *Leg. Agr.* ii. 34; Suet. *Nero* 9; Tac. *Ann.* xiv. 27.

[138] lii. 43.

[139] 177. 13-178. 2.

depredations of the civil war years) was one which Augustus could have used throughout Italy as desired.

Of the 50 or more colonies which seem likely to have been established in Italy between Philippi and the end of Augustus' reign, as many as 11 were already *coloniae* of earlier generations: Capua of B.C. 59, Castrum Novum 264, Dertona 109?, Florentia 59? (below, p. 175), Minturnae 295, Mutina 183, Nola 80, Parma 183, Pisaurum 184, Puteoli 194, Venusia 80?. If we knew more of Sullan colonisation, the total could go higher. Octavian may well have felt obliged in an official document, by which he wished posterity to judge him, to omit these from his own tally, although he was clearly happy to accord them fresh titles to commemorate reinforcement or favours. He might also omit Antonian colonies founded in the latter's interest, which would account for at least six more towns (Pisaurum and Capua were already colonies, and he refounded Bononia). If he in fact chose here to omit Bononia, the genuine foundations of his reign should amount to about 33, sufficiently close perhaps to the group of 28 actually claimed.[140] This line of argument, however ingenious, is perhaps over-subtle. It is much easier to suppose, with Beloch, Cuntz and Gabba, that the 28 colonies were those of the post-Actium programme, together with Aosta, and any later foundations.

We should expect, and have evidence, that Octavian took a considerable interest in all the colonies established in his lifetime, whether or not he had been personally responsible for their creation, so that later in his reign it should have been quite possible for him to claim all 50 or more as particularly his own foundations. It seems that all (or very nearly all) were named in the source used by the Elder Pliny.

The number of recipients in the post-Actium settlement scheme amounted to 40,000-50,000. This was a substantial total, equal to the numbers accommodated after Philippi; they were distributed, it seems, over a larger number of towns. We hear no matching howl of protest, and no record survives of unrest or street fighting. This may be testimony to the weight of contemporary propaganda, the comparative sparsity of the literary sources, or serve as evidence of Octavian's tact and circumspection, and the greater care with which groups of veterans were grafted on to Italian communities, with the lessons of 41 very much in mind. The new era could brook no repetition of the troubles of a decade before. But such a large number of men could not have been settled without disruption and dispossession. Some 21–28 towns received colonists now, and their existing inhabitants were in part removed, to be compensated either with land or in cash. The *Res Gestae* places considerable emphasis on compensation, and we may assume that it was paid, and without much delay, from the spoils of Egypt.

5. *The middle years of Augustus' reign.*

The colonising activity of Augustus did not stop with Actium, either in Italy or in the provinces. Many of the best known provincial foundations date to the middle years of his reign, down to 14 B.C., after which cash gratuities were substituted for the land grants which had continued to be made up to that date (below, p. 208).

---

[140] If all the likely post-Actium colonies were added to those established by or on behalf of Octavian in 41, the resulting total would be about 36.

At present three main phases of activity can be detected, linked in part to the travels of Augustus and of Agrippa, and to the reorganisation of provinces which followed their visits. In 26–25 B.C. we know by chance of the reinforcement of Cirta, the possible establishment of one or more colonies in the new province of Pisidia, and of Augusta Emerita in Lusitania.[141] In Italy itself the final subjugation and expulsion of the Salassi by Terentius Varro Murena made available the valley of Dora Baltea for Roman settlement, and Strabo reports that veterans of the *cohortes praetoriae* were sent there, attaching their name to the new foundation (below, p. 205). Less certainly some of the Mauretanian foundations which bear the title *Augusta* might be assigned to this year.

In 21 B.C. Augustus travelled to Sicily and initiated the foundation of colonies at Syracuse and four or five other towns, partly on land confiscated 15 years before from supporters of Sextus Pompeius.[142] The foundation of Caesarea Augusta can plausibly be linked to Agrippa's presence in Spain in 19 B.C.[143] There is no evidence of settlement in Italy in these years. We may well believe that sufficient land of any quality was difficult to obtain. Only the Praetorians had received land in Italy in the decade after Actium, and that only by the expulsion of the Salassi.

Augustus makes no mention in the *Res Gestae* of money expended in the purchase of land for any foundations of 26–25 B.C. or 21–19 B.C., and we may conclude that it did not cost him, personally, very much. However, outlays for veteran settlement in 14 B.C. (*consulibus M. Crasso et Cn. Lentulo Augure*) are coupled with those following Actium itself.[144] Literary evidence can be adduced to suggest the foundation (or reinforcement) of Patrae, Berytus and perhaps Alexandria Troas in the wake of Agrippa's journey in the eastern provinces,[145] and under 15 B.C. Dio reports that Augustus colonised numerous cities in both Gaul and Spain, activity which must be linked to his sojourn in the west in 16–13 B.C. The colonies of Ilici, Tucci and Astigi are perhaps to be placed at this time, but in Gaul no new foundations can be identified with any certainty. Perhaps existing colonies at Arelate, Narbo, Arausio, Baeterrae, Noviodunum, Lugdunum, Forum Iulii and Raurica were reinforced.[146]

The number of veterans settled in Italy as this time is less easy to establish (Fig. 7). Augustus states that 600,000,000 sesterces were spent in 30 and 14 B.C. combined,

---

[141] For Cirta, *AE* 1955, 202; for the Pisidian colonies, Levick 29; for Emerita, Dio liii. 26 with R. Syme, 'The Spanish War of Augustus (26–25 B.C.)', *AJP* lv (1934), 293–317.

[142] V. Scramuzza, *ESAR* III, 346; Brunt, *IM* 597; R. J. A. Wilson, *Sicily under the Roman Empire* (forthcoming).

[143] Grant, *FITA* 217. Three legions (IV, VI and X) contributed veterans.

[144] *RG* 16. 1.

[145] M. Reinhold, *Marcus Agrippa* (New York, 1933), 110. For Alexandria Troas, see now P. A. Brunt, 'C. Fabricius Tuscus and an Augustan dilectus', *ZPE* xiii (1974), 161–85; for Patrae, see now R. Frei-Stolba, 'Legio X Equestris', *Talanta* x–xi (1978–79), 44–61.

[146] Dio liv. 23. 7; Vittinghoff 100 ff. Three veterans of a legion XX are attested at Emerita within the Augustan period (*CIL* II 22*, 662, 719). These cannot be colonists of 25 B.C., who were drawn from legions V and X, but could document a later reinforcement; cf. Frontinus 51. 18 on successive waves of colonists there. Plancus' colony at Raurica is now known to have borne under the Empire the titles *P[ia Apollin]aris/[Augusta E]merita*; H. Lieb, 'Zum Zweiten Colonia Raurica', *Chiron* iv 1974, 415–23. Perhaps the military colonists implied by the title *Emerita* arrived at Raurica at this time.

▲ Towns where work is ascribed to Tiberius or Drusus
   by the Liber Coloniarum

◆ Towns where work is ascribed to Claudius Caesar
   by the Liber Coloniarum

■ Known settlement sites

□ Possible settlement sites

FIG. 7: SETTLEMENTS OF AUGUSTUS' MIDDLE YEARS

but how much was expended in the latter year is not made clear. The *Liber Coloniarum* has references to Augustan activity in towns which never became colonies; some of this work could be ascribed to 14 B.C. (p. 79, n. 126). The same source has details of settlement work possibly by Tiberius at five towns (Beneventum, Aesernia, Saepinum, Castrimoenium and Atina), and by Drusus at three (Ulubrae, Cereatae, and Anagnia; above, p. 9). Tiberius and Drusus built walls at Saepinum (above, p. 9), and an inscription from Atina records a joint dedication by a legion XX to an Augustan senator P. Tettius Rufus Tontianus. No indication is given that Tettius had ever served in the legion as senatorial tribune or legate, and it could be that he supervised settlement of members of the legion at Atina, but his work cannot be dated.[147] An inscription recording a veteran of Spanish origin from the legion VIIII *Hispaniensis* is known at Cales with the local tribe *Publilia*. The inscription (Sylloge 59) is likely to be Augustan in date, but must be later than the Actium settlement. The most probable circumstance for the man's appearance at Cales would be as a colonist in a small non-colonial settlement at about this time. At Altinum, the young Tiberius gave porticoes and gardens to the municipality in 13 B.C. Recent excavations have produced an epitaph of a veteran of legion IIII *Scythica*, which could belong under Augustus, and may testify to some small-scale settlement.[148] Doubtless more such settlements remain undetected. It is not clear whether any new colonies were now established in Italy. Those listed by Pliny are normally all assigned — with the necessary exception of Aosta — to the aftermath of Philippi, Naulochus or Actium, but some could well be later, perhaps much later. For example, we may wonder whether Turin was a foundation of the middle years of Augustus' reign, and others may fall into the same category.

There is, however, one obstacle, but not perhaps insuperable, to any belief that the settlement programme in Italy in 14 B.C. was of more than minor significance — the absence from the peninsula in that year of Augustus and the chief members of his family. Augustus himself was in Gaul, and did not return until July 13. Agrippa was engaged in a tour of the eastern provinces. Both Tiberius and Drusus were occupied in Raetia, executing a pincer movement against recalcitrant tribesmen. The presence of at least one of the above four would be expected as a sensible precaution in case of trouble. But the schemes may have been carried over, in Italy, to the following year, when Tiberius himself was consul. The main effort, however, was directed to, and the major expense incurred in, the provinces, with Augustus settling veterans from the armies of the western provinces in Gaul and Spain, and Agrippa those of the Danube army and the east.

It has already been noted that several Italian colonies of the post-Philippi and post-Actium schemes bear the title *Augusta*, an epithet which can only have been awarded or adopted in 27 B.C. or later (above, p. 17). The title is not borne by many of the known or suspected post-Actium foundations, and is best seen as denoting additional settlement, or special favours, after 27 B.C. It could be suggested that the title *Augusta* commemorates reinforcement in 14 B.C., but the criteria for the award

---

[147] X 5059–60 = *ILS* 930–930a; Wiseman no. 426.

[148] V 2149 (Tiberius); B. M. Scarpi, 'Altino (Venezia). Le iscrizioni funerarie romane provenienti dagli scavi 1965–69 e da rinvenimenti sporadici', *Att. Ist. Ven.* cxxviii (1969–70), 207–89, no. 1.

or the circumstances are nowhere known. Brixia, Beneventum, Nola, Ariminum, Parma, Capua, Dertona, Puteoli, Sutrium, Turin and Venafrum were all *coloniae Augustae*; a recent inscription has added Placentia to the familiar list (above, p. 17) Doubtless more will become known. If a fragmentary inscription from Dertona is an accurate record, that town had already acquired the title *Augusta* by 22 B.C. (below, p. 205). In general we may suspect that a number of small settlements took place in Italy after 30 B.C., many of them as yet undetected, and in various years.

In the *Res Gestae* Augustus proudly asserts that, in the course of his long reign, substantially above 300,000 veterans had received discharge from his forces, and *praemia* either in the form of land (i.e. up to 14 B.C.) or in cash (from 13 B.C. onwards).[149] We have argued that 120,000 were already in their colonies by 29 B.C., and to that figure we must add men who were already dead by that year and others, mainly Antonians, who had been rewarded with cash but not land. How the remaining figure (which I compute at about 150,000) is to be distributed cannot be determined with any pretence at accuracy.[150] The Augustan army of 28 legions, whose members served a minimum of 16 years (plus four spent *sub vexillo*), would generate about 4,000-5,000 veterans each year.[151] It is very clear that there was no system of annual discharges at least before 13 B.C., and even after that date (when service was fixed at 20 years) the numbers being released probably fluctuated greatly. We can, however, say that about 4,000-5,000 men would become eligible for discharge each year from 29 B.C. onwards (even though none was actually released until 25 B.C. or later). After A.D. 5/6 it is likely that discharges were reduced to a trickle, with only those too old or too weak to continue service being discharged. The numbers entitled to release after 13 B.C., when cash gratuities replaced land grants, can be estimated therefore at about 90,000. The remainder, perhaps some 60,000 in all, must have been released between 29 and 14 B.C. We know that several colonies were established or reinforced in 26-25 B.C., and a second group in 21-19 B.C., but the majority were perhaps released in 14 B.C., if Augustus' testimony has any weight. As has been noted, Augustus coupled the programmes of 30 and 14 B.C. as being especially important, or particularly costly. The recipients in the latter year, perhaps 30,000-35,000 in all,[152] should be recruits who had entered the army to replace Actium veterans (above, p. 37). The very fact that the settlement of 14 B.C. could be linked to that following Actium suggests that the clearance of men following the latter was sufficiently large to require a considerable intake of recruits, despite the radical slimming down of the now amalgamated armies of the Roman world.

---

[149] *RG* 3. 3.

[150] For earlier assessments, E. G. Hardy, 'Augustus and his Legionaries', *CQ* xiv (1920), 187-94; Brunt, *IM* 332-42.

[151] J. F. Gilliam, 'The Veterans and *Praefectus Castrorum* of the *II Traiana* in A.D. 157', *AJP* lxxvii (1956), 359-75.

[152] Hardy's estimate (loc.cit., n. 150) of close to 100,000 men being released at this time represents about two-thirds of the entire legionary force available to Augustus.

CHAPTER FOUR

THE SETTLEMENT PROCESS

1. *Preparations and survey*

The provision of land for veterans took time, considerable time, a fact which the veterans themselves did not always appreciate. We hear repeated complaints at the slowness of the process. Some Caesarian veterans were released in 47 B.C., before Caesar left for Africa, and discharges began in earnest in or soon after July 46. Yet there were men who had not yet gone out to their allotments in March 44; others apparently remained to be provided for by the *lex Antonia* of June of that year.[1] The 18 cities selected for settlement by the Triumvirs—or proscribed, like the human victims[2]—were chosen at Bononia in November 43; commissioners were appointed at once to superintend the work,[3] but we may doubt if any more than token preparations were in hand before the necessary victory had been won. After Naulochus and after Actium there was unrest among veterans waiting in Italy when the promised allotments had not materialised within a few months. In the winter of 31/30 Octavian was compelled to return to Italy to soothe their discontent (above, p. 74).

In earlier centuries the establishment of a *colonia* could take up to three years. Much of the time was occupied by the measuring and survey of the land to be distributed to colonists.[4] Survey remained a necessary prelude to settlement in the later first century B.C., even after Philippi, when we might infer from Appian and Dio that veteran settlers took over existing farmsteads lock, stock, and barrel: μετά τε τῆς δουλείας καὶ μετὰ τῆς ἄλλης κατασκευῆς.[5] The veterans themselves were doubtless concerned to see that allotments were equitably assigned, though some evidently let pass no opportunity of extending their holdings during the first few weeks after arrival.[6] Steadings, farm equipment, and slaves must have been reassigned to suit the new land division, or were supplied from scratch (below, p. 123). It is a tribute to the strength of tradition that the time-consuming survey-process was allowed to take its course.

Land for Caesar's settlements in 47–44 was amassed by the searching out and accumulation of *ager publicus* wherever it might be found, and by purchase (above, p. 54). The task was long and complicated.[7] The establishment of colonies after Philippi by wholesale confiscation must have greatly speeded the process. The procedure adopted after Actium by which land was in part acquired by compulsory purchase would shorten the waiting time for the veterans. The work of organising individual settlements was delegated by the formal *deductores* (Caesar in 47–44, the

---

[1] Even in July 43 there were, according to Appian, Caesarian veterans who had still to receive land (*BC* iii. 87).

[2] Cic. *Att*. xvi. 16A. 2; Focas, *Vita Verg*. 73.

[3] App. *BC* iv. 3, 85; Dio xlvii. 14. 3.

[4] Kornemann 571–8; Salmon 19 ff.

[5] Dio xlviii. 6; cf. App. *BC* iv. 3.

[6] App. *BC* v. 13.

[7] For the problems which had faced the Gracchan land commissioners, App. *BC* i. 18.

Triumvirs after Philippi, and Octavian in 36 B.C. and later) to commissioners or agents usually of senatorial rank, often and perhaps always with the title *praefectus* (above, p. 51). Among the first tasks of the newly appointed commissioner was to visit the designated town or towns, and to set in motion the machinery of survey with the aid of a sizeable staff of surveyors and assistants.[8] The commissioner would investigate the ownership of land, hear claims for exemption from seizure, and arrange for the purchase or exchange of holdings where necessary. The convoying of colonists to the colony (*deductio in agros*) came very late in the sequence of his duties.[9]

Centuriation is the modern name applied to the distinctive Roman system of land survey, which preceded the distribution of land parcels.[10] Grids of *centuriae* have been observed by the study of modern maps or by aerial reconnaissance in the territories of many towns chosen as *coloniae* between 47 and 14 B.C. It might be thought that the study of such a valuable and ever increasing body of information would lead not only to the identification of colonies founded or reinforced at this time, but also to an estimate of the number of colonists settled. However, many of the grids now plotted must belong not to the Late Republic, but to the third and second centuries B.C., and must serve above all as an index of the physical penetration of Roman or Latin settlers throughout the peninsula, whether by the establishment of colonies or the large-scale distribution of *ager publicus* in viritane grants.[11] The appearance of centuriation in the territory of a town is no indicator of its status in the Late Republic or at any other time. The square *centuria* containing 200 *iugera* was in widespread use both in Italy and (later) the provinces, but as the earliest examples date from the third century B.C. and as it remained the standard unit into the Empire, no conclusions on dating from its occurrence are possible. Irregularly shaped *centuriae* were noted by the *Gromatici*, and some have been confirmed by modern research; these too can often be linked to events of earlier generations.[12] Only occasionally can the laying out of a grid be directly associated with the settlement programmes of the later first century B.C.

[8] Under the *rogatio Servilia* of 63 B.C. each commissioner was to have a staff of 20 *finitores* of equestrian birth, and other assistants; Cic. *Leg. Agr.* ii. 32 with C. Nicolet, 'Les *finitores ex equestri loco* de la loi Servilia de 63 av. J.C.', *Latomus* xxix (1970), 70–103.

[9] For some consideration of the costs to the government of land settlement, M. H. Crawford, *Roman Republican Coinage* (Cambridge, 1974), 600; P. D. A. Garnsey, 'Where did Italian Peasants live?', *Proc. Cambr. Phil. Soc.* xxv (1979), 1–25.

[10] Among the ever-expanding body of relevant literature, it should suffice here to cite A. Schulten, *Die römische Flurteilung und ihre Reste* (Göttingen, 1898); E. Fabricius, *RE* XIII (1926), 672–701, *s.v. Limitatio*; A. Castagnoli, *Le ricerche sui resti della centuriazione* (Roma, 1958); idem, *Diz. Epig.* IV (1964), 1379–84, *s.v. Limitatio*. For bibliographies of more recent work, L. B. Brizio, 'Studi sulla centuriazione in Italia', *Arch. Class.* xxi (1969), 92–100; O. A. W. Dilke, 'Archaeological and Epigraphic Evidence of Roman Land Surveys', in *ANRW* II. i (1974), 564–92. Dilke, *The Roman Land Surveyors* (Newton Abbot, 1971) offers a readable general introduction. F. T. Hinrichs, *Die Geschichte der gromatischen Institutionen* (Wiesbaden, 1974) discusses the legal aspects. U. Heimberg, *Römische Landvermessung: Limitatio* (Aalen, 1978) is a well illustrated survey, emphasising the evidence from the western provinces under the Empire.

[11] Castagnoli, *Ricerche* 34.

[12] Toynbee II 563–7 and below, p. 164 on Luceria; Castagnoli, *Ricerche* 24 on Beneventum.

Augustus is credited by the *Gromatici* with extensive survey of the territories of Italian towns. Yet it is clear that much of his work, and that of Caesar, must have consisted in the refurbishing of existing grids, with their extension where necessary. *Augustus eorum* (i.e. earlier colonisers from the Gracchi onwards) *mensuras recensiit, et ubi fuerunt lapides alios constituit, et omnem terram suis temporibus fecit permensurari ac veteranis adsignari.*[13] The importance of terminal stones in guaranteeing allotment sizes is repeatedly stressed; their removal was a punishable offence.[14] Yet Augustus' activity in Italy seems hardly reflected at all in the epigraphic record of inscribed *termini Augustei* bearing his name and titles, in contrast to the small but growing number of Gracchan *cippi* recovered from the southern half of the peninsula.[15]

Existing grids in many older colonies were almost certainly re-used in the Late Republic. Centuriated areas identified, at Parma and Mutina for example, far exceed the area required for the original colonists of 183 B.C.[16] However, as it was normal practice to allow in the initial survey for subsequent reinforcement, and in many instances we know that reinforcement did occur, we cannot tell how far any extensions were required in the Late Republic. Centuriation observed in the *ager Campanus* should belong to the mid-second century B.C., or to Caesar's colony of 59 B.C. at latest, so that the imposition of veterans in later waves would necessitate only modest alterations.[17] Nevertheless grids on the territories of some towns in Transpadana and Venetia (e.g. Turin and Concordia) and in Histria (Pola and Parentium) most easily belong to the foundation of the colonies there in the later first century B.C.

Whenever the land of the selected colony proved insufficient for the numbers of veterans assigned to or arriving at the town, the deficiency was made good by the forcible seizure of parts of the territories of adjacent towns.[18] Datable examples of this procedure seem to belong in the main to the post-Philippi settlement. It must always have been administratively easier, as well as politically less sensitive, to expropriate the land of nearby towns and to extend the grid into their territories than to proceed to the creation of more colonies.

[13] *LC* 242. 13–15.

[14] Sic. Flacc. 165. 10; Latinus et Mysrontius 348. 1L; '*Lex Mamilia*'. 263. 1L; Digest xlvii. 21. 3; Castagnoli, *Diz. Epig.* IV (1964), 1381.

[15] They were recognisable by their distinctive shape, *LC* 240. 20, 242. 12; cf. Hyg. Grom. 172. 3. For boundary stones specifically called *termini Augustales*, ILS 2454–5, 5969–70 (erected in A.D. 6), 5972, *AE* 1946, 11 (A.D. 6), 17–19, etc. For uninscribed stones, possibly of Augustan date, L. Alpago-Novello, 'Resti di centuriazione romana nella Val Belluna', *Rend. Acc. Linc.* ser. 8, xii (1957), 249–69. On the Gracchan stones, D. B. Nagel, 'The Failure of the Roman Political Process in 133 B.C.', *Athenaeum* xlviii (1970), 372–94; *AE* 1973, 222; M. Pani, 'Su un nuovo cippo graccano dauno', *Rend. Ist. Lomb.* cxi (1977), 389–400.

[16] P. Tozzi, *Saggi di topografia storica* (Firenze, 1974), 44–60; idem., 'Indicazioni sul primitivo stanziamento della colonia di Modena', *Riv. Stor. Ant.* v (1975), 47–74.

[17] Castagnoli, *Ricerche* 32; M. A. Levi, 'Una pagina di storia agraria romana', *Atene e Roma* n.s. iii (1922), 239–52.

[18] Frontinus 49. 7; Sic. Flacc. 159. 26, 164. 3; App. *BC* v. 14. U. Laffi has shown that such transfers are not examples of the *contributio* of territory; *Adtributio e contributio* (Pisa, 1966), 153 ff. Hyginus has references to *quaedam divi Augusti edicta* on the transfer of land, which could indicate that such expropriations also occurred later in his reign (119. 24–120. 6).

Historically the best known instance of such expropriation occurred at Cremona where the insufficiency of the *ager Cremonensis* resulted in the annexation of part of the territory of Mantua, including the family property of the poet Vergil (below, p. 191). The extent of the inroads into the *ager Mantuanus* has been recently illuminated by the valuable work of Professor Pierluigi Tozzi who has mapped details of Roman surveying in and around Cremona.[19] In all probability the *ager Cremonensis* was first surveyed at the time of the foundation of the *colonia Latina* (218 B.C.) on a normal grid of square *centuriae* of 200 *iugera,* each measuring 20 by 20 *actus.* Internal subdivisions suggest that the allotments were to be of 25 *iugera.* At a later, undetermined date (which can hardly be dissociated from the known settlement of 41 B.C.) this grid was altered to accommodate *centuriae* of 20 by 21 *actus.* Frontinus and Hyginus Gromaticus make specific mention of these unusual dimensions, and assign the work to the Triumvirs.[20] The purpose of the resurvey was, it seems, to accommodate land parcels of 35 *iugera,* which we may see as the designated allotment size at Cremona. A grid of these distinctive *centuriae* has been observed not only within the natural boundaries of the *ager Cremonensis,* but extending eastwards into the territory of Mantua and (less predictably) northwards into land which may reasonably be considered to have been *ager Brixianus.* It would seem that Mantua was not alone in suffering for *nimia vicinitas* to the new colony. Over 70% of the *ager Mantuanus* was, it seems, covered by the Cremonese grid which extended to within 1 km. of the town itself.[21]

There is literary and epigraphic evidence for the transference of land at other post-Philippi colonies. The *ager Beneventanus* was extended to include the territory of neighbouring Caudium (*muro tenus* as a boastful inscription of Severan date proclaims)[22]; similarly, parts of the territory of Ligures Baebiani, Telesia and perhaps Ligures Corneliani passed to Beneventum (below, p. 158). The territory of Hispellum was extended at the expense of Assisium, and perhaps other towns (below, p. 178). The dispute between Firmum and Falerio, which prompted the well-known Domitianic rescript on the ownership of *subseciva,* may have had its origins in the transference of land at this time (below, p. 183). Frontinus notes what was evidently an extreme example of expropriation of territory: expansion of the *ager Asculanus* took in part of the town-site of neighbouring Interamnia Praetuttiorum.[23] At Dertona on the Alessandria plain, an extensive grid of square *centuriae* was mapped by Plinio Fraccaro; it should belong initially to the *colonia* established there in the later second century B.C. However, *centuriae* on the same alignment were noted west of the River Tanaro on land which seems most naturally to belong to either Valentia or Forum Fulvi. Only further work can determine whether the discovery of these *centuriae* is evidence for the expansion of Dertona at

---

[19] *Storia padana antica* (Milano, 1971), 9 ff.

[20] Frontinus 30. 19; Hyg. Grom. 170. 19; Tozzi 23.

[21] Tozzi 20–23, 59 ff. L. J. F. Keppie, 'Vergil, the Confiscations and Caesar's Tenth Legion', *CQ* lxxv (1981), 367–70.

[22] *ILS* 6488.

[23] 18. 10–19. 1. Schol. Bern. on Lucan *Phars.* iii. 462 states that Caesar rewarded Opitergium for services to his cause by enlarging its territory by 300 *centuriae.*

the expense of one or more of its neighbours in the Late Republic.[24] The *Gromatici* make clear that, in the territories of the neighbouring towns, only land actually assigned to veterans passed into the permanent ownership of the *colonia*; such zones were named *praefecturae*. The remainder was returned to the jurisdiction of the neighbouring town.[25] Some towns however, such as Caudium, lost all their land.

An important aspect of the settlement process was adherence to religious practices and traditions. The commissioner defined the boundaries of the town by ploughing a sacred furrow (*sulcus primigenius*).[26] A coin of 29–27 B.C. depicts on its reverse Octavian as a colony commissioner, in appropriate priestly garb, ploughing the *sulcus primigenius* (Pl. VIIA).[27] Antony could be portrayed by Cicero as grazing the walls of Capua with his ploughshare, when establishing the colony at Casilinum.[28] In Italy, however, when all but a few colonies already existed as towns, such a procedure could be no more than symbolic. The appearance within some colonies of *vici* named after the hills and districts of Rome is an interesting phenomenon, often linked to the colonisation process in the Late Republic. Such *vici* at Pisidian Antioch and at Ariminum have long been known; more recently attention has been drawn to a similar series at Puteoli.[29] The practice was probably not an idea of Augustus and confined to the Late Republic, but does reflect the maintenance of links between colonies and their mother city.[30]

2. *The allotments*

The size of allotments granted to veterans in the settlement programmes of the Late Republic must form an important factor in our assessment of their potential social position in the town concerned. The allowance for colonists in the *coloniae civium Romanorum* of earlier centuries had been very small, but substantial areas could be assigned to settlers in *coloniae Latinae*, especially in Cisalpina, and many soldiers benefited; a basic allowance of 50 *iugera* is attested in the colonies at Bononia and Aquileia.[31]

The amount of land given by Gracchan commissioners is uncertain, though 30 *iugera* have been seen as a maximum allowance, from a passage in the '*Lex Agraria*'

[24]'La colonia romana di Dertona (Tortona) e la sua centuriazione', *Opuscula* III (1957), 123–50; P. Tozzi, 'Per la identificazione di tratti di vie romane', *Athenaeum* liv (1976), 296–9.

[25]Hyg. 119. 24 ff.; Sic. Flacc. 164. 3–14. On this, a lesser known, meaning of the term *praefectura*, Sic. Flacc. 160. 4 ff.

[26]Salmon 27.

[27]H. Cohen, *Description historique des monnaies frappées sous l'Empire Romain* (Paris-London, 1880), I, 81 no. 117; H. A. Grueber, BMC *Roman Republic* (London, 1910), II, p. 17, no. 4363, pl. lx. 8.

[28]Cic. *Phil.* ii. 102.

[29]Levick 76–77; *CIL* XI, p. 77; G. A. Mansuelli, *Ariminum* (Roma, 1941), 47; J. H. D'Arms, 'A new inscribed base from fourth century Puteoli', *PdP* xxvii (1972), 255–70. Cf. at Beneventum, IX 1569.

[30]Cf. at Cales (a Latin colony of 334 B.C.), X 4641. Beneventum, Ariminum and Puteoli had been colonies under the Republic.

[31]Liv. xxxvii. 57. 7, xl. 34. 2. For allotments in Republican colonies, G. Tibiletti, 'Ricerche di storia agraria romana I: la politica agraria dalla guerra annibalica ai Gracchi', *Athenaeum* xxviii (1950), 183–266.

of 111 B.C.; the allowance at the colony of Carthage may have been much greater.[32]

Saturninus had offered 100 *iugera* of provincial land in Africa to veterans of Marius' Jugurthine campaigns,[33] but the amount offered, or granted, to time-served men after the northern campaigns, is not reported.[34] Nor is there any secure evidence on the size of allotments given by Sulla to his men.[35] Only 10 *iugera* of fertile Campanian land were to be distributed under Rullus' bill in 63 B.C., and we know that such an allowance was in fact given to recipients there under Caesar's programme of 59, in part to veterans of Pompey's eastern wars.[36] Perhaps the allowance was kept small to maximise the number of beneficiaries.

The *Gromatici* emphasise that land was allotted to veterans according to the military rank of the recipient and his achievements under arms (*pro portione offici* or *pro merito*) and according to the quality of the land itself (*pro aestimio ubertatis et natura locorum*).[37] Perhaps, therefore, there was no fixed allotment size in any of the Late Republican settlement programmes. In a single entry (for Volaterrae) the compiler of the *Liber Coloniarum* specifies that soldiers settled there *lege trium-virale* received 25, 50, 35 or 60 *iugera*.[38] The only known assignments at Volaterrae belong under Caesar. The variations in allotment-size may reflect the ranks of recipients at that time: *milites gregarii* could thus have received 25, junior officers (e.g. *signiferi* and *aquiliferi*) 35, centurions 50, and tribunes 60 *iugera*. But the variation could be due in part to allowance for differences in the quality of land within the *ager Volaterranus* (or reflect more than a single settlement phase). Siculus Flaccus envisaged that some veterans by virtue of their rank might receive one and a half, others twice, the basic allowance.[39] Centurions often received at least twice the basic cash donatives in these years (above, p. 42), and in general we may think that distinctions in pay would continue to be reflected in the size of land grants on discharge. In 49 B.C., to encourage his troops to fight Caesar, Domitius Ahenobarbus promised them 40 *iugera* each out of his own estates, after victory had been won.[40]

---

[32]'*Lex Agraria*' 13-14 (Italy), 60 (Carthage). For the view of G. D. B. Jones that Gracchan plots around Luceria were of 10 *iugera*, Toynbee II 565.

[33] *De Vir. Ill.* 73.

[34] An anecdote preserved by Plutarch (*Crass.* 2. 8), which speaks of allotments of 14 *iugera* being distributed by Marius, refers rather to the activities of Manius Curius Dentatus; E. Gabba, 'Ricerche su alcuni punti di storia Mariana', *Athenaeum* xxix (1951), 12-24.

[35] Plots of about 100 *iugera* have been suggested at Pompeii, on the basis of the distribution of *villae rusticae* in the Early Empire; F. Day, 'Agriculture in the Life of Pompeii', *YCS* iii (1932), 165-208; E. Lepore, 'Orientamenti per la storia sociale di Pompeii', in *Pompeiana: raccolta di studi per il secondo centenario degli scavi di Pompeii* (Napoli, 1950), 144-66. Not all the *villa* sites need yet be known. F. Castagnoli has studied grids of *centuriae* in the *ager Pompeianus*, 'Tracce di centuriazione nei territori di Nocera, Pompei, Nola, Alife, Aquino, Spello', *Rend. Linc.* ser. 8, xi (1956), 373-8. The grid south of the town has rectangles of 18 x 23 or 18 x 24 *actus*, each containing a little over 200 *iugera*, but the system cannot be dated.

[36] Cic. *Leg. Agr.* ii. 78; *Att.* ii. 16. 1.

[37] Hyg. 114. 1; Sic. Flacc. 156. 9; Hyg. Grom. 176. 13; *LC* 214. 12, 216. 11, 232. 2. After the Hannibalic War soldiers were given 2 *iugera* for each year spent under arms (Liv. xxxi. 49. 5), but this method of calculation was not used again, so far as we know.

[38] *LC* 214. 14-15.

[39] 156. 9-12.

[40] Caes. *BC* i. 17. Brunt has shown good reason to reject a common emendation of XL in this passage to *quaterna* (i.e. 4 *iugera*), 'Two Great Roman Landowners', *Latomus* xxxiv (1975), 619-35. The amount had to be credible in the economic and political climate of the time.

That the Triumvirs made known the size of allotments to be given to their soldiers, to encourage them to victory in the impending struggle against the Liberators, should be a reasonable hypothesis, though the literary sources offer no guidance.[41] The allowance was presumably at least as large as that recently awarded to Caesar's men, and in all probability larger. The *Gromatici* refer frequently to the Triumvirs. For example, Hyginus Gromaticus reports their use of *centuriae* of different sizes *secundum agri amplitudinem*. Sometimes these contained 50 *iugera*, sometimes 200; at Cremona the *centuriae* contained 210 *iugera*.[42] Frontinus also refers to a *centuria* found in some towns in Italy, which was smaller than the norm; it was called the *centuria triumviralis* and contained 50 *iugera*.[43] *Centuriae* of just this size have been recently observed near Cures Sabini, so confirming an entry in the *liber Coloniarum*, where work by Caesar is reported,[44] but not at any post-Philippi colony. However, a four-fold division of the normal *centuria* of 200 *iugera* into square plots of 50 *iugera* has been noted at Florentia, Pola (Pl. IV), Parentium, Concordia and Fanum.[45] It is perhaps to such subdivisions that Frontinus is referring. It would be a simple matter to place terminal stones at appropriate points along the edges of *centuriae* to facilitate subdivision.[46] The colony of Concordia may belong after Philippi, and Florentia may have received settlers at this time, but Fanum in my view belongs after Actium. The territories of Pola and Parentium were perhaps first divided under Caesar (below, p. 203). Thus a subdivision into squares of 50 *iugera* may have been common practice, though it was later to become particularly associated with the work of the Triumvirs.

It is obviously important to establish whether these plots of 50 *iugera* represent allotments actually distributed to colonists,[47] or whether they served merely as a convenient framework to allow distribution to proceed. Perhaps the intention was to subdivide them further. Where, however, these squares have survived into modern times, it suggests that they had some permanency as land boundaries. The same figure, 50 *iugera*, recurs in the *Gromatici* as a typical or minimum allotment size.[48]

At the post-Philippi colony of Cremona, Tozzi has suggested that plots of 35

[41] According to Dio (xlvii. 8. 5) Octavian in 41 B.C. reluctantly agreed to exempt from confiscation farms smaller than the veterans' allowance, which could suggest that the size of the latter was well known. The senatorial decree of January 43 contained a clause to reward loyal troops with land grants equal in size to any previously given (Cic. *Phil.* v. 53).

[42] 170. 17–20.

[43] 30. 20.

[44] M. P. Muzzioli, 'Note sull' *ager quaestorius* nel territorio di Cures Sabini', *Rend. Acc. Linc.* ser. 8, xxx (1975), 223–30; *LC* 253. 18; cf. Sic. Flacc. 136. 18.

[45] For Florentia, F. Castagnoli, 'La centuriazione di Florentia', *l'Universo* xxviii (1948), 361–8; for Pola and Parentium, M. Suić, 'Limitation of Roman Colonies on the Eastern Adriatic Coast', *Zbornik Instituta za historijske nauke u Zadru* i (1955), 32–36 (English summary); for Concordia, L. Bosio, 'La centuriazione dell'agro di Iulia Concordia', *Att. Ist. Ven.* cxxiv (1965–66), 195–260; for Fanum, N. Alfieri, 'Per la topografia storica di *Fanum Fortunae* (Fano)', *Riv. Stor. Ant.* vi (1976–77), 147–71. The same divisions have been discerned at Salonae and Iader, see Suić, loc.cit.

[46] Cf. *LC* 213. 6–214. 2.

[47] So Pais, *Colonizzazione* 338; Castagnoli, *Diz. Epig.* IV (1964), 1380.

[48] Hyg. 110. 10; *LC* 247. 17.

iugera were distributed.[49] But such an allowance cannot have been standard; the *Gromatici* speak of the dimensions of Cremona's *centuriae* as distinctly unusual, if not unique.[50] At the colony of Aquinum, which may belong after Philippi, *centuriae* of 210 *iugera* were identified by Cagiano de Azevedo; more recently, Castagnoli and Coarelli have plotted, in a different part of the *ager Aquinas*, a grid of squares measuring approximately 36 x 36 *actus* which could have been subdivided to produce allotments of about 40 *iugera*.[51] At Arausio, the foundation of which could belong in 35 B.C., the allotments are thought to have been of $33\frac{1}{3}$ *iugera*.[52]

During a description of the *sortitio* process, Hyginus Gromaticus cites, by way of example, the tripartite division of a *centuria* of 200 *iugera* into plots of $66\frac{2}{3}$ *iugera,* and imagines these as being distributed to named veterans of the legion V *Alaudae*.[53] Neither time nor place is specified and the value of the passage has been doubted.[54] The first set of veterans is given the stock-names of Roman Law,. but the second group could well have been excerpted from genuine records.[55] It is not impossible that Hyginus was using as his example the colony of Augusta Emerita, where colonists in 25 B.C. included former members of legion V *Alaudae*.[56] Within Italy itself Alfieri has recently noted a tripartite division of some *centuriae* at Fanum.[57]

The evidence cited above suggests that surveyors might have in mind a basic allotment size when preparing the grids for settlement, but it was not unknown for an allotment to be split among two, three, or even four *centuriae*.[58] The need to provide for soldiers rewarded at a higher rate would disturb the neat distribution suggested above. Land within a single *centuria* might be shared between one or more veterans and a *vetus possessor*. The epigraphic evidence from Arausio is particularly valuable. It would seem that *centuriae* at Arausio accommodated allotments of $33\frac{1}{3}$ *iugera,* but that in almost every *centuria*, some land was left aside

---

[49] Tozzi 23. The existing gird, presumably initially of 218 B.C., was already divided into parcels of 25 *iugera*, which could easily have been 'doubled up', if 50 *iugera* was the intended allotment size here. Parcels of $33\frac{1}{3}$ *iugera* could likewise have been provided without altering the main framework of the existing grid.

[50] Front. 30. 19; Sic. Flacc. 159. 10; Hyg. Grom. 170. 19.

[51] M. Cagiano de Azevedo, *Aquinum* (Roma, 1949), 57 ff.; F. Castagnoli, 'Tracci di centuriazione nei territori di Nocera, Pompei, Nola, Alife, Aquino, Spello', *Rend. Acc. Linc.* ser. 8, xi (1956), 373–8; F. Coarelli, 'Note sulla topografia extraurbana di Aquino', *Quad. Ist. Top. Ant.* i (1964), 51–54. The alignment of the Via Latina was adjusted to suit the centuriation, and Coarelli adduces a milestone-inscription to show that the road was already realigned by 39 B.C. (X 6895), which should prove a useful *terminus ante quem*.

[52] A. Piganiol, *Les documents cadastraux de la colonie romaine d'Orange* (Paris, 1962), 56.

[53] 199. 11–201. 6.

[54] Brunt, *IM* 296.

[55] First group: L. Titius L.f., [T.] Seius T.f. [A.] Agerius A.f. (200. 6). Second group: L. Terentius L.f. Pollia, C. Numisius C.f. Ste. and P. Tarquinius Cn. f. Ter. (201. 3), with C. Thulin, *Corpus Agrimensorum Romanorum* I. i (Teubner ed., 1913), 164, *app. crit.*

[56] Note what must be a reference to Emerita in the following paragraph of Hyginus Gromaticus (201. 9); cf. Front. 51. 23.

[57] Loc. cit. (n. 45 above). I. A. Richmond and C. E. Stevens, 'The Land-Register of Arausio', *JRS* xxxii (1942), 65–77 proposed a tripartite division of *centuriae* at Arausio, but Piganiol has shown good reason to suppose that allotments there were of $33\frac{1}{3}$ *iugera* (above, n. 52).

[58] Frontinus 14. 1–7; Hyg. Grom. 204. 8–13.

for the native population, or became the public domain of the colony.[59] Sometimes, however, the *veteres possessores* were transplanted to other, probably less fertile land, in order to leave large tracts of the most productive areas for veterans alone.

The evidence for allotment sizes is thus confusing. Nevertheless, we may be able to conclude that veterans from Caesar onwards might receive a basic rate of between 25 and 50 *iugera,* depending on the fertility of the ground. Allotments of just 10 *iugera* have sometimes been thought standard throughout this period,[60] on the basis of assignments made in the *ager Campanus* in 59 B.C., but even at Capua it must be highly probable that settlers of 45–44, 41 and 36 B.C. received considerably more than 10 *iugera*. If the plots were insufficient to be viable, the veterans would be likely to desert them before too long.

The allotments, once handed over, became the property of the recipients, and could be passed on to succeeding generations. But they could not be sold, at least for a considerable period. Such a condition, forbidding *abalienatio* (legal transfer of ownership) of former *ager publicus,* became standard practice from the Gracchan period onwards.[61] Under the legislation of Ti. Gracchus, the sale of allotments granted by his commission was forbidden, but the relevant clause was soon annulled.[62] Similarly, Sullan allotments could not be sold, though Cicero implies that the provision had not prevented them falling into the hands of large land-owners at one colony, Praeneste.[63] Rullus' bill contained a similar condition, from which the same may be inferred for land parcels acquired under Caesar's legislation in 59 B.C. Allotments distributed to veterans of Caesar's Gallic legions in Italy (and perhaps to civilian and military recipients in the provinces) could not be sold for 20 years; Brutus and Cassius sought the support of men waiting in Rome for formal *deductio* by a praetorian edict of March 44 annulling the restriction.[64] The provision was thus a particular grievance, well-meant though it may have been. Whether such a condition was imposed on allotments granted after 44 B.C. — when the purely economic motives for colonisation became for a time less important — is not clear. It could be argued that the Triumvirs were in no position to restore it.

Siculus Flaccus reports that land given in 47–44 to Caesarian veterans, who subsequently resumed service and were killed, was repossessed by the state, and assigned to other veterans.[65] Likewise the *Liber Coloniarum* frequently refers to the infusion of fresh waves of veterans *post demortuos milites* or *deficientibus veteranis.*[66] The former were presumably men who had no families, or made no wills, the latter were men who had abandoned their land. Abandoned allotments

---

[59] Piganiol, op. cit. (n. 52), passim.

[60] H. Dohr, *Die italische Gutshöfe nach den Schriften Catos und Varros* (Köln, 1965), 36; R. P. Duncan-Jones, 'Some configurations of landholding in the Roman Empire', in M. I. Finley (ed.), *Studies in Roman Property* (Cambridge, 1976), 7–33.

[61] D. C. Earl, *Tiberius Gracchus* (Bruxelles, 1963), 16 ff.; E. Badian, 'Tiberius Gracchus and the Beginning of the Roman Revolution', in *ANRW* I.i (1972), 669–731, esp. 680.

[62] App. *BC* i. 27.

[63] Cic. *Leg. Agr.* ii. 78.

[64] App. *BC* iii. 2.

[65] 162. 9–15.

[66] Hyg. 131. 14 ff.; Sic. Flacc. 161. 11; Front. 45. 11.

could be re-used in later schemes, and some land of this sort was perhaps available for Octavian to utilise at Capua in 36 B.C. But allotments granted under the Empire could (it seems) be sold at will.[67]

3. Sortitio *and* deductio

When the survey was complete and an accurate record of it prepared, the commissioner would return to Rome to assemble and enrol the intending colonists. A considerable time could have elapsed since formal discharge, with the men returning to their homes to settle up their affairs,[68] and to prepare their families for the move to a new home. Others would doubtless linger in Rome itself, or return there awaiting settlement, obviating financial hardship with the aid of accumulated cash reserves, if any.[69] The location of the land parcels within the *territorium* of a colony was decided by lot (*sortitio*); both Hyginus and Hyginus Gromaticus give details of the process.[70] The precise numbers who would appear at the appointed time were perhaps not known exactly, but a tally must have been made before the veterans were allowed to disperse on discharge. The work of assigning the land could take place in Rome itself. Caesar's death found groups of veterans scattered throughout the city in temple precincts and other large spaces 'under a single standard and one colony-leader' (ὑφ' ἑνὶ σημείῳ καὶ ὑφ' ἑνὶ ἄρχοντι τῆς ἀποικίας).[71] The description is suggestive of veterans of a single legion, identifiable as legion VIII, soon to be established at Casilinum by Antony. They had already received notification of their land and destination, and were in any case on the point of departure.[72] In 41 we find Octavian calling veterans to the Campus Martius ἐπὶ νέμησιν.[73] After Actium he carried out at least a preliminary allocation at Brundisium, to which veterans were summoned in the winter of 31/30.[74] The *adsignatio* complete, the colonists were led out under a special banner, a *vexillum*, with all the traditional ceremony of earlier days.[75] Octavian in 41 made a show of his duties as *deductor* by participating in the settlement of one or more groups in southern Italy.[76]

On arrival at the colony, the veterans and their families were distributed according to the results of the *sortitio*, and exact details of the location, the size and

---

[67] *LC* 209. 12, 216. 5, 223. 3, 224. 2–3.

[68] App. *BC* ii. 120.

[69] Caesar's men received their main donative in September 46, and in the aftermath of his Triumphs were a source of public disorder in the city (Dio xliii. 24. 3). The donative following Philippi was much delayed, if it was ever paid (above, p. 41).

[70] 113. 1–18; 199. 11–201. 6.

[71] App. *BC* ii. 120. This official (ἄρχων) was perhaps a *praefectus* (above, p. 88), and is not to be confused with any of the voluble spokesmen who soon appeared to voice the complaints of the veterans.

[72] App. *BC* ii. 119; Dio xliv. 51. 4. Similarly colonists destined for Buthrotum in Epirus assembled at Rome (Cic. *Att.* xvi. 16A); they did not converge on the colony at will. Under the Empire colonists from a frontier garrison would doubtless travel direct to a provincial colony without first returning to (or visiting) Italy.

[73] App. *BC* v. 16.

[74] Dio li. 4. 5.

[75] E.g. Cic. *Leg. Agr.* ii. 86; *Phil.* ii. 102. The veiled priest, plough and *vexillum* appear frequently as reverse types on the coin issues of provincial colonies; cf. above, p. 52 and Pl. VIIA.

[76] App. *BC* v. 19.

the shape of the allotments were inscribed on a series of bronze tablets, the *forma coloniae*.[77] Individual farmsteads were renamed after the veteran whose name appeared on the *forma,* and the results of this procedure may still be reflected in modern place-names.[78]

The commissioner selected the first magistrates and priests for the town, and an *ordo* of up to 100 *decuriones,* many drawn from the ranks of the colonists, especially (we may imagine) centurions and tribunes.[79] He might himself serve as one of the first pair of *IIviri* of the colony,[80] and in any case presumably remained in the town for some months to ensure a smooth beginning to the settlement (below, p. 106). The *deductor,* his commissioner, and their descendants, automatically became eligible to serve as patrons of the colony.[81] The commissioner also formulated a *lex coloniae,* detailing its constitution, and also the conditions of landholding within the *territorium.*[82] Sections of the *lex coloniae* of Caesar's colony at Urso in southern Spain have survived on bronze tablets now at Madrid; short passages of the laws of Tuder and Florentia are known, and the wording of a single clause of the *lex* of Concordia is preserved by chance in a letter of Fronto.[83] Such *leges* derived their content from the general enabling laws or edicts authorising the settlement programme — with allowance for local conditions. One copy of the *forma,* the *lex coloniae* and other supporting documents was placed on view at the colony itself, and another deposited in the Tabularium at Rome.[84]

4. *The size of colonies*

When colonies had as their principal *raison d'être* the protection or pacification of unsettled border zones, the colonists were regularly numbered in thousands. In many cases Livy preserves detailed figures. A common total envisaged was 3000, though commissioners were not always able to recruit the full number, at least at once. On occasion even larger numbers might be despatched, as 4000 to Vibo and other towns, 6000 to Placentia and Cremona, even 20,000 (though this figure is suspect) to Venusia.[85]

[77] F. Castagnoli, 'Le 'formae' delle colonie romane e le miniature dei codici dei gromatici', *Mem. Acc. Linc.* ser. 7, iv (1943), 83–118; idem, 'Cippo di 'restitutio agrorum' presso Canne', *Riv. Fil.* xxvi (1948), 280–6. Cf. Sic. Flacc. 157. 20 for the *forma* of Pisaurum.

[78] For modern 'toponimi prediali' which could preserve the names of known veterans, see below, p. 179 (S. Andrea d'Agliano/Allianus) at Hispellum; below, p. 203 (Visinada/Vinusius) at Parentium. Cf. Suet. *Reliquiae* (ed. C. L. Roth, Teubner, 1862), 295. 5–9: *L. Accius . . . a quo et fundus Accianus iuxta Pisaurum dicitur, quia illuc ex urbe inter colonos fuerat deductus.* Sic. Flacc. 161. 26 notes the value of *vocabula villarum agrorumque* for determining the ownership of land; cf. *LC* 239. 6; Hor. *Sat.* ii. 2. 133–4.

[79] Cic. *Leg. Agr.* ii. 96; *Lex. Urs.* lxvi; E. Gabba, 'L'elogio di Brindisi', *Athenaeum* xxx (1958), 90–105. Below, p. 107.

[80] Pompey and Piso Caesoninus served as *IIviri* at Capua in 58 B.C. (Cic. *Pis.* 24–5; *Post Red.* 29). For the possibility of Piso as *IIvir* at Pola, below, p. 204.

[81] L. Harmand, *Le patronat sur les collectivés publiques* (Paris, 1957), 156 ff.

[82] Hyg. 117. 12–119. 19; Sic. Flacc. 157. 11 ff., 164. 14 ff.

[83] *ILS* 6087 = Bruns, *FIRA*[7] 28 (Urso); I 1409 = Bruns *FIRA*[7] 32, 33 (Florentia and Tuder); Fronto *ad Am.* ii. 7. 3 (Concordia). Cf. *ILS* 140, line 39 (Pisae), III 12042 (Cnossus).

[84] Sic. Flacc. 154. 13–155. 9.

[85] Kornemann 571–2; Beloch, *It. Bund* 149–50.

Literary evidence for the size of colonies in the later first century B.C. is modest. L. Scipio established 3000 men at Comum, probably in 77 B.C.; a total of 5000 was envisaged for Capua under the proposals of Rullus, and this number was actually sent out in 59.[86] Caesar's colony at Comum in 58 was of similar size.[87] Strabo states that 3000 'Romans' were established at Augusta Praetoria,[88] though we may doubt if there was sufficient land in the plain of the Dora Baltea to accommodate so many (but cf. below, p. 206). The same number was sent to Carthage, in or about 44 B.C.[89] The *Liber Coloniarum* appears to say that 4150 men were sent to Teanum Sidicinum.[90]

The settlements of the later first century B.C. need not have been of uniform size, or necessarily very large. The total of 3000 may be a stock figure. When veterans and their families were grafted on to the population of an existing town (and this was the norm in Italy), we should beware of over-estimating the numbers which could be absorbed by any town.

Caesar deliberately split up the mass of his veterans, at least in Italy, except on the *ager Campanus* where the supply of land was sufficient and public opinion amenable to the settlement of substantial numbers. The groups sent to Capena, Veii, Volaterrae and other towns can have been numbered in hundreds at most. The colonies established after Philippi were much larger. Some 16 or 18 towns received upwards of 40,000 men (above, p. 60). The legionary framework was strictly observed; each colony received the veterans of at least one legion, sometimes two. We may imagine that 3000 or 4000 men could be despatched to a single town. If the land available there proved insufficient, the balance was acquired at the expense of neighbouring communities. The totals sent to any town must have varied considerably.

After Actium up to about 28 colonies provided in Italy for some 50,000 veterans. Legions were again doubled up on occasion, but more often one legion to a colony must have been the norm (above, p. 79). A single Praetorian cohort provided the manpower for the Mauretanian colony at Gunugu, and a legion VII (perhaps Antonian) was split up among at least three colonies on the same coastline.[91]

Other approaches towards estimating the numbers sent to towns in Italy may be available. The size of the town-site, or the capacity of newly erected public buildings, can offer no sure guide, but the evidence of centuriation, if carefully employed, may supply some useful data.[92] The number of *centuriae* in a grid, coupled with a known or notional allotment size, can be used to suggest a maximum for settlers established on it. Some figures are presented below:

[86] N. Criniti, 'L. Cornelio Scipione Emiliano secondo colonizzatore di Como nel 77 a.c. (Strabo v. 1. 6)?', *Contributi dell'Istituto di storia antica* i (1972), 91–97; Cic. *Leg. Agr.* ii. 76.

[87] Strabo v. 1. 6.

[88] Strabo iv. 6. 7.

[89] App. *Pun.* 136.

[90] *LC* 238. 8 with *app. crit.*

[91] Brunt, *IM* 596, nos. 59, 53–5.

[92] Duncan-Jones 259 ff. and Levick 92 ff. discuss the difficulty of calculating city-populations.

town-name	approximate no. of centuriae	size of allotment (in iugera)	maximum number of veterans
Bononia	750	(50)	3000
Brixia	1000	(50)	4000
Concordia	800	50	4000
Cremona	1600	35	3200
Dertona	600	(50)	9600
Fanum	48	50	2400
Florentia	400	50	192
Luca	70	(50)	1600
Mutina	500	(50)	280
Parentium	450	50	2000
Parma	600	(50)	1800
Pisae	75	(50)	2400
Pola	650	50	300
			2600

Note: Where squares of 50 *iugera* have been observed at a colony, these have been assumed to represent the allotment size.

Grids mapped in the colonies listed above[93] seem to cover most or all of the flat land available in the territory of each, and the totals of colonists suggested are based on the assumption that all the *centuriae* were entirely made over to veterans at a basic rate of 50 *iugera*. If allotments were regularly of 25 *iugera*, the number of veterans could be doubled. However, we cannot know how much land was retained by the former owners; it need not always have been small. Allowance must also be made for larger plots given to junior officers, to *evocati*, to centurions and to tribunes. In addition, some land, especially *subseciva* and woodland, was set aside to become the common *ager publicus* of the colony.[94] Not all the grid we see today need have been utilised in the Late Republic. Thus the totals of veterans given above should be substantially reduced.

Cremona must have been among the largest of the post-Philippi colonies, though its holdings seem likely to have been cut back after Actium (below, p. 195); it enjoyed huge prosperity in the early Empire, tragically cut short in the autumn of A.D. 69. Elsewhere, for example at Concordia, Bononia, Pola and Dertona, the

[93] For Bononia, R. Chevallier, 'La centuriazione e la colonizzazione romana dell'ottava regione augustea Emilia-Romagna', *l'Universo* xl (1960), 1077–1104; for Brixia, Tozzi 111; for Concordia, L. Bosio, 'La centuriazione dell'agro di Iulia Concordia', *Att. Ist. Ven.* ccxiv (1965–66), 195–260; for Cremona, Tozzi 26; for Dertona, P. Fraccaro, 'La colonia romana di Dertona (Tortona) e la sua centuriazione', *Opuscula* III (1957), 123–50; for Fanum, N. Alfieri, 'Per la topografia storica di *Fanum Fortunae* (Fano)', *Riv. Stor. Ant.* vi (1976–77), 147–71; for Florentia, F. Castagnoli, 'La centuriazione di Florentia', *l'Universo* xxviii (1948), 361–68; for Luca, F. Castagnoli, 'La centuriazione di Luca', *SE* xx (1948–49), 285–90; for Mutina, P. Tozzi, 'Indicazioni sul primitivo stanziamento della colonia di Modena', *Riv. Stor. Ant.* v (1975), 47–74; for Parentium and Pola, M. Suić, 'Limitation of Roman Colonies on the Eastern Adriatic Coast', *Zbornik Instituta za historijske u Zadru* i (1955), 32–36; R. Chevallier, 'La centuriazione romana dell'Istria e della Dalmazia', *Att. Mem. Soc. Istr.* ix (1961), 11–24; for Parma, P. Tozzi, *Saggi di topografia storica* (Firenze, 1974), 44–60; for Pisae, P. Fraccaro, 'La centuriazione romana dell'agro Pisano', *SE* xiii (1939), 221–29 = *Opuscula* III (1957), 63–70. See below, p. 144 for centuriation in the *ager Campanus*.

[94] Piganiol, op. cit. (n. 52), 145 estimated that, of the area covered by the fragmentary Cadaster B at Arausio, just over 53% was assigned to colonists, just over 36% retained by the former inhabitants, and nearly 11% given to the colony itself. All the best land passed to the colonists.

number of colonists must have run into thousands, and we can surely say the same about other colonies possessing large territories (e.g. Turin and Placentia) where a modern study of the centuriation is still to seek.

In many towns whose holdings of flat land were far from extensive, the laying out of a wide-ranging grid must have been difficult or nigh impossible. We may instance Hadria, Saena, Tuder and Sutrium. A small grid of 70 *centuriae* has been observed at Luca.[95] We know that Luca accommodated the veterans of two legions, XXVI and the evocate VII, probably after Philippi. Even if the representation from the latter was negligible, the combined veterans of the two legions cannot have totalled less than 1,000 or 1,500 men, perhaps more. Similarly at Pisae, the *centuriae* so far observed could accommodate only a few hundred men.[96] At Fanum the visible *centuriae*, perhaps 48 in all, occupy all the flat land north of the Metaurus river.[97] Hardly more than 200 veterans can have been accommodated there. Two legions were established after Philippi at Ancona: even allowing for some expropriation of land from nearby Aesis or Auximum, the task of accommodating their veterans on flat land must have been difficult.

It is evident that not every veteran can have received flat land in the plains. In some or all of the above colonies, veterans must have been settled on isolated plots, on fertile terraces and in narrow valleys, on *ager strigatus* or *scamnatus,* or in the narrow strips which the *Gromatici* call *laciniae* and *praecisurae*.[98] Most of the veterans at Beneventum whose memorials were found away from the town itself come from hill country; the one known epitaph from Pisae was not found in the area covered by the grid of *centuriae* but on higher ground to the south (below, p. 173). The equation between flat land and fertile land is certainly not applicable over wide tracts of Italy. Hillsides could be productive (e.g. for vines and olives), and some veterans may have been well pleased to receive them. On the other hand, flat land in the valley bottoms might be in need of drainage, and be neither productive nor profitable. The study of centuriation has to be linked to an appreciation of local factors in land use, if we are to proceed to more than tentative conclusions on the numbers despatched to any town.

[95] F. Castagnoli, loc. cit. (above, n. 93).

[96] P. Fraccaro, loc. cit. (n. 93).

[97] N. Alfieri, loc. cit. (n. 93). Earlier studies by C. Selvelli, 'Mura e strade della colonia Julia Fanestris', *l'Universo* viii (1927), 923–935.

[98] For the extension of centuriation into hilly areas, *LC* 218. 3, 219. 6, 228. 7, 240. 1; J. P. Bradford, *Ancient Landscapes* (London, 1957), 199. The terminal stone from Amandola (below, p. 183) testifies to a grid which could only have been fitted with great difficulty into the narrow valley where it was found; P. Bonvicini, 'Iscrizioni latine inedite della quinta *regio Italiae*', *Rend. Acc. Linc.* ser. 8, xxvii (1972), 195–205.

CHAPTER FIVE
THE IMPACT OF SETTLEMENT

1. Veteres *and* novi

The designation of a town for veteran settlement, followed by the arrival of sur-veyors, and after no long interval by the colonists themselves, was undoubtedly a great shock for the inhabitants, bringing ruin to many. Even before Philippi the 18 cities named at Bononia sent their young men to aid Sextus Pompeius,[1] and after the battle many of the dispossessed sought refuge in the ranks of his forces. Doubt-less some of those instructed to forfeit their land remained as long as possible, in the hope of exemption or relief; confrontations were inevitable. The arrival of the colonists led to street fighting in the designated towns early in 41, and similar scenes on individual farmsteads can be presumed.[2] The discontent was soon fomented into civil war; continuing skirmishes throughout the year are implied by Appian's narrative.

The hostility felt towards the incoming veterans after Philippi is well docu-mented. Our picture is enriched and our views coloured by the reminiscences of Vergil, Horace and Propertius, all of whom suffered loss and discomfort at this time.[3] Two Vergilian *Eclogues* (i and ix) illustrate the impact of contemporary reality on the ideal pastoral world. Both poems show clearly the hostility of the rural population to, and the contempt for, the incoming veteran in whose agricultural competence the countrymen have little confidence.[4] The soldier is represented as an uncouth boor (*miles barbarus*), under whose inefficient management the value and productiveness of the land would suffer an inevitable and catastrophic decline.[5] The fact that the veteran could possess a cultural background similar, if not superior, to the newly enfranchised Transpadane is ignored. Some of the settlers at Cremona were members of Caesar's Tenth Legion (below, p. 191).

The colonists did not always arrive alone. They might bring their wives or concubines, their children, brothers or sisters, even their parents, and of course slaves. The assignment of land meant a new life for all the family. Others married local women or took slaves, or married the daughters or sisters of other veterans (below, p. 157). But many made no known links after settlement.

An overbearing attitude and high-handed action towards the local populace

---

[1] App. *BC* iv. 25, 85.

[2] Dio xlviii. 9.

[3] *Ecl.* i and ix; Hor., *Epis.* ii. 2. 130–36; Prop. *El.* i. 21, i. 22; iv. 1. 126–30. The misfortunes of Tibullus (*El.* i. 1. 19–20, 41–2) are not certainly to be linked to land settlement. The pictures conjured up by Vergilian scholiasts and biographers have the ring of truth; Servius (ed. Thilo) on *Ecl., Proem.* p. 3 (Vergil and the centurion Arrius); idem on *Ecl.* ix. 1 (Vergil and the veteran Clodius); Focas, *Vita Verg.* 71–80; Probus (ed. Thilo), III p. 328 (Vergil and the *primipilaris* Milienus Toro). For an armed rising against Sullan colonists at Faesulae, Granius Licinianus (ed. M. Flemisch, Teubner 1904), p. 34.

[4] H. Bennett, 'Vergil and Pollio', *AJP* li (1930), 325–42; L. P. Wilkinson, *The Georgics of Virgil* (Cambridge, 1969), 28 ff.

[5] *Ecl.* i. 70–1; L. J. F. Keppie, 'Vergil, the Confiscations and Caesar's Tenth Legion', *CQ* lxxv (1981), 367–70; R. D. Williams, *Virgil: The Eclogues and the Georgics* (New York, 1979), commenting on *Ecl.* i. 71.

characterised the conduct of the newly arrived colonist; he was himself subjected to obstruction and hostility by the townsfolk and the remaining farmers in the *territorium*. In March 44, Brutus could stir the minds of Caesarian veterans in Rome by emphasising the uncertainties of their future life, under the watchful eye of the dispossessed, ever eager to recover their holdings, should the opportunity arise.[6]

The entire population of a town and its *territorium* was not turned out on the arrival of the colonists. The owners or tenants of a sometimes very substantial part of the *territorium* were dispossessed, but the townsfolk might remain largely unaffected by the tremors in the countryside. On the land itself some residue of the pre-colonial inhabitants (the *veteres possessores* of the gromatic writers) would be left, men whom *dignitas aut gratia aut amicitia* had secured exemption, or an exchange of holdings.[7] These *veteres* are mentioned frequently by the gromatic writers, who are careful to define their status.[8] It is impossible to establish their numbers in any colony, but important not to underestimate them. In 41 senators were allowed by Octavian to retain their land where threatened by confiscation, and a similar concession may be presumed for later schemes; their stewards would remain in possession. Time-served veterans of Caesarian and earlier schemes were also exempt from loss, and in 41 B.C. spokesmen for the discharged Philippi veterans obtained the concession that their own relatives, and fathers and sons of fallen comrades, should be allowed to retain any holdings at risk.[9]

In colonies established by Sulla, evidence has accumulated that the importation of veteran colonists produced a two-tiered society. Pliny, in his listing of Italian communities from an Augustan source, records *Veteres* and *Novi* at Clusium, and *Veteres* and *Fidentiores* at Arretium. There is epigraphic confirmation for *veteres* at Arretium, and at another probable Sullan colony, Nola.[10] It has sometimes been averred that we have here evidence for the co-existence in these towns, and others, of two communities, politically and even physically separate, with in each case a *colonia* planted alongside an existing *municipium*.[11] Much of the evidence, however, testifies merely to distinctions and groupings on the *ordo decurionum* of the town, on which the veterans had the upper hand. At Pompeii the two groups of *Pompeiani* and *coloni* remained identifiable and distinct for nearly 20 years. They had squabbled in the past over canvassing and voting rights (*de ambulatione ac de suffragiis suis*), but according to Cicero the dispute had by 62 B.C. been settled to the satisfaction of both sides.[12] There is neither archaeo-

---

[6] App. *BC* ii. 141, v. 13. Cf. Sull. *Or. Lep.* 23 where insults and envy are the lot of the Sullan veteran on his new estate.

[7] Sic. Flacc. 155. 7; *LC* 247. 19.

[8] Front. 5. 9; Hyg. 117. 13, 119. 10; Sic. Flacc. 157. 22; Hyg. Grom. 202. 1.

[9] Dio xlviii. 9.

[10] Pliny *NH* iii. 52; *ILS* 6608, 6344.

[11] Th. Mommsen, *Bürgercolonien* 165; Kornemann 584; H. Rudolph, *Stadt und Staat im römischen Italien* (Leipzig, 1935), 92; A. Degrassi, 'Quattuorviri in colonie romane e municipi retti da duoviri', *Mem. Acc. Linc.* ser. 8, ii (1949), 281–344, esp. 285–89 = *SVA* I, 104–8; F. Hampl, 'Zur römischen Kolonisation in der Zeit der ausgehenden Republik und des frühen Prinzipates', *Rhein. Mus.* xcv (1952), 52–78.

[12] Cic. *Sull.* 60–62. Cf. T. P. Wiseman, 'Cicero, *Pro Sulla* 60-1', *LCM* ii. 2 (Feb. 1977), 21–22, who argues strongly, and perhaps correctly, for *ambulatio* to be translated as 'arcade'. Yet it may be wondered whether such a local topographical allusion would be comprehensible to Cicero's audience in Rome.

logical nor epigraphic evidence for the coexistence of separate municipal organisations at Pompeii. The *Pompeiani* and the *coloni* formed separate strata within a single community.[13] What this might mean in practice is well illustrated again by Cicero, who reports that at Agrigentum in the first century B.C. there existed a division between *Agrigentini veteres* and *coloni novi* in the town. The community's charter had decreed that the decurions of the *Agrigentini veteres* should always form a majority. Verres had disregarded this provision, and the *veteres* were quick to despatch a delegation to him in an attempt to reestablish primacy.[14] The distinction was one which remained important in the context of local political life.

There are hints of a distinction between *veteres* and *novi* in some of the Caesarian and later settlements. The establishment of a colony at Comum in 58 B.C. produced a category of *Novocomenses,* and the town itself bore for a while the name Novum Comum.[15] Pliny reports *Iulienses* alongside the *Veteres* and *Fidentiores* at Arretium, and his entry on Bovianum probably indicated groups of *Veteres* and *Undecumani* there. Distinctions on the *ordo decurionum* at Parentium and perhaps at Puteoli are evidenced by inscriptions.[16]

Nevertheless it is difficult to suppose that any meaningful distinction could have been brought into being at this time, though 'double communities' of citizen colonists and the non-citizen local populace continued to be formed in the provinces.[17] Much of the alleged epigraphic evidence for double communities in Italy belongs to the Empire, when any such distinctions, whatever their original form and purpose, had ceased to have any meaning. Yet the memory of the distinction might be preserved and commemorated by later generations.[18]

[13] G. Onorato, 'Pompei municipium e colonia romana', *Rend. Acc. Nap.* xxvi (1951), 115–56; E. Gabba, *Republican Rome; The army and the Allies* (Oxford, 1976), 204 n. 218 modifies his earlier views on 'double communities' in Italian towns. At the Sullan colony of Interamnia, inscriptions show two members of the *gens Poppaea* as patrons *municipi et coloniai* (*ILLRP* 617–18; IX 5075). Topographic research seemed to reveal two nuclei in the street plan of modern Teramo, suggesting that the arrival of colonists led to an extension of the town site; A. La Regina, *EAA* VII (1966), 712–13; E. Gabba, 'Urbanizzazione e rinnovamenti urbanistici nell'Italia centro-meridionale del I sec. a.C.', *Stud. Class. Or.* xxi (1972), 73–112, at 103. More recent work has suggested that such notions were ill-founded; L. Migliorati, '*Municipes et coloni:* note di urbanistica teramana', *Arch. Class.* xxviii (1976), 242–56. The inscriptions from Interamnia may testify rather to some uncertainty over nomenclature and terminology in the opening years of the new settlement.

[14] *Verr.* II. ii. 123–24. So at nearby Heraclea, recruitment to the *ordo* was carefully regulated (Cic. *Verr.* II. ii. 125). See E. Gabba, 'Sui senate delle città siciliane nell'età di Verre', *Athenaeum* xxxvii (1959), 304–20. At Sullan colonies the *novi* would have the upper hand.

[15] *CIL* V, p. 565; G. E. F. Chilver, *Cisalpine Gaul* (Oxford, 1941), 8; U. Ewins, 'The Enfranchisement of Cisalpine Gaul', *PSBR* xxiii (1955), 73–98. On the other hand the *Fabraterni Veteres* and *Fabraterni Novani* were the inhabitants of two quite distinct towns in Latium, the former at Ceccano, the latter (replacing Fregellae after 125 B.C.) at Isoletta; *CIL* X, pp. 546, 552; F. Coarelli, 'Fregellae, la colonizzazione latina, e i santuari del Lazio meridionale', *Quaderni del Centro di studio per l'archeologia etrusco-italica* iii (1979), 193–230. The significance of two imperial dedications at Ferentinum by *Ferentinates Novani* (X 5825, 5828) is not clear, but could reflect veteran settlement at a date unknown. Notice *ILS* 6195 (Lanuvium).

[16] Pliny, *NH* iii. 52, 107; below, pp. 202, 150.

[17] Salmon 25–26. The title *Gemella* or *Gemina* attached to some provincials colonies may reflect such communities or their later unification; cf. Pliny *NH* iii. 22 on Emporiae.

[18] At Valentia, a colony probably founded by Pompey about 71 B.C., distinctions in the *ordo* between *veteres* and *veterani* were remembered into the third century A.D.; A. J. Wilson, *Emigration from Italy in the Republican Age of Rome* (Manchester, 1966), 40–42.

One effect of colonisation could, however, have been a temporary dichotomy between the population of the town site and of the *territorium,* the latter now in large part occupied by the newly arrived colonists. Dedications of Augustan date at Veii, erected by *municipes intramurani* and separately by *municipes extramurani* of the town, have been adduced.[19] Joint dedications by the *plebs urbana* of a town are commonplace, but parallel activity on the part of the scattered country-based inhabitants is scarce.[20] A particular coherence among the countryfolk of the *ager Veientanus* in the Augustan period may account for these dedications; we know that veterans were settled there by Caesar (above, p. 52), and some later settlement after 27 B.C. may account for the title *municipium Augustum Veiens* already in use by A.D. 1.[21] Equally significant may be two almost identical dedicatory inscriptions from the *municipium* of Atina in Latium, erected by the *Atinates urbani* and by *legio* XX to a senator P. Tettius Rufus Tontianus. Elsewhere at colonies joint dedications by the *coloni* of the town have come to light, and we may well imagine that the common interests of the colonists, whom the turn of fortune's wheel and the shared experience of military service had united, might find subsequent expression in this way.[22]

Caesar had taxed Sulla with making his veterans and the *veteres possessores* lasting enemies (ἀλλήλοις ἐς αἰεὶ πολεμίους).[23] At Venusia in the early 50s B.C. the young Horace was made to feel inferior by the burly and swaggering sons of centurion-colonists whom he encountered in his earliest schooldays.[24] Caesar himself had hoped to obviate the risk of such enmity by care in the selection of sites and in the placing of the veterans, but some initial friction was almost inevitable, however tactful the founder and however carefully the veterans were inserted into the community. It would be natural to suppose that Augustus encouraged the integration of the two groups with all speed.

2. *Veterans in local government and society*

Once the veterans were settled, they disappear almost entirely from the national scene and from the pages of the historians. It becomes extremely difficult to identify individuals, at least during their lifetimes (above, p. 43). A list of *pontifices* of Sutrium, beginning from the colony's foundation year, may well contain the names

---

[19] XI 3797 = *ILS* 922; XI 3798-99. G. D. B. Jones, 'Southern Etruria 50-40 B.C.: an attack on Veii in 41 B.C.', *Latomus* xxii (1963), 773-76 with *LC* 220. 8-11: *ager eius militibus est adsignatus ex lege Iulia. postea deficientibus his ad urbanum civitatem associandos censuerat divus Augustus.* However, I. Bitto 'Municipium Augustum Veiens', *Riv. Stor. Ant.* i (1971), 109-117 prefers to identify the *intramurani* as Veientines who lived in Rome itself.

[20] J. C. Mann, 'City-Names in the Western Empire', *Latomus* xxii (1963), 777-82, at 780 n. 5.

[21] *ILS* 6579, 6582a, c. However, the *extramurani* could merely be citizens of Veii who lived in suburbs just outside the walls of the old town. Cf. *TLL s.v. extramuranus.*

[22] X 5059-60 = *ILS* 930, 930a: above, p. 85 (Atina); Sylloge 93 (Tuder), 91 (Sora); X 7349 (Thermae Himeraeae). Cf. XI 3312.

[23] App. *BC* ii. 94.

[24] *Sat.* i. 6. 72-73. It has sometimes been averred that these centurions were settled at Venusia by Sulla, so forming evidence of a Sullan colony there, but the date of these schoolboy skirmishes ought to be 60-55. The incident ought therefore to testify to Pompeian veterans planted under the *leges Iuliae* of 59 B.C. It would be wise, however, not to press Horace's wording too far.

of veterans, but indication of military service would be out of place. Similarly a fragment of the *Fasti* of Venusia gives the names of the colony's magistrates for 34–28 B.C.; we might expect that among the *IIviri,* aediles and quaestors of the colony some veterans of the post-Philippi foundation might be discovered.[25]

It is clear that the prospect of enhanced social status was one of the most sought after consequences of land settlement, and a powerful incentive to loyalty. An unintentional gesture by Caesar on crossing the Rubicon made some of those present believe that all would be *equites* with a fortune of 400,000 sesterces once the war was over.[26] In 44 Antony made centurions and perhaps other veterans eligible by virtue of completed military service for inclusion in a third decury of jurymen, where a census requirement of at least 200,000 sesterces might normally be sought; the *Tabula Heracleensis* permitted soldiers who had served their full time to stand for office at below the normal age.[27] Here was visible testimony to the special status of the veteran.

Several authors testify that veterans were often settled in strict military formation, with their own tribunes and centurions. The latter groups would be natural leaders in the opening years of the settlement. It was from among the centurions and tribunes that the spokesmen of the veterans were largely drawn, the ἡγεμόνες τοῦ στρατοῦ who figure so prominently in the pages of the historians in the years after Caesar's death.[28] In 36 B.C. Octavian sought to placate the centurions and tribunes of his army in Sicily by the offer of the decurionate in their home towns (βουλευτικὴν ἐν ταῖς πατρίσιν ἀξίωσιν) and its outward trappings.[29] The proposal was carefully framed, in the hope of separating from the rank and file, and muzzling, the most articulate and determined of the mutineers. It was rejected: the veterans, including the tribunes and centurions, did not want simply to return home, but to receive land in colonies, a concession which Octavian was then at pains to avoid.

We might expect to find substantial numbers of veterans participating in the government of their colonies, at least in the first few years after the foundation when, as a result of the dispossessions, the veterans could form a substantial portion of the voting body, and while local families might be cowed and uncooperative. In many, perhaps most, towns decurions had to possess property and valuables to the value of

---

[25] XI 3254 (Sutrium); IX 422 = *ILS* 6123 (Venusia). Less certainly we may look for veterans among prominent citizens at Pisae in A.D. 2–4, named on XI 1420–21 = *ILS* 139–40.

[26] Suet. *Caes.* 33. So nine years earlier, when Caesar put some of his Tenth Legion on horseback to serve as an escort, a wit among them quipped that he had 'knighted' them; (Caes. *BG* i. 42. 6). Above, p. 30.

[27] Cic. *Phil.* i. 19–20, v. 12, xiii. 3. For the normal census requirement, Suet. *Aug.* 32. 2; *Diz. Epig.* II (1910), 1507–8. Veterans settling in the provinces could expect fiscal and other immunities (above, p. 71 n. 98). For the *Tabula Heracleensis, ILS* 6085, line 91 and above, p. 38.

[28] W. Schmitthenner, 'Politik und Armee in der späteren römischen Republik', *Hist. Zeit.* cxc (1960), 1–17; H. Aigner, *Die Soldaten als Machtfaktor in der ausgehenden römischen Republik* (Innsbruck, 1974), 107, 142. Note esp. App. *BC* v. 16 (the centurion Nonius), v. 128 (the tribune Ofillius). Some of the *IIviri* instructed by Antony to carry out arms' inspection in Caesarian colonies were perhaps former centurions and tribunes (above, p. 52).

[29] App. *BC* v. 128; but Dio xlix. 14. 3 mentions only an offer to centurions.

100,000 sesterces, as professed before the local censors.[30] The fact that veterans are found as decurions implies that some did fall within the necessary property valuation (assuming this was rigorously applied). With our growing knowledge of the size of allotments, and some appreciation of land values in Italy in the Late Republic, we can move towards an estimate of their likely financial status, but considerable uncertainty remains. Veterans with allotments of close to 100 *iugera* (i.e. centurions and tribunes) would be brought by virtue of the capital value of their land grant close to, if not within, the property qualification for admission to the *ordo decurionum*, but those with 50 *iugera* or less would not. It would thus be the tribunes and centurions who would be best placed to participate, should they so wish, in the local government of the *colonia*. The first magistrates and decurions of a colony were normally selected by the founding commissioner (above, p. 97). Many of these would be veterans, but not to the exclusion of pre-colonial families and former members of the *ordo*. At the very least veterans could fill gaps left by the dispossessed. As *IIviri* in the first year of settlement, tribunes and centurions would be obvious candidates.

The rôle of tribunes settled with the legions deserves special consideration. Both Tacitus and Hyginus Gromaticus note that tribunes participated in the colonisation of the Late Republic, though neither author specifies a particular settlement scheme.[31] Octavian's offer of the decurionate after Naulochus encompassed in Appian's version both centurions and tribunes. Throughout the first century B.C. the combination of continuous warfare and enlarged armies produced among the equestrian tribunate a group of almost professional officers, some promoted from the centurionate, who might look forward at the end of useful service to settlement with the men under their command.[32] Not every tribune would desire settlement in this way. Two entries in the *Liber Coloniarum* record that tribunes would be found among colonists at the towns concerned;[33] we know from Cicero that under the *Lex Antonia* of June 44 land in the *ager Semurius* was allocated to tribunes who had served twice in Caesar's army; the location of the *ager Semurius* has not been pinpointed, but it clearly lay very close to Rome.[34] The measure was designed not to strengthen a particular colony, but perhaps to keep favoured officers near the capital.[35]

[30] *Diz. Epig.* II (1910), 1524-8; C. Nicolet, *The World of the Citizen in Republican Rome* (London, 1980), 62 ff., 69 ff.; W. Langhammer, *Die rechtliche und soziale Stellung der Magistratus municipales und der Decuriones* (Wiesbaden, 1973), 190 ff.

[31] Tac. *Ann.* xiv. 27; Hyg. Grom. 176. 13.

[32] R. Syme, 'Who was Decidius Saxa?', *JRS* xxvii (1937), 127-37; idem, 'Caesar the Senate, and Italy', *PBSR* xiv (1938), 1-31; J. Suolahti, *Junior Officers of the Roman Army in the Republican Period* (Helsinki, 1955), 55, 137-8; C. Nicolet, 'Armée et société à Rome sous la république: à propos de l'ordre équestre', in J.-P. Brisson (ed.), *Problèmes de la Guerre à Rome* (Paris, 1970), 117-56; Wiseman 145-7. Under the Empire the military tribunate was inserted into a career structure which all but precluded settlement in this way.

[33] 235. 5, 236. 13.

[34] Cic. *Phil.* vi. 14, vii. 17; Macrobius, *Sat.* i. 10. 16. The beneficiaries in gratitude erected a statue to L. Antonius. The detail that they had served *bis* may point to a minimum requirement for participation in the scheme.

[35] For a possible enclave of tribunes at Interamna Nahars, XI 4183a, 4184, 4187, 4189-94, with Gabba, *Ricerche* 248. Not all the inscriptions need have an Augustan date. Cf. also X 7349 (Thermae Himeraeae), III 6097 (Patrae).

Tribunes settled with their men in colonies would naturally be looked to to act as leaders of the community in civilian life. The allotments granted to tribunes must have been in the most generous of all categories. Several tribunes playing a distinguished rôle in the government of colonies at this time can be identified from the epigraphic record (see list, below, p. 109). One such man should be C. Aclutius Gallus at Venafrum, tribune in legion II *Sabina*, twice *IIvir urbis moeniundae*, twice *praefectus* for unnamed *IIviri*, and *IIvir* once in his own right. At Tuder, Q. Caecilius Atticus, perhaps tribune of legion XXXXI, was *IIvir quinquennalis* and *patronus* of the town. He is honoured in a dedication erected by men of the legion, now colonists at Tuder. Much less certainly we may include M. Vecilius Campus at Luceria, *IIvir quinquennalis*, *pontifex* and benefactor, and L. Sergius Lepidus at Pola, tribune in legion XXIX, and aedile of the colony (below, p. 204). However, the tribune L. Firmius, who is honoured at Sora by colonists of IIII *Sorana*, cannot be regarded in quite the same light. The careful wording of the dedication makes clear that he had held the chief local magistracy (*IIIIvir*) before, perhaps long before, the foundation of the colony. After its establishment he became the first *pontifex*, but held no other office. At Placentia the ex-tribune P. Aufudius served as both *IIIIvir* and *IIvir*; if the change in the title of magistracy is indicative of colonial foundation (and this was Degrassi's interpretation), it would appear that Aufudius and the other members of his family named on the dedication were already resident in the town. [36] Several other tribunes are known who may have been settled along with their men, but no secure link can be discovered, and we must beware of trying to link every tribune of Augustan date recorded in a known colony with the settlement programmes. [37] Those with inherited wealth and holdings, for whom the gift of up to 100 *iugera* would be an insufficient temptation, might return home to ancestral properties. A useful example here is of the brothers Tillius, who served as tribunes in Antony's legion X *Equestris*, presumably until Actium. After discharge they settled in Pompeii, a town with which their father had substantial links and where he may recently have taken up residence. [38]

In the later first century B.C., centurions, like tribunes, were rewarded in land and money at well above the basic rates. [39] Men of equestrian status are found serving as centurions, attracted by the prospect of long-term military service, and its rewards. [40] Their rôle was enhanced and applauded by Caesar. Centurions could be

[36] X 1217; A. Degrassi, 'Quattuorviri in colonie romane e in municipi retti da duoviri', *Mem. Acc. Linc.* ser. 8, ii (1949), 281–344, esp. 294.

[37] Gabba, *Ricerche* 248 n. 1 for other possible examples. Note *NS* 1905, 219 for the tribune L. Ancharius C.f. Rom., *IIvir* and *augur* at Ateste.

[38] P. Castrén, *Ordo Populusque Pompeianus* (Roma, 1975), 229 no. 410; idem., 'About the *legio X Equestris*', *Arctos* viii (1974), 5–7; R. Frei-Stolba, 'Legio X Equestris', *Talanta* x-xi (1978–79), 44–61. Note also XI 7495 (Falerii), *AE* 1931, 93 (Saturnia); *ILS* 2228 (Aesernia).

[39] C. Nicolet, loc. cit. (n. 32); B. Dobson, 'The centurionate and social mobility during the Principate', in C. Nicolet (ed.), *Recherches sur les structures sociales dans l'Antiquité classique* (Paris, 1970), 99–115; Wiseman 74. Caesar borrowed money from his tribunes and centurions in 49 B.C. (Caes. *BC* i. 39). Suetonius reports that each centurion offered to pay the cost of hiring a cavalryman to augment his forces (*Caes.* 68).

[40] In the Late Republic, the centurionate was worth purchasing (Cic. *Pis.* 88; *De imp. Cn. Pomp.* 37). On the social status of the centurion in the Early Empire, B. Dobson, 'Legionary centurion or equestrian officer? A comparison of pay and prospects', *Anc. Soc.* iii (1972), 193–207; idem, *Die Primipilares* (Koln-Bonn, 1978), 115–21.

found serving on juries in the mid first century B.C., and in 44 B.C. Antony included them in his third decury of jurymen, whatever their financial status (above, p. 53). The epigraphic record provides but modest confirmation: two centurions as decurions at Ateste and Beneventum are the only testimony to their status in the Italian colonies.[41]

The active rôle played by *milites* is more an occasion for surprise. At Ateste a ranker was decurion, and at Beneventum one was *aedilis*. At Hispellum an *evocatus* is found as *VIvir*, freeborn priest presumably of Augustus himself; at Parma a *veteranus* was *aedilis* and *sexvir*. The centurion and ranker who were decurions at Ateste achieved the office by adlection, i.e. they were not admitted at the five-yearly revision of the roll, but by special cooption. Octavian could bring some veterans within the property qualification for office, but this could not by itself ensure that they obtained it. Some pressure might be required.[42] Land grants of 50 *iugera* or less which *milites* received would probably leave men well short of the census qualification for the *ordo*, unless they had movables, cattle, or slaves to a substantial value, which the censors could take into account. Some might gain admittance to its ranks *beneficio conditoris,* or by a temporary easing of the property qualification, but secure financial backing was a necessary prerequisite for successful tenure. The burdens of office were considerable. Where rankers do appear in local government, we may think to identify them as men highly successful as farmers, perhaps with a diversity of business interests, or buoyed up by booty, by a *patrimonium,* legacy or dowry, and perhaps not entering the *ordo* until many years later.

Particularly illuminating is the *elogium* of L. Antistius Campanus at Capua (Sylloge 65), a man who had served (if Mommsen's ingenious restorations are accepted) as a ranker under both Caesar and Octavian and who was settled at Capua (*deductus in coloniam nostram*) most probably in 41 or 36. Over the following decades he exhibited a quite remarkable generosity; in the surviving text the tenure of no particular magistracy is mentioned, but it is likely that he held them all. Here was an ideal colonist, pursuing after settlement a selfless course of benefaction to the community.[43]

A place on the *ordo*, or a magistracy, brought with it considerable and visible privileges: a special seat at the town's theatre and amphitheatre, participation in municipal banquets and other benefits. This was just the privileged position to which the veterans aspired within local society. By a decree of Augustus, decurions in the colonies obtained the right of voting in absence at elections in Rome. Probably but not certainly decurions in the military colonies of the later first century

[41] Sylloge, 24, 31. Note also *ILS* 2233 (a centurion who became *IIvir* at Urso); *Ath. Ann. Arch.* iv (1971), 112 for a centurion who was *IIvir* at Patrae.

[42] All known decurions at Ateste were *adlecti* (Sylloge 6, 24, V 2395, 2524, 2860, NS 1906, 418 no. 2. For a civilian made decurion at Nola *beneficio dei Caesaris, ILS* 6343 = *ILLRP* 630. Frontinus reports that at some colonies the *conditor* had ordained that *incolae* should be eligible for public office (52. 22): his example is Tuder. Such a privilege, designed to enlarge the pool of worthies from whom office holders might be drawn, was later sought and acquired by other towns, e.g. Fanum (Front. 52. 22–23), Aquileia (*ILS* 1374) and Tergeste (*ILS* 6680). Note at Aequum a man elected to local office in the colony, apparently in its foundation year, *suffragio* [*veteranorum*] (III 2733).

[43] Line 8 of the restored text reads *in* [*cumulatio*]*ne officiorum r*[*ei publicae praestitorum* . . . *co*]*nsenesceret* (X 3903).

B.C. were the beneficiaries here. This concession can have had little practical impact, except in the rarer tribes, but it emphasised and maintained the special link between them and the *urbs Roma*.[44]

Veterans in local government

1. *Tribunes*

name	colony	offices	ref. (Sylloge)
C. Aclutius Gallus	Venafrum	duovir urbis moeniundae bis, praef. iure deicundo bis, duovir iure deicundo	96
Q. Caecilius Atticus	Tuder	IIvir quinquennalis patronus coloniae	93
(L. Firmius	Sora	pontifex	91)
L. Sergius Lepidus	Pola	aedilis	90
M. Vecilius Campus	Luceria	IIvir iure dic., pontifex	81

2. *Centurions*

Avidienus	Beneventum	decurio	31
L. Blattius	Ateste	decurio allectus	24

3. *Milites*

M. Billienus	Ateste	decurio allectus	6
Cn. Decimius Bibulus (evocatus)	Hispellum	VIvir	74
L. Vettidius	Parma	sexvir, aedilis	88
ignotus	Beneventum	aedilis	39
L. Antistius Campanus	Capua	?	65

Direct participation would at most last for a generation, until advancing years took their toll, but the incoming families might maintain their prominence into the next generation, or enhance it. The younger Antistius Campanus at Capua, praised in his father's *elogium* at Capua as *minist[erii eius atque munificen]tiae successor,* was probably *IIvir* of the town in 13 B.C. Less certainly sons of veterans can be identified among known *IIviri* at Beneventum and Venusia.[45] A notable example at Nuceria has recently been highlighted: M. Virtius Ceraunus, *IIvir* of the town, commemorated in a grandiose tomb in the Sarno Valley, was the son of M. Virtius, a veteran of legion XIX, and probable colonist, whose seemingly far less prestigious memorial was located nearby.[46]

The resilience of the pre-colonial families should not be underestimated. The *ordo* of any colony in the years following foundation would contain a combination of both veterans and *veteres* in varying proportions. Cicero notes that, after the foundation of the colony at Capua in 59 B.C., many of the old population stayed on, *nomine commutato,* as *coloni* and *decuriones.*[47] There are many magistrates of

[44] Suet. *Aug.* 46. For the right granted to former auxiliaries to be registered in their absence for the local census, *EJ²* 301-2 and above, p. 71, n. 98. The only two Italian towns known to have been in *Romilia* (Ateste and Sora) were both colonies. Of six towns known to have been in *Lemonia*, up to four were colonies of this time (Ancona, Bononia, Hispellum and Parentium).

[45] X 3803 (Capua); IX 1643 = *ILS* 5734a with Sylloge 35 (Beneventum); IX 422 = *EJ²* 323, line 58 with Sylloge 97 (Venusia).

[46] *ILS* 6446 with Sylloge 86; J. M. Reynolds and E. Fabbricotti, 'A Group of Inscriptions from Stabiae', *PBSR* xl (1972), 127-37.

[47] *Sest.* 9.

Augustan date in the colonies for whom there is no need to assert military antecedents. Only a minority could aspire to such heights even in a local context. The
spotlight is inevitably on the most successful. The majority were preoccupied with
their land, and their epitaphs record merely the terse details of military service.
Some might combine their farms with a variety of business interests, equally hard to
document (see below, p. 126). Here accumulated cash reserves could assist by providing capital for a variety of ventures. [48]

We may be sure that a spirit of comradeship did survive in the colonies. In the
provinces one manifestation was the addition to the colony's titulature of an
adjective formed from the numeral of the legion in which the veterans had once
served (above, p. 18). For Italy we have only Pliny's reference to *Undecumani* at
Bovianum. The titles *Iulia* or *Augusta* maintained the link with the *deductor,* and
other epithets might recall the shared military service of the colonists (above, p. 18).
The inhabitants of a *colonia Iulia* or *colonia Augusta* might come to be known
collectively as *Iulienses* or *Augustini*; such appellations came quickly to identify all
the inhabitants of the town, without implying any personal military antecedents for
the group so described. [49]

It would not be unexpected if the veterans preserved some form of association
after settlement, which commemorated their common origin and past successes.
The Royal British Legion, and more politically-orientated organisations in France
(Association des anciens Combatants de l'Union Française) or in the United States
(The American Legion and The Veterans of Foreign Wars) come to mind. Evidence
from a much later date of *collegia veteranorum* can be adduced in towns where
veterans were wont to congregate. [50] Inscriptions from colonies at Ateste and Beneventum record such *collegia,* but seem likely to date to the second or third centuries
A.D. It would be difficult to think of later infusions of veterans to these particular
towns, and the *collegia* could therefore have had their origins in the Augustan age,
or have been formed very much later by the descendants of the veteran colonists. [51]
For durability we may compare the Society of the Cincinnati (U.S.A.), which was
formed by former members of the Revolutionary Army, called from the plough in

[48] Of potential importance in this context is the numismatic evidence of coin hoards from colonies,
which close early in the Augustan age; M. H. Crawford, 'Coin Hoards and the Pattern of Violence in
the Late Republic', *PBSR* xxxvii (1969), 77–81; idem, *Roman Republican Coin Hoards* (London,
1969), esp. nos. 460, 466, 504, 519, 529, 549. Note also G. Gorini, 'Nuove considerazioni sul tesoretto
di Padova', *Att. Ist. Ven.* cxxvii (1968–69), 29–51 for a hoard from Patavium which stops abruptly in
45 B.C., and which the author suggests could represent the savings of a veteran released in that year;
but we cannot know the status of the owner. Where hoards contain a substantial number of legionary
issues of Mark Antony, it is tempting to think that these may represent the savings of his soldiers, or the
loot acquired at Actium or Alexandria.

[49] Front. 46. 17 (*Lucus Feroniae Augustinorum*); *ILS* 139 (*Iulienses* at Pisae).

[50] J. P. Waltzing, *Étude historique sur les corporations professionelles* (Bologna, 1900), IV 151.
From Italy there is evidence at Ostia (*ILS* 6146), Aquileia (V 784, *ILS* 2471), Puteoli (*ILS* 6328), and
probably Ravenna (*ILS* 7311).

[51] V 2475 (Ateste); less certainly *ILS* 6502 (Beneventum). V 8755 (Concordia) seems related to a
military presence there in the Late Empire; perhaps V 4001 (Brixia). For memories of military origins
preserved into, or revived in, the third century A.D., above n. 18 (Valentia). Cf. *ILS* 9400 (from
Uthina, a Caesarian colony), erected in A.D. 206 to Severus by *cives Romani pagani veter(ani) pagi
Fortunalis/quorum parentes beneficio divi Augusti/[..........] Sutunurca agros acceperunt.*

1776, and has given the name to a major city. That Society, whose membership is restricted to the direct descendants of these officers, has survived despite vicissitudes of fortune for 200 years.

For pride in a shared endeavour a group of five (perhaps six) funerary inscriptions from the neighbourhood of Ateste deserve special mention. Each stone records the military service of a veteran who bears as a surname the title *Actiacus,* in clear commemoration of the sea-battle of Actium.[52] The texts of the five complete (or near complete) inscriptions may be repeated here:

Ref. (Sylloge)	First reported at:	Name and rank, etc.
26	Aquileia	M. Aufustius M.f. Rom. Actiacus Valeriae C.lib. Charidi coniugi
2	Ateste	Q. Atilio Q.f. Rom. Actiaco et . . .
6	Ateste	M. Billienus M.f. Rom. Actiacus legione XI proelio navali facto in coloniam deductus (etc.)
8	Ateste	Q. Coelius L.f. leg. XI Actiacus signifer
27	Patavium	Ossa Salvi [S]emproni C.[f.] Rom. leg. XI A[c]tiaco Licinia L.[f.] f.

The epitaph of M. Billienus is the most specific (Pl. IB), mentioning the sea-battle in which he as a legionary had fought. The adoption of laudatory or descriptive *cognomina* was part of the continuing Roman name-building process. During the Republic successful generals took *cognomina* from a conquered region or tribe, but common soldiers too might seek permanent commemoration of their service in this way.[53]

Three of the stones recording *Actiaci* were recovered from within the *ager Atestinus*; the other two were first reported at Aquileia and Patavium, but the fact that both men belonged to the tribe *Romilia* ensures that they too had been colonists at Ateste. Only one legion is mentioned (legion XI, one of the two which formed the nucleus of the settlement at Ateste), on three of the stones. On the other two the nature of the veteran's military service is not specified—it has been supplanted by the more evocative *Actiacus.* Actium is the only battle in Roman history from which a personal *cognomen* is known to have been formed. According to Orosius (the only source to provide details) Octavian embarked eight legions and five *cohortes praetoriae* on his ships before the battle.[54] The remainder of the army watched the battle from the shore. Only skirmishing took place on land, and the Antonian legions surrendered without bloodshed.[55] Veterans from only one legion

[52] L. J. F. Keppie, 'A Note on the Title *Actiacus*', *CR* lxxxv (1971), 329–30.

[53] C. Valerius *Arsaces* (Sylloge 55; below, p. 159); Cestius *Macedonicus*, a crazed veteran at Perusia (App. *BC* v. 49). For the title *Africani* adopted by a group of soldiers to commemorate or describe their service in Africa, *ILLRP* 146 which E. Gabba, *Republican Rome: The Army and the Allies* (Oxford, 1976), 202 n. 185 now proposes to place in the Sullan era. Cf. under the Empire, M. Helvius Rufus, who adopted the surname *Civica* after the award of a *corona* by Tiberius in A.D. 20 (Tac. *Ann.* iii. 20 with *ILS* 2637).

[54] vi. 19. 8.

[55] Dio li. l. 4.

can as yet be shown to have employed the title *Actiacus,* and not all the veterans of that legion settled at Ateste make use of it.

Another inscription from the *ager Atestinus* may be adduced. The stone (Sylloge 21) was catalogued by Mommsen under Verona, and not under Ateste, as its findspot, at Marega, required. It has not attracted the attention of scholars. The inscription reads:

........IVS T F ROM
.......ER SIBI ET
.......IO T F PATRI AC
.......GN CHOR V̄ ....

This is an epitaph erected by an *ignotus* to himself and to his father who had attained the rank of *signifer* in a *cohors V,* almost certainly a *cohors praetoria.*[56] At the end of the third line appear the letters AC. These could be the first two letters of a split word, rather than the connective *ac,* only rarely employed as an epigraphic equivalent of *et.* The reading PATRI AC/TIACO SIGN CHOR V PR is proposed here, which would add to the list of *Actiaci* a standard-bearer of a *cohors praetoria,* one of the five which according to Orosius served on board Octavian's ships. Veterans of two other *cohortes praetoriae* are already known at Ateste (below, p. 195).

There is, however, no need to imagine that the exploits of veterans styling themselves *Actiaci* had been particularly outstanding. Rather it may be that some of those who fought at Actium and had been settled after the campaign at Ateste chose to adopt for themselves a descriptive title which attained a local vogue. An alternative, that the title was awarded by Octavian to specific veterans in return for sterling service, seems less likely. The very adoption of the title *Actiacus* (Aktium-kämpfer) tells us not a little about the pride felt by its bearers—a Roman equivalent of Μαραθωνομάχης—and something about their attitude to the local population from whom they wished to be distinguished. It was a title they carried with them to the grave.[57]

3. *Augustus and his veterans*

Under the Republic a *deductor* would hope to maintain close links with the colony, the establishing of which he had overseen; he and his descendants would automatically be invited to serve as *patroni* of the colony. In the year of foundation, or shortly afterwards, he might himself act as *IIvir* (above, p. 97). We know that Augustus was patron of two colonies in Italy, and, had the epigraphic record been fuller, he would most probably be revealed as patron of the majority, if not all, of the colonies, including those founded by the friends of Antony. He was of course

---

[56] G. Pietrogrande, *Ateste nella milizia imperiale* (Venezia, 1888), 98 with a sketch by A. Martini. The fragment, now sadly further mutilated by the loss of the crucial right-hand portion, is on view in the Museo Civico at Verona.

[57] For the pride of Caesarian *evocati* in their achievements, see Cic. *Phil.* xii. 29 (*memoriam rerum quas gesserunt pro populi Romani libertate*).

patron of many *municipia* also.[58] In the Julio-Claudian period it became common for the emperor or a member of his immediate family to be elected as sole *IIvir* or *IIIIvir* of a town; the recipient of the honour appointed a distinguished local citizen to act as his *praefectus*. We might expect to find Augustus elected *IIvir* in some of his colonies; evidence is lacking in Italy, though numerous offers must have been made.[59]

Augustus maintained, or wished to be seen as maintaining, a close bond as *patronus* with individual veterans. The historians tell of a number of encounters between the *princeps* and his former comrades in arms. Suetonius preserves the story of Scutarius, *evocatus quondam suus*, on whose behalf Augustus spoke, when Scutarius had been brought to court on a charge of *iniuriae*. The man had a special claim on Augustus' gratitude, and having offered his personal services to the Emperor in his time of need, he was now calling in the debt.[60] Dio has the same tale, in which Augustus' reluctance to make a personal appearance in court was overcome by a timely reminder of the precise nature of the obligation. In Macrobius' version, additional details are supplied, and the obligation stated to have been incurred *Actiaco bello*.[61] Suetonius names the veteran as Scutarius, perhaps simply a nickname for the shield-laden legionary, but the *nomen* is epigraphically attested. In particular, a L. Scutarius served as *quaestor* of the post-Philippi colony at Venusia in 32 and as *IIvir* there in 31 B.C.[62]

Pliny tells of a veteran entertaining Augustus at his house in Bononia.[63] The man had served in Antony's Parthian campaign, and had returned to Italy with his booty intact, no mean achievement in troubled circumstances. The meal they shared was eaten off plates of gold. The setting of the story in Bononia and the allegiance of the host point to a deliberate gesture by Augustus, emphasising the reconciliation of factions. Suetonius has the further story that Augustus entertained to dinner a former member of his bodyguard at whose house he had once stayed.[64] Both these veterans had perhaps risen to high position in their respective towns. We should not be surprised that Augustus strove to retain a special relationship with his

---

[58] *ILS* 79 (Capua), *ILS* 6753 (Aosta). Also *AE* 1966, 73 (Larinum), *ILS* 76 (Saticula), *AE* 1969-1970, 132 (Tarentum), *ILS* 78 (Luna), X 206 (Grumentum), XI 5642 (Camerinum); L. Harmand, *Le patronat sur les collectivités publiques* (Paris, 1957), 24, 134-7. Valerius Maximus reports (ix. 15. 1) that in the spring of 44 many veteran settlements adopted the usurper Amatius as their patron. L. and C. Caesar were patrons at Pisae (*ILS* 139-40) and doubtless at many other towns; XI 6220 shows Germanicus as patron at Fanum. For P. Sulla as patron at Pompeii, Cic. *Sull.* 62.

[59] For Augustus and the young Tiberius as *IIviri* at the colony of Carthago Nova, see Grant *FITA* 158-59. Grant assigned the coins to the *municipium* of Saguntum, but an epigraphic record of the young Tiberius as patron of Carthago Nova (*ILS* 144) may confirm the traditional attribution.

[60] Suet. *Aug.* 56.

[61] Dio lv. 4; Macrobius *Sat.* ii. 4. 27.

[62] *ILS* 6123 = *EJ*[2] 323, col. 2, lines 7, 16; IX 569 records a freedman L. Scutarius Andrea in the town. The suggestion of C. Cichorius, that Scutarius be emended to Scruttarius, need not be entertained; see 'Ein rheinischer Soldatengrabstein als Document für die Lebensgeschichte des Augustus', *Römische Studien* (Leipzig-Berlin, 1922), 282-85.

[63] *NH* xxxiii. 82.

[64] *Aug.* 74.

veterans.[65] A well-known rescript of Domitian alludes to a letter of Augustus *ad quartanos suos,* to men of his own Fourth Legion (the *Macedonica*), settled after Philippi at the Adriatic town of Firmum (below, p. 181). Some 30 years after the foundation of Pisae, its citizens took pains on the occasion of the deaths of their patrons Lucius and Gaius Caesar in A.D. 2 and 4 to record and recall their special link with the imperial family. This attitude is in marked contrast to that evinced by the people of Praeneste who were later to disown and annul the Sullan colony in the town.[66]

Inscriptions from two colonies, Firmum and Iader in Dalmatia, give Augustus the title *parens coloniae.* At Bononia he is simply *parens.* This is welcome evidence of a specific and enduring relationship between Augustus and these towns, and should betoken the high regard in which he as *conditor* was held. The coining of such titles also reflects the general regard for Augustus as universal protector and guardian of the Roman commonwealth.[67] In the worship of Augustus in his lifetime and after his death, it is no surprise to find the colonies playing a leading part.[68] The traffic was not all one-way; as *clientes,* the veterans joined other groups in contributing to the rebuilding of Augustus' house on the Palatine after a disastrous fire.[69]

4. *Benefactions and financial aid*

Augustus' well-known claim that his 28 colonies remained prosperous and populated to the end of his reign should imply a certain amount of concern for their continued well-being. In the following pages an examination will be made of the literary, epigraphic and archaeological evidence for Augustus' interest in and support for the Italian colonies.

Nothing is known of gifts of money or the provision of amenities to the post-Philippi group of colonies in the years immediately after 41. The veterans were mostly settled in old established towns, and the sources specifically state that all necessary equipment and steadings, even slaves, were to be left intact for the incoming colonists.[70] In the years before the final conflict with Antony, Octavian made a special effort to assuage Antonian feeling in the colony at Bononia;[71] this may have included the promise of large-scale public works. It is likely that he made similar gifts to other Antonian colonies. Velleius informs us that after settling veterans on Campanian *ager publicus* in 36, Octavian compensated the town by

---

[65] For a veteran who prevailed upon Caesar in court by a reminder of past services in Spain, and won his case, see Seneca *de Benef.* v. 24.

[66] *ILS* 139–40; Aul. Gell. *Noct. Att.* xvi. 13. 4.

[67] Below, p. 181 (Firmum), *ILS* 5336 (Iader), below, p. 188 (Bononia). At Falerii Augustus was hailed as *pat(e)r patriae et municipi* (XI 3083). The title of *pater* (or *mater*) *coloniae* could be awarded to local citizens in return for munificence (XI 7993, *ILS* 6657).

[68] For temples or shrines to Augustus, V 2533 (Ateste), XI 948 (Mutina), IX 1556 = *ILS* 109 (Beneventum), Vitruvius *de Arch.* v. 1. 7 (Fanum), Tac. *Ann.* iv. 52 (Nola). The dedication to Augustus of the temple on the promontory at Puteoli has been recently challenged (see below, p. 148). All towns, whatever their status, joined in the worship of the emperor.

[69] Suet. *Aug.* 57.

[70] App. *BC* iv. 3; Dio xlviii. 6. 3.

[71] Dio l. 6. 3.

assigning to it land at Cnossus in Crete (which brought in an annual revenue of 1,200,000 sesterces in his day), and by the promise of an aqueduct; Dio adds the detail that the latter was named the *Aqua Iulia*.[72] Both authors comment on the success of the project, on the pride of the colony in the possession of it, and its continuing usefulness. Velleius' near contemporary testimony is particularly welcome. It forms his one detailed reference to the settlement programmes of the age.[73]

For the remainder of Augustus' long reign we are dependent almost entirely on epigraphic and archaeological evidence. The historians are prolific in their praise of the Emperor's generosity to cities but short on specific instances outside Rome itself.[74] Similarly in the *Res Gestae* frequent reference is made to buildings within the city, erected at the expense of Augustus, but, apart from allusions to the improvement to the Italian road network, public works in the peninsula and in the provinces are not recorded.

In the absence of specific literary reference, recourse must be had to the chance survival of epigraphic records, and to imprecise archaeological data, for evidence of a programme of public works and gifts.[75] The epigraphic evidence for construction work in the Italian colonies is tabulated below:[76]

town	structure	date	donated by	ref.
Ariminum	*vias omnes stern[it?]*	A.D. 1	C. Caesar	XI 366 = *ILS* 133
Ariminum	arch	27 B.C.	[Imp. Caesar Augustus]	XI 365 = *ILS* 84
Ariminum	bridge	completed A.D. 22	Imp. Caesar Augustus Ti. Caesar August.	XI 367 = *ILS* 113
Bononia	*balineum*	—	divus Aug. parens	XI 720 = *ILS* 5674
Brixia	*aquas in coloniam perduxerunt*	—	divus Augustus Ti. Caesar Augustus	V 4307 = *ILS* 114
Fanum	*murum dedit*	A.D. 9–10	Imp. Caes. Augustus	XI 6218 = *ILS* 104
Firmum	—	—	Imp. Caesar Augustus	IX 540*
Hispellum	walls and gates	—	[Imp. Caesa]r divi [f.]	XI 5266
Puteoli	*horologi[um] po[suit]*	after 27 B.C.	[Imp. Caesar A]ug.	X 1617
Tergeste	*murum turresque fecit*	33 B.C.	Imp. Caesar	V 525 = *ILS* 77
Venafrum	aqueduct	18–11? B.C.	[Im]p. Ca[esar Augustus]	X 4842 = *ILS* 5743

[72] Vell. ii. 81. 2; Dio xlix. 14. 5; below, p. 145.

[73] Prompted perhaps by a maternal link with the town; *RE* VIIIA (1955), 638.

[74] Suet. *Aug.* 46; Dio liv. 23. 8; Vell. ii. 89. 6.

[75] F. C. Bourne, *The Public Works of the Julio-Claudians and Flavians* (Princeton, 1946), 16–20; R. Paribeni, 'Le opere pubbliche', in *Augustus: studi in occasione del bimillenario augusteo* (Roma, 1938), 405–13: E. Gabba, 'Urbanizzazione e rinnovamenti urbanistici nell'Italia centro-meridionale del 1 sec. a.C.', *Stud. Class. Or.* xxi (1972), 73–112.

[76] Full references will be found under the appropriate headings in Chapters 6–9 below.

The gift of an aqueduct to Venafrum is perhaps the best documented instance of benefaction to a colony, thanks to the survival of parts of two copies of an Augustan *edictum* outlining its use, and of seven *cippi* marking its course (below, p. 138). A study of the text of the edict suggests that it was issued after 18 B.C. and perhaps before 11 B.C.

A new wall circuit, together with at least one monumental gateway, was provided by Augustus for the colony at Fanum Fortunae, and the structures were dedicated in A.D. 9–10. At Tergeste he provided walls in 33 B.C.; he may have financed similar work at Hispellum, and some benefaction to Firmum is implied by a now lost inscription (below, p. 181). At Bononia the emperor gave a *balineum* to the town, a gift which could form confirmation of Dio's testimony on favours given in 32 B.C., but the date of its construction is not known. Late in the reign an aqueduct for Brixia was begun, to be finished by Tiberius. The completion of work on the Flaminia in 27 B.C. was marked at Ariminum by the insertion of a commemorative archway into the walls of the town at its south gate, and a few years before Augustus' death work was begun on a new bridge across the Marecchia for travellers proceeding north-westwards along the Aemilia. Within the town itself C. Caesar is credited with the paving of streets in A.D. 1. Perhaps he was *patronus* there. At Lucus Feroniae and at Pola inscriptions refer to an *Aqua Augusta*; excavated remains of the former suggest that it could be dated to Augustus' reign. However, by itself the title *Augusta* is not evidence that Augustus himself financed such structures or that they were put up during his lifetime.[77] A water-clock at Puteoli completes the list of benefactions attested by epigraphic evidence.

It was normal for Roman towns to look to the wealthiest of their citizens and to their *patroni* to provide amenities, ranging from an amphitheatre to sets of weights and measures.[78] The donors themselves might be senators or even freedmen, and the gifts might be for the benefit of the entire citizen body, or be restricted to members of a particular *collegium* or priesthood. This was normal practice, and we should not suppose that towns looked specifically to Augustus to fill their needs. His initiatives might encourage the public-spirited to resume their traditional rôle. We need not doubt that there had been a lull in such activities during the Civil Wars.

There are many records of private benefactions within colonies in Augustus' reign. A Caesareum was built at Beneventum by Veidius Pollio sometime between 27 and 15 B.C.; at Luceria an amphitheatre was erected at the expense of the tribune M. Vecilius Campus *in honorem imp(eratoris) Caesaris Augusti coloniaeque Luceriae.* Another, much smaller, amphitheatre was provided at Lucus Feroniae by the freedman Silius Epaphroditus. At Dertona a donor, whose name is unfortunately lost, restored the forum and adjacent buildings in 22 B.C. Several other inscriptions, in particular those recording benefactions by *IIviri* to mark the successful completion of a year of public office, could be adduced to swell the

---

[77] Buildings could be so-named in his honour after A.D. 14 (*ILS* 5326, 5919).

[78] Duncan-Jones 120 ff. Among prominent local benefactors of this time, note Sittius at Cales (App. *BC* iv. 47), L. Arruntius at Atina (X 5055), Scribonii Libones at Caudium (*ILS* 5326, *ILLRP* 567–68), T. Labienus at Cingulum (Caes. *BC* i. 15. 2).

total.[79] The town itself might finance and undertake the construction work, if no benefactor came forward: at Capua the amphitheatre was erected by *colonia Iulia Augusta Felix* in or soon after Augustus' reign, and at Sutrium it is likely that the colony paid for the provision of an aqueduct at Vicus Matrini.

Private building in the colonies under Augustus

town	structure	date	donated by	ref.
Beneventum	*Caesareum*	27–15 B.C.	P. Veidius Pollio	IX 1556 = *ILS* 109
Castrum Novum	*curiam tabularium scaenarium subsel-iarium porticus cenacula*	—	L. Ateius Capito (*IIvir*)	XI 3583 = *ILS* 5515
Dertona	*[bib]liotheca porticus forum*	22 B.C.	—	V 7376
Luceria	*amphitheatrum*	after 27 B.C.	M. Vecilius Campus	Sylloge 81
Lucus Feroniae	*...forumque refecit*	—	L. Octavius A.f. (*IIvir*)	below, p. 169
Lucus Feroniae	*statuas fornicesque*	—	C. Didius T.f. M. Vettius M.f. (*IIviri*)	below, p. 169
Venafrum	*aqua Iulia*	—	M. Volcius Sabinus	*ILS* 5759

Public building in Augustan colonies

town	structure	date	donated by	ref.
Capua	amphitheatre	—	[colonia Iu]lia Felix Aug[usta]	X 3832 = *ILS* 6309
Sutrium	aqueduct	—	[colonia? Au]gusta Iul[ia]	XI 3322

If more evidence had been available, we might have learnt of gifts to colonies by local senatorial or equestrian families, e.g. the Volusii Saturnini at Lucus Feroniae (below, p. 169), and by colony commissioners, such as L. Memmius at Luca and L. Munatius Plancus at Beneventum. Augustus encouraged *triumphatores* to carry out improvements to the road network in Italy, apparently without much success, but substantial public buildings in Rome were erected by these men.[80] It might be that they were encouraged to assist the towns of Italy also. Agrippa, foremost among the benefactors through whom Augustus embellished the city, is attested as *patronus* of a number of towns throughout the peninsula, including Rufrae within the territory of Venafrum, but there is little evidence of benefaction.[81]

While the surviving epigraphic evidence for Augustan benefactions does favour the colonies, the *municipia* were of course not excluded, and a policy of benefiting the colonies alone would have been contrary to the general mood of recon-

[79] At the Caesarian colony of Curubis, the *IIvir* L. Pomponius Malcio *murum oppidi totum ex saxo quadrato aedific(andum) coer(avit)* in 45 B.C. (*ILLRP* 580).

[80] F. W. Shipley, 'Chronology of the Building Operations in Rome from the Death of Caesar to the Death of Augustus', *MAAR* ix (1931), 7–60.

[81] F. W. Shipley, *Agrippa's Building Activities in Rome* (St. Louis, 1933); X 4831 (Rufrae). His grandson was patron at Puteoli (*ILS* 933 and below, p. 148).

ciliation.[82] Only a few benefactions to colonies can be dated, and those which do admit of exact dating are scattered across the reign without indication of any concentration in the years immediately after the colony's foundation. The provision and improvement of public buildings was for any town a continuing, never-ending, process.

Our picture of the development of the colonies under Augustus can be substantially augmented by archaeological evidence of buildings which constructional technique or building materials may allow us to place within his reign. This form of evidence is generally unsatisfactory: most buildings cannot be dated with sufficient precision by these means. Excessive reliance should not be placed on excavation reports or observations of the last half century by scholars ever anxious to place a building within the 'epoca augustea'. The circumstances of erection or the source of finance of a building are not supplied by an examination of its standing remains.

The Augustan age was in general one of reconstruction and renewal, with an upsurge of projects involving the replacement on a grander or grandiose scale of public buildings within the towns of Italy. Construction work cannot be equated with colonisation;[83] the archaeological evidence, though incomplete and imprecise, testifies to massive building programmes in colonies and non-colonies alike during Augustus' long and peaceful reign.[84] In the provinces the construction of a city with all its amenities was the normal consequence of the settlement of veterans in its *territorium*; in Italy only a handful of the colonies established from 47 B.C. onwards were planted on what may be termed virgin sites, where full-scale building was a matter of some urgency. Aosta (*Augusta Praetoria*) serves as an example of a town whose walls, gates, forum, theatre and amphitheatre were put up in the Augustan era. Similarly at Lucus Feroniae excavations over the last 30 years have suggested that the entire township was created from scratch in the later 1st century around a nucleus provided by a temple to the rural goddess Feronia. Building work on an equally large scale must have been required at Turin (*Augusta Taurinorum*), Tergeste, Pola, Parentium and Concordia. To what extent the building programme was in such cases financed directly by the emperor is not known, but his contribution must on occasion have been considerable. At Aosta and Turin it has been suggested that military engineers planned and constructed the entire town,[85] but the regular site-layouts reflect the conventions of Roman town-planning, rather than any contemporary military installations.

[82] Note the provision of an aqueduct at Caere (XI 3594), and unspecified work at Cingulum (IX 5680) and Tridentum (*ILS* 86). The young Tiberius was active at Saepinum (above, p. 9) and Altinum (above, p. 85), perhaps in relation to veteran settlement.

[83] Except where the building of a capitolium can be evidenced; see M. Cagiano de Azevedo, 'I 'capitolia' dell'impero romano', *Mem. Pont. Acc.* ser iii, v (1941), 1–76; U. Bianchi, 'Disegno storico del culto capitolino nell'Italia romana e nelle provincie dell'impero', *Mem. Acc. Linc.* ser. 8, ii (1950), 347–415; F. Castagnoli, *EAA* II (1959), 326–30. Not every temple with three *cellae* need be a capitolium, and epigraphic confirmation is desirable. For capitolia in Augustan colonies, Suet. *Tib.* 40; Tac. *Ann.* iv. 57 (Capua), Suet. *Gramm.* 9 (Beneventum), IX 5438 (Falerio), below, p. 119 (Aquinum), p. 141 (Minturnae).

[84] A. Boethius and J. B. Ward-Perkins, *Etruscan and Roman Architecture* (Harmondsworth, 1970), 305–6 (Velleia); Blake 236 (Ocriculum).

[85] I. A. Richmond, *Roman Art and Archaeology*, ed. P. Salway (London, 1969), 249–59; A. Boethius and J. P. Ward-Perkins, op. cit. (n. 84), 302.

At a number of old-established towns there is archaeological evidence for extensive rebuilding, for extension of the town-limits and for the provision of substantial public amenities. At Aquinum a new wall circuit was laid out on the approximate line of the old, new gateways were constructed, and an arch set up on the line of the Via Latina where it entered the city from the south. Within the walls there is evidence for the construction of a capitolium, a theatre and an amphitheatre. At Venafrum a completely new street grid, embracing the Samnite nucleus but extending into the plain below, seems likely to have been laid out at this time. The ex-tribune Aclutius Gallus held an appointment apparently to supervise the construction of walls to embrace the expanded urban zone. At Minturnae excavation in the 1930s produced evidence of reconstruction following an extensive fire; it is not unlikely that the foundation of a veteran colony speeded the reconstruction process. At Tuder in the Umbrian uplands the town site may have been enlarged by about one third. Recent excavations at Rusellae suggest substantial changes in the layout of public buildings at about this time.

Of all the public buildings of a Roman town the amphitheatre was at once the most impressive and has often been the most enduring through the centuries.[86] A few towns, especially in Campania, already had amphitheatres by the mid first century B.C.,[87] but many more were built under Augustus and his successors, so that, by the middle of the second century A.D., hardly a town in the Italian peninsula lacked an amphitheatre. Where structural evidence of its construction is lacking, epigraphy often fills the gap. Among colonies which probably acquired stone-built amphitheatres during Augustus' long reign, we may cite Nuceria, Luceria, Aosta, Aquinum, Asculum, Lucus Feroniae, Paestum, Puteoli (if it was not earlier) and Rusellae; in all probability Ancona, Ariminum, Capua, Venusia and Venafrum can be added to the list (see p. 133 below); many were of great size.[88] On the other hand, a number of colonies, especially in Etruria and Umbria, did not acquire an amphitheatre (at least in stone) until the middle or even the end of the first century A.D. The amphitheatre was the most expensive of amenities which a benefactor might offer to a town. Not every colony might have citizens of sufficient generosity; the costs were often shared out among a consortium. Tacitus bemoans the destruction by fire in A.D. 69 of the fine amphitheatre at Placentia (*pulcherrimum amphitheatri opus*), which he states to be the largest then existing in Italy, and an object of intense envy by neighbouring colonies.[89] Its destruction by fire led Salvatore Aurigemma to suppose that the structure was wholly or partly timber-built,[90] but fittings and furnishings could be sufficient to cause a major blaze. We

[86] L. Friedländer, *Darstellungen aus der Sittengeschichte Roms* (Leipzig, 1922), II 50–112, III 205–40; *Encl. Ital.* III (Milano, 1929), 280–85. G. Forni, *EAA* I (1958), 374–90 provides an extensive bibliography.

[87] Pompeii (*ILLRP* 645); Cumae, see *EAA* II (1959), 972. For Capua, Puteoli and other possibilities, W. Johannowsky, 'La situazione in Campania', in P. Zanker (ed.), *Hellenismus in Mittelitalien* (Göttingen, 1976), 267–89.

[88] Notice Parma (major axis 135 m), Luceria (131 m), Puteoli (130 m), Nuceria (125 m), Ancona (111 m), Aquinum (111 m). If the Capuan amphitheatre proves to be Augustan, it would surpass all these, with a major axis of 167 m.

[89] *Hist.* ii. 21.

[90] S. Aurigemma, 'Gli anfiteatri romani di *Placentia*, di *Bononia* e di *Forum Corneli*', *Historia* vi (1932), 558–87.

are not told the date of its construction; the Augustan era seems the most probable. If Tacitus' testimony is to be trusted here, the Placentian amphitheatre must have been larger than the stone amphitheatre at Capua, which with a major axis of 167 m. was, so far as we know, the biggest then (A.D. 69) standing anywhere in the Roman Empire. Tacitus refers to the jealousy of *vicinae coloniae,* a remark which (if taken literally) suggests that the possession of large public amenities among colonies in particular was a matter of intense competition. The amphitheatre was the supreme status symbol of a town, and testimony to its prosperity, though not by itself the hallmark of a colony, at least in Italy. Nevertheless, of the towns which we know to have acquired amphitheatres at about this time, the great majority were colonies, testimony perhaps to the veterans' taste in entertainments, or more probably to an influx of capital. Among the *vicinae coloniae* envious of Placentia's amphitheatre, Cremona, Mutina and Parma might be identified.[91]

Many towns in southern Italy already possessed stone theatres of the Greek or Hellenistic types well before the Social War. The Augustan age witnessed the construction of many new theatres, for example at Aosta, Aquinum, Asculum, Capua (here replacing an earlier structure), Florentia, Minturnae and Turin, and probably also at Concordia, Pisae, Tuder and Venafrum (see list at p. 133).[92]

The extension or refurbishment of the wall-circuit of a town is frequently datable to the Augustan age, at both *coloniae* and *municipia,* and not only on the northern frontiers of Italy. A desire for security and (more important) tradition and civic pride provided a powerful stimulus. The completion of such work might be followed by the incorporation of monumental gateways or arches (often privately financed) set between the towers of a gateway to greet travellers entering the town.[93]

The provision of aqueducts and the improvement of sanitation within the Italian cities was a matter dear to Augustus' heart. His work on the water supply of Rome itself is well known,[94] but he was prominent in this sphere elsewhere. The provision of aqueducts for Capua in 36 and for Venafrum some two decades later has already been mentioned. Others seem likely from archaeological evidence to have been built in his reign at Lucus Feroniae, Asculum, Minturnae, Aquinum and Nuceria (list, p. 133). His most extensive venture was the so-called Serino aqueduct snaking across the plain of southern Campania from Acquaro to Neapolis and Puteoli, with branches to Nola, Cumae, Pompeii, Atella, Acerrae, Baiae and Misenum. Its construction has been dated to the decade before Actium, but the

---

[91] After the first battle of Cremona in A.D. 69, legion XIII *Gemina* was instructed to build amphitheatres at Bononia and Cremona for use in Vitellius' victory celebrations (Tac. *Hist.* ii. 67). The work was completed in a little over one month. It is hard to suppose that neither town had an amphitheatre before A.D. 69, and perhaps more likely that temporary, additional structures were put up. Cf. Tac. *Ann.* iv. 62, xiii. 31, Suet. *Nero* 12. 1; *AE* 1926, 78: [*in*]*tra duos men*[*ses a*]*mphitheatrum ligne*[*u*]*m fecit* (Antiochia Pisidiae).

[92] E. N. Modona, *Gli edifici teatrali greci e romani* (Firenze, 1961); G. Forni, *EAA Sup.* (1973), 772–89; G. Bejor, 'L'edificio teatrale nell'urbanizzazione augustea', *Athenaeum* lvii (1979), 124–38.

[93] Blake 112–14, 203–9; I. A. Richmond, 'Augustan Gates at Torino and Spello', *PBSR* xii (1932), 52–62; idem, 'Commemorative Arches and City Gates in the Augustan Age', *JRS* xxiii (1933), 149–74.

[94] E. B. Van Deman, *The Building of the Roman Aqueducts* (Washington, 1934); Blake 219–20.

inferred title *Aqua Augusta* should indicate that it was completed, or extended, after 27 B.C.[95]

There can be no doubt that the cities of Italy were in need of support after the depredations of the Civil Wars, when the advertisement of wealth was not without its dangers. But colonies might easily lag behind when peace and with it confidence returned—the redistribution of land was at the very least a set-back to the established local aristocracy to whom the town would normally look for benefactions (below, p. 127). The diminution of resources, or their complete dispersal, must have left a gap which Augustus could help to fill.

We know little of the circumstances surrounding the bestowal of imperial favour on any town. Under the Empire (as before) delegations would come to Rome seeking assistance, particularly after earthquake or flood damage,[96] but whether specific projects were undertaken merely in response to pleas from individual colonies is unclear. Augustus may have attempted to distribute favours as evenly as possible throughout the colonies of the age (and not merely the 28 which he was to claim as particularly his own foundations); the scrappy evidence gives little hint of a definite policy being pursued. After the decision had been taken by Augustus to finance a specific project, a distinguished local citizen might be chosen to supervise the work, perhaps with the title *curator operum*. The holder of such a post, in a provincial context, has recently come to light.[97] The ex-tribune Aclutius Gallus at Venafrum was surely such a man. The surge in building projects was in any case beneficial to Italy, providing work for artisans, contractors, and architects alike. One architect, Vitruvius, supervised the erection of a basilica at the colony of Fanum Fortunae. Details of its ground plan and dimensions are given in the Fifth Book of the *de Architectura*.[98] The construction of the basilica seems likely to date to the last two decades of the first century B.C. We cannot tell whether the project was financed by Augustus, or resulted from local initiatives (below, p. 184).

The colonies not only received financial aid from Augustus. The foundation was frequently accompanied by the enlargement of the *territorium* at the expense of neighbouring towns (above, p. 89). These accretions may not always have been permanent. There might be other, smaller grants of land or resources at various times, by direct gift of the Emperor.[99] Capua gained territory within the territory of Cnossus to offset loss of revenue (and land?) in 36, and perhaps at the same time the colony acquired the chalk-bearing *colles Leucogaei*, the loss of which to Neapolis was offset by a cash grant.[100] The Younger Pliny records that Augustus made over

---

[95] X 1805, with *CIL* X, p. 1009; I. Sgobbo, *NS* 1938, 75–97; *AE* 1939, 151 (*fons Augusteus*); J. H. D'Arms, *Romans on the Bay of Naples* (Cambridge, Massachusetts, 1970), 79–80.

[96] Note Tac. *Ann.* i. 79 (Florentia under Tiberius), xii. 58 (Bononia under Claudius); *AE* 1969/1970, 592 (Sinope under Antoninus Pius; a prominent citizen *misso legato a colonia in urbem sine viatico* on four occasions); F. G. B. Millar, *The Emperor in the Roman World* (London, 1977), 420 ff.

[97] C. Fabricius Tuscus, *praef(ectus) cohort(is) Apulae et operum quae in colonia iussu Augusti facta sunt* (at Alexandria Troas); P. A. Brunt, 'C. Fabricius Tuscus and an Augustan dilectus', *ZPE* xiii (1974), 161–85; *EJ*[2] 368.

[98] v. 1. 6.

[99] Front. 49. 10.

[100] Pliny *NH* xviii. 114.

to the colony at Hispellum ownership of the *Fontes Clitumni* at the southern extremity of the Pianura Umbra, with its sacred grove and temple precinct;[101] Augustus also presented some land to Venafrum, seemingly to support a local cult.[102] A *Liber Beneficiorum* was kept in the Tabularium of each colony, in which such gifts and other benefactions might be permanently recorded.[103]

5. *Veterans as farmers*

To Octavian's offer after Naulochus to the soldiery of increased *dona militaria*, and the promise of enhanced status in their native towns, the reaction of the mass of time-served men was forcibly and succinctly put by their ill-fated spokesman, the tribune Ofillius. Such things were mere 'playthings for boys' (παισὶν ἀθύρματα); a soldier's true rewards were land and money (στρατοῦ δὲ γέρα χωρία καὶ χρήματα).[104] Of the two, land was by far the more important, and the particular object of their desires. When the veterans early in 41 demanded the cities 'which had been chosen for them before the war', it was not the town-sites which they especially wished to receive, but the *territoria,* for it was on the land of the designated colonies that their future homes would be.[105] Appian offers three criteria for the selection by the Triumvirs of towns to become colonies after their victory; they were καὶ περιουσίᾳ (prosperity) καὶ ἐδάφεσι (soil-type) καὶ οἴκοις (houses) εἰς κάλλος διαφέρουσαι.[106] Land remained their chief prospect, until in 13 B.C., on the initiative of Augustus, gratuities in cash were substituted 'in place of the land they were always requesting'.[107]

In the anxious days after Caesar's death, the possibility that the Senate might annul Caesar's grants of land to his soldiers brought a quick and determined reaction from the veterans then concentrated in Rome. Their spokesmen, articulate and insistent, petitioned the Senate, and secured the passing of decrees guaranteeing the rights of those who had already received land, and of those who were waiting to go out to their colonies (the majority of those still in Rome fell into this latter category). The veterans rightly distrusted the motives and attitudes of the Senate which had in the past been persistently hostile to their cause. The prospect of having to give up the land for which they had fought long and hard, at the moment when it seemed finally won, or of never receiving it at all, was sufficient to rouse the veterans to determined action. Throughout the following years the retention of their allotments was an important goal for the spokesmen of Caesar's veterans. For the majority the allotments represented a substantial leap in social status, which they were determined not to endanger. The mere acquisition of land was not enough. The veterans were concerned for its quality, and to demand the best available, on

---

[101] *Ep.* viii. 8.

[102] *LC* 239. 9–10.

[103] Hyg. Grom. 203. 1–2.

[104] App. *BC* v. 128. Cf. App. *BC* v. 13, Dio xlvii. 14. 4, Plut. *Brut.* 46, Oros. vi. 18. 33, Suet. *Aug.* 13. 3, Lucan *Phars.* i. 344–45, Hyg. Grom. 176. 8–9.

[105] App. *BC* v. 12.

[106] App. *BC* iv. 3.

[107] Dio liv. 25. 5.

which they would have a good chance of success and prosperity in the coming years.[108]

The arriving colonists after Philippi took over steadings, farm equipment and even slaves, left behind by the former owners. Not all the farmsteads can have been suitably located, and some reshuffling of buildings, equipment and slaves must have been necessary to suit the new land division (above, p. 87). Caesar in 47 B.C. had promised to provide 'the necessaries' to his colonists, and it would be reasonable to suppose that, in all phases of veteran settlement in the Late Republic, steps were taken to ensure that the suitable equipment was on site for the colonists, or financial aid available from state funds to purchase it. This was important: the veterans thus avoided having to lay out their financial reserves in the opening months of settlement.[109] Where necessary, however, the veterans would set to work to erect or repair their steadings.[110]

Many scholars have held a pessimistic view of the veteran as an agriculturalist, or doubted his serious intention to devote himself to agriculture. In Gabba's earlier view (which has been widely followed) the allotments represented capital, which was quickly realised. The veterans sold up without delay, and departed to live in the towns, in Rome, or in the provinces.[111] However, the eagerness with which the veterans sought land in the Late Republic, and their anxiety not to lose it, implies in my view a serious intention to farm and to develop their allotments. Like the other beneficiaries of land under the resettlement schemes of the Late Republic, their intention was to grasp firmly the opportunity of social improvement. As Brunt has convincingly demonstrated, there is little reason for supposing that veterans in the Late Republic were either inexperienced in, or averse to, the farming life. Some might previously have been owners or tenants of small properties. The duration of service was short in comparison with the long years required of the recruit to the professional army of the Empire (below, p. 210). The veteran might return to the land, young and vigorous, with every intention of making a serious attempt to farm.[112]

Some have thought that the lot of veterans in these years was a life of hard drudgery in the fields (of which on Gabba's earlier views he quickly tired), barely above subsistence level.[113] Others have argued that the veteran was an absentee

---

[108] App. BC v. 13, 22, Dio liii. 25. 5, Prop. El. iv. 1. 129–130, Sic. Flacc. 156. 1–3. According to Sall. Or. Lep. 23, some Sullan veterans had been relegati in paludes et silvas.

[109] App. BC ii. 94. Cf. Plut. Ti. Gracch. 14. 1. Much later Constantine provided seed corn, oxen, and cash ad emenda ruri necessaria (Cod. Th. vii. 20. 3) for veterans who intended to farm. The provision of animals, cereals and household utensils for Italian settlers in Libya in the 1930s may be compared.

[110] Veterans in search of building materials around Capua in 45–44 B.C. disturbed ancient graves (Suet. Caes. 81); even this could be held against them. For colonists as tomb robbers at Corinth, see Strabo viii. 6. 23.

[111] Gabba, Ricerche 181; R. E. Smith, Service in the post-Marian Roman Army (Manchester, 1958), 52.

[112] Brunt, AL 73–5; Gabba, 'The Perusine War and Triumviral Italy', HSCP lxxv (1971), 139–60, esp. 148 for a modification of his earlier views. Caesar prevailed on both Varro and the agronomist Tremellius Scrofa to serve on his land commission in 59–58 B.C.; P. A. Brunt, 'Cn. Tremellius Scrofa the Agronomist', CR lxxxvi (1972), 304–8.

[113] A laboriosa requies (Hyg. Grom. 176. 10). Cf. Frank, ESAR I, 321–22; Brunt, IM 297.

landlord who lived in town (i.e. on the town site of the *colonia*) and managed the allotment through a *vilicus,* or handed it over to a tenant for rent.[114] Our view of the veteran as agriculturalist and his likely social status depends in the first instance on an estimate of the size of the allotments themselves. It has been argued above that Caesarian veterans could have received 25 *iugera* in 47–44, and that those released after Philippi (and in later phases) are likely to have been given up to 50 *iugera* (above, p. 91). Junior officers, *evocati,* centurions and tribunes would be rewarded more generously, up perhaps to 100 *iugera,* or more. Men who had received allotments of this size (tribunes and centurions would be the main beneficiaries here) could well afford to live in town, if they so wished, and to visit their farms as often as fancy or other commitments allowed. This was normal practice for owners of substantial properties.[115] Those who were given smaller allowances of 50 *iugera* or less could have maintained a small establishment in town, or have travelled daily to their steadings if distance or terrain allowed, but a large number are perhaps more likely to have been resident fairly permanently on their farms.[116] The veteran could work 50 *iugera* with his family and a few slaves. Figures offered by Columella suggest that a farm of 50 *iugera,* principally arable, with half lying fallow each year, would need a workforce of two or three slaves, depending on the balance of crops. Holdings of 25 *iugera* cannot have allowed much surplus.[117] The οἶκοι and οἰκήματα which the veteran hoped to obtain after service can be seen as *villae rusticae* which they intended to inhabit.[118] The departure of many landowners might leave vacant some town-houses, and perhaps these too passed to the veterans. Yet families deprived of their land in the *territorium* might retire into the town, to attempt a diversification of interests, or to wait for a hoped-for upswing in their fortunes. Where the old families had left the district, the town-houses might certainly pass to or be sold to veterans.

We lack knowledge of the type of agriculture that the veterans hoped to practise. It is a reasonable conjecture that most practised mixed farming, with a good proportion of the land devoted to cereal crops, but some part must always have been made over to olives and vines. The cultivation of vines and olives could become the chief source of income, especially in areas where their cultivation was traditional and particularly profitable.[119] The incoming colonists would be likely to maintain

[114] W. E. Heitland, *Agricola* (Cambridge, 1921), 176; Rostovtzeff, *SEHRE* 31, 59.

[115] K. D. White, 'Latifundia', *BICS* xiv (1967), 62–79; H. Dohr, *Die italischen Gutshöfe nach den Schriften Catos und Varros* (Koln, 1965), 11 ff., 37. Notice Columella i. 7. 3 on tenants who were city-based.

[116] For similar conclusions, based on a different body of evidence, over a wider time-scale, P. D. A. Garnsey, 'Where did Italian Peasants live?', *Proc. Cambr. Phil. Soc.* n.s. xxv (1979), 1–25.

[117] Columella ii. 12. 7; K. D. White, *Roman Farming* (London, 1971), 336; Duncan-Jones 327–33. Several veteran-epitaphs mention 2, 3 or 4 slaves or freedmen, some at least belonging to the veteran's personal household (Sylloge 26, 30, 37, 41, 51). In the Liri valley around Ceprano (the ancient *ager Fregellanus*), local opinion avers that three hectares (c. 12 *iugera*) would be sufficient to support a family (1981), with part of the ground devoted to crops, part to vines and part to vegetables; those owning less than three hectares had to supplement their earnings as day-labourers, or by other part-time work.

[118] App. *BC* iv. 3, v. 13.

[119] For example, at Venafrum, a famous olive-growing centre. Varro mentions two serving soldiers from the *ager Faliscus* who had business interests in bee-keeping (*RR* iii. 16. 10).

the existing balance of crops which they found on arrival, at least in the short-term. Not all need have been interested in cereal crops. Those with experience in vine or olive growing, or in orchards or the pasturing of animals, would be likely to revert to such activity, if the land was suitable. Recent archaeological surveys, some within the territories of known colonies, suggest that small- to medium-sized farms were still very common in the Italy of the Early Empire. [120] At Sutrium and Lucus Feroniae, it has been possible to detect a break in occupation of many farmsteads in the Late Republic, and subsequent rebuilding on fresh sites, a process which can plausibly be linked to the settlement programmes from Caesar onwards. [121] It is less easy to assess the occupational histories of individual farmsteads in the *ager Lucerinus* as revealed from the air by J. P. Bradford, and more recently studied by G. D. B. Jones, in the absence of dating evidence which may show how many were in use in the Late Republic and Early Empire. [122]

In Vergil's Ninth *Eclogue* the slave Moeris is portrayed driving a flock of kids to town (Cremona rather than Mantua) for inspection by the new master, a newly-arrived colonist. It is the slave not the owner who makes the journey. The rustic and the animals in his care are indispensable ingredients of the pastoral scene, but the story may help confirm Dio's statement that after Philippi slaves and animals passed from the old owner to the new. [123] It suggests that the veteran was primarily a town-dweller. Horace recalls the philosophical reaction of an old friend Ofellus to the expropriation of his ancestral holding at Venusia. [124] The farm was made over to the veteran Umbrenus, but Ofellus stays on as tenant, making a virtue of enforced frugality. The farm was evidently not large, having been worked by Ofellus and his family. Umbrenus meanwhile was content to live in town, and sensibly to leave the day-to-day management to Ofellus. The change in ownership had been accomplished without bitterness; it cannot always have been so.

The principal aim of time-served veterans in the Late Republic was a substantial improvement in social status, the comfortable life of owners, where the work could (if the veteran so desired) be mostly (or entirely) left to others. Had it been otherwise, their enthusiasm for farming would not be so pronounced. The units must have been known to be viable in the conditions of the time. For veterans with any ambitions in the local government of the colony, the possession of a town-house

---

[120] See esp. M. W. Frederiksen, 'The Contribution of Archaeology to the Agrarian Problem in the Gracchan Period', *D. Arch.* iv–v (1970–71), 330–67; idem, 'Changes in the Pattern of Settlement', in P. Zanker (ed.), *Hellenismus in Mittelitalien* (Göttingen, 1976), 341–55; J. Lloyd and G. Barker, 'Rural Settlement in Roman Molise: Problems of Archaeological Survey', in G. Barker and R. Hodges (eds.), *Archaeology and Italian Society* (Oxford, 1981), 289–304; G. Barker, J. Lloyd and D. Webley, 'A classical Landscape in Molise', *PBSR* xlvi (1978), 35–51; S. L. Dyson, 'Settlement Patterns in the *ager Cosanus*', *J. Field Archaeology* v (1978), 251–68; P. D. A. Garnsey, loc. cit. (n. 116); D. W. Rathbone, 'The Development of Agriculture in the "Ager Cosanus" during the Roman Republic: Problems of Evidence and Interpretation', *JRS* lxxi, 1981, 10–23.

[121] T. W. Potter, *The Changing Landscape of South Etruria* (London, 1979), 132; the point is brought out by M. H. Crawford, in a review, *Athenaeum* lxviii (1980), 497–98.

[122] Below, p. 164. For farmsteads plotted in the *ager Bononiensis*, E. Silvestri, *NS* 1971, 17.

[123] xlviii. 9.

[124] *Sat.* ii. 2.

or a suburban residence was a necessary qualification.[125] But not all veterans can have wished it so, or have enjoyed success at their farms. As Brunt has emphasised, conditions were inimical to farming in the Late Republic.[126] A number of men, perhaps a large number, must have found the life difficult, unprofitable, or unsuited to their temperaments; some would persevere, but others might depart to seek alternative employment. Yet we hear little of other full-time occupations.[127]

The first years of the settlement were undoubtedly the most difficult; it was important for the colonist not to give up too soon. The rustics might mock his initial difficulties and mistakes. The veteran needed a few years to work himself into the job. The donative of 29 B.C. paid out on the occasion of Octavian's triple triumph must have come at a good moment psychologically.

The epigraphic evidence, in particular an examination of the find-spots of graveslabs, may provide a corrective to the concept of the absentee landlord. Of the 27 memorials from Ateste (below, p. 200) 18 were found or first reported at various points throughout the *territorium;* five were first seen at the town-site, and of these only one seems certainly to have derived from a cemetery there. The remainder have no reliable provenance (below, p. 201). At Beneventum up to 10 memorials come from the *ager Beneventanus* and its adjuncts, and only one certainly from the vicinity of the town, although a further 16 were first reported there (below, p. 160). It must be likely that several of the latter did derive from cemeteries outside the walls of Beneventum. However, a very substantial majority of all the veteran-inscriptions of this period, for which a precise findspot is known, were first reported well away from the town-site of the colony; presumably the men were buried on their own land.[128] Siculus Flaccus stresses that the tombs of veterans (*monumenta eorum quibus adsignati sunt agri*), scattered in the countryside, could serve as evidence of ownership in cases of dispute.[129] Similarly, in a short passage *De Sepulchris*, an unknown author notes that veterans or their wives were sometimes buried *in praediis suis* close to the farmhouse. This too was helpful towards establishing ownership.[130] Siculus also comments on the tendency to mistake *sepulchra,* lying on the edges of allotments and so on the line of *limites,* as terminal stones.[131] The same point is taken up in a late treatise: *sepulchra veteranorum* were familiar landmarks of the

---

[125] *Lex Urs.* xci; at Tarentum decurions had to possess a house in the town, or in the *territorium,* with a roof supporting at least 1,500 tiles (*Lex Mun. Tar.* 26).

[126] *AL* 82–83. Note the ex-tribune C. Castricius of perhaps mid Augustan date, an active and committed farmer at Forum Livi, who adopted the *agnomen* Agricola, and inscribed on his tomb monument useful precepts for his slave and freedmen workers (XI 600). He is not necessarily a colonist, and we cannot estimate the size of his holdings.

[127] App. *BC* iii. 2, 42; Hyg. 131. 14 ff., Sic. Flacc. 161. 11; Front. 45. 11. For a veteran at Antiochia Pisidiae, who was *scriba* to a *quaestor* there, or perhaps *scriba* then *quaestor* himself, *JRS* vi (1916), 90 n. 1; Levick 74 n. 3. Vespasian's grandfather, a centurion called out by Pompey, who returned home presumably without any formal *praemia,* successfully took up debt collecting (Suet. *Vesp.* 1. 2). For occupations other than farming (in a later age), R. MacMullen, *Soldier and Civilian in the Later Roman Empire* (Cambridge, Massachusetts, 1963), 110.

[128] Cf. Sylloge 73 for a veteran at Hadria *sepultus in suo; ILS* 2259 for a veteran in Dalmatia *occisus in agello.*

[129] 161. 25.

[130] 271. 15–17L.

[131] 139. 23–26.

countryside.[132] There is no proof here of permanent residence on the steadings, but the evidence should indicate that many veterans did not forsake their allotments and move elsewhere.

6. *The longer-term effects of settlement*

Some of the short-term effects have already been discussed. A substantial disruption in agricultural production can be assumed. The designation of 18 cities as the prizes of war in the autumn of 43 would discourage agricultural investment, and planting, during the winter of 43–42, and more so after Philippi in the winter of 42–41. A very real famine in Italy in 41 was caused in part by the depredations of Sextus Pompeius, and partly by the diminution of the normal level of supplies throughout the peninsula.[133] The convoying to Rome of large numbers of veterans by Antony in the spring of 44, and the call to arms by Octavian and Ventidius in the later months of that year, and by Octavian and L. Antonius in the summer of 41, must have hindered the settling-in process. Many of those who followed Antony in the spring of 44 were back at their farms within three months. Members of legion VIII at Casilinum can hardly have had time to locate their allotments and claim ownership before travelling northwards with Antony. Others who followed Octavian and Ventidius were not to see their steadings again until after Philippi. If I am correct to argue that many were then assigned new allotments, the opportunity was thus taken to make a fresh start (above, p. 62). The Perusine War must have interrupted the efforts of many colonists, and further soured relationships with the *veteres possessores*, though they may well have had time to get in any standing crops before being called away. Attempts by Agrippa and Octavian to call out veterans in southern Italy in July 40 were a further nuisance.[134] Well might the spokesmen for the veterans plead for reconciliation and peace; they had urgent work to do on their new farms.

It has already been shown that the arrival of the colonists made for a substantial change in the population of the *territorium* of a town, perhaps less so in the town itself. It is very likely that many of the dispossessed left their land and the town forever, in search of a new home and occupation, in Rome, elsewhere in Italy, or in the provinces. After Actium some were offered land in Macedonia, and perhaps elsewhere. Others may have congregated in the towns in the hope of restitution, or with a view to establishing a new financial base in the area they knew best.[135] The influx of veterans brought to any colony a body of men united by shared military service, but drawn from all over the peninsula and Cisalpina. The totals settled in Italy between 47 and 14 B.C. can only be roughly estimated, at 130,000–150,000.[136]

---

[132] 347. 5L. Other passages in the *Gromatici* imply a country-based veteran (e.g. Front. 51. 25).

[133] E. Gabba, 'The Perusine War and Triumviral Italy', *HSCP* lxxv (1971), 139–60.

[134] A deputation of veterans, perhaps from colonies inclining to Antony, met him at Alexandria in the winter of 41/40, and were detained there for several months (App. *BC* v. 52).

[135] Some of those dispossessed after Philippi, who joined the forces of Sextus Pompeius and subsequently transferred to Octavian in 36, would qualify for land settlement after Actium.

[136] Above, p. 86. For much higher estimates based on Appian and the *Res Gestae*, J. Kromayer, 'Die wirtschaftliche Entwicklung Italiens im II und I Jahrhundert vor Chr.', *NJ Klass. Alt.* xvii (1914), 145–69, at 160–2; E. G. Hardy, 'Augustus and his Legionaries', *CQ* xiv (1920), 187–94.

The great majority of men placed in any colony can have had no previous links with, or knowledge of, the locality. There is little secure evidence that veterans had any choice in their place of settlement, either individually or collectively, or that they could opt (as many might have wished) for settlement close to their home towns, or indeed in the provinces where they may have developed interests or acquired property during service. It would be natural to think that Caesar and Octavian would not be averse to offering cash, in place of land grants, if the disruptive effects on Italian land-holding could thereby be lessened.[137]

Much has been written about the purpose of colonisation in the later first century B.C., and about the 'success' or 'failure' of particular settlements. The purpose of colonisation in Italy from 47 B.C. onwards was simple: the removal from the national scene, with all possible speed, of the veterans of the legions, whatever the disruption and distress that resulted. It is difficult to detect and to document any positive social or economic motives for settlement, or in the selection of sites, to match those of the Gracchi, or of Rullus or Caesar in his earlier work of his consulship.[138] The middle years of Augustus' reign witnessed a change in motivation, but to the strategic and defensive: the colonies once again begin to act as *propugnacula imperii*: in Italy one example of this phase is known, Augusta Praetoria, founded in 25 B.C.[139]

The *Gromatici* sometimes credit Augustus with lofty and carefully nurtured aims: the regeneration of Italy and the boosting of her population. Hyginus Gromaticus praises Augustus for repeopling many old towns exhausted by the Civil Wars.[140] In the *Res Gestae* Augustus can claim that his 28 colonies were prosperous and populous, and Suetonius, paraphrasing Augustus' words, states that he 'peopled' Italy by his colonisation.[141] But there is little sign that the regeneration of Italy or the renewal of her population, or the improvement of her economy or her agriculture, were significant motives for the Triumvirs, or Octavian after Actium, though the latter might later be credited with them. Where some positive economic effects did result, these were largely incidental. Only with Caesar might we expect that some thought would be given to the regeneration of deserted tracts of the peninsula.[142] In 43, it was the prosperity of cities and the fertility of their lands, not desolation and depopulation, that prompted selection. Given the scantiness of our knowledge of Octavian's plans after Actium, and of his activities in 14 B.C., some

---

[137] Some recruits who enlisted around Capua in 44 were evidently sent back there in 36 (below, p. 146), and the title *Sorana* attached to a legion IIII seems indicative of settlement at the town from which it had originally been raised (below, p. 136); also below, p. 197 on Ateste. For a soldier of legion XXX who remained in Spain after service, or returned there later, *ILS* 2233; for Caesar's release of veterans in Africa in 46 B.C., above, p. 50.

[138] One of the hoped-for results of the abortive *lex Flavia* (60 B.C.) was to have been *Italiae solitudinem frequentari* (Cic. *Att*. i. 19. 4).

[139] The defensive needs of Italy were perhaps not forgotten in the foundation of colonies after Philippi or Actium, e.g. at Turin, Tergeste, and Concordia.

[140] Hyg. 113. 22–25; Hyg. Grom. 177. 9–178. 9, 179. 7.

[141] *RG* 28. 1; Suet. *Aug*. 46.

[142] Some of the small towns of south Etruria must have been revived by his work; G. D. B. Jones, 'Civil War and Society in Southern Etruria', in M. R. D. Foot (ed.), *War and Society: Historical Essays in Honour and Memory of J. R. Western* (London, 1973), 277–87.

attention to the long-term economic needs of Italy is perhaps not to be ruled out. Yet we do not find any noticeable attempt to regenerate southern Italy: Lucania, Bruttium, Calabria, and the Apennine heartlands remained largely untouched.

The geographer Strabo, the preliminary compilation of whose work can be placed in the final decade of the first century B.C.[143] is generous in his praise of Caesarian and Augustan colonisation in the provinces; where a colony has been established, this is a starting point for growth and prosperity.[144] But within Italy, Strabo, though he appreciated the importance of colonisation in the expansion of Roman power in the peninsula, has little to say about the settlement programmes from 47 B.C. onwards. He does note the foundation of Aosta and the settlement at Rhegium, where the arrival of colonists boosted the population of the town to its permanent advantage: καὶ νῦν ἱκανῶς εὐανδρεῖ.[145] Perhaps Strabo saw little overall economic importance in the colonisation of Italy, in relation to his wider horizons and particular interests. In general his picture of Italy reflects its condition in the early first century B.C.[146] Several of the towns which became colonies after Philippi or Actium are not mentioned at all,[147] but it is clearly wrong to see in Strabo's account an accurate picture of Italy in the wake of the settlement programmes, and to interpret the presence of some towns in his narrative, and the absence of others, as indicative of their success or failure as colonies.

For the most part the colonies of the later first century were already long established townships. Only a few were created from scratch, or where only a village had stood before. Here we may name Aosta, Turin, Concordia, Tergeste, Pola, Parentium and Lucus Feroniae. All but the last-mentioned were on the very fringes of Italy. Elsewhere we can at most postulate a change in the scale of population. For some colonies, colonisation would bring an influx of capital, some special attention from Augustus, and quite possibly (if the dispossessed stayed on in town) a boost to their overall population. The settlement programmes resulted in a further stirring of the population of Italy, and in the areas affected would represent a final intermingling of races, to the further extinction of local dialects and cultural variations.[148]

Longer-term effects on the prosperity of a town are less easy to assess. It may be that the prosperity of many towns was not greatly altered either way. Towns that

---

[143] E. Pais, 'Straboniana', *Riv. Fil.* xv (1887), 97–246; idem, *Ancient Italy* (Chicago and London, 1908), 379–428.

[144] viii. 7. 5 (Patrae), viii. 6. 21 (Corinth), x. 4. 9 (Cnossus), xii. 3. 11 (Sinope), xiii. 1. 26 (Alexandria Troas), xvi. 2. 19 (Berytus).

[145] vi. 1. 6.

[146] G. Aujac and F. Lasserre, *Strabon, Géographie,* Tome I. i (Paris, 1969), xxxiv–xlii; F. Lasserre, *Strabon, Géographie,* Tome III (Paris, 1967), 4 ff.

[147] Ateste, Rusellae, Florentia, Saena, Suessa Aurunca, Falerio, Parentium, Brixellum, Pisaurum, and Turin. Several doubtless did not exist when his chief sources, Poseidonius and Artemidorus, wrote, but Pisaurum was an old *colonia maritima,* Rusellae was one of the original twelve cities of the Etruscan League, and Suessa was the ancient capital of the Aurunci. Perhaps all had fallen into decay. On the other hand Strabo knew of Lucus Feroniae (v. 2. 9) and Concordia (v. 1. 8).

[148] Rostovtzeff, *SEHRE* 33; Harris 313–18. The disappearance of Venetic name-forms at Ateste must be linked (in part at least) to the colony established there in 30 B.C.; cf. M. Lejeune, *Ateste à l'heure de la romanisation* (Firenze, 1978), with review by M. H. Crawford, *JRS* lxxi (1981), 160.

were important by virtue of their natural position and the fertility of their lands kept their prosperity; others which had been small and unimportant for the most part remained so.[149] Yet where there had been significant accretions of fertile land, some long-term advantage should have accrued to the town. None of the newly established townships was a complete failure; all persisted into the later Empire. For example, Turin and Pola became major cities; but Lucus Feroniae seems to have developed little, and a question-mark must remain over the survival of *colonia Falisca* (below, p. 171).

It might be asked whether the military spirit of the colonists survived into subsequent generations, and whether the colonies of Italy, as did their counterparts in the provinces, made a notable contribution in men to the armies of the Empire. It seems rather that Italian towns with large populations (e.g. Aquileia, Verona, Mediolanium, Cremona) supplied many recruits, whatever their formal status, to the legions, the Praetorian Guard and the Urban Cohorts, while some colonies contributed hardly at all. One interesting exception is Ateste which makes a significant showing in the ranks of all three branches of the army in the early first century A.D.[150] We could expect the survival of the martial spirit for one generation at least, and look for sons of veterans enlisting under arms. No specific examples are to hand, but where inscriptions of mid- or late-Augustan soldiers or veterans are found in known colonies, there could be some suspicion that these are sons of veteran colonists.[151] However, given that the veterans of the Late Republic were not for the most part long-serving professionals, there was less incentive or opportunity for sons to follow a military career.[152]

There is little reason to think that the veteran settlement programmes contributed markedly to the decline of Italian agriculture. In some areas, especially in the north-west and north-east corners of Italy, the arrival of veterans must have helped to open up new areas to agriculture, by the clearing and draining of land. In general the refurbishment of centuriated grids throughout the peninsula could have contributed to an improvement in land use.[153] In my view the epigraphic evidence shows veterans remaining on, or closely associated with, their holdings until death. Surviving epitaphs are concentrated on known or likely colonies, indicating (despite

[149] This seems generally the view of Rostovtzeff, loc. cit.

[150] I rely here on figures culled from G. Forni, *Il reclutamento delle legioni da Augusto a Diocleziano* (Milano-Roma, 1953), with the excellent supplement by the same author, 'Estrazione etnica e sociale dei soldati delle legioni nei primi tre secoli dell'impero', *ANRW* II. i (1974), 339–91; J. C. Mann, *The Settlement of Veterans in the Roman Empire* (London, Ph.D. unpub., 1956); A. Passerini, *Le coorti pretorie* (Roma, 1939); H. Freis, *Die Cohortes Urbanae* (Bonn, 1967) = *Epigr. Stud.* 2.

[151] V 4365 = *ILS* 2272 (Brixia), X 4862 = *ILS* 2690 (Venafrum), X 4872 = *ILS* 2021 (Venafrum), Sylloge 69–70 (Cremona).

[152] The idea that colonies, especially in the provinces, represented a source of skilled military manpower, which could be drawn upon to aid the regular forces in times of need, is often repeated. However, the only specific instance where colonists may have been called upon to take up arms again, apart from the obvious example of Caesarian veterans in 44–42 B.C., concerns Berytus, from which in Quinctilius Varus was able to draw 1,500 ὁπλῖται to bolster his forces when on the march against insurgents.

[153] For the link between centuriation and *bonifica*, J. P. Bradford, *Ancient Landscapes* (London, 1957), 177 ff.; Tozzi 111 ff.

the smallness of the sample) that the veterans did not abandon the allotments for Rome itself or the provinces.[154]

It has been alleged that the arrival of the veterans helped to break up, at least temporarily, large estates in the territories of colonies.[155] One result must certainly have been to establish on the most fertile land of a town a class of middling proprietors resident on their farms or in the nearby town, alike replacing owners, tenants and slave-managers of absent landowners. Multiple holdings in the *territorium* would be broken up, but the land of senators was exempt. Many small farmers, where they had survived, must have been swept away, despite Dio's report that Octavian discontinued the confiscation of holdings below the minimum allotment size. The settlements could have led to a greater regularity of farm sizes, between 25 and 50 *iugera*, with smaller and larger units alike disappearing.[156]

The loss of land, and with it at a stroke a great part of the economic base of many families in the colonies, must have brought to an abrupt halt their rise and progress in society, though, as has already been emphasised, the resilience of the pre-colonial families should not be under-estimated, where their holdings had been sufficiently scattered, or their interests sufficiently diverse, to maintain their position. The Propertii of Assisium weathered the loss of their land in the Pianura Umbra and may have risen to senatorial rank by A.D. 14.[157]

Some examples have already been given of an active rôle played by veterans in government and society at a local level. On the national scene soldiers of Sulla and of Caesar might reach the Senate, but when they did (and genuine examples are few), no period of settlement in a colony can be seen to have intervened.[158] Among men who received land from Caesar, the Triumvirs or Octavian, none can be adduced who reached the Senate by their own efforts. The normal progression for the successful was equestrian rank in one generation, and senatorial in the next. Sons of successful centurions and tribunes might reach the Senate, if they had inherited a secure financial base.[159] At Venafrum, the *primipilaris* Vergilius Gallus

[154] Similarly the failure of Sullan colonists is perhaps overstated. Cicero notes that allotments at Praeneste had fallen into the hands of *pauci* (*Leg. Agr.* ii. 78), but we know that colonists were still to be found in substantial numbers at Arretium, Faesulae and Pompeii at the time of the Catilinarian Conspiracy, nearly 20 years after settlement (Cic. *Sull.* 60–62, *Mur.* 49; Sall. *Cat.* 24, 36).

[155] J. Kromater, loc. cit. (n. 136); Brunt, *IM* 294 ff. According to Probus (ed. Thilo) III, p. 328, Vergil's farm sufficed for 60 veterans.

[156] Dio xlviii. 9; Frank, *ESAR* I, 221, 321; ibid. V, 169.

[157] Wiseman no. 344; for the Aufidii at Placentia, above, p. 107; for a Firmius at Sora, below, p. 136; for Vecilii at Luceria, below, p. 165. Note Suet. *Aug.* 40 for the impoverishment of *equites* during the Civil Wars.

[158] H. Hill, 'Sulla's new Senators in 81 B.C.', *CQ* xxvi (1932), 170–7; R. Syme, 'Who was Decidius Saxa?', *JRS* xxvii (1937), 127–37; idem, 'Caesar, the Senate and Italy', *PBSR* xiv (1938), 1–31; J. Harmand, 'Le soldat prolétarian et le barbare dans le senat à la fin de la République', in C. Nicolet (ed.), *Recherches sur les structures sociales dans l'Antiquité classique* (Paris, 1970), 117–31.

[159] Cf. Tac. *Ann.* iii. 75 on the antecedents of the consular Ateius Capito whose grandfather was a Sullan centurion and his father a senator; Suet. *Vesp.* i. 2 for the Flavii of Reate; Pliny *NH* xxii. 11 for a Cn. Petreius, a centurion in the Cimbric War, probably father of the Pompeian legate M. Petreius; Tac. *Hist.* iv. 5 for Helvidius Priscus, son of a *primipilaris* who retired to Cluviae in Samnium.

Lusius married his daughter into the rising equestrian family of the Vettuleni Cereales, and it is likely that two of his grandsons were consuls under Vespasian. Vergilius himself was not a veteran colonist, but it is conceivable that his father had been.[160] Even where senatorial or equestrian families can be linked to a colony, it would be rash to suppose that a colonist was necessarily the founder of the family fortunes; nevertheless many genuine cases must remain shadowy, or unrecognised.[161] At Brixia, C. Pontius Paelignus became a senator before Augustus' death, and held the aedileship early in Tiberius' reign. Wiseman has plausibly suggested that his *cognomen* reflects immigration to Brixia from central Italy at the foundation of the colony, i.e. after Actium; if so, the advance of this family was indeed swift.[162] The upward rise of families in the fluid society of the early Empire is a familiar phenomenon, but an allotment of 25–50 *iugera* was a modest foundation.

Without doubt veterans were unpopular in the initial years of settlement, but the benefits which colony-status and the favour of Augustus could bring were a powerful palliative. Within each town we may imagine a conflict between *veteres* and colonists for local office and influence, until, with the passing of years, differences of origin became blurred and unimportant (though perhaps never quite forgotten), so that all citizens of the town could boast of the bond between the colony and its illustrious and now legendary founder, whatever their own antecedents. It is often said to have been one of Augustus' greatest achievements that he took the army out of politics. It may equally have been to his credit that he defused the antagonisms engendered by the settlement programmes in a general mood of reconciliation, as the prosperity of Italy was restored.

---

[160] *ILS* 2690; *PIR*[1] V 278; *PIR*[2] L 434, 445; R. Syme, 'Antonine Relatives: Ceionii and Vettuleni', *Athenaeum* xxxv (1957), 306–15. The *primipilaris* was born A. Lusius Gallus, but was adopted by M. Vergilius. The adoption may have strengthened his financial position, but *primipilares* were notoriously wealthy (cf. Suet. *Tib.* 37. 3, *Cal.* 38. 2).

[161] The Flavian consular Corellius Rufus, seemingly a Cisalpine, could be a descendant of the equestrian Corellius of Ateste, mentioned by Pliny (*NH* xvii. 122); A. N. Sherwin-White, *The Letters of Pliny* (Oxford, 1966), 111–12.

[162] Wiseman no. 336; cf. Vibius Viscus Thurinus, perhaps also from Brixia (Wiseman no. 493); the Palpellii at Pola (Wiseman no. 304). For the Vitellii of Nuceria, one of whose members was alleged to made a fortune from the sale of confiscated estates as an agent for the Roman Treasury, Wiseman no. 503.

BUILDING WORK IN THE COLONIES UNDER AUGUSTUS
(literary, epigraphic and archaeological evidence).

town	walls, gates, arches	capitolium	theatre	amphitheatre	aqueduct	other buildings
Ancona						
Aquinum	x	x	x	x	x	baths
Ariminum		x				
Asculum		x	x	x	x	baths, bridges, temples
Ateste						
Aug. Praetoria	x	x	x	x	x	
Aug. Taurinorum		x	x			
Beneventum		x				*Caesareum*
Bononia						baths
Bovianum						
Brixellum						
Brixia					x	
Capua			x	x?		
Castrum Novum						portico etc.
Concordia		x	x			
Cremona						
Dertona						forum, porticoes
Falisca				x	x	roads
Fanum Fortunae		x				basilica, *aedes Augusti*
Falerio			x?			
Firmum						*Augusteum*
Florentia		x				
Hadria						
Hispellum		x				
Luca			x			
Luceria				x		
Lucus Feroniae	x			x	x	baths, basilica, forum
Minturnae	x		x	x	x	temple
Mutina				x?		
Nola						
Nuceria				x	x	
Paestum				x?		
Parentium						
Parma				x		
Pisae		x	x	x		*Augusteum*
Pisaurum						
Placentia						
Pola		x		x	x	temple
Puteoli				x	x	mole, temple
Rusellae				x		forum, basilica, portico
Saena						
Sora						
Suessa						
Sutrium						
Teanum						
Tergeste		x				
Tuder		x	x			
Venafrum		x	x	x	x	
Venusia				x?		

PART TWO

SITES AND SETTLERS 47–14 B.C.

PREFACE

The epigraphic evidence for veteran settlement in Italy under Caesar, the Triumvirs and Augustus down to 14 B.C. is discussed below in a local context of what is known about those towns which seem likely to have acquired or reacquired colonial status in this period. The towns have been grouped geographically according to the Augustan *regiones*. Discussion is restricted to those matters having a direct bearing on the status of the town, the date when the colony was established, the identity of the colonists, and their impact on each town. Pliny's list forms the basis of selection. However, no mention will be found of Antium, Aquileia or Ostia (where there seems no real evidence of colonisation at this time), or of Rhegium (where some colonists were settled in 36 B.C.), or any of the small-scale settlements carried out by Caesar, or by Augustus in the middle years of his reign. The evidence for such work has, it is hoped, been adequately noted elsewhere in these pages. On the other hand, two of the towns discussed below (Cumae and Ausculum) are rejected as colonies, and doubt is thrown on the relevance of others to the present study.

   In the preparation of individual entries recourse has been made in the first instance to Nissen's *Italische Landeskunde* and to entries in the Pauly-Wissowa *Realencyclopädie*. Early entries in the latter work are often mere paraphrases of Nissen, but the more recent essays can have considerable merit. Recent archaeological work in individual towns is often conveniently summarised in the *Enciclopedia dell'Arte Antica* (1958–1966) or in its *Supplemento* (1973), or both.

   Reference to the above works has been kept to a minimum, except where the views propounded deserve special commendation, or are refuted. Local Italian literature has been surveyed wherever possible, but no attempt is made in the footnotes to cite all the works looked at. Some major studies of the later nineteenth and early twentieth centuries retain lasting value. The series *Forma Italiae*, conceived over 60 years ago, makes only moderate progress in the survey and documentation of archaeological remains of the Italian towns and their countryside, and though a goodly number of towns have been the subject of *tesi di laurea* by university students, the results are not always accessible. Many more systematic and comprehensive studies of individual towns, by scholars competent to assess the literary, archaeological and epigraphic record, are much to be desired.

CHAPTER SIX

LATIUM AND CAMPANIA

Sora

The town of Sora, a *colonia Latina* of 303 B.C., lies on the right bank of the Liris where it emerges from the narrow Val Roveto gorge and descends for a while into more open country.[1] Sora's status as a colony in the early Empire is reported by Pliny, and confirmed by the *Liber Coloniarum* and by epigraphic evidence. Its foundation has been assigned to the aftermath of Philippi.[2]

Of special interest is a slab from the town honouring the tribune L. Firmius, who had served as *IIIIvir iure dicundo* at Sora before the establishment of the colony (Sylloge 91). After its foundation he became the first *pontifex* to be appointed under its new charter. The slab was set up jointly by members of a legion IIII *Sorana*. This title is not found elsewhere attached to any legion, but must derive from the town-name. Some have argued that legion IIII adopted this title after discharge, to commemorate its place of settlement.[3] Others have preferred to see here a legion originally raised at Sora, where with singular appropriateness it was settled after service.[4] This seems the more likely explanation. The formation of this Soran legion can best be placed in 43 B.C. when Pansa was raising fresh legions for the Senate against Antony (above, p. 26). Founder members could thus expect to be released after Naulochus at the earliest, or after Actium. In 41 B.C. members of the only known legion IIII then requiring settlement, the *Macedonica,* were established at Firmum. Most probably, therefore, the colonists commemorated at Sora arrived there in or about 30 B.C.

Firmius had seen service as a *primus pilus* and later as a *tribunus militum*. It would be tempting to see in him a tribune settled in the town along with members of his legion, who later dedicated the stone to him in commemoration of their former association, but no direct link is specified. His rôle in the government of the colony is modest. It may be that Firmius, a local worthy at Sora with some previous military service as centurion, was persuaded in 43 B.C. to serve as tribune in IIII *Sorana* at its creation. By the time of the colony's foundation, he may have been too old, or disinclined, to play more than a ceremonial rôle in its administration.

An inscription honouring Otacilia Severa, wife of Philippus Arabs, and so datable with precision to the years A.D. 244–249, was erected *numini maiestatique eius* by [*col*]*onia Iulia Pra*[.......]; the letters *Pra* are most convincingly expanded to

---

[1] A. Lauri, *Sora, Isola del Liri e dintorni* (Sora, 1914).

[2] Mommsen, *CIL* X, p. 560, p. 561 on X 5713; Pais, *Colonie militari* 38; Ritterling, *Legio* 1564. The colony was established *iussu Caesaris Augusti,* as reported by the *Liber Coloniarum* (237. 17). An entry in the *Liber,* which seemed to record survey work in the *ager Soranus* in 34 B.C. (244. 5), was shown by Mommsen (*CIL* X, p. 560) to refer to the activities of a military surveyor under the orders of the *Praefectus Urbi* in 126 A.D. The epitaph X 5728 from Sora records a Q. Cassius Scaeva, perhaps Caesar's centurion (for whom see below, p. 142), or a relative, but the inscription makes no mention of military service.

[3] A. Von Domaszewski, 'Die Heere der Bürgerkriege in den Jahre 49 bis 42 vor Christus', *NHJ* iv (1894), 157–88, at 183; Ritterling, *Legio* 1564.

[4] Mommsen on X 5713; Dessau on *ILS* 2226; Degrassi on *ILLRP* 498a.

Praetoria.[5] On the analogy of Aosta, *colonia Augusta Praetoria*, the title should indicate settlement in the colony of veterans of one or more of the *cohortes praetoriae* who may have shared the colony with legion IIII, but we cannot tell when either title was adopted.

Aquinum

Aquinum (the modern Aquino) lies astride the Via Latina between Casinum and the site of Fregellae.[6] A theory that under the Republic Aquinum occupied a site on the heights above, and was transferred to its present location in the middle of the Liri valley when the colony was founded, has met with slight acclaim, and conflicts with both the literary and archaeological evidence.[7]

Pliny includes Aquinum in his list of inland colonies of Latium and Campania; the *Liber Coloniarum* assigns a Triumviral date.[8] No veterans are explicitly attested, but one inscription published in the Tenth Volume of the *Corpus* deserves close attention (Sylloge 1, Pl. VIII). It reads:

C AIEDIVS C F

LEM

L III̅ V D P S

Mommsen could make little of the letters L III V in the final line. '*Litteris quid significetur, nescio; fortasse aedificium id quod C. Aiedius de pecunia sua fecit*".[9] The stone is now built in horizontally to the south wall of the twelfth century church of S. Maria della Libera at Aquino. It is clearly a gravestone, and is most easily interpreted as recording the military service of a veteran of a *legio* III. The overall layout suggests that the inscription dates to the later first century B.C. The *nomen* is not found again at Aquinum, and the tribe *Lemonia* could indicate an origin at Bononia, Ancona or in Umbria. Evidently Aiedius did not adopt the local *Oufentina* of Aquinum upon settlement.

The Augustan age witnessed wholesale construction of major public buildings within the town (above, p. 119), including an aqueduct, theatre, baths, amphitheatre and capitolium.[10] Centuriation observed in the *ager Aquinas* was already, it would seem, laid out by 39 B.C.[11] If the colony belongs after Philippi, as might seen probable on this evidence, legion III could be a member of Caesar's consular series of 48 B.C., perhaps to be equated with the later III *Gallica* (above, p. 28). In the

[5]X 5711; PRA was read by Mancini, PR by Marcilli and Helbig. An alternative expansion would be PRIMA (cf. below, p. 154).

[6]M. Cagiano de Azevedo, *Aquinum* (Roma, 1949); C. Giuliani, 'Aquino', *Quad. Ist. Top. Ant.* i (1964), 41–49; *Atl. Aereofotografico*, tav. cv.

[7]G. Säflund, 'Ancient Latin Cities of the Hills and the Plains: a study in the Evolution of Types of Settlement in Ancient Italy', *Opuscula Archaeologica* i (1935), 64–86.

[8]Pliny *NH* iii. 63; *LC* 229. 13.

[9]On X 5407. The remaining letters of line 3 are best expanded to *vivus de pecunia sua* (or *vivus de proprio suo*). Less probably V could be the abbreviated title of a legion.

[10]Cagiano, op. cit. (n. 6), 33 ff.; G. Cressedi, *EAA* i (1958), 522.

[11]F. Coarelli, 'Note sulla topografia extraurbana di Aquino', *Quad. Ist. Top. Ant.* i (1964), 51–54. Above, p. 000.

Early Empire, as under the Republic, Aquinum was a populous town, well deserving the laudatory appellations accorded to it in the sources. It could easily have merited inclusion in the group of 18 prosperous cities designated for land settlement after Philippi.[12]

Venafrum

Venafrum lay at the western edge of the largest plain in the valley of the Volturno north of the main *ager Campanus*. The town was famed for its olive groves, among the most productive in Italy. That a colony was established here in the last generation of the Republic is not open to doubt: a series of *cippi* testifying to *vectigalia publica colonorum* give its titulature as *colonia Iulia Venafrana*. An inscription of undefined date and fragmentary condition describes the town as *colonia Augusta Iulia*.[13]

It is likely that the foundation of the colony had a considerable impact on the town, with the enlargement of the urban area, the construction of a wall-circuit to enclose it, and the building of a theatre and amphitheatre (cf. above, p. 119).[14] An aqueduct, of which considerable though mainly subterranean remains survive, was provided by Augustus, bringing to the town the waters of the Monte della Rocchetta, 30 kms. to the north. Two copies of an *edictum*, one complete but partly illegible, the other a mere fragment, prescribe regulations for its use and main-tenance. A series of *cippi*, erected *iussu imperatoris Caesaris Augusti*, were set up to mark out a strip eight feet wide on either side of the conduit, to be left *vacuus*.[15] The edict names two farm-owners along the course of the aqueduct-conduit, as Q Ceionius L.f. Ter. and L. Pompeius M.f. Ter. Sulla; one or both may easily be veterans.[16] At a date unknown, but probably before 27 B.C., the ex-tribune Volcius Sabinus provided a separate aqueduct, named as the *Aqua Iulia*, for villagers at Rufrae within the territory of Venafrum. Whether Volcius himself was a colonist is not known. Rufrae has also yielded a dedication of 29 B.C. to Octavian.[17]

Closely concerned with the government of the colony in its opening years was C.

---

[12]Cic. *Phil.* ii. 106; Strabo v. 3. 9; Sil. Ital. viii. 403.

[13]X 4875, 4894. The *Liber Coloniarum* displays no knowledge of Venafrum's colonial status (239. 7), but records work by *quinqueviri*, perhaps Caesarian in origin and testifying to settlement work in 59–58.

[14]A. La Regina, 'Venafro', *Quad. Ist. Top. Ant.* i (1964), 55–67; idem, *EAA Sup.* (1970), 894–95; *Atl. Aereofotografico*, tav. cviii.

[15]The first copy of the *edictum* was found at the village of S. Maria Oliveto near Venafro (*ILS* 5743 = *EJ*[2] 282), the second at S. Vincenzo al Volturno, close to the source of the aqueduct; A. Pantoni, 'L'editto augusteo sull'acquedotto di Venafro, a una sua replica alle fonti del Volturno', *Rend. Pont. Acc.* xxxiii (1960–61), 155–71; *AE* 1962, 92. Seven *cippi* are attested (X 4843, *NS* 1926, 434, *AE* 1962, 91). On the date of construction, Th. Mommsen, 'Römische Urkunden: 1. Edikt Augusts über die Wasserleitung von Venafro', *Zeitschrift für geschichtliche Rechtswissenschaft* xv (1850), 287–371; A. Maiuri, V. Cimorelli, F. Frediani, 'L'acquedotto augusteo di Venafro', *Campania Romana* i (Napoli, 1938), 165–86; F. de Martino, 'Note sull'Italia augustea', *Athenaeum* liii (1975), 245–61.

[16]*ILS* 5743, line 16, with Pantoni, loc. cit.

[17]*ILS* 5759; *ILS* 80. Rufrae (mod. Presenzano) lies c. 12 kms. S of Venafro, and separated from the latter by Monte Calvello. It is hard to suppose that Volcius merely extended to Rufrae the major aqueduct described above.

Aclutius Gallus, who held the posts of *duovir urbis moeniundae bis, praefectus iure deicundo bis* and *IIvir iure deicundo* (Sylloge 96). Michael Grant has asserted that the title *duovir urbis moeniundae* was drawn directly from the terminology of the *deductio* process, and identified Gallus as an *adsignator coloniae* specially charged by the *deductor* with the organisation of settlement and distribution of allotments to veterans on arrival, one of those 'confidential city-governors' whom he discerned at work at a number of colonies.[18] Such notions are ill-supported by the evidence. More probably the title *duovir urbis moeniundae* reflects a special responsibility for the provision of the new wall circuit to which archaeology now testifies. Although his tenures of office could have been spread over many years, it is tempting to think that Aclutius enjoyed a number of successive terms, twice acting as deputy for unnamed *IIviri*. Yet he never became *IIvir quinquennalis* of the town. In addition to holding these municipal posts, Aclutius was tribune in two legions, a *legio prima* and *legio secunda Sabina*. It must be very likely that he was tribune in the latter at the time of settlement. As the legion II *Sabina* is most easily seen as another of Pansa's consular series of 43 B.C. (above, p. 26), the colony at Venafrum could be placed after Actium.

Teanum

Teanum, on a low spur to the south-east of Roccamonfina, was a major centre under the Republic, as recent excavations have confirmed. Strabo could describe Teanum as the second most important inland city of Campania (after Capua).[19] Teanum is listed as a *colonia* by Pliny, and numerous *IIviri* are attested, but the date of the bestowal of colonial rank is disputed.[20] Two inscriptions give the town's titulature under the Empire as COL CL FIRMA TEANUM, confidently expanded by Mommsen to *colonia Claudia Firma Teanum*, which indicated a Claudian date for the colony.[21] The alternative expansion of CL to *Classica* was preferred by Beloch and Pais, who drew attention to nearby *Iulia Felix Classica Suessa* (below, p. 143), and to Teanum's entry in the *Liber Coloniarum*, which records the establishment there by *Caesar Augustus* of *milites metyci* (i.e. non-citizen troops). Pais identified the latter as peregrine or newly enfranchised sailors from Octavian's fleets.[22] This appeared to settle the matter: several inscriptions recording *IIIIviri i.d.*, which Mommsen had made pre-Claudian, might easily be restricted to the Late Republic.[23] However, settlement at Teanum of peregrine sailors would be as surprising here as at nearby Suessa (see below, p. 143); perhaps the reference to *metyci* arose from a misunderstanding of the title *Classica*, which should record settlement by a legion whose members had seen service with a naval squadron (above, p. 31).

Subsequently, however, Degrassi adduced a small fragment of municipal *Fasti* said to originate from Teanum, and covering the years A.D. 45–46. For the latter

[18] *FITA* 285, 293, 422.
[19] A. de Monaco, *Teano osco e romano* (Teano, 1960); *Atl. Aereofotografico*, tav. cvi.
[20] *NH* iii. 63; *CIL* X, p. 471.
[21] Mommsen, *CIL* X, p. 471; idem, *Bürgercolonien* 195.
[22] Beloch, *RG* 514; Pais, *Colonizzazione* 263–65; *LC* 238. 6–9.
[23] X 4796, 4797 = *ILS* 6298; X 4798, 613* = *EE* VIII 575. However, Teanum was still governed by *IIIIviri* at a time when Iader had already become a colony (*AE* 1908, 218 = *ILS* 9389).

year two *IIIIviri iure dicundo* and two *aediles* are listed as the chief officials; also in
A.D. 46 two members of the senatorial *gens Vipstana* served as magistrates, possibly
as *quaestores*.[24] Degrassi concluded that the *IIIIviri* must be magistrates of Teanum
as a *municipium,* and that the Vipstani had been appointed (perhaps at the insti-
gation of Claudius) to supervise the foundation of a *colonia Claudia*, which we could
thus date precisely to A.D. 46.

Nevertheless, there are good reasons for supposing that Teanum did become a
colony in the later first century B.C., most probably after Philippi. A veteran C.
Cabilenus C.f. Fal. Gallus is known, who had served in legion VIII *Mutinensis*
(Sylloge 92). He is most easily identified as a former member of Caesar's Eighth
Legion, which was re-formed around a nucleus of veterans at Casilinum on
Octavian's behalf in the autumn of 44 B.C. The title *Mutinensis* (which seems
attached to the legion rather than the man) should result from its participation in
the campaign of Mutina in 43.[25] The tribe *Falerna* suits an initial settlement at
Casilinum, but not Teanum (which was in *Teretina*), or Mutina (in *Pollia*). Perhaps
Cabilenus received a fresh allotment at Teanum in 41, after service in the re-formed
legion VIII. No naval service by members of this particular legion is reported in the
sources, so that the epithet may derive from the exploits of the younger legion with
which VIII presumably shared the colony.

Appian's narrative for the early months of 41 B.C. includes a proposal for a
conference between Octavian and L. Antonius at Teanum.[26] The initiative came
from representatives of the post-Philippi colonists, at a time when Octavian was preoccupied with the supervision of one or more colonies in Campania or southern
Italy. The sequence of events in Appian's narrative could suggest that Octavian was
then precisely at Teanum establishing colonists there (above, p. 59).

That Teanum was already a *colonia* by the middle years of Augustus is the
natural conclusion to be drawn from an inscription first seen at Teanum in 1753
and now lost.[27] It is one of the two that give versions of the colonial titulature of the
town. The stone was noted and its text reported by the English scholar Sir Richard
Colt Hoare and the local antiquarian Michele Broccoli in 1819 and 1821. It read:
IMP CAESAR D F AVG/ PONT MAX TRIB POT XX COS XIII/DESIGNATO
PATRI PATRIAE/ COL CL FIRMA TEANUM.[28] Mommsen rejected the first two
lines out of hand, having already decided upon a Claudian date for the colony,
though elsewhere he conceded that Hoare was a reliable witness. There are difficulties over the precise dating of the inscription, but Hoare and Broccoli indepen-

---

[24] A. Degrassi, 'Problemi cronologici delle colonie di Luceria, Aquileia, Teanum Sidicinum', *Riv.
Fil.* lxvi (1938), 129–43 = SVA I, 79–97. The fragment (*AE* 1905, 192) was first seen at Le Curti
outside Capua Vetere. Hülsen, in an early discussion of its significance, argued that it should belong to
Cales, where parts of similar *Fasti* were already known; 'Consularfasten aus Campanien', *Röm. Mitt.*
xix (1904), 322–27. For the Vipstani, conceivably a local family, Wiseman nos. 498–99.

[25] The word order requires that *Mutinensis* be taken as the title of the legion. Contrast ILS 2249
Q. Annaeus Q.f. Pol. Balbus Faventinus ann. LIII meiles leg. V. The surname *Gallus* can be no sure
guide to origin — or place of service.

[26] *BC* v. 20.

[27] X 4781 with Mommsen ad loc.

[28] R. C. Hoare, *A classical Tour through Italy and Sicily* (London, 1819), 188; M. Broccoli,
Teano Sidicino antico e moderno (Napoli, 1821), I, 69–70.

dently report the text, with interesting variations in reading; there must be a case for rehabilitation.[29] It is distinctly possible that Teanum achieved colonial status after Philippi.

Minturnae

At Minturnae the Via Appia, having passed through the gap between the Monti Aurunci and the sea, crossed the Garigliano about 2 kms. from its mouth. In 295 B.C. a Roman colony was planted at Minturnae to guard the crossing. Some picture of Roman Minturnae in the last years of the Republic can be built up from the published results of excavation of the central area of its town-site in 1931–33 by a team from the University of Pennsylvania under Professor Jotham Johnson, in conjunction with the Italian authorities.[30]

It seems clear that about the middle of the first century B.C. the heart of the town was gutted by fire. Comprehensive redevelopment followed: the 'capitolium' was rebuilt, a theatre complex and an aqueduct (bringing water from Cap d'Acqua to the north-west) were constructed, and it is possible that a less congested forum precinct was laid out on the southern side of the Appia. Other buildings too can be given an Augustan date.[31] Professor Johnson placed the fire within the decade 55–45 B.C., and dated the rebuilding programme to shortly after.[32] It would be natural to think that the desolate condition of the town centre, visible to every traveller along the Appia, may have prompted the despatch of colonists, and that their arrival speeded the rebuilding of the burnt-out zone, but it may be doubted whether the archaeological evidence allows such a close dating to be attached either to the fire or to the subsequent reconstruction programme. The rebuilding of a town even on the Via Appia may have been delayed by the events of the Civil War years.

Further information on the date of settlement is provided by Hyginus Gromaticus, in his discussion of Octavian's colonial programme after Actium; he notes that the status of some towns was changed at this time from *municipium* to *colonia,* but some existing colonies, *quas bellorum civilium interventus exhauserat,* were reinforced, *dato iterum coloniae nomine,* and occasionally also boosted by an extension of their *territoria.* Minturnae is cited as his example: *sicut in Campania finibus Minturnensium, quorum nova adsignatio trans fluvium Lirem limitibus continetur.*

[29] So Pais, *Colonizzazione* 263–65. Augustus was TR P XX from July 4 B.C. to June 3 B.C., and COS XIII in 2 B.C. (hence XIII DESIGNATO in 3 B.C.), but did not formally become *pater patriae* until February 2 B.C.

[30] *Excavations at Minturnae* I (Philadelphia, 1935), II. i (Rome-Philadelphia, 1933). At least one further volume by A. Maiuri was promised, but did not appear. See, however, Maiuri's summary in *EAA* V (1963), 105–7.

[31] Op. cit. (n. 30), I, passim: idem, *RE Sup.* VII (1940), 458–94, *s.v. Minturnae*; I. A. Richmond, 'Commemorative Arches and City Gates in the Augustan Age', *JRS* xxiii (1933), 149–74; H. C. Butler, 'The Roman Aqueducts as Monuments of Architecture', *AJA* v (1901), 175–99. For doubts on Johnson's whole interpretation, see the review by L. R. Taylor, *AJA* xl (1936), 284–85.

[32] Op. cit. I, 5 ff., 34.

At a later date there was some reallocation of previously centuriated land *citra Lirem* (Pl. VI).[33]

Hyginus Gromaticus seems to suggest that the *ager Minturnensis* of the Republic was confined to the northern bank of the river and that, as a result of Octavian's attention to the town, it was extended southwards, at the expense (no doubt) of Suessa or Sinuessa. However, it is more probable that his reference to *nova adsignatio* is based on a report that the *ager Minturnensis* to the south of the Garigliano was only now parcelled up into *centuriae;* as a maritime Roman colony of a few hundred families Minturnae would have required only a small amount of centuriated land, all of which may have lain on the more secure northerly side of the river. Already by the Augustan Period it would seem that a suburb of the town had grown up on the south bank.[34] Hyginus' report implies two phases of settlement. Perhaps an initial wave of settlers arrived in 47–44 B.C., which would confirm a reference to activity of 'C. Caesar' in the *Liber Coloniarum*. Minturnae could have been one of those Caesarian 'colonies' visited by Octavian in the autumn of 44 B.C. (above, p. 53). Perhaps at this time veterans were planted on newly surveyed land on the southern side of the Liris.[35] At a later date, most probably after Actium, Minturnae's colonial status was formally renewed, with further settlement, this time to the north of the river.[36] Alternatively, if the first wave of settlers arrived after Actium, there may have been a further infusion in 14 B.C.

A military gravestone of the Late Republic is recorded at the town; it commemorates Q. Ancharius, an *evocatus* of citizen stock from Narbo, who had served in the *ala Scaevae* (Sylloge 85), and who died at the age of 23. Caesar's doughty centurion Scaeva, after whom this military unit is apparently named, served at Pharsalus in legion VI, which was later settled at Arelate in the province of Narbonensis.[37] Perhaps he was seconded to raise and command a cavalry regiment when Lepidus was organising fresh forces in the province after Caesar's death, which would be a useful *terminus post quem* for Ancharius' arrival at Minturnae.[38] It is, however, difficult to believe that Ancharius could have completed a basic term of service, have been 'called out', and have qualified for land settlement, in any

---

[33] 177. 13–178. 9. Rudorff's Fig. 150 (here Pl. VI) shows the walled town of *Mynturnae* straddling a river and lying between a mountain chain and the sea. On the river's southern bank is a grid of *centuriae* with the designation *nova adsignatio*. The illustration incorporates a place-name not in the text (*mons Vescini*) and displays a commendable knowledge of local topography; F. Castagnoli, 'Le 'formae' delle colonie romane e le miniature dei codici dei gromatici', *Mem. Acc. Linc.* ser. 7, iv (1943), 83–118, no. 3; O. A. W. Dilke, 'Maps in the Treatises of Roman Land Surveyors', *Geog. J.* cxxvii (1961), 417–26 no. 1.

[34] Pliny *NH* iii. 59; *RE Sup*. VII (1940), 460; *Atl. Aereofotografico*, tav. cv.

[35] A statue was erected at Minturnae *deivo Iulio iussu populi Romani e lege Rufrena, RE Sup*. VII (1940), 478.

[36] In an ingenious paper, E. Staedler linked a group of altars at Minturnae (*ILLRP* 724–46), re-used in the foundations of a temple of Tiberian date, to the process of *nova adsignatio*, which he dated to precisely 28 B.C.; 'Zu den 29 neu ausgefundenen Inschriften von Minturnae', *Hermes* lxxvii (1942), 149–96. However, his arguments can carry no weight. See also E. Badian, 'Marius' Villas: the Testimony of the Slave and the Knave', *JRS* lxiii (1973), 121–32.

[37] Caes. *BC* iii. 53. 5; *RE* III (1899), 1744, *Sup*. I (1903), 278.

[38] For the history of the *Ala Scaevae*, E. B. Birley, '*Alae* named after their Commanders', *Anc. Soc*. ix (1978), 257–73.

formally constituted branch of the Roman army, by the age of 23.[39] We could suppose either that the *evocatus* died while in transit with his unit,[40] or that the age as recorded on the stone (now lost) was misread, and that he was a genuine settler in the town.

Suessa

Little is known about settlement at the old Latin colony of Suessa Aurunca, high above the Liris valley at the south-western edge of Roccamonfina; the monuments of the town have attracted scant attention.[41] Suessa reacquired colonial status, with the titulature *Colonia Iulia Felix Classica Suessa,* some time after 43 B.C.; it is recorded as a colony by Pliny.[42] The title *Classica* is perhaps indicative of settlement by veterans of a *legio classica* (cf. above, p. 31), but its numeral is not known.

Capua, Calatia and Casilinum

The *ager Campanus,*[43] the most extensive and most fertile tract of public land available to the Roman state in the Late Republic, naturally loomed large in the land reallocation schemes of the times.[44] Survey work for land settlement was carried out in the *ager Campanus* by the Gracchan land commissioners in 132–130 B.C., though Cicero denies any formal colonial foundation.[45] In 83 B.C. self-government was restored, under the guise of a colony, by Marian politicians, but it was quickly suppressed.[46] It seems that Sulla, though he extended the holdings of the temple-complex of Diana Tifatina, did not sanction any general reallocation within the *ager Campanus.*[47] However, the latter was destined to play a leading rôle in the abortive programme of Rullus,[48] and Capua finally reacquired formal self-government in 59 with the establishment of a colony under the agrarian legislation of Julius Caesar. Cicero asserts that a maximum of 5,000 settlers, each receiving a small plot of 10 *iugera*, could be accommodated within the boundaries of the *ager Campanus* at this time. About 25% of the total land area would have been needed to accommodate them; the remainder was presumably retained by existing owners

---

[39] Mommsen, 'Evocati Augusti', *EE* V (1884), 142–54; Dessau on *ILS* 2490; Degrassi on *ILLRP* 498.

[40] Schmitthenner 36, 187 n. 11.

[41] M. della Corte, 'Le iscrizioni graffite del criptoportico del teatro di Sessa Aurunca', *Campania Romana* i (1938), 189–204; A. Maiuri, 'Il criptoportico di Sessa Aurunca', *Rend. Acc. Nap.* xxxvi (1961), 55–62.

[42] *NH* iii. 63; X 4832. It was a *municipium* in April 43 B.C. (Cic. *Phil.* xiii. 18).

[43] Of the extensive modern literature, see esp. Th. Mommsen, *CIL* X, pp. 365–70; K. J. Beloch, *Campanien* (Breslau, 1890), 295–374; J. Heurgon, *Recherches sur l'histoire, la religion et la civilisation de Capoue préromaine* (Paris, 1942); M. W. Frederiksen, 'Republican Capua: a Social and Economic Survey', *PBSR* xxvii (1959), 80–125.

[44] For a general discussion of the impact of the various land settlement schemes of the Late Republic, U. Laffi, *Adtributio e contributio* (Pisa, 1966), 99–109.

[45] D. Curreri, 'Capua e l'Ager Campanus nella legislazione agraria e colonaria di Caio Gracco', *Epigraphica* xxxiii (1971), 33–47.

[46] Gabba, *Ricerche* 256–61.

[47] Cic. *Leg. Agr.* ii. 81; *ILS* 251, 3240.

[48] Cic. *Leg. Agr.*, passim; Brunt, *IM* 312 ff.

or tenants. An unknown proportion of the new settlers were veterans of Pompey's campaigns in the East.[49]

Neither Calatia nor Casilinum is mentioned by the sources in conjunction with land reallocation in 59 B.C., though allusions to Capua may easily be taken to include other townships within the *ager Campanus*. Centuriation observed in the *ager Campanus* is orientated on Capua, and covers the *territoria* of Capua, Calatia, Atella and probably Casilinum.[50] Calatia lay on the Appia, 10 kms. south-east of Capua, Casilinum only 5 kms. to the north, at the point where the Latina and the Appia united to cross the Volturno river; neither town can have possessed an extensive *territorium*. In particular Casilinum lay at the extreme northern edge of the *ager Campanus* — only a narrow strip of land between Capua and the Volturno seems available for it, unless some land in the *ager Stellas* or the *ager Falernus* north of the river fell within its control.[51]

Both Calatia and Casilinum were selected by Caesar to receive substantial numbers of his Gallic veterans; members of legion VII were established at Calatia, and of VIII at Casilinum (above, p. 52). One result was to move the boundary of the latter southwards almost to the walls of Capua; given the apparent meagreness of its territory, some extension was perhaps inevitable if veterans were to be accommodated in any number. The selection of Calatia and Casilinum need not have been random; it was a combination which effectively bracketed Capua (δύο τάσδε Καπύης ἑκατέρωθεν), thus counteracting any residue of pro-Pompeian sympathies among earlier settlers at Capua itself.[52] Both towns now acquired colonial rank, if they did not already possess it from 59 B.C.[53]

Neither Calatia nor Casilinum long retained independent status; both were perhaps too close to the Campanian metropolis to remain viable. The Elder Pliny mentions Casilinum in a list of Italian towns which had all but disappeared by his day (*sunt morientes Casilini reliquiae*). The *Liber Coloniarum* has preserved a record of the absorption of Calatia by Capua, though the date and circumstances are garbled.[54] Neither town is included by Pliny in his regular town-lists; in all probability both were absorbed by Capua before the death of Augustus. Urbana in the *ager Falernus*, and perhaps one other town (not yet identified), were soon to

[49] M. A. Levi, 'Una pagina di storia agraria romana', *Atene e Roma* n.s. iii (1922), 239–52; L. R. Taylor, 'Caesar's Agrarian Legislation and his Municipal Policy', in P. R. Coleman-Norton (ed.), *Studies in Roman Economic and Social History presented to A. C. Johnson* (Princeton, 1951), 68–78.

[50] F. Castagnoli, 'Note al Liber Coloniarum', *BCAR* lxxii (1946–48), App. pp. 49–58; W. Johannowsky, 'La situazione in Campania', in P. Zanker (ed.), *Hellenismus in Mittelitalien* (Göttingen, 1976), 267–99; C. Bencivenga, 'Un nuovo contributo alla cognoscenza della centuriazione dell' Ager Campanus', *Rend. Acc. Nap.* li (1976), 79–90. J.-P. Vallat, 'Le vocabulaire des attributions de terre en campanie: analyse spatiale et temporale', *MEFR* xci (1979), 977–1013; idem, 'Cadastrations et contrôle de la terre en campanie septentrionale (IVᵉ siècle av. J.-C. — Iᵉʳ siècle ap. J.-C.)', ibid. xcii (1980), 387–44.

[51] The town of Casilinum in fact straddled the river (Liv. xxii. 15, xxiii. 17, Dion. Hal. xv. 4. 2).

[52] App. *BC* iii. 40. Pompey gathered troops at Capua during his retreat before Caesar in 49 B.C. (Caes. *BC* i. 10).

[53] In October 43 B.C., Cicero (*Phil.* ii. 102) could describe Casilinum as having been founded as a colony *paucis annis ante*. Given that Cicero would be likely to understate the time-gap, the reference should be to 59 B.C., rather than to a Caesarian plan of 47–44.

[54] *NH* iii. 70; *LC* 232. 4.

follow.[55] An illustration preserved in the gromatic corpus could show other holdings (above, p. 14).

Capua was among the towns marked out for settlement after Philippi; presumably allocation took place.[56] Again in 36 B.C. colonists were accommodated there—in Velleius' words, a *speciosum adiectum supplementum Campanae coloniae*.[57] The *ager publicus* utilised for settlement may have included abandoned allotments of earlier schemes. Compensation in the form of land in Crete and the promise of an aqueduct followed. More land was acquired by purchase. The transfer of the chalk-bearing *colles Leucogaei* from Naples to Capua may belong now.[58] Octavian's work at this time was commemorated by the erection of a sequence of *cippi* set up *iussu imp. Caesaris qua aratrum ductum est*, which would mark the formal re-ploughing of the sacred furrow round the city.[59] Octavian may also have taken the opportunity to effect a radical reappraisal of land-holding in the *ager Campanus*, with the establishment of a colony at Puteoli, and an enlargement of its *territorium* (below, p. 148).

Here as elsewhere the Augustan period witnessed some building activity: Capua's theatre was replaced and an amphitheatre perhaps built now, on such a scale that it was probably upon completion the largest in the Roman world.[60] The aqueduct funded by Octavian attracted the praise of Velleius and Dio. Capua became *Colonia Iulia Felix Augusta;* there is later evidence for the title *Concordia*.[61] How the sequence of titles was built up is not clear. The first element to be awarded must have been *Iulia*, perhaps in 59 B.C., or more probably in 41. Refoundation in 36 would confirm that title, and may have added *Felix* or *Concordia* or both. The title *Augusta* may indicate some reinforcement or benefits accruing to the town after 27 B.C. (see above, p. 85).

Several epitaphs, erected by or for veterans of the Triumviral and Augustan ages, are known. The earliest is probably that of the brothers Canuleius (Sylloge 61); its precise findspot is not known. The stone (Pl. IA) commemorates two brothers who enlisted in one of Caesar's Gallic legions. The elder was killed almost at once, at the

---

[55] Pliny *NH* xiv. 62 (*Urbanam coloniam Sullanam nuper Capuae contributam*). For a sculptured relief of five city personifications, perhaps identifiable as Capua, Calatia, Casilinum, Urbana and Atella?, found among the ruins of the amphitheatre at Capua, P. Veyne, 'Contributio: Bénévent, Capoue, Cirta', *Latomus* xviii (1959), 568–92, with pl. xxxvi.

[56] App. *BC* iv. 3.

[57] Vell. ii. 81; Dio xlix. 14. 5.

[58] Pliny *NH* xviii. 114.

[59] X 3825 = *ILS* 6308 = *ILLRP* 482.

[60] For the theatres of Capua, *NS* 1943, 149–52; A. de Franciscis, 'Commento a due nuovi 'tituli magistrorum campanorum'' in *Studi in onore di Calderini e Paribeni* (Milano, 1956), III 353–58; idem, *NS* 1952, 307; M. W. Frederiksen, loc. cit. (n. 44). Scholars are divided on the date of construction of the amphitheatre, which is obscured by Hadrianic rebuilding. W. Johannowsky advocates a date in the later second century B.C.; see 'La campania', *D. Arch.* iv–v (1970–71), 460–71; however, the main dedicatory inscription ascribes its construction to *colonia Iulia Felix Augusta Capua* (*ILS* 6309); political reasons militate against any amphitheatre in the town before 59 B.C. Notice that most of the fragments of the *elogium* of L. Antistius Campanus derived from the amphitheatre; another fragment (vi), if correctly assigned to the *elogium*, may refer to [*lu*]*dos* and to an [*amphith*]*eatr*[*um*] (X 3903).

[61] *ILS* 6309–10.

age of 18, but Gaius Canuleius survived the fighting in Gaul and against Pompey, to be settled by Caesar, presumably at Calatia in 45–44. After Caesar's death he was persuaded to re-enlist by Octavian or Ventidius; no wife or family is mentioned to distract him, and at his age (less than 35) a further period of military service might not have seemed unattractive. In 43 B.C., Octavian's legion VII, *constituta ex veteranis*, is found fighting under Hirtius, scoring signal success at Mutina.[62] Canuleius' *dona militaria*, appropriate to an *evocatus*, may have been acquired at this time or at Philippi. The difference in wording between *mortuus est* (applied to C. Canuleius) and *occeisus est* (applied to Q. Canuleius) suggests that the former survived additional service, dying soon after a return to Capua. The *monumentum* to the two brothers was erected by their father, who had perhaps followed the surviving son to his allotment, and so was on hand to set up the memorial.

When legion VII was re-formed by Octavian in October 43, and a rival formation rather later by Ventidius, many new recruits must have been required to fill out the legions. Once such may be M. Britius Spuri f. (Sylloge 60). His *nomen*, the Campanian-type stele, and the particularly Campanian funerary formula combine to suggest that Britius was linked to a local family; his father was a *libertus*.[63] Britius is described as MILES DE L(*egione*) VII P; the final letter may be suitably expanded to *Paterna* (above, p. 31), which must demonstrate that he had joined Octavian's re-formed legion. As a recruit of 44 he could have secured release in 36 B.C.

No less interesting is the veteran L. Antistius Campanus (Sylloge 65), who fought both for *deus Caesar* and for Octavian before being *deductus in coloniam* to Capua.[64] No rank or legion is ascribed to him, but the restored phrase [*emeritis omnibu*]*s militiae stipe*[*ndiis*] strongly suggests that he began service in the ranks. He is congratulated for selfless benefaction to the community (above, p. 108). His success in local politics (*cumulatio officiorum*) and the wealth upon which he was able to draw—the text mentions a *patrimonium*—suggests an established local family, though there can be no proof.[65] The date of his return to Capua after service can best be placed in 41 or 36 B.C.

Other memorials of veterans belong to the later first century B.C. From Le Curti, the cemetery area outside Capua, comes the tombstone of Q. Felsinius L.f. Fal. who ended his military service as *signifer* in a legion X (Sylloge 62). The *nomen*, not otherwise attested outside Rome, is manifestly Etruscan.[66] Another veteran, L. Magius M.f. Fal. who bears the name of a family long established in the town,[67] served in legion X *Fretensis* (Sylloge 63). Felsinius and Magius could have been settled at Capua after Naulochus, in which the legion X *Fretensis* almost certainly participated (above, p. 31). Finally, from a cemetery outside Capua comes the slab

[62] Cic. *Phil.* xiv. 27, *Fam.* x. 30.
[63] M. W. Frederiksen, loc. cit. (n. 43), 101.
[64] X 3903 = *EJ*² 329 for a full text.
[65] Frederiksen, loc. cit., 119. L. Antistius Campanus, probably his son, less certainly the veteran himself, was *IIvir* at Capua in 13 B.C. (X 3803; above, p. 109).
[66] Schulze, *Eigennamen* 163.
[67] Frederiksen, loc. cit., 117; P. Castrén, *Ordo Populusque Pompeianus* (Roma, 1975), 187.

of C. Sertorius C.f. Labeo (Sylloge 64), described as *class(iarius?)*, perhaps a *miles classicus* of a legion serving on shipboard. He too might have been a settler at Capua in 36.

Puteoli

The promontory round which lay Roman Puteoli first entered history as the site of the Greek colony Dicaearchia, established from Samos. Direct Roman control from 194 B.C., with the foundation of a *colonia maritima,* assisted the growth of the town which quickly became a principal trading centre of peninsular Italy, bustling and cosmopolitan, an entrepôt for expanding trade with the eastern Mediterranean and an outlet for the manufactured goods of Campania.[68] The *ager Puteolanus* in the Late Republic appears to have consisted of a narrow strip of land between the sea and the Phlegraean Fields, extending in the west to the Lucrine Lake and in the east to the chalk and sulphur producing *Colles Leucogaei.*[69]

Given the absence of an extensive *territorium*, it might seem unlikely that Puteoli could ever have been selected as the site of a military colony in the Late Republic. The *Liber Coloniarum* indicates land reallocation by *Augustus*, but the entry has been seen as a casually worded reference to Nero or (better) to Vespasian, long known to have honoured Puteoli.[70] Though Pliny names Puteoli as a *colonia* in a coastal section, Triumviral or Augustan settlement was considered improbable. Indeed Tacitus' description of Nero's work at Puteoli, which reports that the *vetus oppidum* there was given *ius coloniae* in A.D. 60, had prompted some scholars to suppose that Puteoli must have forfeited its colonial status, and so have been eligible for an award in A.D. 60;[71] others had identified, in the phrase *vetus oppidum*, a separate community peopled by the descendants of Greek colonists of Dicaearchia, which was only now brought into equality with the Roman inhabitants.[72] But such ingenuity is quite unnecessary. Tacitus' use of the phrase *vetus oppidum* is non-technical, as elsewhere. He alludes rather to the great antiquity of Puteoli, without constitutional overtones.[73] The status of Puteoli as a *colonia* of the later first century B.C. has been placed beyond all doubt by the occurrence, on a wax tablet dated A.D. 39 from the archive of the Sulpician banking firm at Pompeii, of what may be assumed to be the Julio-Claudian titulature of the town, *colonia Iulia Augusta Puteoli.*[74]

The despatch of colonists may have been accompanied by a substantial extension to the *ager Puteolanus*. It has often been asserted that Vespasian rewarded Puteoli for her prompt adherence to the Flavian cause in 69 by transferring to her

---

[68] C. Dubois, *Pouzzoles Antique* (Paris, 1907); M. W. Frederiksen, *RE* XXIII (1959), *s.v. Puteoli,* 2036–50; R. Annecchino, *Storia di Pozzuoli* (Pozzuoli, 1960); F. Castagnoli, 'Topografia dei campi flegrei', in *I campi flegrei nell'archeologia e nella storia* (Roma, 1977), 41–79.

[69] Dubois, op. cit. (n. 68), 366–71.

[70] *LC* 236. 11.

[71] Pliny *NH* iii. 61; Tac. *Ann.* xiv. 27. Nissen, *IL* II 738–39.

[72] Kornemann 538; Dubois, op. cit. (n. 68), 40; F. Sartori, *Problemi di storia costituzionale italiota* (Roma, 1953), 62 f.

[73] So Frederiksen, loc. cit. (n. 68), 2041. Cf. Tac. *Ann.* xiv. 17, xiii. 48 (*oppidani* at Puteoli), xv. 22 (Pompeii described as *oppidum*).

[74] C. Giordano, 'Nuove tavolette cerate pompeiane', *Rend. Acc. Nap.* xlv (1970), 211–31, no. 6.

jurisdiction a sizeable corridor of Campanian land lying between Liternum and Atella, extending as far north as modern Aversa.[75] Literary evidence makes it tolerably clear that this corridor belonged to Capua in the Late Republic, but inscriptions honouring *cives Puteolani* have been adduced to show that by the late first century A.D. it had passed to Puteoli.[76] The revelation that Puteoli was a *colonia* of the Triumviral or Augustan age provides an alternative and more suitable occasion for the expansion of the *ager Puteolanus*, which would become available for veteran settlement.[77]

Panciera has tentatively linked the above-mentioned transfer of land, from Capua to Puteoli, to the statements of Dio and Velleius on Octavian's activity in the *ager Campanus* in 36 B.C.[78] He supposes that the gift to Capua of Cretan land, and the promise of an aqueduct, were not manifestations of Octavian's generosity and concern for public opinion, but direct compensation for the permanent loss of territory in favour of Puteoli, so that the colony there can best be placed in 36. Yet Dio and Velleius make no reference to Puteoli in their accounts of Octavian's activity in 36, which is described by both as a great boon to Capua. Nevertheless Panciera's suggestion is attractive. Puteoli must have been at a low ebb in the mid 30s, with the cutting of sea communications by Sextus Pompeius, so that the infusion of veterans, and accretions of land, leading to a more balanced economy and a more equitable division of the rich agricultural land of Campania, can be warmly commended. Agrippa's grandson was later patron of the town, which could suggest a connection established in 36; Agrippa's activities on the Campanian coastline are well attested.[79] The famous arched mole at Puteoli (the richly decorated *opus pilarum*) dates from the Augustan period.[80] An amphitheatre of considerable size may belong to this time but could be earlier.[81] On the promontory itself a major temple (the capitolium?) was refurbished at the expense of one member of a prominent merchant family.[82]

Cumae

The acropolis at Cumae, rising in abrupt isolation to the north-west of the Phleg-raean Fields, affords a magnificent view along the Campanian coastline. In its heyday Cumae controlled considerable tracts of the fertile interior, but under

---

[75] Nissen, *IL* II 706, 739 and all commentators down to (and including) Frederiksen, loc. cit. (n. 68), 2053; Laffi, *Adtributio e contributio* (Pisa, 1966), 105.

[76] Cic. *Leg. Agr.* ii. 36–37; *ILLRP* 722, X 1807, 1873 = *ILS* 6331 (Marano), X 3750 = *ILS* 8351 (Aversa), X 3735 (Grumi).

[77] The *Liber Coloniarum* reports (236. 12–13) that allotments were given *veteranis et tribunis legionariis*, apparently under Augustus.

[78] S. Panciera, 'Appunti su Pozzuoli romana', in *I campi flegrei nell'archeologia e nella storia* (Roma, 1977), 191–211.

[79] *ILS* 933; *Atl. Aereofotografico*, tav. 135–36.

[80] Dubois, op. cit. (n. 68), 249–61.

[81] V. Spinazzola, *NS* 1915, 409–15; F. Castagnoli, 'Topografia dei campi Flegrei', in *I campi flegrei nell'archeologia e nella storia* (Roma, 1977), 41–79. This amphitheatre is not to be confused with the larger, and better known, Flavian structure in the town.

[82] For the temple, until recently considered, on the basis of Mommsen's reading of *CIL* X 1613, to have been dedicated to Augustus during his lifetime, see F. Castagnoli, loc. cit. (n. 81).

Roman domination the *ager Cumanus* was confined to the Bacoli peninsula and a strip of low-lying marshy ground along the coast, below the town itself.[83]

It has often been stated, sometimes with confidence, that Cumae became a colony before the death of Augustus, a status it certainly enjoyed by the close of the third century A.D.[84] Agrippa had been active in the *ager Cumanus* and had restored its port-facilities in the troubled years of war against Sextus Pompeius, but by the end of the first century A.D. Cumae was largely deserted, though retaining some charm as a peaceful coastal retreat.[85] The case for including Cumae in any list of military colonies of the Triumviral or Augustan ages depends principally on the interpretation of a group of inscriptions which include the abbreviation C I, normally expanded by scholars into *colonia Iulia*. Two inscriptions bearing this abbreviation were published by Mommsen in the Tenth Volume of the *Corpus* and placed under Cumae. Two more were discovered recently at Puteoli during clearance work in and around the temple on the promontory. All four are listed below:

1. X 3703 = *ILS* 6388   *Sextiae   L.f.Kani/   monumentum   publice/   factum D D C I/ quod ea munifica erga/coloniam fuit*
2. X 3704 = *ILS* 5054   *..Veratio A.f.Pal.Severiano/ equiti Rom. cur.rei p. Tegianensium.....et diem felicissim.III id.Ian.natalis/ dei patri n. venatione .....largiter exhibuit/ Ad honorem quoque duumviratus ....libenter accessit....L D D D C I*
3. Unpublished   *..........Nigro IIIIvir..../ D D C I*[86]
4. Unpublished   *......VII....../......D D C I*

It is evident that the letters D D C I form a fixed group, of which the first two letters can be expanded *decreto decurionum*, and L D D D (on no. 2) as *loco dato decreto decurionum*. The expansion of C I as *coloniae Iuliae* has a number of epigraphic and numismatic parallels, sufficient to show that this would be a recognised abbreviation.[87]

But the connection of the inscriptions with Cumae is open to considerable doubt. Of the two published inscriptions, one was recovered from the *ager Cumanus* (no. 1), the other first seen at Naples (no. 2); but the two recently discovered stones came from Puteoli. The inscription honouring Veratius Severianus (no. 2), first noted at Naples but assigned by Mommsen to Cumae, may also be attributed to Puteoli: the tribe *Palatina* and the mention of a *duumviratus* are appropriate to Puteoli, but not to Cumae where *praetores* governed the town throughout the Empire. Veratius exhibited games to mark the *natalis dei patri n(ostri)*; a cult of *deus patrius* is now firmly anchored at Puteoli.[88] On the other hand, the inscription of Sextia L.f. Kani was discovered *prope lacum Fusari in sepolcreto Cumano;* one

[83] R. F. Paget, 'The Ancient Ports of Cumae', *JRS* lviii (1968), 152–69.

[84] Mommsen, *CIL* X, p. 351 on X 3698 = *ILS* 4175; Pais, *Colonizzazione* 222–23.

[85] Juv. *Sat.* iii. 1–3; Stat. *Silv.* iv. 3. 65–66.

[86] Alluded to by J. H. D'Arms, 'A New Inscribed Base from Fourth Century Puteoli', *PdP* xxvii (1972), 255–70, at 267 n. 41.

[87] Similarly CIS = *colonia Iulia Secundanorum* (Arausio); CIP = *colonia Iulia ?Pia* (Thapsus); CIH = *colonia Iulia Hadrumetum*.

[88] J. H. D'Arms, loc. cit. (n. 86).

need not doubt that the stone was recovered from within the *ager Cumanus*. The Sextii were a prominent family at Puteoli, but are not otherwise known among the few inscriptions from Cumae.[89] Perhaps Sextia had a villa there to which she retired in later life.

The designation C I seems therefore most likely to have belonged to Puteoli, given that the latter is now known to have been a *colonia Iulia*. But difficulties remain: Puteoli's titulature was changed in A.D. 60 to include *Neronensis*, and again under Vespasian to include *Flavia;* the title *Iulia* went out of use. While the inscriptions of Sextia and perhaps Niger may reasonably be assigned to the Julio-Claudian age (the latter on palaeographic grounds), that of Veratius Severianus must have been erected long after the title *Iulia* was replaced. Perhaps the letters C I should be expanded to *colonorum Iuliensium*. The abbreviation occurs in the context of the *ordo decurionum,* and may serve as evidence of a division therein between the *decuriones* of the *Puteolani Veteres* and those of the incoming *Iulienses,* similar to that detected at other colonies in the Late Republic (above, p. 103). The traditional groupings might have been maintained long after the titulature of the town itself had changed.

If, as seems likely, this group of inscriptions is assignable to Puteoli, the remaining evidence in favour of a *colonia* at Cumae is meagre.[90] The town is not accorded this status by the Elder Pliny; the *Liber Coloniarum* records a *colonia* and the despatch of veteran settlers under 'Claudius Caesar', which could refer to work by the young Tiberius, but it is perhaps more likely that the entry relates to the separation of Misenum from the *ager Cumanus* by Claudius himself.[91]

The earlier part of the first century B.C. brought considerable expansion to Cumae, with a new forum area and public buildings laid out to the north-east of the Greek town; a large amphitheatre was constructed outside the wall-circuit to the south. Under Augustus the temples on the acropolis (to Jupiter and to Apollo) were restored and the latter was reorientated to face the forum area.[92] It would be natural that a site rich in association for the Roman people should have received attention at this time, but promotion to colonial status need not have been (and probably was not) a result.

Nuceria

Roman Nuceria lay at the eastern edge of the triangular plain of the River Sarno, cut off by Vesuvius from the main *ager Campanus,* and astride the Via Annia, a natural line of communications with Lucania.[93] A recent ground survey of the

---

[89] For a *porticus Augusti Sextiana* at Puteoli, C. Giordano, 'Nuove tavolette cerate pompeiane', *Rend. Acc. Nap.* xlv (1970), 211–31.

[90] X 3711 reports the town as *municipium*; X 3697 (dating probably to A.D. 7) describes its citizens as *municipes.*

[91] Pliny *NH* iii. 61; *LC* 232. 12; below, p. 210.

[92] W. Johannowsky, *EAA* II (1959), 970–73; A. Gallina, ibid. *Sup.* (1973), 273–74; F. Castagnoli, loc. cit. (n. 81).

[93] M. and A. Fresa, *Nuceria Alfaterna* (Napoli, 1974), the product of a lifetime's investigation by two local antiquaries.

Roman remains of the town has traced the wall-circuit and identified a number of public buildings, including a large amphitheatre whose reticulate facings may date it to the Augustan era.[94]

Appian names Nuceria among the 18 cities designated for settlement after Philippi. The outstanding fertility of the Sarno plain, together with the strategic position of Nuceria astride the Annia, are reasons enough for its selection at that time. Traces of centuriation have been observed by Castagnoli, suggesting a grid containing squares of 200 *iugera*.[95]

Nuceria appears in a Plinian coastal list, but it is not given the designation *colonia*. Pliny's inland list for Campania includes the *Alfaterni*, which should conceal a second reference to the town.[96] The epithet *Alfaterna* is found attached to Nuceria from at least the third century B.C.; its employment was prompted by the need to distinguish between Campanian Nuceria and Nuceria Camellaria, the modern Nocera Umbra.[97] The Nuceria Alfaterna of the Republic was transformed under the Empire into Nuceria Constantia, an epithet which surely derives from the titulature of the post-Philippi *colonia*. The town may therefore have been *colonia Iulia Constantia* (or *Constans*) *Nuceria*.[98] The earliest known inscription which attaches the new epithet to the town has the word-order *Constantia Nuceria*, but other references, from the mid first century A.D. onwards, reverse this order, and it is evident that *Constantia* by then served merely as the distinguishing epithet of the town.[99]

A potential veteran of this time was buried in a family plot in the Sarno valley north of Gragnano (Sylloge 86); it was covered by the ash of Vesuvius in A.D. 79. The chief monument in the group testifies to the local prominence of the veteran's son M. Virtius M.f. Men. Ceraunus, who had been *aedilis* and *IIvir* at Nuceria, being excused the normal *summa honoraria* for the latter post in recognition of his benefactions to the town.[100] The veteran, M. Virtius L.f. had served in legion XIX. A legion bearing this numeral was recruited by Caesar in 49 B.C.; its founder members would be eligible for discharge after Philippi (see above, p. 23). If Virtius

---

[94] M. and A. Fresa, 'Primo contributo alla topografia di Nuceria Alfaterna', *Rend. Acc. Nap.* xxxiii (1958), 177–202; idem, 'L'anfiteatro sepolto di Nocera nel villaggio Grotte', *Att. Acc. Pontaniana* n.s. xix (1969–70), 87–99. The authors prefer to date the amphitheatre to the mid first century A.D., or later.

[95] F. Castagnoli, 'Tracce di centuriazione nei territori di Nocera, Pompei, Nola, Alife, Aquino, Spello', *Rend. Acc. Linc.* ser. 8, xi (1956), 373–78.

[96] *NH* iii. 62, 63.

[97] *CIL* XI, p. 822.

[98] For the epithets *Constantia Iulia* attached to provincial towns, Pliny *NH* iii. 11, 14. The designation *colonia Iulia Constantia* is applied to an illustration in the treatise of Hyginus Gromaticus (Rudorff, Fig. 187). For Santa Constantia in local legend at Campanian Nuceria, a martyr under Nero, G. Orlando, *Storia di Nocera dei Pagani* (Napoli, 1884), 220.

[99] IV 3882 = *ILS* 5146. Also VI 2379b, col. 9, 5–6; VI 32526a, col. 1, 18; *AE* 1926, 122; *NS* 1958, 144 no. 349; *LC* 235. 20. For a freedman with the *nomen* Constantius, above, p. 19.

[100] J. Reynolds and E. Fabbricotti, 'A Group of Inscriptions from Stabiae', *PBSR* xl (1972), 127–34 no. 10. The name Ceraunus could derive from his father's military service; it was also a surname given to or adopted by great rulers (Plut. *Arist.* 6).

is accepted as a recipient of a post-Philippi allotment, the findspot of the monument near Gragnano should be a pointer to the location of the allotment itself in the *ager Nucerinus*.[101]

Nola

The town of Nola lay also on the Via Annia, its fertile *territorium* stretching from the summit of Vesuvius to the Samnite foothills.[102] Various strands of evidence point to the establishment of a *colonia* by Sulla.[103] Colonial status from the later first century B.C. is undisputed; Nola is recorded as a *colonia* by Pliny, and *IIviri* are attested under the early Empire.[104] One inscription of Diocletianic date reports the town as *col(onia) Fel(ix) Aug(usta) Nola*. The date or dates at which *Augusta* and *Felix* were awarded to the town remain unclear; other less durable epithets may have been suppressed before the close of the third century A.D. (above, p. 19). Nola became a cult centre of *divus Augustus*, who died there in a house which had belonged to his father; a temple to him was consecrated there by Tiberius in A.D. 26.[105] Little is known about the town itself: an amphitheatre of tufa bricks but with *opus reticulatum* foundations is recorded. Roman Nola probably extended somewhat further to the west and south than its modern counterpart, but much has disappeared since the early sixteenth century when the antiquarian Ambrogio Leone noted substantial remains.[106]

---

[101] On the findspot, F. di Capua, 'Contributi all'epigrafia e alla storia della antica Stabia', *Rend. Acc. Nap.* xix (1938–39), 102, with the review by A. Degrassi, *Epigraphica* i (1939), 353–54. The *nomen* Virtius could suggest an origin in north Italy (Schulze, *Eigennamen* 253).

[102] E. La Rocca, *Introduzione allo studio di Nola antica* (1972), 13 ff.

[103] E. Gabba, *Ricerche* 235; *LC* 236. 5; *ILS* 6344 (above, p. 102).

[104] *NH* iii. 63; X 1233, 1236 etc.; CIL X, p. 142.

[105] Beloch, *Campanien* (Breslau, 1890), 404 with Tac. *Ann.* iv. 57; Suet. *Tib.* 40; Dio lvi. 46.

[106] Beloch, op. cit. (n. 105), 402–6; E. La Rocca, op. cit. (n. 102), 71 ff.; G. Cressedi, *EAA* V (1963), 537. For centuriation in the *ager Nolanus* on two alignments, so confirming Sic. Flacc. 162. 3–5, F. Castagnoli, loc. cit. (n. 95).

CHAPTER SEVEN

LUCANIA, SAMNIUM AND APULIA

Paestum

The southern part of the coastal plain of the Sele river formed in antiquity the territory of a single city, Paestum, long flourishing as the Greek colony Poseidonia. [1] In his authoritative survey of southern Italy under the Empire, Ulrich Kahrstedt described the Late Republic and Early Empire as 'die Zeit der grossen Depression' in the history of Paestum, [2] a conclusion based to a considerable degree on the scantiness of the epigraphic material available for study. This conclusion must now be viewed with some scepticism; the publication in 1968 of the enlarged epigraphic corpus for Paestum increased sevenfold the number of inscriptions available for study. [3] Kahrstedt's thesis, of an indifferent existence for Paestum in the first and second centuries A.D., followed by a revival in the third and fourth, can no longer stand, as at least half of the known inscriptions date from the former period. [4]

A Latin colony from 273 B.C., Paestum presumably became a *municipium* after the Social War, but its status in the last decades of the Republic has been the subject of much scholarly debate. The town is described as an *oppidum* by Pliny. [5] Our knowledge is enriched (some would say confused) by numismatic data: almost alone among the towns of Italy, Paestum after the Social War is found issuing a bronze coinage, the emission of which was kept up until the reign of Tiberius. [6] A majority of coins carry the names of magistrates responsible for their issue; many are specifically described as *IIIIviri* and *IIviri,* the latter forming a substantial majority. This change in title has been taken as an indication of the alteration in Paestum's status from *municipium* to *colonia.* Mommsen argued from a combination of the numismatic and epigraphic evidence accessible to him that this change could best be placed under Caesar or the Triumvirs, though elsewhere he left open the possibility that Paestum might have been a Sullan foundation. [7] The latter alternative, already proposed by Beloch, was enthusiastically adopted by Rudolph, while Nissen had

---

[1] P. C. Sestieri, *Paestum* (Roma, 1968); M. Mello, *Paestum romana* (Roma, 1974); *Atl. Aereofotografico,* tav. lxii–iii.

[2] *Die wirtschaftliche Lage der Grossgriechenlands in der Kaiserzeit* (Wiesbaden, 1960 = *Historia Einzelschriften* 4), 8; idem. 'Ager Publicus und Selbstverwaltung in Lukanien und Bruttium', *Historia* viii (1959), 174–206.

[3] M. Mello and G. Voza, *Le iscrizioni latine di Paestum* (Napoli, 1968); hereafter cited as *ILP.*

[4] Paestum's amphitheatre, which could be assigned an Augustan date, lies next to the forum, a siting which may be indicative of depopulation. Strabo reports (v. 4. 13) that the town-site of Paestum was malarial, but possible effects on the inland *ager Paestanus* are not known. Bradysism as a factor in the supposed decline of Paestum is now largely discounted; A. Maiuri, 'Origine e decadenza di Paestum', *PdP* vi (1951), 274–86; M. Mello, 'Strabone v. 4, 13 e le origini di Poseidonia', *PdP* xxii (1967), 401–24.

[5] *NH* iii. 71.

[6] R. Garrucci, *Le monete dell'Italia antica* (Roma, 1885), 179–82, tav. cxxii–iii; R. S. Poole, BMC, Greek Coins, *Italy* (London, 1873), 274–82.

[7] *CIL* X, pp. 52–53; idem, *Bürgercolonien* 167.

earlier made the improbable suggestion that a colonial foundation might have followed in the wake of the devastation of Lucania by Spartacus.[8]

Serious study of the coinage was initiated by Grant, who professed to be able to show that the town was governed by *IIIviri* until about 60–55 B.C., after which there was a change to *IIviri,* though he envisaged no transfer to colonial status at that time.[9] His conclusions were based on the double criteria of coin-types copied from Rome-mint issues, and a gradual decrease in weight throughout this period, the latter allowing the coins to be placed in an approximate sequence, the former establishing a *terminus post quem* (though not necessarily any closer connection in date) for the Paestum issues. One issue he linked directly to be foundation process of the colony, which he dated to 36–25 B.C.[10] However, M. H. Crawford has demonstrated recently that the numismatic evidence provides no real clue to the date of colonial foundation; the issue adduced by Grant reports rather a banquet given by representatives of two prominent local families.[11] It is Crawford's thesis that the coinage at Paestum was primarily euergetic, i.e. minted for distribution to *cives Paestani* on the occasion of shows and festivals. Hence the frequency of issue could be indicative of fluctuations in the fortunes of the well-to-do local families.

Until recently, no evidence was available on the titulature of the town. However, Mello and Voza included in their corpus of inscriptions two fragments of a marble slab honouring a military tribune who settled veterans at Paestum on Vespasian's behalf in A.D. 71.[12] The town is described as *colonia Flavia Prima,* i.e. 'First in loyalty to the Flavian dynasty'.[13] Neither *Iulia* nor *Augusta* appears, but we could suppose that one or both were suppressed at the foundation of Vespasian's colony.

Effectively the case for the inclusion of Paestum as a colony of the Late Republic rests on the alteration in the titulature of its magistrates from *IIIviri* to *IIviri.* A number of Italian towns were reconstituted as *municipia* in the Caesarian age, and their magistrates appear subsequently as *IIviri,*[14] but there is no direct parallel for such activity in a former Latin colony, which presumably already possessed all the normal machinery of a *municipium* in the aftermath of the Social War.

From the epigraphic evidence we know of the *IIviri* Claudius and Sex(s)tilius, whose inscribed fountainheads testify to improvements in the system of water

---

[8] Beloch, *RG* 512; H. Rudolph, *Stadt und Staat im römischen Italien* (Göttingen, 1935), 93 n. 3; Nissen, *IL* II 894.

[9] *FITA* 200–4, 284–89.

[10] *FITA* 284. The legend reads: L VENE/ D FAD EPVL DED, expanded by Grant to *L. Venedius D. Fadius epulo deduxerunt.*

[11] 'Paestum and Rome: The Form and Function of a subsidiary Coinage', in *La monetazione di bronzo di Poseidonia-Paestum,* published as a *Supplemento* to *AIIN* xviii–xix (1973); idem., 'The imperial bronze coinage of Paestum', *AIIN* xxiii–iv (1976–77), 151–59. Crawford expands the coin legend as *L. Venedius D. Fadius epulum dederunt.*

[12] *ILP* 86.

[13] Cf. Pliny NH v. 69: *Caesarea . . . ab Herode rege condita, nunc colonia Prima Flavia a Vespasiano deducta;* Galsterer-Kröll, *Beinamen,* no. 527; ibid. no. 499 on Comama.

[14] A. N. Sherwin-White, *Roman Citizenship* (Oxford, 1973), 159 ff.; M. W. Frederiksen, 'Changes in the Pattern of Settlement', in P. Zanker (ed.), *Hellenismus in Mittelitalien* (Göttingen, 1976), 341–55.

distribution in the town; Claudius and Sex(s)tilius seem unlikely to have held office much after 50 B.C.[15] A tribune, probably of Augustan date, is revealed as a magistrate and *patronus municipi;* another inscription refers to *municipes viri,* but is less easy to date.[16] A stone honouring Q. Ceppius Maximus as *patronus coloniae* has been considered Augustan, but it could belong much later.[17] A scrutiny of the combined epigraphic and numismatic evidence suggests a continuity in the leading families of the town from the period of the Latin colony to the Empire, without any hint of disruption caused by a colonial foundation.[18]

In order to reconcile the apparently conflicting strands of evidence, it could be supposed that Paestum became a colony with *IIviri,* perhaps under Sulla, but that the colony was soon suppressed in favour of a *municipium,* which persisted until Vespasian established the *colonia Flavia Prima.* Decisive proof of a Late Republican foundation is still to seek.

Beneventum

That Beneventum, a centre of Roman communications in the South, received veteran colonists in 41 B.C. after Philippi is not open to doubt; it was one of the 18 designated cities. The memorial to L. Munatius Plancus at Gaieta states that he *agros divisit in Italia Beneventi.*[19] No date is given for this activity, but it can hardly belong to any other point in time. We may assume that the town now acquired some or all of its titles *Iulia Concordia Felix;* later it became a *colonia Augusta.*[20]

A substantial number of veteran-epitaphs have survived from the *ager Beneventanus* and its adjuncts (below, p. 160). Most belong to one or other of two legions, VI and XXX. In only one instance is a title found attached to a legion — VI *Ferrata,* thus identifying the legion VI to which all the veterans of that legion at Beneventum presumably belonged (Sylloge 36). In my view both legions were settled at Beneventum after Philippi. Caesar's Sixth legion, raised during the later stages of the Gallic War, was temporarily reduced after the Alexandrian campaign to an active strength of less than 1,000 men; in 45 B.C. its members received land at Arelate in Narbonensis (above, p. 50). Re-formed by Lepidus, it passed in 43 B.C. to Antony, and remained with him thereafter, fighting in the Parthian War; after Actium it was incorporated into Octavian's army.

---

[15] X 480, *ILP* 144–53; *ILLRP* 636.

[16] *ILP* 68–69. Scrutiny of the enlarged epigraphic corpus could suggest that the tribune was the husband of, or otherwise related to, the benefactress Mineia, whose family was prominent in the town in the Augustan age, which would help to date his holding of the patronate. His *nomen* is restored by Mello and Voza as Flaccinius (*ILP* 68), but could be Flacceius (cf. *ILP* 156–58).

[17] *NS* 1890, 92 = *EE* VIII 288; *ILP,* p. 196 n. 3.

[18] A. Degrassi, 'Il collegio di cinque questori della colonia latina di Paestum', *Rend. Acc. Nap.* xli (1966), 71–72 = *SVA* IV, 65–66; G. Voza, 'Questori della colonia di Paestum', *Arch. Class.* xix (1967), 98–105; M. Mello, *Paestum romana* (Roma, 1974), 89 no. 159. Notice a Ciceronian reference to Fadii and Sexstilii (*Fin.* ii. 55), who could perhaps be localised at Paestum.

[19] App. *BC* iv. 3; *ILS* 886. For the town and its monuments, A. Meomartini, *I monumenti e le opere d'arte della città di Benevento* (Bergamo, 1889); M. Rotili, *Il museo del Sannio* (Roma, 1967).

[20] Above, p. 20. The *Liber Coloniarum* reports work initiated by *Nero Claudius Caesar* (231. 6) which may be datable to the Augustan age (above, p. 9).

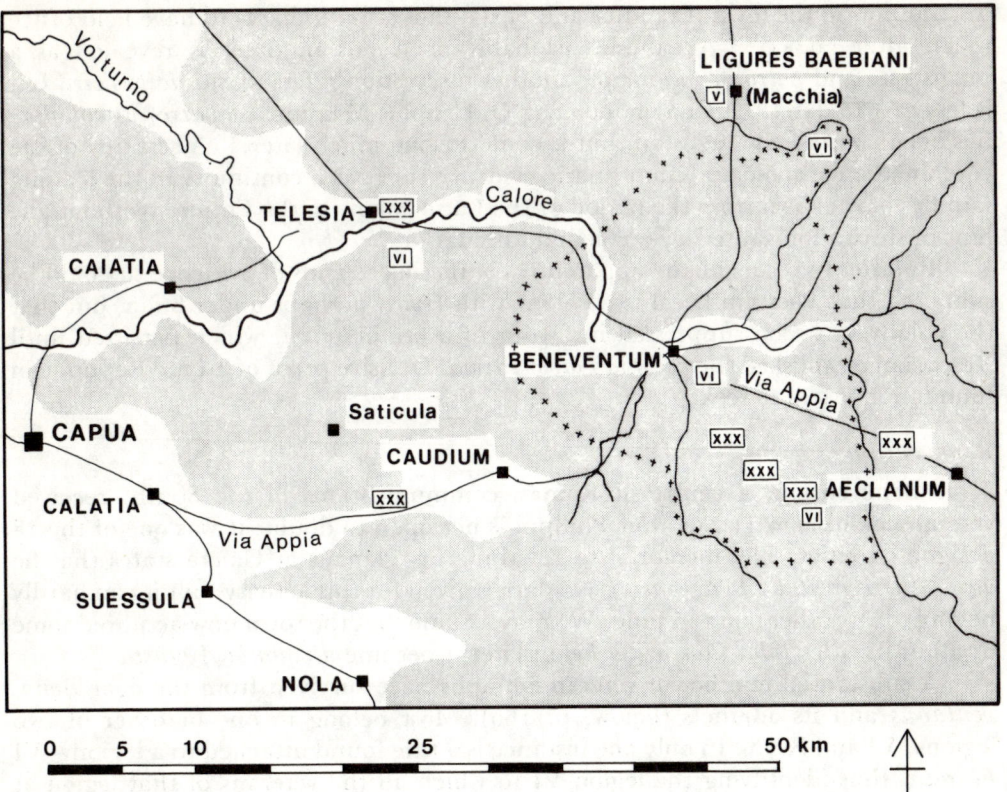

+ + + Suggested boundaries of the **ager Beneventanus** before 41 B.C.

☐VI Findspot of inscription, with numeral of legion

FIG. 8: VETERANS AT BENEVENTUM

The date of formation of legion XXX can be established without difficulty: it was one of those legions raised in 49 in preparation for the struggle against Pompey.[21] Almost at once it was despatched to Spain, and in 44 was one of the legions under the command of Asinius Pollio in the province of Hispania Ulterior. As a unit of Pollio's command, legion XXX would naturally pass to Antony after Mutina. Its founder members could expect release after Philippi; we do not know that it survived the reorganisation after that battle.[22] The land commissioner at Beneventum in 41 was L. Munatius Plancus, praetorian governor of Transalpine Gaul for Antony in 44–3, and consul in 42.[23] His presence at Beneventum in 41 by itself suggests that the *ager Beneventanus* has been set aside for Antonian veterans among the soldiers of Caesar. It is unlikely that Octavian would have considered Plancus suitable to supervise the settlement of his own veterans.

[21] Ritterling, *Legio* 1821.

[22] For Sylloge 76, the epitaph of a veteran of legion XXX *Classica* at Locri, above, p. 71. Coins reporting a legion XXX with Antony are not now accepted as genuine (above, p. 27).

[23] R. Jullien, *Le Fondateur de Lyon* (Lyon, 1892); A. Masi, 'La 'praefectura urbi' di Lucio Munazio Planco e l'iscrizione del Mausoleo di Gaieta', in *Studi in onore di Edouardo Volterra* v (Milano, 1971), 239–50, with bibliography at 240 n. 10.

Nine inscriptions referring to men of legion VI (11 if the restoration of V to VI is allowed in two cases) have been recovered from Beneventum and the *ager Beneventanus,* and 11 from legion XXX (14 if restorations are permitted). The large proportion of damaged stones will be noticed. In two instances, only the use of a distinctive format allows positive inclusion (Sylloge 45, 50). All but one of the known veterans have adopted the local tribe *Stellatina.*

At least 10 memorials were first reported well away from Beneventum itself (see Fig. 8). Three members of legion XXX are reported south of the town at Le Pastine, Sciarra and at Pietra de' Fusi, another on the line of the Appia over against Aeclanum. Two from legion VI were found further out from the town, at Pago to the north-east and at Venticane to the south.[24] If it is possible to draw any valid conclusions from the distribution, it may be that a block of land south-east of Beneventum was distributed to men of legion XXX. Another veteran is reported at Arpaia on land which must originally have belonged to Caudium (legion XXX), and two on *ager Telesinus,* at Telesia itself and at Solopaca (XXX and VI). A veteran of the legion V *Alaudae* is known at the town-site of Ligures Baebiani, but it is not clear that he need have had any link with the colony at Beneventum (below, p. 159).

An examination of nomenclature is of little help in establishing the origins of individual veterans or the recruiting grounds of either legion. Many of the *nomina* are so rare that no other certain occurrences are known. The veteran Tetarfenus has a distinctly Etruscan name, and Figilius could be a local man, from Samnium or Lucania. The name Aequanius may suggest a Central Italian background.[25] Brothers and parents are recorded, who may have shared in the work of the new allotment; *liberti* and *libertae* of veterans abound, but only in a very few cases can any picture of the family and social connections of the veterans be built up. M. Crassicius Castellus may have been the father or grandfather of L. Crassicius who became *IIvir* of the colony early in the first century A.D. Castellus' wife seems to have come from a local family.[26] C. Lisidius M.f. supervised the erection of a tombstone for himself, his parents, and members of his *familia*; his father's tribe *Publilia* could indicate an origin in Latium or Cisalpina — the father might assist Lisidius on the farm and a home was thus provided for his parents in their old age; in Italy the *nomen* recurs in this spelling only once outside Rome, at nearby Ligures Baebiani where a C. Lisidius Modestus served as decurion. His activity there could testify to the general location of the veteran's allotment within the enlarged *ager Beneventanus.*[27] M. Albius, *signifer* of legion XXX, was buried alongside two freed-women, one Albia Hilara manumitted by himself, the other Curtia P.l. Chila, the latter conceivably deriving her name from the family of the veteran Sal. Curtius L.f. As Curtius' own monument was erected by his daughter Polla, who died at the age of 12, it is not clear that this family was able to become established in the town, though *liberti* and *libertae* are attested.[28] The *nomen* Clodius, never rare, occurs frequently

[24] Another (Sylloge 36) was reported by Pratilli as seen on the line of the Appia east of Beneventum, between the first and second milestones.

[25] Schulze, *Eigennamen* 242 (Tetarfenus), 261 (Figilius), 355 (Aequanius).

[26] IX 1643 (son?), 2008. Wife's family: IX 1650, 1828, *AE* 1925, 116.

[27] IX 1462, 1693 (Beneventum); Schulze, *Eigennamen* 181 for Lissidii at Spoletium.

[28] IX 1807–9, 2086.

at Beneventum: two veterans bear the name — P. Clodius P.f. Pius, for whom no family is indicated, and C. Clodius P.f., who was buried with his wife Valeria Diodora. The two veterans may have been brothers: both served in legion XXX. The veteran C. Numisius Q.f. was buried with his freedmen around him; no family is known, but the *nomen* recurs frequently in the town. Other names do not re-appear at all within the territory of Beneventum, despite the enormous epigraphic corpus available. Two inscriptions state that veterans held municipal office at Beneventum: the centurion Avidienus became *decurio*; and a ranker whose name is lost was elected *aedilis* (above, p. 109; Sylloge 31, 39).

It has long been perceived, from the literary and epigraphic evidence, that the territory of Beneventum was enlarged at this time.[29] Confirmation is provided by the findspots of the veteran-epitaphs, several of which come from beyond the natural boundaries of the *ager Beneventanus*. That the entire *ager Caudinus* was earmarked for settlement and transferred to the jurisdiction of Beneventum is an obvious deduction from a boastful inscription of Severan date, giving the grandiose titulature of the colony, which was set up by the *colonia Beneventana* close to the western extremity of the *ager Caudinus* (near Arpaia in the Caudine Forks), to greet the traveller on the Appia arriving from the west.[30]

Some land belonging to Ligures Baebiani also passed to Beneventum. Evidence for reallocation derives from the well known Alimentary Table of Trajanic date. From details of land holding which it contains, Mommsen concluded that the territory of Ligures Baebiani passed likewise in its entirety to Beneventum, and in a more recent study P. Veyne, after some initial hesitation, appears to concur.[31] Each entry in the Alimentary Table gives the general geographical location of every farm pledged, sometimes simply with the name of the *pagus* in which it lay, in other cases giving the additional information that the *pagus* lay *pertică Beneventanā, finibus Beneventanorum*, or *in Beneventano*.[32] There is no agreement on the precise meaning of each phrase, but the term *pertica Beneventana* seems best used to describe the former territory of Ligures Baebiani, which had passed to Beneventum;[33] *in Beneventano* could be applied to the original nucleus of Bene-ventane territory, and the term *finibus Beneventanorum* may identify a district lying on the border between the two towns.[34] Many of the *pagi* have no extra descriptive phrase attached and it is simplest to suppose that these were lands under the jurisdiction of Ligures Baebiani. Only those areas not under the latter's control required a special description. Nine *pagi* are described as being *in Beneventano*, but the phrase *pertica Beneventana* occurs with reference to only a single *pagus*,

[29] Beloch, *RG* 541; Thomsen, *It. Regions,* 75.

[30] *ILS* 6488.

[31] *ILS* 6509; Mommsen, *CIL* IX, p. 128; P. Veyne, 'La table de Ligures Baebiani et l'institution alimentaire se Trajan', *Mél. d'Arch. et Hist.* lxix (1957), 81–135; ibid. lxx (1958), 177–241; idem, 'Contributio: Bénévent, Capoue, Cirta', *Latomus* xviii (1959), 568–92.

[32] Nine *pagi* are named as lying partly or wholly *in Beneventano*, one as lying *pertică Beneventanā*, and one as lying *finibus Beneventanorum*.

[33] Cf. Sic. Flacc. 160. 8 ff. One farmstead is described as lying *pertica Nolana*, which may imply some transference of land to Nola, perhaps when the latter became a colony. Nola shared no border with Ligures Baebiani.

[34] Or in the ownership of the *respublica Beneventanorum*.

and *finibus Beneventanorum* is found only once. This could suggest that the
expropriation of land at the expense of Ligures Baebiani was not extensive. The
frequent reference to land lying *in Beneventano* may testify rather to the poverty of
Ligures Baebiani, which had to call upon landowners within the territory of Beneventum to make up a viable alimentary scheme. Other details on the settlement at
Beneventum may perhaps be culled from the Alimentary Table: something can be
learnt of estate sizes in the territory of Beneventum, which may offer a clue to the
size of allotments distributed in the Late Republic;[35] the farm-names listed on the
Table may serve to identify veterans not attested epigraphically.[36]

Whether the same (partial) annexation of territory in the interest of Beneventum applied to the shadowy town of Ligures Corneliani is unknown.[37] Both the
ager Cornelianus and the *ager Baebianus* were allotted to veterans according to the
Liber Coloniarum, which places that event *post bellum Augustianum*.[38] It is
probable that part of the *ager Telesinus* passed to Beneventum. A veteran of legion
XXX has long been known at Telesia itself; another, of legion VI, has recently come
to light at Solopaca.[39]

The town-site of Ligures Baebiani has yielded the epitaph of C. Valerius C.f.
Aem. Arsaces, a veteran of legion V *Alaudae* (Sylloge 55). The *cognomen* suggests
service in the East under Antony, in his Parthian War. The *nomen* may indicate a
provincial enfranchised to join the legion when Italian recruiting grounds were
denied to Antony.[40] On the other hand, we may prefer to see Valerius as an Italian
who adopted a distinctive surname to commemorate his participation in the
Parthian War. His tribe *Aemilia* is not apparently that of Ligures Baebiani itself
(probably *Velina*) nor of Beneventum (*Stellatina*).[41] Valerius could be an *evocatus*

---

[35] Of 13 single estates lying *in Beneventano* or *perticā Beneventanā*, nine are given a value of
50,000 or 60,000 sesterces. Perhaps these represent allotments given to veterans after Philippi. If a
satisfactory valuation per *iugerum* could be established for land in Italy at this time, we might
calculate their extent. Cf. J. Kromayer, 'Die wirtschaftliche Entwicklung Italiens im II und I
Jahrhundert vor Chr.', *NJ Klass. Alt.* xvii (1914), 145–69.

[36] The following names were attached to farms lying *in Beneventano*: Pomponius, Rubrius,
Caesius, Albius, Amarantius, Surius, Annius, Veiaeus, Curius, Munatius, Profius, Bassius, Valerius,
Plinius, Vettius, Nonius, Petronius, Vergilius, Vedius. A *fundus Sestianus* is reported as lying *finibus
Beneventanorum*, and a *fundus Pastorianus* as lying *perticā Beneventanā*. The *fundus Munatianus* can
be linked to the colony's founder, and the *fundus Vedianus* to P. Ve(i)dius Pollio (below, p. 160). In four
cases, farm-names in the Table coincide with names of known veterans (*Albianus*, *Clodianus*,
Curtianus, *Flavianus*), but none of the latter are stated to lie in Beneventane territory. If the farm-
names do reflect their veteran-owners of 41 B.C., then comparison with the names of owners under
Trajan reveals a substantial turnover in the century and a half which had elapsed.

[37] *CIL* IX, p. 125.

[38] *LC* 235. 9.

[39] Sylloge 53–54. Mommsen considered that Solopaca lay within the old territory of Beneventum
(*CIL* IX, end map), but Thomsen placed it within the *ager Telesinus* (*It. Regions*, 75–76). A
sculptured panel on Trajan's Arch at Beneventum portrays four turreted city-personifications, who
look on while Trajan distributes loaves to his subjects. If the relief has any local significance, the city to
whom the central position is assigned can plausibly be identified as Beneventum. Candidates for the
other three, who are subordinate but not subservient, should be Caudium, Ligures Baebiani, Ligures
Corneliani and Telesia; P. Veyne, 'Contributio: Bénévent, Capoue, Cirta', *Latomus* xviii (1959),
568–92.

[40] Ritterling, *Legio* 1565.

[41] For *Velina*, IX 1465, *EE* VIII 92; but *Aemilia* recurs on *EE* VIII 91.

returning after extended service to an allotment of an earlier, perhaps Caesarian, scheme (above, p. 80). But note two other veterans (Sylloge 28, 40), perhaps of the same legion. Extensions to the *ager Beneventanus* are perhaps not surprising, if veterans of two (or more) legions were to be accommodated in a conspicuously hilly terrain. The flat plain below Caudium would be a welcome accretion, so also would be the low-lying ground west of Telesia. A grid of *centuriae* is reported by the *Liber Coloniarum*; it could belong to the Latin colony of 268 B.C., but no traces have been observed on the ground.

Of public buildings of the Augustan age we are ill-informed. Some of the town-gates were probably built or rebuilt at this time.[42] The rich and influential P. Veidius Pollio, agent and one-time friend of Augustus, financed the construction of a Caesareum dedicated *imperatori Caesari Augusto et coloniae Beneventanae*; one of his freedmen was an *augustalis* of the town and could have officiated at sacrifices in the Caesareum.[43]

LIST OF VETERANS AT BENEVENTUM
(a) Stones first reported at Beneventum itself

Sylloge	name	legion	rank	family, etc.
29	L. Acilius A.f. Ste.	VI	(miles)	wife
30	M. Albius M.f. Ste.	XXX	signifer	liberti
31	Avidienus T.f. Ste.	...	centurio	—[44]
32	C. Clodius P.f. Ste.	XXX	(miles)	wife
33	C. Figilius L.f. Ste.	VI	(miles)	wife
34	T. Flavius T.f. Ste. Titullus	XX	(miles)	libertus[45]
35	M. Crassicius M.f. Ste. Castellus	XXX	(miles)	wife[46]
38	...[P]ompeius T.f. Ste.	XXX	(miles)	—
39	.........Stel.	VI	(miles)	wife
40	T. Ruf.....ius	V..	(miles)	wife
41	......ius C.f. Ste.	VI	(miles)	liberti, son
42	A. Silanus ..f. Ste.	II?	signifer	brother[47]
43	Q. Tetarfen[us L.f. Ste.]	VI	(miles)	brother
44	.......inius T.f. Ste.	XXX	(miles)	heres
45	.........Sp.f. Ste.	..X	(miles)	wife?[48]

[42] Blake 203.

[43] *ILS* 5067. Pollio seems to have maintained an establishment at Beneventum, and may have been a local man; IX 1702, 1894, 2018, *EE* VIII 101; R. Syme, 'Who was Vedius Pollio?', *JRS* li (1961), 23–30.

[44] The *nomen* is probably complete; Schulze, *Eigennamen* 105; Hor. *Sat.* ii. 2. 55.

[45] The 'Flavian' nomenclature could suggest a later period, but formulae and format require an Augustan dating.

[46] As printed in *CIL* IX 1610, lines 2–3 are read as:
    M CRASSICIO M F STE CASTELLO
       VIRO   PRO   LEG   XXX
The letters PRO were expanded by Mommsen to *probo,* an adjective in agreement with *viro.* Mommsen had evidently not seen the stone himself, but adopted the reading of Verusius, in preference to the testimony of other scholars. In fact line 3 of the stone, now at the Museo del Sannio in Benevento, reads VIRO LEG XXX.

[47] Mommsen proposed that line 2 of the inscription should read L F STE LEG II, but any link with such a legion remains tenuous. SICIL could be an abbreviated *origo* or *cognomen*.

[48] Not classified in *CIL* IX as a military inscription. The format, however, suggests that it commemorates a veteran of the later first century B.C.

Sylloge	name	legion	rank	family, etc.
50	L. Romanius	XX.	(miles)	family[49]
51	C. Numisius Q.f. Stel.	VI	(miles)	liberti[50]

(b) Stones first reported in the *ager Beneventanus*

28	......onius P.f. Ste.	V	(miles)	liberti
Pago				
36	L. Labicius L.f. Ste. Celer	VI	(miles)	—
on the Via		*Ferrata*		
Appia, east of				
Beneventum				
37	C. Lisidius M.f. Ste.	XXX	(miles)	parents, liberti
on the Via				
Appia, over				
against				
Aeclanum				
46	P. Sertorius M.f. Ste.	VI	(miles)	brother
Venticane				
47	.....lius ..f. Ste.	XXX	(miles)	—
Pietra de'				
Fusi				
48	P. Clodius P.f. Ste. Pius	XX.	(miles)	—
Sciarra				
49	Sal. Curtius L.f. Stel.	XXX	(miles)	wife,
Le Pastine				daughter[51]

(c) Stone first reported in the *ager Caudinus*

52	Sex. Aequanius Sex. f. Stel.	XXX	(miles)	—
Arpaia				

(d) Stones first reported in the *ager Telesinus*

53	P. Manlius P.f. Stel.	XXX	(miles)	—
Telesia				
54	L. Caienus Q.f. Vel.	VI	(miles)	—
Solopaca				

(e) Stone first reported at Macchia (town-site of Ligures Baebiani)

55	C. Valerius C.f. Aem. Arsaces	V	(miles)	concubina
		Alaudae		

Bovianum

The town site of Bovianum (modern Boiano) lies on the north-eastern flank of the Monte del Matese massif, in the uppermost reaches of the Biferno valley. The plain immediately below the town, the most extensive area of flat land in central Samnium, formed its *territorium*. The modern name, geographical position, and general context in Livian narratives combine to prove beyond serious doubt that modern Boiano is the site of Roman Bovianum, *caput Pentrorum Samnitium*.

[49] Published by Fr. Ribezzo, 'Epigrafia latina. Iscrizioni inedite di Benevento', *Rivista Indo-Greco-Italica* viii (1924), 147–50 no. 9; never included in *AE*.

[50] For the readings adopted here, P. Cavuoto, 'Iscrizioni inedite di Benevento', *Epigraphica* xxx (1968), 126–55 no. 10. The editors of *AE* 1968 (at no. 127) suggest LEONI for LEG VI in line 3, without good reason, as autopsy makes clear.

[51] Note a reference to this stone in *Epigraphica* iii (1941), 169 no. 1490, recording a change of location; hence *AE* 1945, 121 where the stone is acclaimed as a fresh discovery, as it is by Gabba, *Colonie triumvirali* 104 n. 2.

Little is known of its street-layout or monuments; alluvium and earthquake damage have removed almost every vestige.[52]

Until recently it had been accepted by scholars that there were somewhere in central Samnium two towns bearing the name Bovianum, i.e. Bovianum Vetus and Bovianum Undecumanorum, the latter located at Boiano itself, the former at Pietrabbondante, 40 kms. to the north. This belief was based principally on Pliny's testimony: *Samnitium . . . colonia Bovianum Vetus et alterum cognomine Undecumanorum.* That Pliny was here listing two separate towns, one or both as colonies, was endorsed by Mommsen, who adduced Oscan and Latin inscriptions in support, and sought to assign literary references to 'Bovianum' to one or other of these sites. He concluded that Bovianum Vetus (at Pietrabbondante) was a *colonia* of the later first century B.C., and that Bovianum Undecumanorum achieved that status at the hands of Vespasian.[53]

However, recent archaeological work at Pietrabbondante, while highlighting that site's function as a religious and festival centre for the population of highland Samnium, has indicated that occupation ceased almost completely in the early first century B.C.[54] Mommsen's translation of an Oscan inscription which appeared to name this site as Bovianum had already been questioned, and rejected, by Vetter.[55] The ancient name for Pietrabbondante is not known. Geographical considerations count heavily against the selection as a *colonia* of this rather bleak highland site, isolated from any known Roman highway, and with little good agricultural land in its immediate vicinity.[56]

Pliny nevertheless appears to state that there were two towns called Bovianum. He could be recording a township which moved downwards from its hill-top site in the last century of the Republic, perhaps as a direct result of the establishment of the *colonia*; the nucleus of Samnite Bovianum is thought to lie on one or all of three hills immediately above the Roman and modern town.[57] However, the descent to a lower site was a common occurrence; we should not expect Pliny to make special reference to it. Another solution is preferable: Pliny's 'inland' lists frequently record the inhabitants of individual towns in adjectival form, a practice which may reflect arrangement of material in his Augustan source (see above, p. 5). The inland list for Samnium which Pliny had available could therefore have read *Bovianenses Veteres, Bovianenses cognomine Undecumani,* or *Bovianenses Veteres et qui*

---

[52] Nissen, *IL* II 791; M. Floriani Squarciapino, *EAA* II (1959), 122–23.

[53] Pliny *NH* iii. 107; Mommsen, *CIL* IX, pp. 257, 239.

[54] A. La Regina, 'Le iscrizioni osce di Pietrabbondante e la questione di Bovianum Vetus', *Rhein. Mus.* cix (1966), 260–86.

[55] E. Vetter, *Handbuch der italischen Dialekte* I (Heidelberg, 1953), no. 150; A. La Regina, loc. cit. (n. 54).

[56] The attempt by A. di Iorio, *Bovianum Vetus oggi Pietrabbondante* (Roma, 1974) to reinstate Pietrabbondante as Bovianum Vetus need not be entertained. M. M. Chiari, 'Terventum', *Quad. Ist. Top. Ant.* vi (1974), 143–82 argues that Pietrabbondante lay in antiquity within the territory of Terventum.

[57] E. T. Salmon, *Samnium and the Samnites* (Cambridge, 1967), pl. 2. Some polygonal walling has been noted on one of the hillocks, the modern Civita Superiore.

cognominantur Undecumani.[58] On analogy with his entries for Clusium and Arretium, this description should indicate a distinction at Bovianum between *Veteres* and *Undecumani.*

It was Mommsen's contention that Boiano (which he identified as Bovianum Undecumanorum) achieved colonial status only in the Flavian period, with the establishment of veterans of legion XI *Claudia pia fidelis.*[59] The belief in a Flavian settlement has been endorsed even by the most recent commentator, La Regina, who has argued that Pliny refers here to a reinforcement under Vespasian of an existing, Triumviral or Augustan, *colonia.*[60] Mommsen had adduced a slab commemorating Marcellus, a centurion of XI *Claudia,* who died at Boiano.[61] However, Marcellus did not finish off his military career in that post, but went on to be prefect of a small district in Pannonia, and to the command of an auxiliary cohort. There is no good reason to suppose that Marcellus was settled at Bovianum with soldiers of XI *Claudia,* and no proof of a Vespasianic colony in the town has been forthcoming.[62]

The epithet *Undecumanorum* must refer to settlement by veterans of a legion XI; no other explanation seems probable. Presumably the veterans were placed at Bovianum in the Late Republic. After Actium veterans from a legion XI were established in northern Italy at Ateste; the settlement by legion XI at Bovianum may therefore have taken place after Philippi, or under Caesar himself.[63] The latter may be more likely, in that we have no evidence that legion XI was re-formed after Caesar's death. The settlement may have been upgraded later to colonial status, perhaps (like Lucus Feroniae?) after Actium.

A slab from Al Pagliarone near Vastogirardi records members of a *gens Papia,* of whom one, or more probably two, brother(s) had served as centurions in a legion XXXIII (Sylloge 57). The stone was catalogued by Mommsen under 'Bovianum Vetus' (Pietrabbondante); with the demise of this site as an independent township, the stone seems best assigned to Terventum.[64] The legion is among those which must have been released after Philippi (above, p. 26). The family is perhaps of local origin, and the slab cannot be used as evidence for the settlement of legion XXXIII at Bovianum (Boiano) which lies too far to the south.

Venusia

Venusia lies among the eastern spurs of the Vulture Range in Apulia. Appian names it as a city marked out before Philippi for veteran settlement; his testimony is confirmed by Horace whose property was not unjustifiably confiscated at that time.[65] One possible recipient of a Venusine allotment is recorded: C. Oppius T.f.

---

[58] Cf. *NH* iii. 63, 105, 106.

[59] *CIL* IX, p. 239.

[60] See his comments in *Sannio: Pentri e Frentani dal vi a i sec. a.C.* (Roma, 1980), 29–33.

[61] IX 2564; hence its appearance as *MW* 354.

[62] But see Sic. Flacc. 131. 14–132. 6 for Vespasian's work in Samnium.

[63] Above, p. 55. Sullan settlement in the town could be envisaged on the basis of App. *BC* i. 51. but *ILS* 70 = *ILLRP* 406 shows Bovianum as a *municipium* in 48–46 B.C.

[64] The tribe *Voltinia* suits this attribution.

[65] App. *BC* iv. 3; Hor. *Epis.* ii. 2. 49–50; N. Jacobone, *Venusia* (1909). Little is known about Roman monuments in the town, but see *NS* 1936, 450 for a segment of its amphitheatre.

Hor. who had served in a legion XII (Sylloge 97), and who ended his military service as an *optio* in a century of that legion's *cohors prima*. L. Oppius, conceivably a son, was *IIvir quinquennalis* at Venusia in 29 B.C.[66] If the veteran Oppius belongs to the post-Philippi colony, his legion must be Caesar's XII, which, as has been argued from other evidence, was re-formed after his death, perhaps in Narbonensis (above, p. 24 n. 4).

Luceria

Luceria lies close to the western edge of the broad expanses of the Tavoliere, occupying a double hillock overlooking the plain.[67] The *ager Lucerinus* has in recent years formed the focal point for a study of the Tavoliere from the air initiated by J. P. Bradford and continued by G. D. B. Jones. Of the patterns of centuriation detected from the air, the basic layout east of Luceria is likely to date to the establishment of the *colonia Latina* in 315/4 B.C.; later systems may belong to Gracchan assignments.[68] Bradford's findings indicate steadings of modest size (sometimes overlying native compounds of uncertain date), a part of whose land (not always small) was set aside for vines and olives. The use of the rest is uncertain, but cereal production could account (as today) for much of it. For the present purpose the lack of dating evidence to determine how many of the farmsteads were (or remained) in use as separate entities under the Empire is a major drawback (above, p. 125).

Luceria is named as a *colonia* by Pliny, but the epigraphic record of *IIIIviri* convinced Mommsen that it could not have acquired colonial status before the reign of Vespasian, and this view had found acceptance.[69] However, confirmation of an Augustan date was forthcoming in 1934 with the publication of the first of two dedicatory inscriptions from the gateways of a newly-excavated amphitheatre, lying just outside the town to the east (Sylloge 81). These describe the town as *colonia* and provide a *terminus ante quem* of A.D. 14 for its foundation and for the construction of the amphitheatre.[70]

Several inscriptions are reported, which may refer to veterans settled at Luceria in the later first century B.C. (Sylloge 77–84), but four are now lost, of which three were in any case incomplete. Of those lost, only L. Anicius and Q. Nonius (Sylloge 77, 79), whose epitaphs are identical in format, can be accepted with confidence as

---

[66]IX 422 = *ILS* 6123. The *nomen* recurs in the town (IX 463, 649).

[67]G. Gifuni, *Lucera* (Urbino, 1937); idem, *Lucera Augustea* (Urbino, 1939); E. de Ruggiero-A. Garzetti, *Diz. Epig.* IV (1973), 1950–52, s.v. *Luceria*.

[68]J. P. Bradford, 'Siticulosa Apulia', *Antiquity* xx (1946), 191–200; idem, 'Buried Landscapes in Southern Italy', *Antiquity* xxiii (1949), 58–72; idem, 'The Apulian Expedition: An Interim Report', *Antiquity* xxiv (1950), 94–95; C. Delano Smith, 'Ancient Landscapes in the Tavoliere, Apulia', *Trans. Inst. Brit. Geog.* xli (1967), 203–8; Toynbee II, 563–67. Publication by G. D. B. Jones in *Arch. Class.* is now imminent.

[69]*CIL* IX, p. 74; idem, *Bürgercolonien* 194; Beloch, *RG* 515.

[70]R. Bartoccini, *BCAR* lxii (1934), *Notiziario*, p. 46 = *AE* 1937, 64; *AE* 1938, 110 = Sylloge 81. For a discussion, A. Degrassi, 'Problemi cronologici delle colonie di Luceria, Aquileia, Teanum Sidicinum', *Riv. Fil.* lxvi (1938), 129–43 = *SVA* I, 79–95. Excavation showed that the amphitheatre overlay some earlier buildings; *Fasti Arch.* xii (1957), 2831 with Pl. xvii. The buildings may have belonged to, or were bought up by, the tribune Vecilius, who put up the amphitheatre *loco privato suo*, as the dedicatory inscriptions proclaim.

settlers at Luceria. Q. Nonius served in a legion VI; if he is envisaged as part of a
sizeable contingent, processes of elimination suggest that it was settled after Actium.
The centurions L. Licinius and Q. Helvius (Sylloge 80, 78) may be veteran settlers,
potential leaders of the new community, but there can be no certainty.

Preserved in the courtyard of the Museo Civico G. Fiorelli at Luceria, but
lacking a secure provenance, is a recently published limestone slab (Sylloge 82),
from the front of a tomb monument, divided into three sections by pilasters topped
by Corinthian capitals.[71] It commemorates L. Curius and his two sons L. Curius
L.f. and Q. Curius L.f., both of whom had served in a legion I. Curius père could
have followed his sons to their new homes. Two inscriptions from hilly country
north-west of Luceria (Sylloge 83–84), near its border with Teanum Apulum,
record other veterans of legion I, Q.Le(g)genius Sta.f. and Lollius L.f.Libo.[72]
Perhaps a group of veterans of legion I were settled in that area, but no centuriation
has been detected thereabouts. The legion may perhaps be identified as a member
of the group of five legions raised by the consul Pansa in 43 B.C.; its founder
members would become eligible for discharge after Naulochus or after Actium
(above, p. 26).

The tribune, M. Vecilius M.f. L.n. Campus, who financed the construction of
the Lucerian amphitheatre *in honorem imperatoris Caesaris Augusti*, naturally
attracts attention as a possible colonist, settled with the centurions and soldiers of
his legion, a leading personality in, and bulwark of, the new community. However,
although the *nomen* Vecilius or Vecillius is rare, Degrassi has pointed out that
one of its few occurrences is on a stone recorded at Volturara Appula, some 25 kms.
west of Luceria and almost certainly within the *ager Lucerinus*.[73] This slab names
four *IIIIviri quinquennales*, among them a L. Vecillius; palaeographic considerations suggest that the inscription can be dated to the mid first century B.C. If this L.
Vecillius can be considered grandfather of the tribune M. Vecilius M.f.L.n., this
branch of the *gens Vecilia* would be revealed as an established local family of some
prominence, which survived the colonial foundation with sufficient success to
expend generous sums on the construction of a public building during the lifetime
of Augustus. Almost nothing is known of other buildings of this time.

Ausculum

Ausculum, the modern Ascoli Satriano, occupies a hillock above the Carapelle river
in the highlands of Apulia. The town is not described by Pliny as a *colonia*, but an
inscription found in 1935 (though only more recently the subject of scholarly
scrutiny) has been thought to testify to the establishment there of veteran settlers in

[71] M. Torelli, 'Contributi al supplemento del *CIL* IX', *Rend. Acc. Linc.* ser. 8, xxiv (1969), 9–48,
Luceria no. 4, with tav. vi, fig. 3; *AE* 1969/1970, 158. Also preserved at the Museo Fiorelli is another
slab from the same monument, decorated with pilasters and Corinthian capitals in identical style.

[72] A. Russi, *Teanum Apulum: Le iscrizioni e la storia del municipio* (Roma, 1976), 210 no. 1,
212 no. 2 = *AE* 1976, 168–69. The *nomen* Le(g)genius is rare, if not unique; note Legiannius at
Bononia (XI 721), and the Gallic Leuconius (V 4902, XI 765, VIII 9665). The filiation *Sta.f.* marks
out Le(g)genius as of central Italian stock.

[73] IX 936; Degrassi, loc. cit. (n. 70).

the Late Republic.[74] The stone was recovered during excavation of the bath suite of a *villa rustica* at Serra di Fico 5 kms. south-west of Ascoli Satriano, where it had served as a threshold; a coin of Hadrian was found in association.

The inscription is best quoted:

```
.......... E D V S
                  > I I V I R
.......... M F
.......... LVM TABERN PORTIC
.......... N COLONEIS FIRMAN
.......... VNT
```

It would seem likely that about half the slab has been lost. The inscription appears to reveal the existence of an otherwise unsuspected *colonia* at (or near) Ausculum, whose members might be officially described as *colonei Firmanei*. The 'centurial' sign (>) was taken as evidence for service as leaders of the new community of two former centurions. There seems no reason to suppose that the stone had been carried any great distance before its humble re-use; the *colonia* therefore must have been either at Ausculum itself or an unknown town whose *territorium* was sandwiched between the *ager Ausculanus* and the *ager Vibinus*. Bartoccini considered the inscription, and hence the *colonia*, to be Sullan in date; more recently Panciera has drawn attention to the entry for Ausculum in the *Liber Coloniarum*, where it is asserted that settlement had taken place *lege Sempronia* and *lege Iulia*.[75] Aerial reconnaissance has revealed (by way of confirmation) two superimposed grids of *centuriae* west of Ausculum in the valley of the Carapelle.[76] Panciera concluded that the *colonei Firmanei* were settled after Philippi or under Augustus at a town subsequently swallowed up by Ausculum. The epithet *Firmanei* prompted him to suggest that the name of the *colonia* was probably Firmum, perhaps even Firmum Apulum.

Several difficulties lie in the way of accepting this new town, Firmum Apulum, as a *colonia*. Firstly the need to postulate the existence of a town which has otherwise passed unrecorded in ancient literature and the Itineraries, and which is not listed by Pliny. Secondly, and more significantly, the proximity of Serra di Fico to Ausculum must count against the existence of an independent township there. The site of Serra di Fico (i.e. 'Firmum Apulum') was identified by Panciera with the unmetrical *oppidulum* at which Maecenas' party halted on their journey to Brundisium, but the latter is more probably to be identified with Herdoniae.[77]

It is much more likely that the *colonei Firmanei* were established at Ausculum itself. Its civic status is not directly attested; Pliny lists the *Ausculani* among the

[74] R. Bartoccini, 'Un ignorata colonia militare in Apulia', *Arch. Stor. Pug.* viii (1955), 17–24 with a photograph of the stone and a map to illustrate its findspot; hence *AE* 1961, 310. Bartoccini's readings were improved by Degrassi, on *ILLRP* 592.

[75] *LC* 210. 10–14; S. Panciera, 'Miscellanea storico-epigrafica II', *Epigraphica* xxiv (1962), 78–105.

[76] Information from Prof. G. D. B. Jones.

[77] Panciera, loc. cit. (n. 75); G. Radke, 'Die Erschliessung Italiens durch die römischen Strassen', *Gymnasium* lxxi (1964), 204–35; idem, *RE Sup.* XIII (1973), 1505–6; on the possible identification of the *oppidulum* with Ausculum, G. Lugli, 'Osservazioni sulle stazioni della Via Appia antica da Roma ad Otranto', in *Festschrift für R. Egger* (Klagenfurt, 1952), I, 276–93.

inland peoples of Apulia, apparently as a *municipium,* and though its chief magistrates were *IIviri,* as a recently published inscription reveals, this is no sure index of colonial status.[78] The epithet *Firmanei* may derive from a title attached to the *colonia* itself, or (less probably) from a *legio Firmana* or *legio Firma.*[79] A more apposite parallel to the *colonei Firmanei* could be the *Fidentiores,* the Sullan colonists at Arretium who maintained their individuality into the Augustan period.[80] Perhaps it is necessary to envisage at Ausculum an enclave of Sullan or Caesarian colonists. The shops, porticoes and other buildings were most probably erected at Ausculum itself. The re-use of the stone (or part of it) in the construction of a bath suite, which was in use (if the archaeological evidence is believed) in the mid second century A.D., suggests that at least one of the buildings paid for by the *IIviri* had already passed out of use and that its dedicatory slab had been discarded. Finally, the identification by Bartoccini of the > sign as indicating the rank of centurion for the *IIviri* remained unchallenged by Panciera and Degrassi. A recent commentator was rightly unconvinced; the sign is merely decorative shorthand, and provides no evidence for the participation of centurions in local government at Ausculum.[81]

[78] *NH* iii. 105; *AE* 1969/1970, 150.

[79] No legion with the required title is yet known. The epithet *Firma* was borne by the colonies at Astigi, Arausio and Teanum. The adjective *Firmana* is otherwise found applied to persons or property belonging to Firmum Picenum (Cic. *Phil.* vii. 23; Liv. xliv. 40. 6; Pliny *NH* iii. 111).

[80] Pliny *NH* iii. 52.

[81] J. M. Reynolds, 'Roman Epigraphy 1961–65', *JRS* lvi (1966), 116–21; further discussion by A. Degrassi, 'L'epigrafia latina in Italia nell'ultimo quinquennio (1963–1967)', in *Acta of the Fifth Epigraphic Congress, Cambridge 1967* (Oxford, 1971), 153–74, at 162 = *SVA* IV, 39–64. For the convention, cf. X 6679, IX 5019, X 123 with *Epigraphica* xxxviii (1976), 135; 1^2 1902 with G. Susini, *The Roman Stonecutter* (Oxford, 1973), 47. Sylloge 76 (Locri) seems the earliest example of the use of the 'centurial' sign.

CHAPTER EIGHT

ETRURIA, UMBRIA and PICENUM

Lucus Feroniae

The site of Lucus Feroniae, in the Tiber plain 25 kms. north of Rome, was identified on the ground in 1952, in the wake of clandestine activity. Large-scale excavation subsequently opened up to view the forum and adjacent structures.[1] Literary references indicate that the sacred grove and shrine of the rural goddess Feronia flourished from at least the third century B.C. onwards; the newly acquired archaeological evidence concurs. Before the later first century B.C. Feronia's grove lay within the *territorium* of the hill-town of Capena, for which it formed a cultural and religious centre.[2] In 46 B.C. Caesarian agents, according to Cicero, *Veientem quidem agrum et Capenatem metiuntur*. It would be reasonable to suppose that these preliminaries to veteran settlement took place partly or wholly on the flat plain beside the Tiber; an unusually specific entry in the *Liber Coloniarum* may provide confirmation.[3] Field survey has suggested that here, as at nearby Sutrium, there was a noticeable break in the occupation of rural sites in the Late Republic, perhaps the direct result of veteran settlement (above, p. 125).

Pliny reports Lucus Feroniae as a colony, and inscriptions record that it bore under the Empire the titles *colonia Iulia Felix*.[4] On the basis of the titulature, and other literary and epigraphic evidence, Renato Bartoccini suggested that the colony was established after Actium. However, L. R. Taylor preferred a Caesarian date, and this view was developed by G. D. B. Jones in his major study of the *ager Capenas*.[5] Jones' thesis was based on Cicero's testimony, on the inclusion of *Felix* in the titulature of the town, and on the apparent occurrence at Capena of *ludi Victoriae Caesaris*. However, these arguments, individually or cumulatively, have no force. Cicero says nothing about the formal establishment of a *colonia*; the title *Felix* is not particularly Caesarian (above, p. 16), and the *ludi* are more probably to be identified as *ludi sevirales*; Feronia had in any case a special brief for freedmen.[6]

The settlement of 46 B.C. is more likely to have formed the nucleus of a later *colonia,* established after Philippi or (better) after Actium. Perhaps Capena was thought unsuitable as the focal point for colonists whose allotments were concentrated in the plain. The establishment of the *colonia* brought a change of tribe:

---

[1] R. Bartoccini, 'Colonia Iulia Felix Lucus Feroniae', *Atti VII congr. int. di arch. class.* (Roma, 1961), II 249–56; G. D. B. Jones, 'Capena and the Ager Capenas, Part I', *PBSR* xxx (1962), 116–207.

[2] *CIL* XI, p. 570; R. Bloch and G. Foti, 'Nouvelles dédicaces archaiques à la deesse Feronia', *Rev. de Phil.* xxvii (1953), 65–77; A. M. Sgubini Moretti and G. Bordenache Battaglia, 'Materiale archeologici scoperti a Lucus Feroniae', in M. Moretti (ed.) *Nuove scoperte e acquisizioni nell'Etruria meridionale* (Roma, 1975), 93–174.

[3] Cic. *Fam.* ix. 17. 2; *LC* 216. 11–13: *colonia Capys . . . termini variis locis sunt adpositi, id est in planitia ubi miles portionem habuit.*

[4] Pliny *NH* iii. 51; above, p. 21. Bartoccini reports a stone on which Trajan is hailed as *restitutor c(oloniae) I(uliae) F(elicis) L(uco)f(eronensis); Autostrade* 1963, vii–viii, 14.

[5] Bartoccini, loc. cit. (n. 1); Taylor, *VDRR* 322; Jones, loc. cit. (n. 1). So also M. Torelli, 'Feronia e Lucus Feroniae in due iscrizioni latine', *Arch. Class.* xxv–vi (1973–74), 741–50.

[6] For the games, *CIL* XI, pp. 571, 578.

Voltinia replaced the Capenate *Stellatina*.[7] Though Frontinus seems to describe the population of Lucus Feroniae as *Augustini*, which would suggest that the titulature of the town included *Augusta*, inscriptions show that it remained *Iulia Felix Lucus Feroniae* under the Empire (above, p. 21).[8]

Our knowledge of the town is far from complete. Only the forum and some adjacent buildings have been cleared, together with a small circular amphitheatre which could belong to the Augustan age but may be later; a freedman *patronus sevirum Augustalium* financed its construction.[9] An unpublished inscription mentions a theatre, and gives details of the supply of water to baths, a basilica and a record office; another testifies to an *Aqua Augusta*.[10] Repairs to the Forum, paid for by a *IIvir* within the Augustan age, and the provision of statues and archways there by a pair of *IIviri*, may be testimony to the embellishment of the town centre in the wake of the colonial foundation.[11] However, no formal street grid or wall circuit has been identified and the general impression is of buildings put up rather haphazardly around an existing road junction. Below the town to the north-east lay an elaborate agricultural establishment, belonging to the senatorial Volusii Saturnini,[12] but there is little to show that Lucus Feroniae was ever a place of any real importance.[13]

Sutrium

Sutrium, an old Latin colony of 383 B.C., is listed by the Elder Pliny as a *colonia*, and the encyclopaedist's testimony is amply supported by epigraphic evidence. The antiquities of Sutrium and the *ager Sutrinus* have been the subject of detailed survey.[14] Little of Roman date can be detected in the town itself; outside to the south-east is a small rock-cut amphitheatre but its date is not established. A large marble slab from the town preserves the names of over 30 *pontifices* of the colony in order of appointment; examination of their nomenclature and of the orthography

[7] Harris 308–9.

[8] 46. 14, 47. 19.

[9] *Atl. Aereofotografico*, tav. cxix; R. Bartoccini, 'L'anfiteatro di Lucus Feroniae e il suo fondatore', *Rend. Pont. Acc.* xxxiii (1961), 173–84.

[10] Bartoccini, *Autostrade* 1963, vii–viii, 17.

[11] For the repairs to the forum, Bartoccini, loc. cit. (n. 1); for the statues and arches, A. M. Sgubini Moretti and G. Bordenache Battaglia, loc. cit. (n. 2), at 104, with tav. 28.

[12] *Autostrade* 1968, viii, passim; J. M. Reynolds, 'Roman Inscriptions 1966–1970', *JRS* lxi (1971), 136–52 with fig. 14; W. Eck, 'Die Familie der Volusii Saturnini in neuen Inschriften aus Lucus Feroniae', *Hermes* c (1972), 461–84. L. Volusius Saturninus, consul in 12 B.C., was patron of the colony; R. Bartoccini, *Atti III congr. int. epig. gr. e lat.* (Roma, 1959), p. xxxviii. For a brief notice of centuriation observed near the town, D. Adamesteanu, 'Contributo della aereofototeca archeologica del Ministero della Pubblica Istruzione alla soluzione di problemi di topografia antica in Italia', in *Int. Archives of Photogrammetry* xv. 7 (1965).

[13] For impressions of the history and development of Lucus Feroniae in the Early Empire, G. D. B. Jones, 'Civil War and Society in Southern Etruria', in M. R. D. Foot (ed.), *War and Society: Historical Essays in Honour and Memory of J. R. Western* (London, 1973), 277–87; B. Nagel, 'Towards a Sociology of Southeastern Etruria', *Athenaeum* lvii (1979), 411–41.

[14] G. C. Duncan, 'Sutri(*Sutrium*)', *PBS*ᴰ xxvi (1958), 63–134; M. Andreussi, *Vicus Matrini* (in series *Forma Italiae;* Roma, 1977). For a fresh study of the town-site, and a zone of its territory to the south-east, see now C. Morselli, *Sutrium* (in series *Forma Italiae;* Firenze, 1980).

of the inscription suggests that it was set up during or not long after the reign of
Augustus. While some names are manifestly of local families, others could be of
veteran colonists. [15] Above this list there survives the strangely worded heading
pontifices a colonia Coniunc(ta) Iulia Sutrin(a) in ord(inem) relat(i), which reveals
the titulature of Sutrium in the Augustan period as *colonia Coniuncta Iulia Sutrina*.
Attempts at interpreting the unique title *Coniuncta* have been numerous, but in
varying degrees unconvincing. Duncan saw the word as implying a joint foundation
by the Triumvirs; Nissen and Philipp as indicating a union or fusion between
settlers owing allegiance to Octavian and to Antony. G. D. B. Jones (following Pais)
postulated union between veteran settlers and the existing population of the town. [16]
On the other hand, it could be thought of as emphasising the closeness of the bond
between the colonists and the *gens Iulia*. A fragmentary inscription from Vicus
Matrini, a small settlement on the Via Cassia 10 kms. north-west of Sutrium,
appears to record the construction of an aqueduct for the local *vicani* by *colonia
Augusta Iulia Sutrina*; [17] an alternative interpretation, that the stone records some
benefaction by the empress Livia, is in my view less probable. [18] *Augusta* may
therefore have replaced *Coniuncta* in the titulature of the town.

During the Perusine War in 41 B.C. Agrippa forcibly occupied Sutrium on the
grounds that the town was (or was likely to be) 'useful' to Lucius Antonius. Gabba
interpreted this passage as indicating that Sutrium was then in the hands of
Antonian veterans. [19] More probably the 'usefulness' consisted in the position of
Sutrium astride the Cassia, facilitating communication with the capital. The precise
date of the re-acquisition by Sutrium of colonial status must remain unknown. [20]

Falerii

The Faliscan capital of Falerii, which until 241 B.C. occupied the easily defended
promontory of Civita Castellana, was moved westwards in that year by the Romans
to a new site astride the Via Amerina, which received the name Falerii Novi. [21] Pliny
includes Falerii in his inland list of colonies in the seventh Augustan region: *intus
coloniae Falisca Argis orta ut auctor est Cato quae cognominatur Etruscorum,
Lucus Feroniae, Rusellana, Seniensis, Sutrina*. [22] The *Liber Coloniarum* also
describes Falerii as a colony, attributes its foundation to the Triumvirs, and attaches
to it the title *Iunonia*. [23] The designation as a colony is not by itself significant, as
all the towns in this section of *Provincia Tuscia* are so described, but the appearance
of a title (which derives from the local cult of Juno Curitis) provides stronger

[15] XI 3254.
[16] G. C. Duncan, loc. cit. (n. 14), at 68 n. 9; Nissen, *IL* II 355–56; Philipp, *RE* IVA (1931), 995;
Pais, *Colonizzazione* 174; Jones, loc. cit. (n. 13), 282.
[17] XI 3322 with restorations by Garrucci; M. Andreussi, op. cit. (n. 14), 70.
[18] Duncan, loc. cit. (n. 16) following Zangemeister.
[19] App. *BC* v. 31 with Gabba, *Appiani V*, ad loc.; idem, *Colonie triumvirali* 103.
[20] Harris 310.
[21] Bormann, *CIL* XI, p. 464; M. W. Frederiksen and J. B. Ward-Perkins, 'The Ancient Road
System of the Central and Northern Ager Faliscus', *PBSR* xxv (1957), 67–203, at 131.
[22] *NH* iii. 51.
[23] 217. 5.

evidence. Where the *Liber* offers details of titulature, these are usually correct, but we cannot establish the date of the award.

Pliny's reference is so specific that it is hard to imagine that he is in error, or to suppose, with Mommsen, that he confused Falerii with Picene Falerio, with which (it is imagined) Pliny was less familiar.[24] If Falerii appeared in Pliny's Augustan source as *Falisca* — and this must be likely — it is hard to see how any confusion need have arisen. We cannot ascribe Pliny's account of its status to Cato — *Falisca* appears at the head of an alphabetical list drawn directly from the Augustan source. It might seem that there is an excellent case for including *Falisca* in any list of Triumviral or Augustan colonies.

However, epigraphic evidence seems to indicate that Falerii Novi had in the Late Republic and Early Empire the status of a *municipium*. On one stone Augustus is commended as *pater patriae et municipi*.[25] The amphitheatre at Falerii Novi was built under Augustus, chiefly at the expense of two patrons of the *municipium,* one a former *primus pilus* of legion VIIII *Hispaniensis,* with a non-local tribe. Other inscriptions could suggest that colonial status was acquired only later, perhaps in the reign of Gallienus.[26]

One solution to the apparent conflict of evidence, that a colony was established by the Triumvirs or Augustus on the old site of Civita Castellana (Falerii Veteres) was proposed by Beloch.[27] However, the revival of town life there seems contradicted by archaeological evidence: part of the town-site was sufficiently deserted in the later second century A.D. to be used for burials.[28] There is no epigraphic record or surface trace of public buildings to match those at Falerii Novi; Pliny names only one town within the *ager Faliscus.*

From the dedication to Augustus as *pater municipi* it seems likely that he was active in the *ager Faliscus,* conferring benefits on the town or its people. Cicero names the *ager Faliscus* as an area in which Rullus contemplated land allocation in 63 B.C.;[29] it could be that some did take place, perhaps under Caesar in 59–58 or 47–44 B.C. The appearance of *Falisca* in Pliny's list still requires explanation. A recent commentator has suggested that a colony was in fact established at Falerii Novi, which maintained an indifferent existence alongside the better known *municipium* until revitalised by Gallienus.[30] On the other hand, a short-lived colony there could be postulated, which reverted to the status of a *municipium* after no

---

[24] *Bürgercolonien* 176. So also Frederiksen and Ward-Perkins, loc. cit. (n. 21); Harris 307.

[25] XI 3083 = *ILS* 5373. For a tribune of a *legio Gemella,* who served as *IIIIvir* in the town, XI 7495.

[26] XI 3112. For a good plan of the town, *Atl. Aereofotografico,* tav. cxx. For the activity of Gallienus, XI 3091–94; A. Alföldi, 'The Numbering of the Victories of the Emperor Gallienus and of the Loyalty of his Legions', *NC* ser. 5, ix (1929), 218–79. Note, however, that the inscriptions praise Gallienus as *redintegrator* not *conditor* of the colony, which lacks any distinctive title accruing from that emperor.

[27] *It. Bund,* 11.

[28] Frederiksen and Ward-Perkins, loc. cit. (n. 21).

[29] *Leg. Agr.* ii. 66.

[30] I. de Stefano Manzella, 'Un'iscrizione di Falerii sul mercato antiquario romano', *Rend. Acc. Linc.* ser. 8, xxvi (1971), 751–68; idem, 'I nomi attributi alle due *Falerii* dalla tradizione litteraria antica e dalle epigrafi', *Rend. Pont. Acc.* xlix (1976–77), 151–62.

long interval, and was revived later. Such possibilities are worth exploring, but more evidence must accrue before any positive conclusion can be reached.

Rusellae

Rusellae occupies a hill-top site on the eastern edge of the plain of Grosseto, overlooking that plain and the *Lacus Prilius* which covered some considerable proportion of it in Roman times.[31] Pliny records *colonia Rusellana* in an inland list; epigraphic evidence provides confirmation of its status.[32] Recent excavations have illuminated the history of the town from the initial Etruscan settlement of the seventh/sixth centuries B.C., through what was perhaps the period of its greatest prosperity in the third/second centuries, until the Empire.[33] In the later first century B.C. a paved forum (somewhat truncated in shape owing to the unevenness of the ground) was laid out in the hollow between the two hillocks embraced by the town walls, sweeping away earlier buildings; ranged round the southern end of the forum were a basilica, a possible Augusteum and a covered portico.[34] Close by, occupying one of the two summits, was a small oval amphitheatre, itself in part overlying a house of the third/second centuries B.C.[35] This activity can probably be linked to the foundation of the *colonia*, but the date of the latter cannot be established.

Castrum Novum

The coastal site of Castrum Novum, a *colonia maritima* of about 264 B.C., lies at Torre Chiaruccia, on the western edge of the modern resort and harbour of Santa Marinella.[36] Inscriptions of the reign of Gallienus give it the title *Iulia*.[37] As Castrum Novum is not recorded as a colony by Pliny, commentators have sometimes postulated settlement there under Caesar,[38] but no positive evidence on the date or circumstances of veteran settlement has been forthcoming. Under the Late Republic, or during Augustus' reign, a *IIvir quinquennalis* provided a *curia*, a record office, and seating for theatrical performances, on his own land within the town, but the occasion for his benefaction is not known.[39] Perhaps some small-scale Caesarian settlement is commemorated in the title *Iulia*, which need not have been officially adopted until very much later.

[31] A. Mazzolai, *Roselle e il suo territorio* (Grosseto, 1960); *Atl. Aereofotografico*, tav. l–li, cxxix.

[32] *NH* iii. 51; XI 2618; *AE* 1964, 254; Harris 310. The inscription *AE* 1960, 329 offers in my view no guide to the titulature of the town. Recent epigraphic discoveries, including an impressive series of dedications to the Julio-Claudian imperial family, have been published by V. Saladino, 'Iscrizioni latine di Roselle', *ZPE* xxxviii (1980), 159–76, ibid. xxxix (1980), 215–36, ibid. xl (1981), 229–48.

[33] Reports by C. Laviosa in *SE* from 1959 to 1971. Summaries, with full bibliography, by Laviosa in *EAA* VI (1965), 1026–29; *Sup.* (1973), 676–77.

[34] *SE* xxxi (1963), 53, xxxiii (1965), 49 ff., xxxvii (1969), 584 ff.

[35] *SE* xxvii (1959), 8 ff., xxxiii (1965), 92 ff. The location of the amphitheatre within the wall circuit could be testimony to depopulation.

[36] S. Bastianelli, *Centum Cellae-Castrum Novum* (Roma, 1954); P. A. Gianfrotta, *Castrum Novum* (in series *Forma Italiae*; Roma, 1972).

[37] XI 3576–78; above, p. 21.

[38] E. T. Salmon, 'The *coloniae maritimae*', *Athenaeum* xli (1963), 1–36, at 22; Harris 306.

[39] XI 3583 = *ILS* 5515 (above, p. 117). For archaeological evidence of public buildings in the town, Gianfrotta, op. cit. (n. 36), 85 ff.

Saena

In contrast with the ample remains of medieval Siena, little is yet known of its Roman predecessor Saena, amid the rolling uplands of central Tuscany. Saena would not appear to have ranked among the great cities of Etruria before the Roman conquest: only modest settlement on the town-site is implied by the archaeological evidence. The few references in Latin literature belong entirely to the Empire, and inscriptions are few.[40]

Of its colonial status there can be no real doubt: Pliny includes *colonia Seniensis* in an inland list; a passage in Tacitus provides confirmation of its status.[41] The *Tabula Peutingeriana,* in order to distinguish Saena from Sena Gallica on the Adriatic, attached to the former the epithet *Iulia.* We can hardly doubt that from the Augustan period onwards the town bore the titulature *colonia Iulia Saena.* Long ago Nissen suggested that Saena was a fresh creation of Octavian with a *territorium* carved from the *ager Volaterranus* which was earmarked for settlement on a number of occasions during the Late Republic (above, p. 55), with some resulting confusion as to its legal status:[42] but the appearance of senatorial Saenii in Saena's own tribe, the *Oufentina,* under the Republic may count against this view.[43]

Pisae

The town-site of Pisae, centrally placed in the Arno delta between the rivers Arno and Serchio, was defended on two if not three sides by water.[44] The geography of the delta in Roman times has been much discussed; lagoons, lakes and canals have been identified in such profusion that Pisae could easily be envisaged as the Tyrrhenian Venice.[45] However, it is clear that drainage and silting had reclaimed for cultivation the greater part of the delta by the Late Republic.[46]

Two inscriptions describe the town as *colonia Opsequens Iulia Pisana*; they are datable to A.D. 2 and A.D. 4, and lament the deaths of Augustus' step-sons L. and C. Caesar, both patrons of the *colonia.*[47] Little has been recovered of the public buildings and monuments to which both inscriptions refer.[48] A veteran of the Late Republic, who served in legion XIX, Sex. Anqurinnius, is commemorated at

---

[40] R. Bianchi Bandinelli, *EAA Sup.* (1973), 718-20.

[41] Pliny *NH* iii. 51; Tac. *Hist.* iv. 45.

[42] Nissen, *IL* II 312.

[43] Harris 323-24; Wiseman no. 370.

[44] N. Toscanelli, *Pisa nell'Antichità* (Pisa, 1933-34); L. Banti, 'Pisae', *Mem. Pont. Acc.* ser. 3, vi (1943), 67-141; eadem, *RE* XX (1950), 1756-72; A. Neppi Modona, *Pisae* (in series *Forma Italiae*; Roma, 1953); idem, *Inscriptiones Italiae* VII. i (Roma, 1953).

[45] A. Toniolo, 'Le variazioni storiche del litorale toscano tra l'Arno e la Magra', *Atti X congr. geog. ital.* (Milano, 1927), 314-30.

[46] P. Fraccaro, 'La centuriazione romana dell'agro pisano', *SE* xiii (1939), 221-29 = *Opuscula* III (1957), 63-70; *Atl. Aereofotografico*, tav. cxxviii.

[47] XI 1420-21 = *ILS* 139-40 = *EJ*² 68-69 = *IIt.* VII. i. 6-7. Freed *servi publici* were given the *nomen* Obsequentius (above, p. 18).

[48] A forum, Augusteum, arch, temples, baths, shops, and (by implication) a theatre and circus. For monuments in the town, A. Neppi Modona, *Pisae* (Roma, 1953), carta 3, and no. 27.

Castelnuovo della Misericordia on high ground at the southern edge of the *ager Pisanus* (Sylloge 89); the rare *nomen* recurs in the town itself.[49] The colony perhaps belongs after Actium (above, p. 77).

Luca

Luca lay on a large elongated island formed by the temporary bifurcation of the Serchio as it emerged from the Garfagnana into the broad expanses of the Arno valley. Archaeology now appears to confirm Velleius' statement that Luca became a *colonia* (with Latin rights) in the early second century B.C.[50]

Luca appears in the Plinian list as a *colonia*: an inscription too gives it this title.[51] Further confirmation is provided by a commemorative tablet now in the Galleria Lapidaria of the Vatican Museum (Pl. IIIA), which identifies both the organiser of the settlement and the legions involved.[52]

> L MEMMIVS C F GAL Q TR PL [PR]
> FRVMENTI CVRATOR EX S C
> PRAEFECTVS LEG XXVI ET VII
> LVCAE AD AGROS DIVIDVNDOS
> PONTIFEX   ALBANVS
> MEMMIA FILIA TESTAMENTO SVO FIERI IVSSIT

L. Memmius C.f. Gal. cannot be securely linked with any known member of the senatorial *gens Memmia,* but may be a descendant of one of the brothers L. C. Memmii L.f. Gal., *monetales* in the Sullan era.[53] His appointment as *frumenti curator,* which on the stone precedes his duties as *praefectus legionum,* has been dated by Gabba precisely to 41 B.C., when Sex. Pompeius' control of sea routes precipitated a food shortage in Rome.[54]

There has been some discussion on the identity of the legions under his control. Though it seems clearly stated that legion XXVI and legion VII were established in the town, Dessau and later Ritterling argued from the sequence of numerals that reference was here being made to legions XXVI and XXVII, the latter's numeral abbreviated to VII. Their verdict has been taken up and repeated.[55] But no parallels can be adduced for such an abbreviation and Von Domaszewski was surely right long ago to reject it.[56] The order in which the legions are reported may have a special significance (above, p. 64). The only legion XXVII of which we have

---

[49] XI 1440 = *IIt.* VII. i. 31; Schulze, *Eigennamen* 122.

[50] P. Sommella and C. F. Giuliani, *La pianta di Lucca romana* = *Quad. Ist. Top. Ant.* vii (1974), 19, 46; F. Castagnoli, 'La centuriazione di Lucca', *SE* xx (1948–49), 285–90; G. Samonati, *Diz. Epig.* IV (1972), 1873–80, *s.v. Luca.*

[51] *NH* iii. 50; XI 1525.

[52] VI 1460 = XIV 2264 = *ILS* 887 = *EJ*² 188.

[53] *PIR*¹ M 336; T. P. Wiseman, 'Prosopographical Notes', *NC* ser. 7, iv (1964), 156–58; M. H. Crawford, *Roman Republican Coinage* (Cambridge, 1974), 320–21, 363–64.

[54] *Appiani V,* p. lxiii n. 1.

[55] Dessau, as cited by Ritterling, *Legio* 1820–21. So Passerini, *Diz. Epig.* IV (1949), 554, *s.v. Legio*; Gabba, *Appiani V,* p. lxiii n. 1; Samonati, loc. cit. (n. 50).

[56] 'Die Heere der Bürgerkriege in den Jahre 49 bis 42 vor Christus', *NHJ* iv (1894), 157–88, at 188 n. 3. For the order L(egiones) II I reported on coins issued by the colony of Acci, A. Vives y Escudero, *La moneda hispánica* IV (Madrid, 1924), 120.

knowledge was raised in 49 B.C., and as part of the garrison of Egypt at Caesar's death, passed to the Liberators. Its members would not qualify for settlement in Italy after Philippi. The two legions VII and XXVI were part of Octavian's forces from July 43; it is only at this time that the two legions can be juxtaposed, and the conclusion must be that they were settled together by Memmius on Octavian's behalf at Luca in 41 B.C.[57]

Florentia

The foundation-dates of the town and of the *colonia* at Florentia continue to be the subject of intense discussion. The all-important factor in the town's development was the reclamation of the water-logged Golfolina Plain on whose agricultural land the city has always relied for its prosperity. The name Florentia could reflect the hoped-for productiveness of the newly-won fields. The successful completion of the drainage work has been ascribed to Julius Caesar,[58] but there remains no real evidence of the rate at which reclamation progressed or regressed during the Late Republic.

Some have thought that the foundation of Florentia as a town should be dated to the second century B.C.;[59] others have argued that the town and the *colonia* belong under Sulla,[60] or the town under Caesar, with the formal status of *colonia* being conferred by Octavian in or about 41 B.C.[61] Sulla established colonists at Faesulae, the old established township on the hills above, and it is sometimes claimed that the Sullan veterans were in fact based on Florentia, a new centre of population on the Arno. But at the time of Catiline's conspiracy in 63 B.C. Faesulae, not Florentia, was the centre of his support; a *Faesulanus* not a *Florentinus* was one of his chief lieutenants.[62] The settlers may well have been established on land in the valley, but it would seem that it constituted *ager Faesulanus*. Florentia receives no mention in the literary sources before the Empire. Florus, writing in the early second century A.D., records that the lands of four *splendidissima municipia* (Spoletium, Interamnium, Praeneste and Florentia) were sold up by Sulla.[63] The reference to Florentia may be anachronistic, and refer to land which only later became *ager Florentinus*. On the other hand, Sulla may have sold up the lands of Florentia to provide allotments for colonists at nearby Faesulae, which would suggest that Florentia already existed as a town before his time.

The *Liber Coloniarum* describes Florentia as a *colonia*, but in a section where this title is indiscriminately applied; it is also said to have been *deducta a*

[57] Apart from an extra-mural theatre, no monuments in the town can be dated to the Augustan age. The well-known amphitheatre appears to have been erected towards the close of the first century A.D.

[58] C. Hardie, 'The Origin and Plan of Roman Florence', *JRS* lv (1965), 122–40. For a discussion of the town and its monuments, G. Maetzke, *Florentia* (Roma, 1940).

[59] Toynbee II, 666–67.

[60] Beloch, *RG* 511; Brunt, *IM* 711.

[61] Hardie, loc. cit. (n. 58); Harris 342.

[62] Sall. *Cat.* 59. 3, 60. 6.

[63] ii. 9. 27. The epithet *splendidissimus* need not be taken at face value. C. Hardie, loc. cit. (n. 58) argues unnecessarily for textual corruption, and substitutes Ferentinum. See the discussion by E. Gabba, 'Commento a Floro II. 9, 27–28', *Stud. Class. Or.* xix–xx (1970–71), 461–64. Gabba favours a Sullan date for the colony.

triumviris.[64] The entry for Florentia follows directly upon a Triumviral edict on land settlement, but the sequence may be fortuitous. Subsequent entries in this section for Tuder, Luna and Ancona describe the territories of these towns as distributed *ea lege qua et ager Florentinus.*[65] The *lex* named in the entry for Florentia is a *lex Iulia.* Now, Ancona is securely attested as a post-Philippi colony; Tuder must belong later, but no settlement at Luna is attested. The *Florentini* are listed by the Elder Pliny among the inland peoples of Etruria, but the title *colonia* is not attached to the town.[66] The omission coupled with the reference to a *lex Iulia*, has prompted some scholars to favour a Caesarian date for the colony in 47–44 B.C. On the other hand, Lopes Pegna saw the colony as a creation of Caesar's consulship of 59 B.C., founded under the agrarian legislation of that year.[67] This is an attractive suggestion. Land abandoned by Sullan colonists who had supported Catiline could have formed the basis of the settlement. Whether further colonists were established by the Triumvirs or Octavian has to remain uncertain.[68]

Tuder

The hill-town of Tuder rises like an island at the western edge of a broad undulating highland plateau, overlooking the Tiber as it winds its way south from Perusia.[69] Tuder is accorded the status of *colonia* by Pliny; inscriptions confirm.[70] The *Liber Coloniarum* specifies assignments at Tuder *ea lege qua et ager Florentinus* (see above). A post-Philippi date is normally accepted for Tuder on this evidence.[71] An inscription shows that Tuder bore the titles *colonia Iulia Fida Tuder,* and *Fida* is reported also by the *Liber Coloniarum.* Colonists in the town were drawn from, or included, a legion XXXXI, of which a centurion, Edusius, and less certainly a tribune, Caecilius Atticus, are recorded (Sylloge 93–94).

It has been argued elsewhere that the date of the legion's formation would be too late to allow settlement of its members after Philippi and that its disbandment can best be placed in 36 B.C. or after Actium (above, p. 27). The reference by Edusius to service in a *legio Augusti Caesaris* is necessarily anachronistic; legion XXXXI can hardly have continued to exist as late as 27 B.C. The centurion merely records service under Octavian, which may be dated at any time between 44 and 27 B.C. He had also served as *centurio classicus,* which may testify to naval service by the legion at Naulochus, or Actium, or over a longer period (above, p. 31). The epitaph came from S. Valentino, south of Todi, beside the Arnata river. A native of nearby Mevania, Edusius was thus no stranger to the Umbrian terrain.[72] Another

---

[64] 213. 6–7.

[65] 214. 3, 223. 14, 225. 4.

[66] *NH* iii. 52.

[67] M. Lopes Pegna, *Firenze dall'origini al medioevo* (Firenze, 1962), 44.

[68] For centuriation in the *ager Florentinus,* with some subdivision of *centuriae* into blocks of 50 *iugera,* F. Castagnoli, 'La centuriazione di Florentia', *l'Universo* xxviii (1948), 361–68. The chronological implications are uncertain (above, p. 93).

[69] G. Becatti, *Tuder-Carsulae* (in series *Forma Italiae;* Roma, 1938).

[70] *NH* iii. 113; *ILS* 2230 = Sylloge 93; XI 4646; *LC* 214. 3; Front. 52. 22.

[71] *LC* 214. 9; Mommsen, *Bürgercolonien* 183; Nissen, *IL* II 399; Harris 313.

[72] For Edusii at Mevania, C. Pietrangeli, *Mevania* (Roma, 1953), 34–35.

potential veteran is the centurion C. Allienus, who bears the non-local tribe *Voltinia*, and served in an unnamed legion (Sylloge 95). His epitaph came to light at S. Terentiano, north of the town.[73]

The colonists of legion XXXXI erected an honorary inscription (most probably from its dimensions, a statue base) to the tribune Q. Caecilius Q.f. Atticus, evidently a leading personality in the town in the years immediately after the colonial foundation; other inscriptions reveal Caecilius as *patronus coloniae* and *IIvir quinquennalis*.[74] It is attractive to suppose that he had served in legion XXXXI. His partner in office as *quinquennalis* was an Attius Bucina; it is a pleasant speculation to see in this *cognomen* a military nickname, but no army service is hinted at.[75]

In the Augustan period it seems that the town was enlarged by the construction of a new wall-circuit, adding 30% to the urban area, evidence perhaps of increased prosperity and population. The theatre was built at about this time, but the small amphitheatre well outside the walls to the south-east (on what was probably the nearest available stretch of level ground) evidently belongs much later.[76]

Hispellum

Hispellum occupies the end of a spur of the Monte Subasio range, overlooking the long narrow plain of the Pianura Umbra. Ancient writers report glowingly on the fertility of the plain, the edges of which were dotted in antiquity with small towns, sharing in the agricultural opportunities provided.[77] The town-site of Hispellum is long and narrow, sloping down towards the south as the spur on which it lies descends into the plain. The Roman wall-circuit is well preserved, and includes six gateways, of which two (the 'Porta Consolare', through which travellers turning off the Flaminia would approach the town, and the 'Porta Venere') are massive triple-arched structures (Pl. IIIB). The walls and gateways are generally thought to be Augustan in date; a fragmentary inscription may show that their construction was financed by Octavian.[78]

That Hispellum became a colony under the Triumvirs or Augustus is certain; inscriptions refer to the town as *colonia Iulia Hispellum*, and Pliny names Hispellum along with Tuder as *coloniae* of the Umbrian hinterland.[79] Hyginus Gromaticus instances Hispellum to illustrate a method of overcoming topographical difficulties in laying out a grid at an old established town:[80]

[73] Taylor, *VDRR* 321 argued that the appearance of the tribe *Voltinia* on several inscriptions from Tuder and its territory was evidence of Caesarian settlement in 59 B.C.

[74] XI 4650–53; *ILS* 2230.

[75] Cf. I² 2642 (Perusia), V 2544 (Ateste).

[76] Becatti, op. cit. (n. 69), 10, 22 ff.

[77] Prop. *El.* i. 22. 9; iv. 1. 130; Sil. Ital. iv. 544–45, viii. 456–60; Stat. *Silv.* i. 4. 126–30; Lucan *Phars.* i. 473.

[78] XI 5266; I. A. Richmond, 'Augustan Gates at Torino and Spello', *PBSR* xii (1932), 52–62; idem, 'Commemorative Arches and City Gates in the Augustan Age', *JRS* xxiii (1933), 149–74; G. Bonasegale Pittei, 'Indagini sulla struttura di Spello medioevale', *Riv. Ist. Arch.* ser. 3, i (1978), 153–98.

[79] *NH* iii. 113.

[80] 178. 19–179. 10.

> *antiqui enim propter subita bellorum pericula non solum*
> *erant urbes contenti cingere muris, verum etiam loca*
> *aspera et confragosa saxis eligebant, ubi illis amplissimum*
> *propugnaculum esset et ipsa loci natura. haec vicina*
> *urbibus rupium multitudo limites accipere propter loci*
> *difficultatem non potuit, sed relicta est ut aut silvas rei*
> *publicae praestaret aut si sterilis esset vacaret. his urbibus*
> *ut haberent coloniarum vastitatem vicinarum civitatium*
> *fines sunt adtributi, et in optimo solo decimanus maximus*
> *et kardo constituti; sicut in Vmbria finibus Spellatium.*

Two related points are being made in this passage: firstly that, as old Italian towns frequently (and with good reason) occupied hill-top sites, the laying out of a grid which had the town itself as its nodal point was impractical; secondly, that the *territoria* of such towns were often enlarged (at the expense of *vicinae civitates*) to give them lands commensurate with their new status as colonies. *Sicut in Umbria finibus Spellatium.* Though it could be argued that Hispellum is cited as an example of the second point only, i.e. that a colonial foundation might be accompanied by an appropriate enlargement of territory (the pre-colonial *ager Spellas* cannot have been extensive), general topographical considerations should indicate that it is meant as an example of the first point also. An interesting illustration accompanies the passage (Pl. V).[81]

One of the *vicinae civitates* which may reasonably have been expected to suffer loss of land to an expanded Hispellum is Assisium, astride a prominent ridge within easy view. A poem of Propertius (a native of Assisium) appears to provide confirmation of expropriation of part of the *ager Assisinus* in the Late Republic and its survey for land settlement.[82] The poet's boyhood experiences ought to date from the period of disturbance after Philippi.[83] However, his family was not totally impoverished, as its members continued to be prominent in the town.[84]

This Propertian passage may be linked to two other poems on the death of at least one *propinquus* in the Perusine War of 41 B.C.[85] The Propertii of Assisium, recently deprived of a substantial part of their property (or under threat of deprivation) are easily envisaged as supporters of L. Antonius, rallying to his aid in nearby Perusia. Propertius makes no specific reference to the foundation of the colony at Hispellum, but, given that the *ager Spellas* is known (from the passage of Hyginus Gromaticus) to have been extended at the expense of its immediate neighbours, the misfortunes of the Propertii seem best associated with the

---

[81] Rudorff, Fig. 152 (in Blume, *Feldmesser* I).

[82] *El.* iv. 1. 127–30: *ossaque legisti non illa aetate legenda/patris et in tenues cogeris ipse lares./ nam tua cum multi versarent rura iuvenci/abstulit excultas pertica tristis opes.*

[83] U. Ciotti, 'Un iscrizione duovirale e la data della costituzione di Hispellum a colonia', *BCAR* lxxi (1943–45), App. pp. 53–57; G. Williams, *Tradition and Originality in Roman Poetry* (Oxford, 1968), 172.

[84] *CIL* XI, p. 785; Wiseman no. 344; G. Binazzi, 'Una nuova iscrizione nel museo del Foro Romano di Assisi', *Arch. Class.* xxix (1977), 188–90. Above, p. 131.

[85] *El.* i. 21, i. 22.

foundation of the *colonia*, an event which may be confidently placed in 41 B.C. Much less certainly Hispellum may also have acquired some land at the expense of nearby Arna at this time.[86] Traces of a grid of *centuriae* noted in the plain by Castagnoli offer no guide to the extent of the *ager Spellas*, or of inroads into the territories of other towns.[87] To the south and west, the *ager Spellas*, in so far as its limits can be determined, occupied no more than its fair share of the Pianura even under the Empire.[88] The Younger Pliny records that *divus Augustus* made over to the town ownership of the *Fontes Clitumni* south of Trebiae (above, p. 121); no indication is given of the date of the award. That the *ager Spellas* could have stretched uninterrupted to the *Fontes*[89] is inconceivable. This was an isolated accretion.

From Fiamenga at the southern limit of the *ager Spellas* has come the gravestone of Cn. Decimius Cn. f. Lem. Bibulus, an *evocatus* of legion XIII and *VIvir* (Sylloge 74). The lettering is not securely datable, and the inscription could belong to the Early Empire. However, a second veteran of legion XIII, the centurion C. Allius L.f. Lem. (Sylloge 75), is attested at S. Andrea d'Agliano to the north-west of Torgiano within the *ager Perusinus*;[90] for this inscription an Augustan date may be suggested. The appearance of the tribe *Lemonia* establishes in both cases a link with Hispellum. Legion XIII had served with Caesar in Gaul, and must have been disbanded in 47–44. There is no evidence of re-formation in 44–42. Octavian's army against Sextus Pompeius included a legion XIII, perhaps the forerunner of the imperial XIII *Gemina*, from which veterans would be available for settlement after Actium.[91] But, as we have seen, Hispellum seems likely to have become a colony after Philippi. Allius and Decimius could be Caesarian *evocati* established after Philippi (though their legion was not apparently re-formed under that numeral), but the evidence is too slight to permit any secure conclusion. The appearance of Allius within the *ager Perusinus* could testify to land settlement there in the wake of the Perusine War, when the *Perusini* were deprived of most of their territory (above, p. 69).

Hadria

Hadria—the modern Atri—a Latin colony from *c.* 290 B.C.—lies like many of its fellow Roman towns of the Adriatic coast amid the eastern spurs of the Apennines. Little can be said about the town itself in Roman times. Topographical restrictions make it likely that the street network was much as today; only the most meagre traces of public buildings have been detected.[92]

Hadria appears as a *colonia* in Pliny's lists, in a coastal section.[93] An inscription recording as *patronus coloniae* a consul of 11 B.C. establishes a *terminus ante quem*

---

[86] XI 5291 from Civitella d'Arne records *fin(es) col(oniae) Hisp(ellatium)*.

[87] F. Castagnoli, 'Tracce di centuriazione nei territori di Nocera, Pompei, Nola, Alife, Aquino, Spello', *Rend. Acc. Linc.* ser. 8, xi (1956), 373–78.

[88] For the boundary with Mevania at Fiamenga, C. Pietrangeli, *Mevania* (Roma, 1953), 126.

[89] Nissen, *IL* II 396.

[90] The place-name d'Agliano should derive from the veteran's *nomen* (above, p. 97).

[91] Dio xlviii. 14. 6.

[92] L. Sorricchio, *Hatria = Atri* (Roma, 1911).

[93] *NH* iii. 110.

for its foundation.[94] There could be some suspicion of an earlier Sullan settlement: a public slave of the town was given on manumission the *nomen* Venerius, as in Sullan Pompeii. Yet the *nomen,* if not simply reflecting a prominent cult of the town, may indicate titulature in use at Hadria under the Empire.[95]

From Mosciano S. Angelo west of Giulianova has come a fragmentary sepulchral inscription (Sylloge 73) to ... arius Pius of the tribe *Maecia* who had seen military service in legion XXIX.[96] Almost certainly Mosciano lay within the *territorium* of Castrum Novum, but the tribe *Maecia* indicates a connection by birth or settlement with Hadria. The stone is unfortunately not now traceable — in an account of its discovery Pius is described as 'forse *trib.mil.* della legione XXIX',[97] but it is not clear what part (if any) of the abbreviation *trib.mil.* appeared on the stone. Only two other members of legion XXIX are known, both tribunes.[98] We must consider the possibility that the legion was settled at Hadria, and that a part of the *ager Castronovanus* had passed into the colony's possession. As the legion belonged to Caesar's recruitment programme of 49 B.C., its members could expect release after Philippi. The text of the inscription was never published in full. Dr. Bruno Trubiani, Direttore of the Biblioteca Capitolare at Atri, who very kindly investigated the whereabouts of the stone on my behalf, ascertained that it had disappeared from sight towards the end of the Second World War.[99] Its overall layout may be tentatively restored (see Sylloge 73).

Asculum

Asculum, now Ascoli Piceno, high up in the valley of the Tronto, occupies a promontory formed by the junction of the Castellano tributary with the main stream of the Tronto; their winding and deeply-cutting courses protect the town on three sides. All around, mountains tower above the town, the hillsides clothed in antiquity with olives.[100] Strabo notes the strength of the town-site at Asculum, but emphasises the difficulty of access in his time.[101] It was not until the middle years of Augustus' reign that a new highway across the Apennines provided Asculum with a direct link to the capital; the traveller entered the town through a new gateway, the 'Porta Gemina'.[102]

[94] Paullus Fabius Maximus (*ILS* 919); *PIR*[2] F 47. For long-established links between the Fabii and Hadria, *RE* VI (1909), 1771, nos. 81–83.

[95] IX 5020; above, p. 18.

[96] F. Savini, *Rivista abruzzeze di scienze, lettere ed arte* xix (1904), 596; G. Gatti, ibid. 598; L. Sorricchio, op. cit. (n. 92), 204.

[97] G. Gatti, loc. cit. (n. 96): "L'altra iscrizione e sepolcrale di un . . . ARIVS PIVS della tribu MAEcia, forse *trib. mil.* della legione XXIX . . . La formula 'hic sepultus est in suo' indica semplicemente che il defunto aveva la proprieta dell'area in cui il monumento fu fatto".

[98] Sylloge 90 (Pola); *AE* 1931, 95 (Saturnia).

[99] Letter of November 18th, 1972: 'E probabile che la stessa sia andata perduta durante il periodo 1943–44, quando il Palazzo Savini in Teramo (where the stone had lain for many years) fu prima sede del Comando Generale Adriatico Tedesco e poi devastato dagli sfollati che ivi ebbero per breve tempo dimora'.

[100] U. Laffi and M. Pasquinucci, *Asculum* I (Pisa, 1975) replaces all earlier work. A second volume, on the *ager Asculanus,* is in prospect.

[101] v. 4. 2.

[102] T. P. Wiseman, 'Roman Republican Road-Building', *PBSR* xxxviii (1970), 122–52; I. A. Richmond, 'Commemorative Arches and City Gates in the Augustan Age', *JRS* xxiii (1933), 149–74; Laffi and Pasquinucci, op. cit. (n. 100), 10 ff.

The Elder Pliny names Asculum as a colony, and attaches the laudatory epithet *nobilissima*.[103] Numerous buildings, including temples, a theatre and an amphitheatre, were put up in the Augustan age.[104] There is some evidence that land was transferred to Asculum, presumably in the Late Republic, at the expense of Interamnia. Frontinus notes that public land belonging to a town was normally inalienable. Exceptionally, when a large part of the *territorium* had been transferred to one of its neighbours, some *loca publica* within the walls of the losing town might also be handed over, *ex voluntate conditoris*. As an example Frontinus cites Interamnia: *sicut in Piceno fertur Intermnatium Praetutianorum quandam oppidi partem Asculanorum fine circum dari*.[105] We may reasonably infer from this passage that a considerable portion of the territory of Interamnia had been given to Asculum. Large-scale expropriation could suggest a date after Philippi for the colony.[106]

Firmum

The Latin colony of Firmum Picenum was established in 264 B.C. on a ridge between the valleys of the Tenna and the Etevivo, overlooking both, some 7 kms. from the sea. Over 70 years ago G. Napoletani identified four complete or partial wall-circuits, testifying to expansion from an original nucleus down the slopes on the western and eastern sides of the ridge.[107] None of these circuits can be dated with precision, but the arrival of colonists in the later first century B.C. may be easily seen as an occasion for expansion.[108]

That Firmum was a *colonia* of the later first century B.C. is beyond doubt; the apparent omission by Pliny of Firmum in a coastal list was shown by Mommsen to be illusory.[109] *IIviri* are attested, and in the Domitianic rescript from Falerio (below, p. 182) there is a specific reference to *quartani*, veteran settlers from a *legio* IIII, who, it is clear, must have been established at Firmum. The *quartani* were sufficiently numerous or influential at Firmum for Augustus to employ that description for the citizen body at the town. An inscription mentioning Augustus as *parens coloniae* and benefactor was perhaps unjustly damned by Mommsen.[110]

The legion IIII which formed part of the garrison of Macedonia in 44 B.C. belonged most probably to Caesar's consular series of 48 B.C. Brought back to Italy by Antonius, it defected to Octavian and fought enthusiastically on his behalf at

[103] *NH* iii. 111.

[104] Laffi and Pasquinucci, op. cit. (n. 100), 20, 27, 43, 50.

[105] 18. 10–19. 1.

[106] So Nissen, *IL* II 427; Mommsen, *CIL* IX, p. 494. Notice that Asculum was the home town of the Antonian partisan Ventidius Bassus, who might have been expected to shield it from loss; Wiseman no. 474.

[107] G. Napoletani, *Fermo nel Piceno* (Roma, 1907) with map; G. Annibaldi, *EAA* III (1960), 624–25.

[108] For other buildings, Napoletani, op. cit. (n. 107), 131–32; P. Bonvicini, 'Iscrizioni latine inedite della quinta *regio Italiae*', *Rend. Acc. Linc.* ser. 8, xxvii (1973), 195–205.

[109] *Bürgercolonien*, 192 n. 1.

[110] IX 540*. Mommsen rejected the inscription as fabricated by Cyriacus in or soon after 1437. However, Napoletani, op. cit. (n. 107), 185 reports the discovery of a medieval inscription of 1235, the wording of which indicates a knowledge of this text.

Mutina, though suffering heavy casualties; later Brutus could (falsely) claim its total annihilation at Philippi.[111]

From Monte Sampietrangeli to the north-west of Firmum has come the inscription of C. Vettius L.f. Vel. Tuscus, *aquilifer* of the legion IIII *Macedonica* (Sylloge 72). Whatever interpretation of the Domitianic rescript is accepted (see below), the settlement of the *quartani* at Firmum seems best placed after Philippi. Founder members of legion IIII *Macedonica* would be eligible for discharge at this time; a post-Actium settlement — Ateste — is already known. Cicero reports the enthusiasm shown by the *Firmani* in 43 B.C. for the ill-fated senatorial cause against Antonius;[112] this activity may have turned the attention of the Triumvirs to Firmum after their victory.

Falerio

Falerio lay on the northern flank of the Tenna valley, about 30 kms. from its mouth; along with Firmum, it had at its disposal the flat land of the valley floor. The town is not mentioned in any classical author before Pliny; excavations (admittedly slight) have revealed nothing of Republican date. The survival of numerous inscriptions could suggest that Falerio flourished in the first and second centuries A.D., but in the medieval period repeated devastation led to abandonment; now only the Falerone hamlet preserves the name.[113]

Pliny does not accord the town colonial status. The *Falerienses* appear among the inland peoples of Picenum. Yet *IIviri* are known, and an inscription testifies to a *colonia*; another stone of Hadrianic date records a capitolium, so that colonial status by the beginning of the second century A.D. seems secure.[114]

The Domitianic rescript to the *Falerienses* issued in A.D. 82 forms an invaluable backcloth to any study of the town's status.[115] Its issue followed an attempt by nearby Firmum to draw attention to *subseciva* within the *ager Firmanus* occupied by *Falerienses*. The action by the *Firmani* can be seen as an attempted display of loyalty to Vespasian (or Titus) at the expense of their immediate neighbours. In the event it backfired. Vespasian's policy on *subseciva*, though endorsed by Titus, was repudiated by Domitian who endeavoured to smooth over the ill-feeling aroused. The *Firmani* moreover had omitted to refer to (or had forgotten) an instruction from Augustus to sell off their *subseciva*. As Domitian reminded them, Augustus had sent a letter to his colonists at Firmum, *qua admonuit eos ut omnia subseciva sua colligerent et venderent quos tam salubri admonitioni paruisse non dubito*. Thus their claim to legal ownership was unsound.

[111]Cic. *Fam.* x. 33. 4; App. *BC* iv. 117. The consul Hirtius carried the *aquila* of IIII *Macedonica* during the opening moments of the battle at Mutina (Cic. *Phil.* xiv. 27). Suetonius reports that Octavian himself seized the *aquila* of an unidentified legion during the same battle, when its bearer was seriously wounded (*Aug.* 10).

[112]*Phil.* vii. 23.

[113]G. de Minicis, 'Teatro di Falerone', *Ann. dell'Ist.* xi (1839), 5–61; G. Cerulli Irelli and P. Moreno, 'Alcune iscrizioni di Falerone', *Arch. Class.* xiii (1961), 159–67.

[114]Pliny *NH* iii. 111; P. Bonvicini, 'Il teatro ed altri monumenti di Falerio Picenus', *Studia Picena* xxii (1954), 33–44; IX 5428, 5438–40, 5444–45.

[115]IX 5420 = Bruns, *FIRA*[7] 82 = *MW* 462. For a small fragment of what may be a *lex agraria* from Falerio, A. Piganiol, 'La table de bronze de Falerio, e la loi Mamilia Roscia Peducaea Alliena Fabia', *CRAI* 1939, 193–200.

It is important to determine what type of *subseciva* was the subject of dispute. The gromatic writers note that the term was applied (a) to awkward plots of land on the very edge of centuriated ground, or (b) to land within a grid, which was left unassigned because of its poor quality or the presence of natural obstacles. Further (c), when a colony had expanded into the territory of its neighbours, any land belonging to the latter, which was not assigned, would be returned forthwith. This land too could be terms *subsecivum*.[116]

Mommsen argued that the third category was meant here, and that, when Falerio was made a colony, its territory must have been extended at the expense of Firmum.[117] Whatever land was left unassigned in the expropriated area reverted to Firmum, but Augustus, sensibly seeking a rationalisation of land-holding, instructed the *Firmani* to sell off such *subseciva* to the *Falerienses*. The explanation is ingenious, and seemingly supported by a passage in Siculus Flaccus.[118] However, it might seem more economical to suppose that the *subseciva* were the result of settlement at Firmum itself, which may have expanded along the valley of the Tenna at the expense of Falerio. According to the *Gromatici*, such *subseciva* should have reverted to the *Falerienses* as a matter of course, but elsewhere we are told that *subseciva* could be retained in the ownership of the colony's founder, i.e. in this case, Octavian.[119] It may be therefore that Augustus, in an attempt to re-establish an economic balance between the towns of Firmum and Falerio, 'advised' the *Firmani* to dispose of their *subseciva*, to their own profit; hence he could be described as *indulgentissimus erga quartanos suos*. The date and circumstances of the promotion of Falerio to colonial status remain quite uncertain.

Slight traces of centuriation have been observed in the Tenna valley near Falerio but are of no assistance in defining the boundary between the *ager Faleriensis* and *ager Firmanus*.[120] A cylindrical boundary *cippus* of allegedly Augustan date, found at Cese near Amandola in 1955, on what must have been *ager Faleriensis*, can have no relevance to centuriation in the Tenna valley, but may show that land was sought at some time for colonists away from the plain, in the narrow inland valleys.[121] But there is no clear proof of its Augustan date.

---

[116] F. T. Hinrichs, *Die Geschichte der gromatischen Institutionen* (Wiesbaden, 1974), 128 ff.

[117] *CIL* IX, pp. 518–19.

[118] 163. 5–14.

[119] Hyg. 133. 2 ff.; Sic. Flacc. 162. 20 ff., Hyg. Grom. 202. 5.

[120] P. Bonvicini, 'La centuriazione del territorio faleronese sotto Augusto', *Studia Picena* xxvi (1958), 135–43.

[121] *AE* 1958, 41; G. Cerulli Irelli and P. Moreno, 'Alcune iscrizioni di Falerone', *Arch. Class.* xiii (1961), 159–67; P. Bonvicini, 'Iscrizioni latine inedite della quinta *regio Italiae*', *Rend. Acc. Linc.* ser. 8, xxvii (1972), 195–205. A passage in Hyginus Gromaticus, which describes the use of triangular *arae* at the junction between the territories of three towns (199. 5–7), is illustrated by a drawing which names (as the three communities sharing a boundary) *Iulienses*, *Falerenses* and *Vettonenses* (Rudorff, Fig. 192). The *Falerenses* could be seen as the people of Falerio, the *Iulienses* as those of Firmum, but Vettona (in the Pianura Umbra) shares no border with either. Most probably the names are introduced *exempli causa*, without any precise locality being intended; so O. A. W. Dilke, 'Falerone presso gli agrimensores romani', *Abruzzo* xiii (1975), 101–5. There is no proof here that Firmum was *colonia Iulia*. Cf. above, p. 15, n. 42.

Ancona

The port of Ancona owed its prosperity in Roman times to its rôle as staging post for Adriatic shipping, and as an embarcation point for the Dalmatian coast.[122] Strabo records that Ancona possessed fine wheat and wine, but by the Late Republic its *territorium* was closely confined by the colonies at Sena Gallica and Auximum.[123] Pliny and inscriptions testify to the creation of a colony in the Late Republic. The testimony of Appian places it after Philippi, and provides the useful detail that two legions were settled there (above, p. 64), but their identity is not known.[124]

Fanum Fortunae

Fanum Fortunae lies on the Umbrian coastline between Sena Gallica and Pisaurum, in the valley of the Metaurus river, 4 kms. north of its mouth. At Fanum Fortunae the Via Flaminia, after skirting the northern edge of the valley, reached the Adriatic and turned sharply north-west towards Ariminum.[125]

The early history of the town is obscure; it is mentioned first by Caesar.[126] Some scholars, pointing to an absence of early material from Fanum, have asserted that the town-site lay initially on M. Giove, 3 kms. from the sea, and was transferred to the present site by Octavian at the foundation of the colony.[127] More probably the town grew out of a *statio* on the Flaminia named after a shrine to Fortuna.[128]

Before the death of Augustus, Fanum Fortunae had been advanced to the status of *colonia* with the title *Iulia*.[129] In the opening section of Book V of the *de Architectura*, Vitruvius provides a detailed description of a *basilica* at Fanum, designed and built under his supervision.[130] The whole section, almost certainly an insertion made by Vitruvius himself or by an editor at least a decade after initial publication, provides interesting details of the interrelationship of some of the public buildings around the forum at Fanum Fortunae, including an *aedes Augusti* of which some traces are believed to have been recovered by excavation.[131] It would be pressing the evidence too far to suggest that Vitruvius had general charge of the provision of amenities for the new *colonia*, but his special interest in the town, and resulting knowledge of its status, could account for the fact that Fanum alone is accorded the designation *colonia* (in one case with the title *Iulia* added) in the *de Architectura*, while that title appears to be denied to other old-established colonies

---

[122] M. Moretti, *Ancona* (Roma, 1945).

[123] Strabo v. 4. 2.

[124] Pliny *NH* iii. 111; IX 5898, 5841; App. *BC* v. 23. According to the *Liber Coloniarum*, land at Ancona was assigned *ea lege qua et ager Florentinus* (225. 4), i.e. by a *lex Iulia* (cf. above, p. 176).

[125] N. Alfieri, 'Per la topografia storica di *Fanum Fortunae* (Fano)', *Riv. Stor. Ant.* vi–vii (1976–77), 147–71. Note also B. Mencoboni, *Fanum Fortunae nell'Antichità* (tesi di laurea, Bologna, 1957); copy in the Biblioteca Comunale Federiciana at Fano.

[126] *BC* i. 11.

[127] C. Selvelli, 'Determinanti storici nell'urbanistica Fanese', *Studia Picena* xxii (1954), 51–77.

[128] The *fanum* is most easily associated with the Roman victory over Hasdrubal in 207 B.C. For Gracchan activity in the *ager Fanestris*, *ILLRP* 474.

[129] An additional title *Flavia* was acquired later, probably under the House of Constantine, *CIL* XI, p. 924.

[130] *De Arch.* v. 1. 6.

[131] F. Krohn, *Vitruvii De Architectura* (Teubner ed., 1912), introduction; P. Thielscher, *RE* IXA (1961), 431–32, *s.v. Vitruvius*.

in Italy.[132] The publication date of the *de Architectura* clearly post-dates Actium, so that no useful *terminus ante quem* is provided for the colony at Fanum.

An acephalous inscription first reported at Ginestreto, north of Monteciccardo, and used for many years in an unbroken state as a church altar, may identify the legion whose members were established at Fanum. It is now in the courtyard of the Biblioteca Oliveriana at Pesaro (Sylloge 71). It records a veteran of legion VIII from Tuder, registered in the tribe *Pollia*. Ginestreto lies high above the Foglia valley, almost certainly within the *ager Pisaurensis,* but the tribe *Pollia* should indicate a connection with Fanum. It seems likely that the veteran, by origin an Umbrian from Tuder, adopted the local tribe of Fanum on settlement there, in place of the Tudertine *Crustumina.* The letters VETERAN on the stone are best expanded to *veteranus,* rather than (with Ritterling) to *Veteranae* or *Veteranā,* a title of the legion itself.[133] The appearance of this veteran within the *ager Pisaurensis* could be indicative of land allocation in the hills at the expense of Pisaurum, but the stone may have been carried northwards from the Metaurus valley in more recent times.[134]

The building of a new wall-circuit at Fanum can be dated to the Augustan era. A monumental archway, to greet the traveller arriving on the Flaminia from the west, was dedicated in A.D. 9–10 (above, p. 116).[135] To what extent the new walls replaced, or enlarged, an existing circuit is unknown.

Pisaurum

Pisaurum, at the mouth of the river Foglia (the ancient Pisaurus), was a *colonia maritima* of 184 B.C. Sullan activity there, recently postulated by Zicàri, remains unproved.[136] Plutarch provides a *terminus ante quem* for the reinforcement of Pisaurum in the later first century B.C.; among portents which he notes as preceding the Actium campaign was a severe earthquake at Pisaurum, which is stated to have been one of Antony's colonies.[137] The destruction wrought in a colony owing allegiance to Antony could be held (no doubt after the event) to presage the fall of the man himself.[138] The *colonia* therefore should date from 41 B.C. A few years earlier, the poet Catullus had described Pisaurum as a *moribunda sedes,*[139] but this verdict should not be over-hastily accepted as evidence for the lack of prosperity of the town in the Late Republic; the context required Catullus to contrast a quiet

---

[132] V. 1. 6; ii. 9. 16.

[133] *Legio* 1644.

[134] For centuriation in the *ager Fanestris,* N. Alfieri, loc. cit. (n. 125), and above, p. 100.

[135] XI 6218–19 = *ILS* 104; I. A. Richmond, loc. cit. (n. 102).

[136] I. Zicàri, *RE Sup.* XI (1968), 1092–98, *s.v. Pisaurum,* with plan.

[137] *Ant.* 60.

[138] For an earthquake at Pisaurum in 97 B.C., Obsequens *Prod. Lib.* 48. The activities of an Antonian partisan, Insteius, at Pisaurum in 43 (Cic. *Phil.* xiii. 26) form no good evidence that the colony should be dated to that year, as Harris 299. Cicero offers only a chance allusion to his origin; Insteii are epigraphically attested at Pisaurum.

[139] lxxxi. 1–4.

town with the populous capital. In any case the precise meaning of *moribunda* is disputed.[140] From the large numbers of inscriptions recovered from the town it would seem that the *colonia* prospered under the Empire. The titulature *colonia Iulia Felix Pisaurum* is attested by two inscriptions.[141]

---

[140] C. J. Fordyce, *Catullus* (Oxford, 1960), 370. Pisaurum would lie on Catullus's most natural route between Verona (his home-town) and Rome. On possible meanings of *moribundus*, I. Zicàri, 'Moribunda ab sede Pisauri', *Studia Oliveriana* iii (1955), 57–69; A. Massimi, 'Nota Catulliana', *Giorn. It. Fil.* x (1957), 336–38; I. Zicàri, Postilla catulliana', *Studia Oliveriana* vi (1958), 87.

[141] XI 6377, 6335 = *ILS* 7218; above, p. 22. For public buildings, Zicàri, loc. cit. (n. 136).

CHAPTER NINE

AEMILIA, TRANSPADANA, VENETIA AND LIGURIA

Ariminum

Ariminum (modern Rimini) lies at the mouth of the Marecchia at the point where the Apennines bid farewell to the Adriatic and usher in the broad expanses of the Po valley. A *colonia Latina* from 268, Ariminum was a vital control point for Italy's invaders and her defenders; Toynbee has aptly compared it to Thermopylae.[1] Ariminum is named by Appian as one of the most prominent of the cities selected for allocation to veterans after Philippi.[2] Under the Empire it bore the titles *col(onia) Aug(usta) Arim(inensis)* (above, p. 20). The absence of *Iulia* prompted Mommsen to query the correctness of Appian's testimony, or at least to doubt that allocation of land had in fact taken place at any time before 27 B.C.; but as the earliest inscription to give titles dates from the later first century A.D., it is perhaps more probable, as Mommsen himself allowed, that *Iulia* had by then fallen out of use.[3]

The completion of Augustus' programme of repairs to the Via Flaminia in 27 B.C. was commemorated at Ariminum by the erection of a monumental gateway where the road entered the town from the south. An earlier gate structure was demolished to accommodate it.[4] The continuing importance of Ariminum as a road centre brought further imperial attention; in or soon after A.D. 1, C. Caesar is credited with paving all the streets within the town; in the last years of Augustus' reign a beginning was made on the construction of a new bridge across the Marecchia, by which the Aemilia left Ariminum for the north; it was completed in A.D. 22 by Tiberius.[5] Of public buildings in the town, the theatre is likely to be Augustan in date; the amphitheatre is later.[6]

Bononia

Bononia, a *colonia Latina* from 189 B.C., lies on the Via Aemilia, close to the northern exit from the Futa Pass, the most direct route from Arretium and Florentia to the Po Valley.[7] Literary evidence testifies to the reacquisition of colonial status in the later first century B.C., but different interpretations have been put on it. Dio records that Octavian, when organising Italian support in the build-up towards Actium, took pains to win over Antonian veterans; as an example he cites Bononia,

---

[1] G. Mansuelli, *Ariminum* (Roma, 1941); Toynbee I, 281; U. Ewins, 'The early Colonisation of Cisalpine Gaul', *PBSR* xx (1952), 54–71; R. Chevallier, 'Problèmatique de la colonisation romaine: l'example de l'Emilia-Romagna', in *Studi archeologici riminesi* (Faenza, 1964), 19–46; M. Zuffa, 'Nuove scoperte di archeologia e storia riminese', ibid., 47–94.

[2] *BC* iv. 3.

[3] XI 408, 414 = *ILS* 6656; XII 1529; Mommsen, *Bürgercolonien* 170.

[4] XI 365 = *ILS* 84 = *EJ²* 286; Dio liii. 22. 2.

[5] XI 366 = *ILS* 133; XI 367 = *ILS* 113 = *EJ²* 82; above, p. 115.

[6] Zuffa, loc. cit. (n. 1).

[7] P. Ducati, *Storia di Bologna* (Bologna, 1928); F. Bergonzoni—G. Bonora, *Bologna Romana*, I (Bologna, 1976).

which was formally refounded at this time by Octavian.[8] It should be clear that Octavian had no veterans for settlement at this juncture, and Dio does not say that he established any; the refoundation can be seen as an attempted counter to Antonian sympathies. Suetonius notes that Octavian specifically exempted the *Bononienses* from the general oath of allegiance in 32–31 *quod in Antoniorum clientela antiquitus erant*.[9] Though it could be argued that Antonius had acquired these *clientes* precisely in 41 B.C., the word *antiquitus* suggests that, for Suetonius, the relationship was of somewhat longer standing. Mommsen argued that Dio, finding in a source a reference to Antonian *clientela* at Bononia and aware of its status as a colony, connected the two items and concluded that it had been an Antonian foundation, after Philippi. In his view no colony was established at Bononia before Actium.[10]

Certainly no meaningful connection between Bononia and any member of the *gens Antonia* is known.[11] Cicero refers to the anti-senatorial stance of Bononia and neighbouring towns in 43 B.C., but this forms no evidence for *clientela,* only for their proximity to the Antonian stronghold at Mutina.[12] However, the testimony of Dio and Suetonius need not conflict; a long-standing connection with the Antonii was perhaps bolstered by the establishment of a *colonia* after Philippi. Pliny's story that Augustus was entertained at Bononia off gold plate by a veteran of Antony's Parthian War (above, p. 113) confirms the allegiance of the colony.

Activity of Augustus at Bononia is confirmed by one or (possibly) two inscription(s) from the town. The first records the construction of baths by *divus Aug(ustus) parens,* and their repair by an emperor who must be Caligula or Nero.[13] The second, published more recently, may describe Augustus, living or dead, as *pater*.[14] The baths themselves could be evidence of his favour to the town before Actium.

Mutina

The town of Mutina, a minor stronghold of the Boii, became along with Parma a *colonia Civium Romanorum* in 183 B.C.; both towns were envisaged as intermediate control points along the newly-built Via Aemilia.[15] A city of some distinction in the Early Empire, Mutina lay close to the important market site of *Macri Campi*.[16] The town is named as a colony by Pliny, but no confirmation of refoundation is forth-

[8] Dio. l. 6.

[9] *Aug.* 17.

[10] *Bürgercolonien* 172–73.

[11] Wiseman 39.

[12] *Fam.* xii. 5. 2.

[13] XI 720 = *ILS* 5674; Ducati, op. cit. (n. 7), 379–80. Identification with Nero is supported by Tac. *Ann.* xii. 58; Suet. *Ner.* 7. 2. For some remains of the structure, recovered by excavation, *NS* 1892, 257.

[14] A. Donati, 'Sulla colonia augustea a Bologna', *Arch. Class.* xviii (1966) 248–50; *AE* 1969/1970, 194.

[15] G. Mancini, *Emilia Romana* II (Firenze, 1944), 67–73; G. Mansuelli, *I Cisalpini* (Firenze, 1962), 41 ff.; P. Tozzi, 'Indicazioni sul primitivo stanziamento della colonia di Mutina', *Riv. Stor. Ant.* v (1974), 47–74.

[16] *CIL* XI, p. 170 n. 1; M. Corradi Cervi, *Arch. Stor. Parm.* ser. 3, iv (1939), 9 ff.

coming from other sources.[17] The siege of Mutina by Antony in 43 must have been detrimental to both town and *territorium,* and could account for later interest, but the precise date of the refoundation is not known. Little of significance is known about Roman buildings in the town.[18]

Parma

Like Mutina, its sister colony to the south-west, Parma lies on the Aemilia, on the eastern bank of an eponymous tributary flowing northwards into the Po.[19] An inscription reveals that Parma was reinforced in the later first century B.C., as *colonia Iulia Augusta Parmensis* (above, p. 22). From Baganzola north of the town a tomb monument records L. Vettidius C.f., a veteran of legion XII *Paterna,* and his wife Tertia (Sylloge 88). The title of the legion may suggest a unit raised by Octavian to match Antony's XII *Antiqua;* it would therefore have been available for settlement after Actium (above, p. 31). Vettidius, whose *nomen* hints at an Umbrian or Picene origin, became *sexvir* and *aedilis* in the town.[20]

Cicero reports that Parma suffered considerably at the hands of the troops of L. Antonius in 43, when in the aftermath of the battle of Mutina it was taken by stealth and pillaged.[21] Cicero indeed maintained that part of the male population was massacred, and the women and children maltreated, but there can be no grounds for thinking here of wholesale depopulation.

Brixellum

Brixellum lies on the southern bank of the Po north-east of Parma. Little is known about the town itself; inscriptions are few and literary references sparse.[22] Pliny gives Brixellum colonial rank; the attribution was doubted by Hülsen, but Mommsen was to remind scholars of the lack of contrary evidence.[23]

In 1932 an elaborate tomb enclosure of Julio-Claudian date, the 'Tomb of the Concordii' was discovered close to modern Brescello.[24] The principal dedication was to C CONCORDIVS BRIXIL L PRIMVS VIVIR AVG. Evidently *publici servi* of Brixellum were awarded upon manumission the *nomen* Concordius. It has been noted elsewhere that *liberti* of colonies sometimes assumed a *nomen* derived from one of the colony's titles (above, p. 18). It might therefore be thought that

[17] *NH* iii. 115.

[18] An inscription from Mirandola north of the town records the construction of a *Caesareum* and *xysti Augustei* by a group of prominent local citizens (XI 948).

[19] M. Corradi Cervi, *NS* 1941, 105; ibid. 1943, 199; P. Tozzi, *Saggi di topografia storica* (Firenze, 1974), 44–60.

[20] Schulze, *Eigennamen* 428; R. Syme, 'Sabinus the Muleteer', *Latomus* xvii (1958), 73–80 for a branch of the family settled at Auximum.

[21] *Phil.* xiv. 8–9; *Fam.* x. 33. 4, xi. 13b. For suggested archaeological evidence of the sack, *NS* 1949, 19–20.

[22] A. Solari, 'Brixellum', *Athenaeum* ix (1931), 420–25; G. Mancini, *Emilia Romana* II (Firenze, 1944), 78–79.

[23] *NH* iii. 115; Hülsen, *RE* III (1899), 884; Mommsen, *Bürgercolonien* 194.

[24] S. Aurigemma, 'Il monumento dei Concordii presso Boretto', *Riv. Ist. Arch.* iii (1931–32), 268–98; *NS* 1932, 171–82; *AE* 1933, 154.

Brixellum possessed the title *Concordia* in the Julio-Claudian Age, confirmings its status as a colony,[25] but the *libertus* may have been named after a prominent local cult, as elsewhere.

Placentia

Placentia, a *colonia Latina* from 218 B.C., lies on the southern bank of the Po some 6 kms. east of the junction of the Trebbia with the main stream of the river. The strategic importance of the town can be seen from the concentration upon it of all the Roman highways from the west. The *ager Placentinus* comprised a sizeable but elongated strip extending on the west to modern Casteggio.[26] Little is known of the splendid monuments or of the walls, which Tacitus records in his account of the siege of Placentia by Vitellian forces in A.D. 69.[27] The status of *colonia* is accorded to Placentia by Pliny, and *IIviri* are known under the Empire.[28] An inscription published in 1958 should assure Placentia of inclusion here; it reports M. Petronius of the tribe *Voturia* as having been decurion at *Augusta Placentia*.[29]

Early in 41 B.C. a mutiny among troops of Salvidienus bound for Spain broke out at Placentia.[30] It was not quelled until the inhabitants of the town had supplied the troops with money, perhaps to encourage them to depart elsewhere. If Placentia had already received veterans in any number, it is difficult to imagine that newly arrived settlers would supply money to their former comrades, so that a date for the colony after Actium may be more likely.[31]

Cremona

Cremona lies on the northern bank of the Po, 30 kms. down-stream from Placentia on the other bank.[32] Rome's first outpost beyond the Po, it was founded along with Placentia as a *colonia Latina* in 218 B.C. Cremona is named as a *colonia* by Pliny and by Tacitus; no titles are known.[33] Hyginus Gromaticus specifically ascribes survey work at Cremona to the Triumvirs, and the knowledge that in the aftermath of Philippi the family of the poet Vergil in the adjacent *ager Mantuanus* was confiscated allows the colony to be dated securely to 41 B.C. Servius' commentary seems to place the colony after Actium, but he consistently confuses the two main phases of

---

[25] G. Susini, 'Colonia Concordia Brixillum', *Riv. Stor. Ant.* i (1971), 119–25.

[26] P. Tozzi, 'Sul confine-occidentale di *Placentia*', *Rend. Ist. Lomb.* cix (1975), 362–64. Tozzi shows that Placentia's centuriation extended to its extreme western border.

[27] *Hist.* ii. 17–23; M. Corradi Cervi, 'Placentia', *Arch. Stor. Parm.* ser. 3, iii (1938), 45 ff.

[28] *NH* iii. 115; *CIL* XI, p. 242.

[29] P. Fraccaro, 'Un iscrizione di *Clastidium* e *Augusta Placentia*', *Athenaeum* xxxvi (1958), 117–22; *AE* 1959, 36.

[30] Dio xlviii. 10.

[31] For the suggestion that the Velleia Alimentary Table provides evidence of the transfer of land to Placentia in the later first century B.C., R. Hanslik, *RE* XX (1950), 1906. For the military epitaph of a soldier or veteran of legion VI *Ferrata* from the town, which could be Augustan in date, *Boll. Stor. Piac.* xxxiii (1938), 83.

[32] Tozzi 9 ff.; also G. Pontiroli, 'Cremona e il suo territorio in età romana', *ACeDSIR* i (1967–68), 163–218, with a valuable appendix by M. A. Levi.

[33] *NH* iii. 130; Tac. *Hist.* iii. 19. An illustration preserved in the gromatic corpus may describe the people of Cremona as *Iulienses* (Rudorff, Fig. 190; above, p. 15, n. 42).

settlement in the Late Republic.[34] Recent work by Tozzi on centuriation in the plain between Cremona, Mantua and Brixia has revealed that Cremona expanded at the expense of both these towns (above, p. 90). It was already clear from the scholiasts that Mantua lost a considerable amount of land, and that the surveyors had advanced almost to the walls of the town. According to Servius' commentary, Cornelius Gallus mounted a bitter onslaught on the land commissioner Alfenus Varus: *cum iussus tria millia passus a muro in diversa relinquere, vix octingentos passus aquae, quae circumdata est, admetireris, reliquisti.*[35] The broad sweep of the Mincius was all that remained in Mantua's possession. Vergil's family property, close to the *vicus Andicus,* which medieval tradition placed at Pietole 3 miles southwest of Mantua, but which scholars have relocated with some plausibility north-west of the town, was seized. Whichever location is preferred, its closeness to Mantua helps to confirm Servius' testimony on the comprehensiveness of the expropriations.[36] Susini has recently identified from the territory of Bononia a small group of epitaphs of the Late Republic or Early Empire, of persons bearing the tribe *Sabatina* of Mantua, two in a style which can be paralleled at Mantua itself.[37] Susini suggested that these people could be dispossessed *Mantuani* who fled to Bononia in 41. However, as Bononia itself was an Antonian colony of the post-Philippi programme, it may be rather that Octavian gave them land there somewhat later.

From Bagnolo 35 kms. north of Cremona (see Fig. 9 at p. 193) has come the epitaph of C. Lanius C.f., a veteran of legion X *Veneria,* and his son by a slave mother. The stone is now at Brescia (Sylloge 66). The *nomen* is rare and not otherwise found in Cisalpina; two occurrences in Umbria may suggest an origin there.[38] The title should indicate that his legion is the Caesarian legion X re-formed by Lepidus, which passed to Antony in 43; Lanius may be envisaged as an *evocatus* recalled from Narbo. His appearance at Cremona could suggest that he had received an enlarged allotment at a new colony in return for service in 44–42 (above, p. 62). Now, Bagnolo might seem on both topographical and epigraphic grounds to lie well inside the *ager Brixianus,*[39] but the tribe *Aniensis* in which Lanius was registered indicates a connection with Cremona. Moreover, Tozzi's researches have indicated that Cremona's new grid extended north from the Oglio (the natural boundary between Cremona and Brixia), at least as far as Manerbio.[40] It may then have extended to Bagnolo.

A stone now at Brescia commemorates C. Domitius, a veteran of legion II; it

---

[34] At *Vita Verg.* 17 Servius reports that the *Cremonenses* were punished *quia pro Antonio senserant,* which is hardly a reason for selection after Philippi; he names the surveyor appointed *ab Augusto* as Octavius Musa (on *Ecl.* ix. 7), perhaps implying a *libertus* of Octavian.

[35] Servius (ed. Thilo), on *Ecl.* ix. 10.

[36] B. Nardi, *Mantuanitas Vergiliana* (Roma, 1963), 21 ff., 53; L. P. Wilkinson, *The Georgics of Virgil* (Cambridge, 1969), 28; K. Wellesley, 'Virgil's Home', *WS* lxxix (1966), 330–50.

[37] G. Susini, 'I profughi della *Sabatina*', *Athenaeum* (fascicolo speciale, 1976) = *Convegno in memoria di Plinio Fraccaro,* 172–76.

[38] Schulze, *Eigennamen* 192.

[39] Inscriptions with the Brixian *Fabia* have been recovered from Manerbio (V 4165), Gambara (V 4129–30), Scorzarolo (V 4145), and Ghedi (V 4156).

[40] Tozzi 101 ff.

was first reported north of the Oglio and west of Manerbio, within an area which seems likely to have been covered by Cremona's centuriation (Sylloge 67); unfortunately Domitius' tribal registration is not given. If Domitius was settled at Cremona after Philippi, the legion should be Antony's legion II, formerly of the Macedonian garrison. However, as the grids of Cremona and Brixia overlap at Manerbio, it could prove equally probable that Domitius was settled at Brixia.

Of more likely relevance here is a partially preserved slab from Ricengo, northwest of Cremona, which commemorates Naevius Ter.f., a veteran of XV *Apollinaris* (Sylloge 68); the nomenclature reveals Naevius as of native Gallic stock. He could have been settled after Philippi when veterans of that legion were eligible for discharge. On the other hand, the title *Apollinaris* has been thought of as a reminiscence of Actium.[41] Naevius could of course have adopted it retrospectively. Other stones from Cremona of early or mid Augustan date (Sylloge 69–70) commemorate a *signifer* Arruntius Maxumus of legion IIX and an Aponius who served in legion IX *Hispaniensis*.[42] Both epitaphs may testify to later settlement at Cremona under Augustus, or to military service by sons of the original colonists.

Brixia

Brixia, nestling in the Alpine foothills to the south-west of Lake Garda, derived its prosperity from sheep grazed on the subalpine slopes and from the fertile plain stretching southwards from the town towards the Oglio.[43] Recent surveys of the town site have helped to define its layout and to identify major buildings. Evidence of construction work under Augustus is not yet forthcoming, except that an aqueduct presented by him was completed by Tiberius; some remains of it have been located.[44]

Interest in the colony at Brixia has centred upon its titles, *colonia Civica Augusta Brixia*, which two inscriptions attest, the earlier datable to the second half of the first century A.D.[45] The title *Civica* is unique, and has generally been interpreted as implying a civilian as opposed to military colony at Brixia, peopled perhaps by Italians dispossessed after Actium.[46] Dispossessed owners are known to have been settled in Macedonia at that time, but no settlements are known within Italy itself (above, p. 76).

The precise date of the colony cannot be securely established from other evidence; it is noted by Pliny, and the title *colonia* is attached to the town on an inscription of Tiberian date.[47] Tozzi's researches have suggested that centuriation

---

[41] Ritterling, *Legio* 1747.

[42] V *Sup.* 1264 (first reported at Cremona); G. Pontiroli, 'Stele di *T. Aponius signifer legionis IX Hispaniensis* nel territorio cremonese', *Rend. Ist. Lomb.* cv (1971), 149–56 (from Genivolta north-west of Cremona).

[43] A. Albertini, in *Storia di Brescia* I (Brescia, 1963), 129–84; Comune di Brescia, *Brescia Romana* (2 vols. Brescia, 1979).

[44] E. Arslan, 'Considerazioni sulla strutturazione urbanistica di Brescia romana', *Latomus* xxvii (1968), 761–85; P. Tozzi, *Saggi di topografia storica* (Firenze, 1974), 29–43. The Flavian capitolium in the town overlies a similar temple datable to the early first century B.C.

[45] V 4212 = *ILS* 6714; V *Sup.* 1273 = *ILS* 4910.

[46] Nissen, *IL* II 197; Mommsen, *CIL* V, p. 439; Vittinghoff, 24 n. 3; Brunt, *IM* 322 n. 1.

[47] *NH.* iii. 130; *ILS* 114.

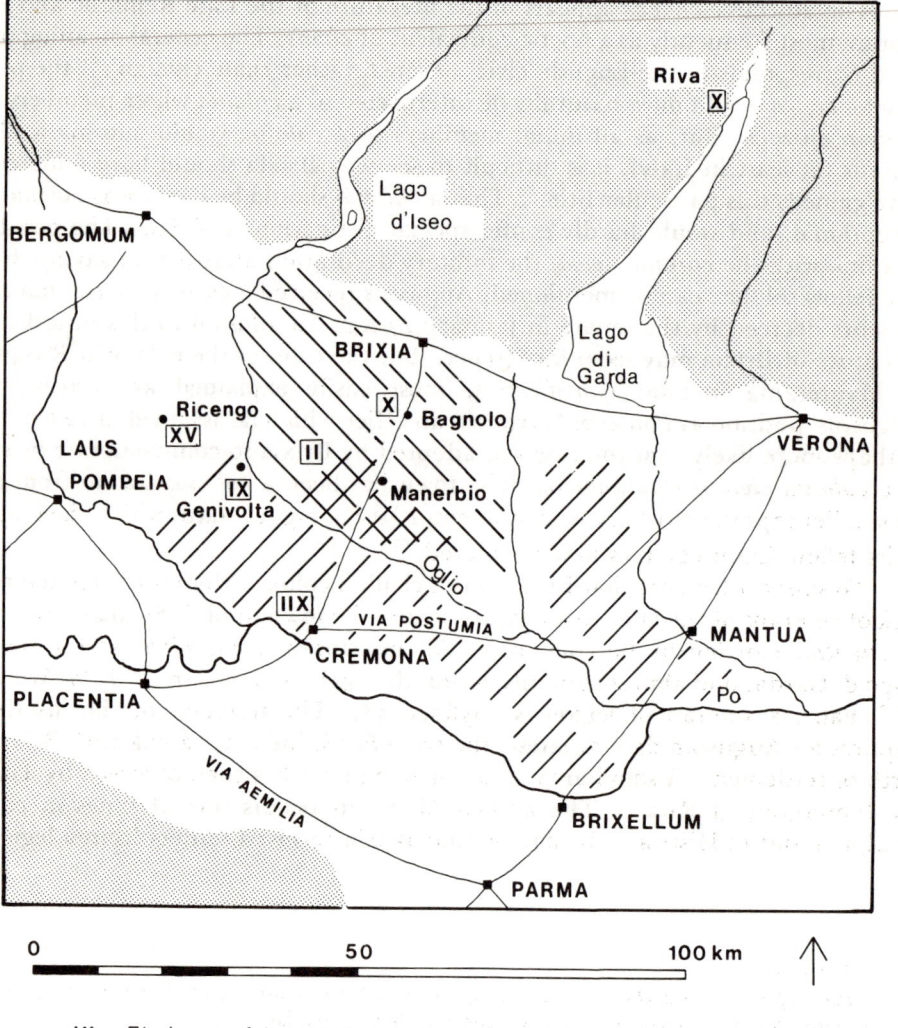

IX   Findspot of inscription, with numeral of legion

\\\   Centuriation on Brixia grid

///   Centuriation on Cremona grid

FIG. 9: VETERANS AT CREMONA AND BRIXIA

orientated on Brixia stretched southwards under the Empire almost to the Oglio, overlapping the system laid out to the benefit of Cremona in 41 B.C.[48] If this sequence is correct, it suggests that the colony at Brixia belongs at the earliest to the post-Actium settlement programme.

The adjective *civicus* appears in the literature of the Late Republic and Early Empire most frequently as a poetic equivalent of *civilis*. The general meaning of the word corresponds to the English 'civic' or 'civil' rather than 'civilian';[49] the phrase *colonia civica* would most naturally be interpreted as a *colonia* whose members were Roman citizens. But, as all initial members of a *colonia* would automatically be citizens (at least in Italy), it is difficult to see why Brixia should have adopted, or have gained, this particular title.[50] That a *colonia* should be *civica* was normal, not exceptional, and would hardly confer special distinction on Brixia. The possibility of a link with the *corona civica*, the military decoration awarded for saving the life of a fellow soldier, can be mentioned. Augustus received a *corona civica* among the honours decreed by the senate in January 27 B.C. An allusion to this award in the titulature of Brixia may seem far-fetched, but the titles of the colony at Rusguniae in Mauretania include *Pontificensis*, most easily explained as deriving from Augustus' position as *Pontifex Maximus*, an office which he assumed in 12 B.C.[51] It is perhaps more likely that the title was adopted by Brixia to commemorate its status as a *colonia civium Romanorum*. The town has been a *colonia Latina* from 89 to 49 B.C. Perhaps the citizenry wished to emphasise a higher status which the majority of its fellow Latin colonies never achieved.[52]

To support his view that Brixia was a civilian colony, Mommsen pointed to the lack of veterans of the later first century within the town itself.[53] Such an argument, *ex silentio*, can hardly be conclusive. An inscription from Riva, at the head of Lago di Garda, and almost certainly within the *ager Brixianus*, records M. Mutellius M.f. Fab., a veteran of legion X (Sylloge 58). The terseness of the inscription requires an Augustan date at latest; the tribe *Fabia* indicates a link with Brixia, by birth or settlement. A small area of centuriated land has been observed by Tozzi in the hinterland of Riva.[54] The *nomen* Mutellius occurs several times in eastern Cisalpina and in Histria.[55] It may be that Brixia received settlers from a legion X,

[48] Tozzi 111.

[49] Hor. *Epis.* i. 3. 23; *Od.* ii. 1. 1, iii. 24. 26, etc. Note, however, Ovid, *Fasti* i. 22 (*civica pro trepidis cum tulit arma reis*) where the weaponry is that of civil law.

[50] Commodus renamed the colony at Carthage *Alexandria Commodiana Togata* (SHA *Vit. Comm.* 17. 8); the last mentioned title presumably emphasised links with Rome.

[51] *AE* 1956, 160; P. Salama, 'La colonie di Rusguniae d'après les inscriptions', *Rev. Afr.* xcix (1955), 5–52. Salama proposes that the colony was named after Lepidus, *pontifex maximus* at its creation, and that it must have served to house one of his legions. For the veteran M. Helvius, who adopted the *agnomen* Civica after an award from Tiberius, above, p. 111, n. 53.

[52] M. A. Levi, in *Storia di Brescia* I (Brescia, 1963), 191 suggested that the title was adopted to commemorate the promotion of the *Brixiani* to full citizenship in 49 B.C.

[53] *CIL* V, p. 439.

[54] Tozzi 115 with his tav. xiv.

[55] Schulze, *Eigennamen* 442, 451 n. 1.

perhaps after Actium (but Mutellius could have been a local man) and from legion
II, if the epitaph of C. Domitius (Sylloge 67) belongs here (above, p. 192).[56]

Brixia was an important town under the Empire with a substantial *territorium*
and large population. Tozzi has identified up to 1,000 *centuriae* in the *ager
Brixianus* of the Empire, and his researches could suggest that Brixia recovered
most, if not all, the land north of the Oglio lost after Philippi; the dominance of its
bloated southern neighbour may have been short-lived.[57]

Ateste

Ateste, modern Este, lying on the northern bank of the Adige (Athesis) river (from
which it derived its ancient name) was an important commercial and artistic centre
of the Venetic Iron Age. It reached the peak of its prosperity in the fifth century
B.C.; thereafter a decline set in, with Ateste eclipsed by its increasingly powerful
neighbour, Patavium.[58]

A glance at a modern map would be misleading in any attempt to account for
the importance of Venetic and Roman Ateste. The river Adige now flows well to the
south of the town, but local antiquarians of the eighteenth century had already
divined that the Adige had in earlier times (probably up to A.D. 589) flowed past
Ateste (as the very name would seem to imply), leaving evidence of its passage in the
form of dunes and sandbanks.[59] The accounts of Mommsen and Chilver are vitiated
by ignorance of this change — Chilver attributed the 'failure' of Ateste as a colony to
the fact that it did not lie on a major river.[60]

There survive from Ateste and the *ager Atestinus* some 27 memorials to
veterans of the later first century B.C. (for a list see below, p. 200). Several legions are
represented, but two predominate: legion V, sometimes bearing the title *Urbana*,
and legion XI. Six veterans of each are commemorated, together with three from
legion IIII *Macedonica,* two from legion XII, and one each from IX, XIV, XV and
XIIX. Where only a single veteran of a legion is recorded, it would be rash to
postulate settlement by large numbers; the epigraphic evidence, in its present state,
suggests a nucleus from legions V and XI, supplemented by smaller groups from
others.[61]

Apart from legionary veterans it is likely that a detachment of Praetorians was

---

[56] Sylloge 56 reports a veteran of legion XIX (or XIV) at Bergomum. He could be a stray from
Brixia, which lies immediately to the east; alternatively the man may simply have returned home after
service.

[57] For Brixia under the Empire, A. Garzetti, 'Epigrafia e storia di Brescia romana', in *Atti conv.
int. per il XIX cent. della dedic. del 'Capitolium'* (Brescia, 1974), 19–61.

[58] G. Pietrogrande, *Ateste nella milizia imperiale* (Venezia, 1888); G. Fogolari, *Il museo nazionale
atestino in Este* (Roma, 1957).

[59] A. Alessi, *Ricerche istorico-critiche dell'antichità di Este* (Padova, 1776), 6 ff.; A. Gloria,
Intorno al corso dei fiumi . . . nel territorio padovano (Padova, 1877), 144 ff.

[60] Mommsen, *CIL* V, p. 240; G. E. F. Chilver, *Cisalpine Gaul* (Oxford, 1941), 31, 33 n. 1. For
archaeological evidence of drainage and of attempts to hold back the turbulent waters in Roman
times, *NS* 1882, 5–6; ibid. 1896, 120; ibid. 1906, 171; ibid. 1924, 8.

[61] Omitted from consideration here are V 2500 (a veteran of legion VI), and *NS* 1915, 145 (a
speculator of a *cohors praetoria*), both of which seem likely to postdate the Augustan age.

also settled at Ateste. *Milites* of a *cohors* I and of a *cohors* II seem certain veterans of this date; a fragmentary stone commemorates a *signifer* of a *cohors* V (above, p. 112).

From the occurrence of epitaphs commemorating *Actiaci* (above, p. 111) it can be concluded that the colony was founded in or about 30 B.C. This dating can be confirmed by examination of what is known of the legions V *Urbana* and XI. The title *Urbana* is known only from the Atestine inscriptions, and not all veterans of legion V settled there employ it. During the Republic, forces left to defend Rome in the absence of the consular legions were called *legiones urbanae*. [62] An explanation along these lines can be made to fit the events of 43 B.C. When D. Brutus was besieged in Mutina, the consul Pansa raised an army of four legions with which he hastened north against Antony (above, p. 26). Obsequens provides the information that a fifth legion was left behind by Pansa *ad urbis praesidium*; Appian confirms. [63] Pansa would not leave a veteran legion to guard Rome when he had only *legiones tironum* with which to face Antony; it may be presumed that this reserve legion was likewise composed of *tirones* and part of the same series. Given that Pansa would most naturally employ the consular numerals I–IV as the basis of his series, it must be likely that the legion left *ad urbis praesidium* had a numeral no higher than V. The case for this legion being the V *Urbana* seems sufficiently strong to overcome the scepticism of Ritterling. [64] It would be only after Naulochus or Actium that even founder members of this *legio Urbana* could look for discharge.

Caesar had raised a legion XI immediately upon arrival in Cisalpine Gaul in 58; its veterans must have received allotments in 47–44 B.C., and there is as yet no clear evidence that it was re-formed after Caesar's death (see above, p. 66). A legion with this numeral formed part of Octavian's forces at Perusia, but its later movements are not recorded. Members of it could ordinarily expect settlement after Actium.

We can say little about the background of individual veterans. None of the inscriptions contains certain reference to an *origo*, though the text of the unfortunately broken epitaph of M. Billienus (Pl. IB) has sometimes been thought to conceal one. [65] We are thrown back on an investigation of *nomina*. The name *Billienus* is found in several towns of southern Italy, and in the north *Billieni* are attested in Pola, Aquileia, Atria and Mediolanium. [66] The family of this veteran may have come north before the Late Republic. M. Tudicius can be seen as a north Italian; the family of L. Caltius can be plausibly domiciled at Praeneste, M. Aufustius in Campania, L. Villius in Etruria, and L. Blattius Vetus, less

[62] T. Steinwender, 'Die legiones urbanae', *Philologus* xxxix (1880), 527–40.

[63] Obsequens 69; App. *BC* iii. 91.

[64] *Legio* 1587. Note that a small hamlet west of Ateste is today named Urbana.

[65] Line 8 of the text (see pl. IB) reads ....MO ERVC.... (or ERVG), inviting a restoration DOMO ERVC (OR ERVG), but no satisfactory place-name is available. Mention of an *origo* is strangely placed in the inscription, and we might look rather for details of other members of the family, but an emendation to BILLIE]NO ERVC[.... is not acceptable. Scrutiny of the stone (now standing upside down in the courtyard of the Museo Civico at Vicenza) confirms the traditional reading. Veterans of this time rarely give details of their origin.

[66] *CIL* V, index; V *Sup.*, index.

securely, in south-east Italy.[67] Some *nomina* cannot be pinpointed because of their very rarity; others are too common.[68] One man, C. Rutilius T.f., could have originated from a family already domiciled at Ateste itself.[69] It could be tempting to suppose that the profusion of legions at Ateste resulted from the deliberate settlement there of Cisalpines from various formations, in a familiar terrain, but (as we have seen) there is only a little support for such a view in the epigraphic evidence. Rather there may have been some reinforcement for the town in 14 B.C.

As Mommsen noted, the boundaries of the *ager Atestinus* can be more accurately determined than those of most Transpadane towns, because of the abundant scatter throughout the *territorium* of inscriptions bearing the rare voting-tribe *Romilia*, their findspots carefully recorded by zealous local antiquarians.[70] Of the 27 memorials, nine have no reliable provenance, or were first seen at Este itself; the remaining 18 were reported at cottages and farmhouses throughout the *territorium*.[71] An examination of the provenances of these memorials may provide useful information on the location of allotments within the *ager Atestinus*. The accompanying figure (Fig. 10) shows their distribution. There is some hint that veterans of the same legion may have been kept in the same general areas within the *territorium*. Three tombstones of members of V *Urbana*, found away from Este itself but within the *ager Atestinus*, were recovered in the south-east part of the *territorium*, at Vigghizolo, Villa Estense and Solesino; two known veterans of IIII *Macedonica* are recorded in the vicinity of Monselice, another at Montagnana west of the town. Two out of three probable members of the *cohortes praetoriae* were found in the south-west of the *territorium* at Minerbe and Marega; the other was discovered near Monselice. Memorials of veterans of legion XI are more scattered: from Moladiriemi and Vetta to the east of Ateste, and from Poiana and Urbana to the west. Nothing can be deduced from the single occurrences of other legions.

Out of the 24 inscriptions which survive more or less intact, only seven mention wives, and only two make direct reference to children. This dearth encouraged Chilver in his view that Ateste was a failure as a colony, and that the town was only momentarily revitalised by the injection of fresh colonists, and was soon in decline once more. The epitaph of C. Talponius (Pl. IIA) gives no hint of a family, but a second inscription (found with it) testifies to a son and grandson, both dying young, perhaps before the veteran himself.[72] The veteran Q. Coelius is commemorated on a stone from Moladiriemi; a memorial to P. Coelius Q.f. Rom. Aper was first seen at nearby Monselice—the exact provenance is not recorded. He could be the son of the veteran, though the latter's tombstone provides no details of any family; the *nomen*

---

[67] Schulze, *Eigennamen* 44 n. 6 (Tudicius); I² 100–2 (Caltius), Schulze, *Eigennamen* 211 (Aufustius), 267 (Villius), 519 (Blattius).

[68] See the tables prepared by G. Mansuelli, 'La civilisation en Italie septentrionale après la conquête romaine', *Rev. Arch.* 1962, 141–78.

[69] *NS* 1933, 121, *CIL* I² 2780. M. Lejeune, *Ateste à l'heure de la romanisation* (Firenze, 1978), 132 f.

[70] *CIL* V, p. 240.

[71] Among those without a secure provenance, I include Sylloge 19, first reported in the collection of T. Obizzio at Cataio (Battaglia Terme), and now in the Este museum.

[72] Sylloge 14 with V 2701.

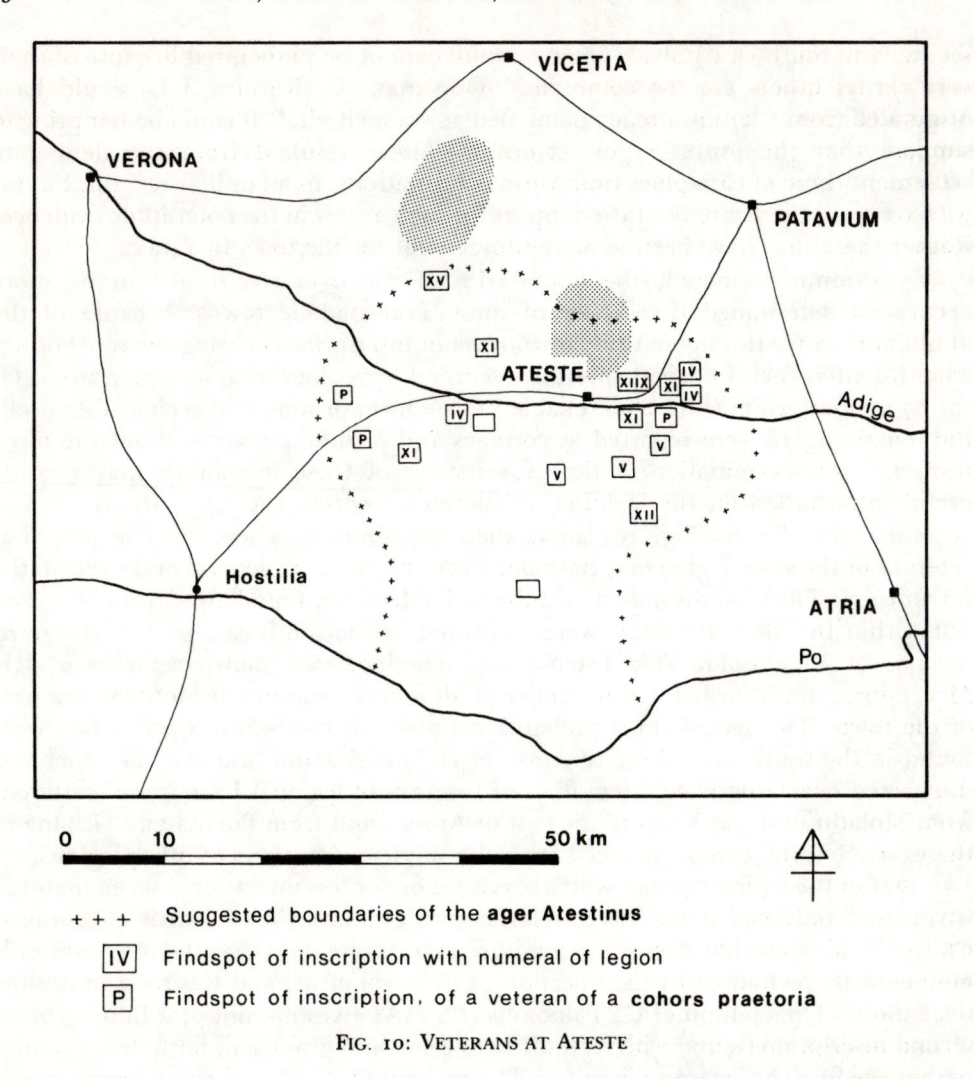

+ + +   Suggested boundaries of the **ager Atestinus**

IV   Findspot of inscription with numeral of legion

P   Findspot of inscription, of a veteran of a **cohors praetoria**

FIG. 10: VETERANS AT ATESTE

recurs at Ateste.[73] The elaborately decorated tombstone of L. Blattius (Pl. IC) came to light at Fregose, south of Monselice, together with a memorial to Blattia Facilis, clearly a *liberta* of the veteran.[74] No marital relationship is hinted at; Blattia's tombstone was erected by her own (slave) mother. From precisely the same location has come the stone erected by L. and M' Blattius to their grandparents Q. Terentius and Calventia Rufa.[75] It may be suggested that the mother of these Blattii (a Terentia) married a Blattius, conceivably the veteran. Evidence would thus be provided for land-holding at Fregose over at least two generations. The veteran

[73] Sylloge 8 with V 2609; V 2575, V *Sup.* 531.
[74] *NS* 1893, 57–60.
[75] V 2704.

C. Veturius was accompanied to Ateste by his parents. Two of the wives specified on veteran-inscriptions can plausibly be shown to have belonged to local families at Ateste (Sylloge 4, 18). Another stone may provide evidence of a marital link between families of known veterans.[76] Two veterans, Billienus and L. Blattius (a centurion), became *decuriones* of the town (cf. above, p. 109).

Two inscriptions have survived from the *ager Atestinus* which relate to repair work by gangs of labourers on embankments of the Adige west of Ateste.[77] It has been assumed by some scholars, almost without discussion, that this work was carried out by squads of newly arrived veterans, perhaps men whose allotments lay in the vicinity of the river, so supplying us with names of other colonists at Ateste.[78] The texts may be quoted:

D E C V R I A	DIIC CLOD
Q ARRVNTI	IANI CV
SVRAI CVR	R Q NAII
Q ARRVNTIO	VIO L SIII
C SABELLO	O PIG C A
PIG T ARRIO	N T I I S T I
SVM H XCIIX	O S H
IN SING HOM	LXXXVIII
OP P XLIII S	IN SING
P ∞IIICCXIV	H P XXVII
	S OP P
	∞∞ CCC
	XCVIII

These stones, found respectively at Saletto di Montagnana and at Ospedaletto close to the ancient line of the Adige, record (with orthography that suggests a date in the Late Republic) the activities of labouring squads (*decuriae*) and were set up to mark the successful completion of 4214 and 2398 *pedes* of an unspecified *opus*; the names are given of the leader of each group, two *curatores* in charge of its administration, and the *pignerator,* perhaps a man who pledged property for the due completion of the work. Also specified are the numbers of men in each gang and the total number of *pedes* which each man might regard as his contribution to the whole.

Undoubtedly these inscriptions refer to the strengthening of the banks of the Adige; their provenances, combined with the known violence of the river, render this conclusion inescapable. There is, however, nothing military in the organisation of the gangs or in the names and titles of their overseers. No doubt repair work to the embankments was a recurring problem, with remedies undertaken by the *colonia Atestina.* The foundation of the *colonia* might prompt some initiative in land improvement, but we have no proof that the veteran settlers themselves bore the weight of the work.[79]

[76] V 2678.

[77] V 2603 = *AE* 1916, 61; *NS* 1915, 137 = *AE* 1916, 60.

[78] F. Barnabei, *NS* 1915, 137; R. Cagnat, *AE* 1916, p. 16; most recently K. D. White, *Roman Farming* (London, 1970), 170.

[79] A third stone, now lost but first seen at Migliadino north of the old line of the Adige, may have been a record of similar work (V 2482).

LIST OF VETERANS AT ATESTE

Sylloge	name	legion	rank	family, etc.
(a) Stones first reported at Este itself				
3	C. Aebutius C.f. Rufus	XI	aquilifer	—
4	C. Allius C.f. Rom.	XIIII	(miles)	wife[80]
7	L. Caltius Sex.f. Rom.	XII	signifer	—
11	L. Mestrius C.f. Rom.	IX	(miles)	—
12	L. Osidius L.f. Rom.	V	(miles)	—
(b) Stones first reported in the ager Atestinus				
2 Lendinara	Q. Atilius Q.f. Rom. Actiacus	—	(miles)	(broken)
5 Baone	T. Atidius T.[f.] Rom. Porcio	XIIX	(miles)	—
6 Poiana	M. Billienus M.f. Rom. Actiacus	XI	(miles)	?
8 Moladiriemi	Q. Coelius L.f. Actiacus	XI	signifer	—
9 Stortola	T. Fannius C.f. Rom.	coh.I pr.	(miles)	liberta
10 Minerbe	M. Gellius L.f. Rom.	coh.II pr.	(miles)	brother
13 Solesino	C. Rutilius T.f. Rom.	V	(miles)	—
14 Monselice	C. Talponius P.f. Rom.	XI	(miles)	—
15 Villa Estense	C. Titius C.f. Ro[m]. Magnus	V Urb.	signifer	—
17 Orgiano	L. Valerius T.f.	XV	(miles)	—
18 Vighizzolo	C. Veturius A.f.	V Urb.	(miles)	wife, parents
19 Museum at Cataio	T. Vibius T.f. Ro[m].	V	centurio	—
20 Stanghella	...Q.......f. Rom.	XII	(miles)	—[81]
21 Marega	....ius T.f. Ac[tiacus?]	coh.V [pr.]	signifer	son
22 Vetta	M' Caesius L.f. Rom.	IIII Mac.	aquilifer	—
23 Urbana	L. Villius P.f. Rom.	XI	(miles)	—
24 Fregose	L. Blattius L.f. Ro[m].	I[V] Mac.	centurio	above, p. 198
25 Montagnana	......	IIII Mac.	....	—[82]

[80] Known only from a manuscript source, the inscription read: ROM C ALLI C F LEG XIIII CLODIAE C L VXORI. Most probably ROM is the misplaced abbreviation of Romilia.

[81] The first letter Q, if not an abbreviated praenomen, could be the initial letter of the nomen Qusonius or Querennius, both occurring at Ateste (V 2675-76).

[82] G. Fogolari, Fasti Arch. ix (1954), no. 4954 gives a brief report of its discovery. I am grateful to Dr. Chieco Bianchi of Este museum for information on the text, and photographs.

NS 1906, 419, ...	...		*centurio?*	...[83]
no. 8				
Migliadino				

(c) Stones first seen outwith the *ager Atestinus*, with no record of discovery

16	M. Tudicius M.f. Rom. Niger	V *Urb.*	(*miles*)	wife
Venice				
26	M. Aufustius M.f. Rom.	—	(*miles*)	wife,
Aquileia	Actiacus			daughter
27	Salvius [S]empronius	XI	(*miles*)	wife?
Patavium	C.[f.] Rom. A[c]tiacus			

Concordia

Concordia lay on the Via Annia, at its junction with the Postumia, midway between Altinum and Aquileia.[84] The origins of Concordia are disputed; the name has been thought to suggest a new town founded after Philippi, but it would not be out of place as a foundation of the second century B.C.[85] The *ager Concordiensis* can be envisaged as carved out of the territory of Opitergium, and the town seen as a former *statio* at the junction of two major roads upgraded.[86] No buildings have been identified which can be dated earlier than the second half of the first century B.C.[87] Several inscriptions attest the titulature of the town in the Early Empire, as *colonia Iulia Concordia* (above, p. 21).

Tergeste

It is likely that Tergeste, at the head of the Adriatic, became a colony before the death of Augustus, but the date of foundation is disputed.[88] Some have asserted that Tergeste gained that status during Caesar's governorship of Gaul and Illyricum.[89] More probably the town became a *municipium* in 49 B.C. along with other towns of Venetia, and a colony after no long interval.[90] A monumental inscription records that Octavian provided a wall circuit and towers; the work was completed and the slab erected in 33/32 B.C.[91] On this evidence the colony has been dated to

[83] The inscription is totally lost, but military emblems on the stone, which is similar in style and decoration to that commemorating the centurion L. Blattius Vetus (Sylloge 24), include a *vitis*, suggesting that the deceased was himself a centurion.

[84] G. Brusin–P. Zovatto, *Monumenti romani e cristiani di Iulia Concordia* (Pordenone, 1960); B. Scarpa Bonazza et al., *Iulia Concordia dell'età romana a età moderna* (Treviso, 1962). On the road network in the vicinity of the town, L. Bosio, *Itinerari e strade della Venetia romana* (Padova, 1970), 37–38.

[85] Mommsen, *CIL* V, p. 178, 936.

[86] For an award of land to the *Opitergini* by Caesar during the Civil War, Schol. on Lucan *Phars.* iv. 462. and above, p. 90, n. 23.

[87] Blake 288; S. Panciera, 'Una nuova iscrizione ed il teatro di Iulia Concordia', *Atti III congr. epig. grec. e lat.* (Roma, 1959), 313–20; For centuriation in the *ager Concordiensis*, which fills the ground between the Livenza and the Tagliamento rivers, L. Bosio, 'La centuriazione dell'agro di Iulia Concordia', *Att. Ist. Ven.* cxxiv (1965–66), 195–260.

[88] V. Scrinari, *Tergeste* (Roma, 1951); P. Sticotti, *Inscriptiones Italiae* X. 4 (Roma, 1951); A. Degrassi, *Il confine nord-orientale dell'Italia romana* (Bern, 1954), 49–53.

[89] Sticotti, op. cit. (n. 88), vii–viii; A. Tamaro, *Storia di Trieste* (Roma, 1924), 9 ff.

[90] A. Degrassi, 'Il nuovo fascicolo delle iscrizioni di Trieste romana', *La Porta Orientale* xxi (1951), 264–70 = *SVA* II, 943–49; idem, 'Epigraphica II', *Mem. Acc. Linc.* ser. 8, xi (1965), 233–76 = *SVA* III, 35–87.

[91] *ILS* 77 = *ILLRP* 418 = *EJ*² 57 = *IIt* X. 4. 20. Cf. V 526 = *IIt* X. 4. 22.

the period of Octavian's Illyrian wars, but it must be doubtful if Octavian could contemplate the release of veterans, unless incapacitated, in 33/32 B.C., on the eve of his final conflict with Antony. More precisely the inscription can serve as a *terminus ante quem* for the colony which is best placed after Philippi or Naulochus (above, p. 63).

Parentium

The modern Parenzo, now Poreč in Yugoslavia, occupies a promontory on the west coast of Histria, about half way between Trieste and Pula. Its *territorium* is hilly, with some level but probably marshy ground in the Val del Quieto.[92] Centuriation has been observed on land to the north-east of the town despite its unevenness.[93] Not all can have been suitable for cultivation.

Uncertainty surrounds the status of Parentium in the Early Empire. The town is mentioned by Pliny in his account of Histria, but it and neighbouring Aegida are described as *oppida civium Romanorum,* which could suggest that his Augustan source regarded the towns as provincial communities not yet added to Italy. In the same section Pliny correctly notes the colonial status of Pola.[94] However, in an inscription datable to the second century A.D. or later, Parentium is described as *colonia Iulia,* and the same stone records a *curial(is) veter(um) Par(entinorum),* which should confirm an influx of colonists and testify to a long-lasting division in the ranks of the *decuriones* there.[95] It has become customary to adjudge Pliny at fault as regards the status of the town.[96] However, in 1942 there came to light at Parenzo fragments of a marble sarcophagus commemorating M. Claudius Acerrentinus who had been *IIIIvir aedilicia potestate* and almost certainly *IIIIvir iure dicundo,* presumably at Parentium, which would suggest that the town was then a *municipium.*[97] The sarcophagus ought to date, at earliest, to the second half of the second century A.D., or later. The discovery prompted Degrassi to rehabilitate another inscription of a *IIIIvir,* preserved in a manuscript source.[98]

In order to reconcile the apparent conflict of evidence between the title *Iulia* and the quattuorvirate in the town, Degrassi proposed that the colony should belong to the reigns of Tiberius or Gaius, more probably the former.[99] However, there is no

---

[92] A. Degrassi, *Inscriptiones Italiae* X. 2 (Roma, 1934); A. Šonje, 'Le iscrizioni romane trovate dopo la seconda guerra mondiale a Poreč e nei dintorni', *Ziva Antica* xii (1962), 157–64; idem., 'Comitium coloniae Iuliae Parentium' (*sic*), *Ziva Antica* xv (1965), 397–404.

[93] M. Suić, 'Limitation of Roman Colonies on the Eastern Adriatic Coast', *Zbornik Instituta za historijske nauke u Zadru* i (1955), 32–36 (Eng. summary); R. Chevallier, 'La centuriazione romana dell'Istria e della Dalmazia', *Att. Mem. Soc. Istr.* ix (1961), 11–23.

[94] NH iii. 129.

[95] *ILS* 6678 = *IIt* X. 2. 242. On Mommsen's authority, an expansion to *curialis vetus Parentinorum* has been preferred (*CIL* V, p. 36).

[96] So Mommsen, *CIL* V, p. 35; Degrassi, op. cit. (n. 92), p. ix.

[97] A. Degrassi, 'Parenzo municipio romano', *Athenaeum* xxiv (1946), 44–49 = *SVA* II, 925–30; *AE* 1947, 51.

[98] Loc. cit. (n. 97).

[99] A. Degrassi, 'Quattuorviri in colonie romane e in municipi retti da duoviri', *Mem. Acc. Linc.* ser. 8, ii (1950), 281–344, at 295 = *SVA* I, 116.

positive evidence for a Tiberian date, and other possibilities deserve consideration. From the Val del Quieto near Visinada has come the epitaph erected by a veteran, Vinusius of legion VIIII *Triumphalis,* to his wife and to his daughter who died young (Sylloge 87). The title of the legion is unique and could commemorate its participation in Caesar's triumphs of 46 B.C. or those of Octavian after Actium.[100] The distribution of the name Vinusius and its cognate forms suggests that the veteran was a local man from Venetia or Histria, but that he was established in the Val del Quieto as part of an official settlement is suggested by the nearby place-name Visinada which it is tempting to think was formed from his name (above, p. 97).

If the legion is Caesar's Ninth (and this seems the best solution), we could imagine a small group placed in the territory of Parentium (as yet within the boundaries of Caesar's old province of Illyricum), perhaps as part of a mainly proletarian colony which Pliny's Augustan source chose to ignore.[101] Alternatively we may prefer to envisage a non-colonial enclave of veterans in the *ager Parentinus,* with the promotion of the town to colonial status coming at a very much later date. The title *Iulia* would thus commemorate a long past but never-forgotten settlement of Caesarian legionaries.[102]

Pola

Pola, now Yugoslavian Pula, lies at the southern tip of Histria and at the innermost recess of a fine natural harbour, which should account for much of its development under Roman domination.[103] That Pola was selected as the site of a colony in the later first century B.C. can be inferred from Pliny who gives it colonial status and notes that it had been renamed *Pietas Iulia.* Degrassi placed the colony after Philippi, on the basis of the titles and an examination of the family history of the Sergii, prominent in the colony in its early years.[104] He saw the title *Pietas* as given by Octavian in or about 41 B.C. to emphasise his special relationship to the now deified Caesar.[105] The Arch of the Sergii, which was erected outside one of the newly built gates of the town, commemorated the brothers L. and Cn. Sergius, both *IIviri* of the colony (in separate years), and the son of L. Sergius who had been *aedilis* and

---

[100] B. H. Isaac argued that this legion IX gained the title from Munatius Plancus, by whom it was subsequently settled at Raurica; see 'Colonia Munatia Triumphalis and legio nona Triumphalis?', *Talanta* iii (1971), 11–43. The argumentation is unsound. Caesar gave the name *Triumphale* to the town of Isturgi in 45 B.C., and is probably to be counted the founder of *colonia Iulia Urbs Triumphalis Tarraco*; Galsterer-Kröll, *Beinamen* nos. 111, 194.

[101] A number of possibly Caesarian colonies on the Dalmatian seaboard have *IIIIviri* as their chief magistrates; Degrassi, loc. cit. (n. 99).

[102] Under the Empire, the Dalmatian *municipium* of Risinium bore the title *Iulium* (III 12695), but the circumstances of the award are not known.

[103] B. Forlati Tamaro, *Inscriptiones Italiae* X. 1 (Roma, 1947).

[104] *NH* iii. 129. A Degrassi, 'La data della fondazione della colonia romana di Pola', *Att. Ist. Ven.* cii (1942–43), 667–78 = *SVA* II, 913–20.

[105] Cf. S. Weinstock, *Divus Julius* (Oxford, 1971), 248–53. Octavian did not have sole use of the title, which was adopted by Pompey's sons in memory of their father, and was employed by L. Antonius in 41 to emphasise the closeness of the bond with his absent brother. By the later first century A.D., *Pietas* had been replaced in the titulature of the colony by the epithets *Pollentia Herculanea* (above, p. 22).

a tribune in legion XXIX (Sylloge 90).[106] A legion with this numeral was attached to Octavian from July 43, but it seems not to have survived the reorganisation after Philippi.

It is, however, by no means clear that the Arch provides any sure evidence for settlement of the legion at Pola. Examination of family relationships prompted Degrassi to conclude that the brothers L. and Cn. Sergius had been colonists after Philippi, and that L. Sergius could easily have had a son old enough to serve in legion XXIX before its disbandment, which he placed after Actium at the latest.[107] The tribune, it is clear, died young before holding the more senior magistracies which military rank and family influence should have secured.

However, if the brothers Sergius were military colonists in the town after Philippi, it is strange that no mention is made of their military rank at a time when such antecedents remained important in the local context. It may be wondered whether Pola was a civilian colony of Caesarian origin, belonging to 47–44 rather than after Philippi. Recorded as *IIviri* in the town are L. Cassius Longinus and L. Calpurnius Piso, who is separately recorded as having constructed some public edifice in the town. The latter is almost certainly Caesoninus, the father-in-law of Caesar.[108] It is tempting to see one or both as organisers of the colony. Of the two, Piso Caesoninus had been closely associated with Caesar's agrarian schemes of 59 B.C., and was *IIvir* along with Pompey at Capua in the following year (above, p. 97). He would be a natural candidate, despite advancing years, to supervise later settlement for Caesar, or for Octavian. A date for the colony under Caesar may be preferable, in that Piso is not known to have been alive after 43 B.C. L. Cassius was the brother of Caesar's assassin, and fled to join the Liberators in 43.[109] Though he was reconciled to Antony by 41, no friendly association with Octavian seems likely. Thus he too could be more easily placed at Pola before Caesar's death. If Pola in fact belongs under Caesar, its new name *Pietas Iulia* fits well into the range of titulature employed by Caesar for his provincial foundations.[110] Centuriation in the *territorium* of Pola, which has the same alignment as the grid in the *ager Parentinus*, comprises square *centuriae* of 200 *iugera* (see Pl. IV), some subdivided into plots of 50 *iugera*, probably the designated allotment size at the colony (above, p. 93).[111]

The Augustan age saw the construction of a number of public buildings in the town. The walls and gates belong to this time, together with an amphitheatre (enlarged later), a temple to Roma and Augustus, and very probably an aqueduct, named the *Aqua Augusta*.[112]

---

[106] *ILS* 2229 = *IIt*. X. 1. 72; G. Traversari, *l'Arco dei Sergi* (Padova, 1971).

[107] Loc. cit. (n. 104).

[108] *ILLRP* 639 = *IIt* X. 1. 81; *ILLRP* 423–24; Broughton, *MRR* II 350 for some details.

[109] Broughton, *MRR* II 324; *RE* III (1899) 1739, no. 65. More prosaically, a link for both men with Pola by patronage or business interests cannot be ruled out. Cassius' ancestor, as consul of 171, had campaigned in Histria.

[110] Galster-Kröll, *Beinamen* 65 ff.

[111] For centuriation in the *ager Polensis*, Suić, loc. cit. (n. 93); Chevallier, loc. cit. (n. 93); J. P. Bradford, *Ancient Landscapes* (London, 1957), 175–78.

[112] E. Polaschek, *RE* XXI (1965), 1219 ff. S. Mlakar, *The Amphitheatre in Pula* (Pula, 1973).

Dertona

Dertona, a road centre of some importance in Roman times, lies at the base of a spur of the Ligurian Apennines, on the eastern edge of the modern Alessandria Plain.[113] Whatever reservations are implied by Velleius' well-known comment on the status of Dertona, it is highly probable that the town enjoyed the rank of a Roman colony from the later second century B.C.[114] That it was reinforced by an infusion of colonists, presumably veterans, in the later first century is not open to doubt. Dertona became *colonia Iulia,* and probably *colonia Iulia Augusta,* the latter title being acquired before 22 B.C.[115] Little is known of public buildings, but a street grid aligned on the Via Postumia has been recognised.[116] No veterans are attested, though Mommsen professed to see, in a veteran of the Praetorian Guard who died at Rome, a colonist of the later first century B.C.[117] Almost certainly, however, the man was a native of Dertona who was settled elsewhere under the Julio-Claudians.[118]

Augusta Taurinorum (Turin)

Turin, *colonia Iulia Augusta Taurinorum,* occupies a site of obvious importance at the junction of the Po with the Dora Riparia, close to the point where the road from the M. Genèvre Pass emerges into the Po valley.[119] Turin is named as a colony by Pliny; the precise date of foundation cannot be established. It could belong immediately after Actium, or may be later.[120] The 'playing card' town plan may suggest a complete resurvey of the site by military engineers, or (better) the close relationship between civilian and military planning techniques at this time; we have no evidence that it ever served as a military encampment. The walls and a theatre are Augustan in date.[121]

Augusta Praetoria Salassorum (Aosta)

Aosta lies at the junction of the Buthier tributary with the Dora Baltea, *iuxta geminas Alpium fores,* where the Roman road from the Po splits to ascend to the Greater or Lesser St. Bernard. The town itself occupies a position almost midway

---

[113] P. Fraccaro, 'La colonia romana di Dertona (Tortona) e la sua centuriazione', *Opuscula* III (1957), 123–50.

[114] Vell. i. 15. 5; U. Ewins, 'The early Colonisation of Cisalpine Gaul', *PBSR* xx (1952), 52–71.

[115] V 1636, 7376; above, p. 21.

[116] P. Barocelli, 'Iulia Dertona', *Boll. Soc. Piem. Arch.* xv (1931), 94–113; ibid. xvi (1932), 168–84. Note also C. Guerra, *Tortona antica attraverso le sue iscrizioni* (tesi di laurea, Pavia, 1963).

[117] VI 2466: DIIS MANIBVS L ENNI L F POMPTINA OPTATO DERTONA TRIBV SCAPTIA; U. Ewins, loc. cit. (n. 114), at 68 n. 77, following Mommsen, *CIL* V, p. 832.

[118] G. Forni, '"Doppia tribù" di cittadini e cambiamento di tribù romane', in *Tetraonyma: miscellanea graeco-romana* (Genova, 1966), 139–55, at 143 n. 20.

[119] G. Bendinelli, *Torino romano* (Torino, 1929).

[120] *NH* iii. 123; F. Rondolino, *Boll. Soc. Piem. Arch.* xiv (1930), 157 suggested that it was one of Caesar's colonies; G. E. F. Chilver, *Cisalpine Gaul* (Oxford, 1941), 20–21 preferred to see Turin as a civilian colony founded in 27 B.C.

[121] Bendinelli, op. cit. (n. 119), 32 ff.; I. A. Richmond, 'Augustan Gates at Torino and Spello', *PBSR* xii (1933), 52–62.

along a narrow fertile plain to either side of the Dora Baltea, with mountains towering high on all sides.[122]

The Celtic Salassi, excluded from the Po valley in 100 B.C. by the foundation of the colony at Eporedia, long remained troublesome, endangering travellers and exacting tolls for the use of both St. Bernard Passes. They were finally crushed in 25 B.C. by M. Terentius Varro Murena. It was on the site of Varro's camp, at the junction of the two roads, that a *colonia* was founded, *Augusta Praetoria Salassorum*, with 3,000 veteran settlers.[123] The foundation of this guard-post on the Alpine routes is best placed in 25 B.C., less certainly in 24. Dio provides an explanation of the title *Praetoria*: the land was given τῶν δορυφόρων τισὶν, i.e. to former members of the *cohortes praetoriae*.[124] A derivation from the *praetorium,* or general's tent occupied by Varro, is improbable. The resemblance of the town-plan to a military encampment has often been noticed, and could indicate that military engineers supervised the laying out of its street grid or extended the existing encampment, but here too we may see rather the common traditions of military and civilian planning (above, p. 205).

Dio records that all the Salassi of military age were sold into slavery, Strabo that the entire population was sold off, at Eporedia. Nevertheless it would appear that some were permitted to remain within the *territorium*. Dio states that the colonists received merely the best of the available land, clearly the flat land along the valley floor. A statue to Augustus was erected in 23/22 B.C. by *Salassi incol(ae) qui initio se in colon(iam) con[t](ulerunt)*, thus providing general confirmation of the date of foundation.[125] A number of Salassi were, it seems, permitted even in the immediate aftermath of the foundation to live in the town, with official approval. Another inscription could suggest that there were Salassi, perhaps a pro-Roman faction among the tribal aristocracy, who obtained the citizenship within the reign of Augustus or shortly after.[126]

A force of 3,000 Praetorians would represent at least one third of the total strength of the *cohortes* under Augustus (above, p. 35); we may wonder whether they were sent out in batches, over a number of years; Dio's total of 3,000 may be a stock figure. Though it might seem unlikely that 3,000 men could have been found land in the long, straggling valley of the Dora Baltea, Beretta has calculated that there was sufficient cultivable land belonging to the modern commune of Aosta to provide allotments of 50 *iugera,* or a little more, to this number.[127] We must imagine

[122] Pliny *NH* iii. 123; P. Barocelli, *Inscriptiones Italiae* X. 1 (Roma, 1932); idem, *Augusta Praetoria* (in series *Forma Italiae;* Roma, 1948); I. Beretta, *La romanizzazione della valle d'Aosta* (Milano-Varese, 1954); I. A. Richmond, *Studies in Roman Art and Archaeology* (ed. P. Salway, London, 1969), 249–59; R. A. Van Royen, 'Colonia Augusta Praetoria and Augustus' *Cohortes Praetoriae*', *Talanta* v (1973), 48–71.
[123] Pliny *NH* iii. 123; Strabo iv. 6. 7.
[124] Dio liii. 25. 5.
[125] *NS* 1894, 369 = *ILS* 6753 = *IIt* X. 1. 6 = *EJ*² 338. For discussions, Beretta, op. cit. (n. 122), 23 ff.; Richmond, loc. cit. (n. 122); U. Laffi, *Adtributio e contributio* (Pisa, 1966), 202.
[126] *V Sup.* 916 = *IIt* X. 1. 112.
[127] Op. cit. (n. 122), 29–30.

that the colonists were spread out along the narrow valley to its extremities. Dio says that the colonists received the 'best' of the land. If the allotments were of 50 *iugera,* there can have been little left for the Salassi except mountain and steep hillside. None of the colonists can be identified, but a survey of Roman nomenclature in the Valle d'Aosta could provide some clue to origins. Nevertheless we cannot tell how many names belong to families who arrived after, perhaps long after, the colonists themselves. [128] Walls and imposing public amenities were provided without delay, perhaps at Augustus' expense, so that within a few years a complete Roman town had sprung up in a clear Alpine setting. [129]

[128] Among families recorded on stones dating to the Early Empire are Arruntii, Ofilii, Pompullii, Virii, Terentii, Lucretii, Cassii, Petilii, Baebatii, Salvii, Avillii, and Vinesii; Beretta, op. cit. (n. 122), 71.

[129] Beretta, op. cit. (n. 122), 33 ff.

CHAPTER TEN

EPILOGUE: LATER SETTLEMENT IN ITALY

The programme of 14 B.C. (however little its scope is understood) marked the end of land settlement in Italy for half a century. In the following year, Augustus announced measures by which 16 years of service in the legions, following by four years as a reservist (*sub vexillo*), would be rewarded by a cash gratuity payable by himself. We are not told the amount.[1] In Dio's account this was the first matter Augustus put to the Senate on his return from Gaul in July 13 B.C., which should suggest that it was of some importance at that juncture. The decision to abolish land grants was perhaps prompted by difficulties in securing sufficient land of any reasonable quality in the previous year, in the provinces or in Italy, or both. Certainly the establishment of colonies was expensive, unpopular with the mass of the population, and time-consuming. The predominantly Italian legionaries would doubtless have preferred land grants to continue, as Dio makes clear.[2]

There was also, it seems, a lull in the establishment of provincial colonies. After 14 B.C., the remaining years of Augustus' reign are completely blank.[3] The *Res Gestae* record the provision of cash awards to a substantial number of soldiers in five separate years between 7 and 2 B.C.; these veterans were, to paraphrase Augustus' wording, *in sua municipi*[*a deducti*]. Presumably by this hybrid phrase he wished to emphasise that the soldiery were still receiving their proper *praemia*, without the need for formal establishment of colonies.[4] The cash totals recorded could suggest that some 30,000 men may have benefited.[5] A number of veterans of Augustus' last years can be pinpointed, some of them perhaps released at this time. But the record is disappointingly slight for the 28 years between the introduction of cash grants and the death of Augustus, a period hardly shorter than that considered in detail in the preceding pages.[6]

In A.D. 5 further adjustments were made to the conditions of military service. The term of service in the legions was extended to 20 years, and each man had to spend a further five as a reservist. The cash gratuity was fixed at 12,000 sesterces, to be financed by new taxes, and administered by an *aerarium militare*.[7] The amount of land a veteran could purchase with this sum cannot be established, but there must remain a suspicion that the introduction of gratuities represented a saving,

[1] Dio liv. 25. 5; Brunt, *IM* 333–34. Praetorians were now required to serve 12 years.

[2] liv. 25. 5.

[3] Unless some of the Pisidian group of colonies belong after 13 B.C.; E. L. Bowie, *JRS* lx (1970), 204. It is difficult to suppose that Augustus was at any time averse to establishing veterans on newly conquered territory where the land would cost him almost nothing.

[4] *RG* 16. 2. In the Greek version, the wording is κατήγαγον εἰς τὰς ἰδίας πόλ(ει)ς, which seems to require that *deduxi* be restored rather than *remisi* (by analogy with *RG* 3. 3).

[5] The sum specified (about 400,000,000 sesterces) could provide something over 30,000 gratuities of 12,000 sesterces, more if the level of payment was substantially less.

[6] XI 6056, XI 348, XII 259, V 4365, V 4923; ?Sylloge 56 (Bergomum), ?Sylloge 69–70 (Cremona). There could be a suspicion that some of the veterans at Ateste, of legions occurring only once, are sons of colonists, returning home after service (Sylloge 4, 5, 11, 17, 20).

[7] Dio lv. 23. 1; *RG* 17. 2. Service in the Praetorian Guard was increased to 16 years. See now M. Corbier, *L'aerarium Saturni et l'aerarium militare* (Roma, 1974).

perhaps a substantial saving, for Augustus.[8] Moreover, the new gratuity took the place of both the land and the cash awards which had become common under the stress of Civil War conditions.

Yet it is evident that land grants were not entirely discontinued. At the very end of Augustus' reign one *colonia* was founded for veterans of the Danube army group at Emona, at that time just inside the border of Pannonia.[9] The colony received the title *Iulia Emona*.[10] The date of foundation cannot be taken as absolutely certain, but circumstantial evidence has been adduced to place it precisely in A.D. 14. An inscription testifies to the provision, by Augustus and Tiberius jointly, of a wall-circuit for the town, the work being complete by May A.D. 15.[11] Among the complaints of the mutinous legionaries of the Balkan army, which lay not far from Emona in A.D. 14, was that upon completion of service they were being given *per nomen agrorum uligines paludum vel inculta montium*. The grievance is far from unique, but it has been argued that the bitterness of the time-served men arose not a little from witnessing the activities of surveyors laying out a grid on the nearby *ager Emonensis* which consisted largely of marshland and bare plateau.[12] The mutineers demanded cash, to be paid out before the veterans left the camp, in preference to rough land on the frontier. It seemed to be Augustus himself who was reneging on the promises made in 13 B.C. and A.D. 5.[13] Yet we may suspect that land in Italy would still have been acceptable, if offered, to many.

Under the earlier Julio-Claudians, evidence for veteran settlement in Italy is sparse.[14] No colonies can be ascribed to either Tiberius or Caligula.[15] Claudius founded several colonies in the provinces,[16] but was not certainly active in this sphere in Italy itself, though suggestions have been made from time to time for

[8] If one *iugerum* of average land could be bought for 500 sesterces, the gratuity would be sufficient to purchase 24 *iugera* (cf. above, p. 76). Some money would have to be set aside to purchase animals, seed corn and other equipment (above, p. 123).

[9] B. Saria, 'Noricum und Pannonia', *Historia* i (1950), 436–86; J. Šašel, *RE Sup.* XI (1968), 540–78, *s.v. Emona:* A. Mócsy, *Pannonia and Upper Moesia* (London-Boston, 1974), 40, 74 ff. For some doubts on the dating, C. M. Wells, 'Emona and Carnuntum: Evidence for the Start of Roman Occupation', in E. Birley, B. Dobson and M. Jarrett (eds.), *Roman Frontier Studies* 1969 (Cardiff, 1974), 185–90.

[10] Galsterer-Kröll, *Beinamen* no. 352.

[11] J. Šašel, 'Drusus Ti. f. in Emona', *Historia* xix (1970), 122–24.

[12] J. J. Wilkes, 'A Note on the Mutiny of the Pannonian Legions in A.D. 14', *CQ* lvii (1963), 268–71.

[13] L. J. F. Keppie, 'Vexilla Veteranorum', *PBSR* xli (1973), 8–17.

[14] L. J. F. Keppie, 'Colonisation and Veteran Settlement in Italy in the First Century A.D. (forthcoming).

[15] For Tiberius, the *Liber Coloniarum* reports small-scale work at Tibur, Tifernum Tiberinum and Campi Tiberiani (258. 18, 224. 1, 218. 9), but in each case the compiler is presumably misled by false etymology. Work in the Balkan provinces can be ascribed to Tiberius at Iulia Scarbantia (Pliny *NH* iii. 46), and Narona (*AE* 1950, 44), perhaps in the aftermath of the mutinies.

[16] Ptolemais, Cologne, Camulodunum, Savaria, Aprum, Aequum, Lixus and Oppidum Novum. The existing colonies at Narbo and Lugdunum (the emperor's birthplace) received the title *Claudia*; perhaps they were reinforced, as was Dalmatian Salonae.

colonies at Iulium Carnicum, Cumae and Velitrae.[17] It was under Nero that colonisation in Italy was resumed. Veterans were sent to Antium (his birthplace) and Tarentum, and several Triumviral or Augustan colonies received additional settlers.[18] At the close of the Civil Wars of A.D. 68–69, Vespasian reinforced many Triumviral or Augustan colonies and added to their titulature.[19] He also sent men to his own birthplace, Reate.[20] Interestingly, with the possible exception of Paestum, no new colonies were established by either emperor. Among the popularity-seeking measures introduced by Nerva was a scheme to buy up Italian land, and to distribute it to the needy, but there is no evidence that veteran colonists were involved.[21] These settlements were not a success despite the effort expended; the veterans' own lack of enthusiasm and their often prompt desertion of the new settlements have coloured many modern commentators' views on the Augustan programmes also, leading to a more pessimistic view of the latter schemes than the evidence really justifies. The settlement programmes of the first century A.D. were initiated by the emperors and, if our evidence is correct, found little support among the veterans themselves. Tacitus notes that those established at Tarentum and Antium preferred to return to the provinces in which they had served half a lifetime, and which they knew as home.[22] It is evident that they did not find Italy, or at least southern Italy, an attractive place to spend their remaining years.

The reasons for this change in attitude can be found in part in the changing trends in recruitment and conditions of army service from the Augustan period onwards. The settlers of Philippi or Actium were almost exclusively Italians, from the peninsula or from Cisalpina; most were in their early to mid thirties, or younger (above, p. 38).

The later decades of Augustus' reign had witnessed a lengthening out of army service, to 25 years; some men were retained even longer. After Actium the legions took up a rôle of frontier defence; by the end of his reign the movement of legions from one province to another, and even within a province, was slowing down. The legions were established in static *hiberna,* which over the years began to assume a more permanent nature.[23] A man might spend the 25 years of his army service on a

---

[17]For Iulium Carnicum, Nissen, *IL* II 237; H. Philipp, *RE* X (1917), 105. Mommsen, in *CIL* V, p. 172 is suitably cautious. Substantial rebuilding in the town can be dated to the mid first century A.D., P. M. Moro, *Iulium Carnicum* (Roma, 1956), 52 ff.; L. Beschi, *EAA* VII (1966), 1290, *s.v. Zuglio.* The tombstone of a Praetorian veteran, of undefined date, is known (V 1840). For Cumae, *LC* 232. 10; *CIL* X, p. 317. For Velitrae, S. Panciera, 'Miscellanea storico-epigrafica II', *Epigraphica* xxiv (1962), 78–105.

[18]Tac. *Ann.* xiii. 31 (Capua and Nuceria), *Ann.* xiv. 27 (Antium, Tarentum and Puteoli). Luceria may also have been reinforced, if IX 799 records a colonist of this time.

[19]Above, p. 22 (Puteoli); P. Ducrey, 'Trois nouvelles inscriptions crétoises', *BCH* xciii (1969), 841–52 (Capua); *ILP* 86–87 and above, p. 154 (Paestum); X 1263 with Ritterling, *Legio* 1286–87 (Nola).

[20]IX 4682, 4683, 4684 = *ILS* 2460, IX 4685, 4687, 4689, 4754.

[21]Dio lxviii. 2; Pliny *Ep.* vii. 31. 4; *ILS* 1019, *ILS* 5750 (colony at Scolacium).

[22]*Ann.* xiv. 27.

[23]G. Webster, *The Roman Imperial Army* (London, 1969), 51 ff.; H. Schönberger, 'The Roman Frontier in Germany: an Archaeological Survey', *JRS* lix (1969), 144–97; J. C. Mann, 'The Frontiers of the Principate', in *ANRW* II. i (1974), 508–33.

single posting, amid fairly peaceful conditions. Ties with the local population, and attachment to the station, grew in strength. When the Italians among them were finally released, they were in their late 40s or early 50s, and less willing to return to a homeland they had all but forgotten.[24] A second reason for declining interest in settlement within Italy is the falling away of the percentage of Italians serving in the legions, which had declined to 50% or less by the close of the Julio-Claudian period; by the reign of Hadrian their contribution was negligible.[25]

In his account of Nero's colonisation programme of A.D. 60, Tacitus criticises the lack of cohesion in the settlements. This could have been achieved if, as of old (*ut olim*), all the colonists had been drawn from a single legion, and the formation settled *en masse*.[26] The criticism, a familiar Tacitean device to undercut the value of an emperor's policy, is both anachronistic and unfair. The legions were now self-perpetuating formations which could no longer be disbanded *en masse*. Even at the time of Philippi or Actium, the number of colonists from a single legion might well number no more than 1,000, perhaps 2,000 at the most (above, p. 98). Even if, as Tacitus advocated, it had been possible to settle a *universa legio* at Tarentum or Antium, it must be doubted whether the settlements would have been any more successful. Tacitus represents Nero's work as a mere parody of earlier settlements, the success of which is elevated by comparison. The motives for the colonisation programmes of Nero and Vespasian, and of Nerva's land commission, were primarily economic, and recall the schemes of an earlier age (above, p. 128). The veterans of the early and mid first century A.D. were utilised by the emperors as part of the sporadic and not always whole-hearted campaign to regenerate and repopulate areas of Italy, especially southern Italy, where economic decline was most evident.[27]

The formal settlement of veterans in Italy appears on present evidence to have ceased with Vespasian, but the promotion of Italian towns to colonial status, and the conferment of fresh titles on existing colonies continued, so that, by the close of the third century A.D., the number of colonies in Italy had risen to at least 120, numerically well above one quarter of all Italian communities.[28] The institution of colonisation retained its prestige — prestige which the success of the Caesarian and Augustan schemes, especially in the provinces, had done much to foster — but the colonists themselves became an increasingly unwanted and unwilling element in the equation, and were eventually deleted from it. A town which received the *ius coloniae* could expect one or more titles linking it to the current emperor, a fresh constitution embodied in a *lex coloniae,* and perhaps some benefactions or other favours, but the physical despatch of colonists did not take place.

[24] On this familiar topic, reference may be made to G. Forni, *Il reclutamento delle legioni da Augusto a Diocleziano* (Milano-Roma, 1953), 65 ff.; idem, 'Estrazione etnica e sociale dei soldati delle legioni nei primi tre secoli dell'impero', in *ANRW* II. i (1974), 339–91.

[25] Forni, op. cit. (1953), 41 ff.; J. C. Mann, in his unpublished doctoral thesis, *The Settlement of Veterans in the Roman Empire* (London, 1956), has analysed province by province the evidence both for recruitment and for settlement under the Empire. Italians continued to form the great majority of recruits for the Praetorian Guard and Urban Cohorts.

[26] *Ann.* xiv. 27.

[27] L. J. F. Keppie, loc. cit. (n. 14).

[28] For lists, not wholly accurate or complete, Kornemann 520–39; Salmon 161–63. For an excellent discussion on the eagerness with which provincial communities vied to secure colonial status, A. N. Sherwin-White, *The Roman Citizenship* (Oxford, 1973), 413.

SYLLOGE OF INSCRIPTIONS

Listed below are inscriptions recording veterans who seem likely to have been officially settled in Italy with land grants between 47 and 14 B.C. Tribunes who, it has been argued, were settled along with their men, find a place here, but men who probably returned home in the later years of Augustus' reign are excluded. Where more than one veteran is known from a town or its *territorium,* the inscriptions are listed in the order in which they appear in *CIL,* followed by more recent publications. The inscriptions have been reproduced with their original line divisions, and some attempt has been made to indicate general format. Missing portions have been restored where the content seems reasonably secure. It is readily accepted that there can be no substitute for autopsy, or for a photograph or accurate line drawing, but it is hoped that the Sylloge will aid consultation of the epigraphic evidence discussed in the foregoing pages.

SYLLOGE OF INSCRIPTIONS

Veterans of Caesar, the Triumvirs and Augustus down to 14 B.C.

Aquinum

1. C AIEDIVS C F
   LEM
   L IIĪ V D P S

   X 5407; Pl. VIII

Ateste

2. Q ATILIO Q F ROM
   ACTIACO   ET
   .....

   V 2389

3. C AEBVTIVS C F
   RVFVS AQVIER
   LEGIONE X̄Ī

   V 2495

4. ROM
   C ALLI C F
   LEG XIIII
   CLODIAE C L
   VXORI[S]

   V 2497

5. T ATIDIVS T [F]
   ROM PORCIO
   MILES LEG XIIX

   V 2499 = *ILS* 2268

6. M BILLIENVS M F
   ROM   ACTIACVS
   LEGIONE X̄Ī PROE
   LIO NAVALI FACTO
   IN COLONIAM DE
   DVCTVS AB ORDI
   NE DECVRIO ALLEC
   [TVS] ..MO ERVC..

   V 2501 = ILS 2243; Pl. IB

7. L CALTIVS
   SEX F ROM
   LEG XII SIGNIFER

   V 2502

8. Q COELIVS L F
   LEG X̄Ī ACTIACVS
   SIGNIFER

   V 2503 = *ILS* 2336

212

9.   T FANNIO C F ROM
      CHORT Ī PRAET
      FANNIA T L FESTA PATRONO
      ET SIBI VIVA FECIT

      V 2505

14.   C TALPONI
      VS P F ROM
      LEG XI

      V 2512; Pl. IIA

10.   M GELLIO L F ROM
      CHORTE ĪĪ
      M' GELLIVS FRATER

      V 2506

15.   C TITI C F RO[M]
      MAGNI LEG V̄
      VRB SIGNIFER

      V 2514 = *ILS* 2236

11.   L MESTRIVS
      C F ROM
      LEG IX

      V 2507

16.   M   TVDICIVS   M   F
      ROM NIGER LEG V VRB
      SIBI ET GRANIAI M L
      APHRODISIAI   VXORI

      V 2515

12.   L OSIDI L F ROM
      LEG V̄

      V 2508

17.   L VALERIVS
      T F LEG XV
      T F I

      V 2516

13.   C RVTILIVS T F
      ROM LEG V

      V 2510

18.   A VETVRIO A F PATRI
      PETRONIAI A F TANNIAI MATRI
      TERENTIAI T F SECVNDAI VXORI
      C VETVRIVS A F LEG V̄ [VRB]
      TESTAMENTO FIERI IV[SSIT]

      V 2518

19.   T VIBIO T F RO[M]
      CENT LEG V̄

      V 2519

21.   .....IVS T F ROM
      ....ER SIBI ET
      ....IO T F PATRI AC
      .....GN CHOR V̄...

      V 8846

20.   ..Q.....F   ROM
      [LEGI]ON[E] XII

      V 2520

22.   M' CAESIVS L F
      ROM LEG IIII
      MACEDONIC
      AQVILIFER
        T F I

      V *Sup.* 514

23. L VILLIVS P F
    ROM LEG
       XI̅

NS 1891, 217

24. L BLATTIVS L F RO[M]
  VETVS   CENT   LEG I[V]
  M[AC]EDON   ADLE[CT]
    [DE]CVRIO

NS 1893, 58; Pl. IC

25. ....
  LEG IIII MACED
      F

(above, p. 200, n. 82)

26. M   AVFVSTIVS
    M F ROM
      ACTIACVS
  VALERIAE   C   LIB
  CHARIDI   CONIVGI
  CRYSIDI F ANN XX OCCISAE
  C ALBIO C LIB SABINO
    CONTVBERNALI

V 890 (Aquileia)

27.   OSSA
  SALVI [S]EMPRONI
   C [F] ROM
  LEG XI A[C]TIACO
  LICINIA L [F] F

V 2839 (Patavium)

Beneventum

28. .....ONIVS P F STE LEG V
  .....BANO ET SECVNDO
  .....T L ORIGO CONCVBINA ANTONIA T L CALE

IX 1502

29. L ACILIO A F STE LEG VI
    MARCIA TERTIA
    VXOR FECIT

IX 1601

30. M ALBIO M F STE LEG
    XXX SIGNIFERO
  ALBIAE M L HILARAE
  CVRTIAI P L CHILAE
  EPAPHRODITVS ET CELER
  LIBERTI F C

IX 1603 = *ILS* 2235

31. AVIDIENO T F STE LEG ..
    CENTVRIONI
    DECVRIONI

IX 1604 = *ILS* 6491

32. C CLODIO P F STE LEG XXX
  ET VALERIAE SEX L
    [DI]ODORAE
    H   F   C

IX 1605

33. C FIGILIO L F STE LEG VI
    MANLIAI P F
    H   F   C

IX 1606

34. T FLAVIO T F STE
  TITVLLO LEG XX
  T FLAVIVS T L FAVSTVS
  SIBI ET PATRONO

IX 1608

35. FVFIA Ɔ L LYCHNIS SIBI ET
    M CRASSICIO M F STE CASTELLO
            VIRO LEG XXX
    TESTAMENT SVO FIERI IVSSIT

    IX 1610

36. L LABICIO L F STE CELERO
            LEG VI FERRATA

    IX 1613

37.   EX TESTAMENTO
    C LISIDIO M F STE LEG XXX
    M LISIDIO Q F PVB PATRI
    HELVIAE C L RVFAE MATRI
    LISIDIAE   C L   PRIMAE
    LISIDIAE C L CHRESTAE
    C LISIDIO C L FAVSTO
        H   M   H   N   S

    IX 1616

38. ..[P]OMPEIVS T F STE
            LEG XXX

    IX 1620

39. ....
    .....STEL LEG VI
            AED
    ....E VXSORI ET
    ..... Ɔ L QVARTAE

    IX 1622

40. T   RVF.......
      LEG V̄...
      FVTILI[A]......
          IA.....

    IX 1623

41. ....O C F STE L VI ET
    ....O C L L PILOMVSO ET
    ....E C L EDONIONI ET
    ....AE CN L SATVRNINAE
    ....VM M SEMMIVS M F ET P SEXTVLEI[VS]
          [F]   C
    [QVOD PR]O SVA PARTE FACERE NO[LVERVNT]

    IX 1624

42. A S I L A N V S
    I S T E S I C I L
    SIGNIFER SIBI
    ID SILANO ET
    FRATRI SVO IN
    FR XII IN AGR XII
            P   P

    IX 1625

43. Q   TETARFEN[VS L F STE]
            LEG VI
    C TETARFENVS L F FR[ATRI]
        FACIVNDVM C[VRAVIT]

    IX 1626

44. ....INIO T F STE
    LEG XXX
    TESTAMENTO
    H   F   C

    IX 1629

45. ....SP F STE
   X
    ....F SECVNDA

    IX 1957

46. P SERTORIO   M   F   STE
    LEG   VI   M'   SERTORIVS
    M F STE FRATER TESTAMEN
        SVO FIERI IVSSIT

    IX 2091

47. ....LIVS
......F STE
LEG XXX
HEIC SITVS
IN AG P XII
IN FRO P X

IX 2099

48. P CLODIVS P F STE PIVS LEG XX[X]
DVM VIXI VIXI QVOMODO
CONDECET INGENVOM QV
OD COMEDI ET EBIBI TANTVM MEV EST

IX 2114 = *ILS* 8155

49. SAL CVRTIO L F STEL
LEG XXX ET
CVRTIAE VXORI
CVRTIA SAL F
POLLA VIXIT ANN XII

IX 2115

50. L ROMANIO........
XX...
L ROMANIO L......
ROMANIAE L.......
ROMANIA L ....
SIBI E[T SVIS]

Rivista Indo-greca-italica
viii (1924), 148, no. 9

51. C NVMISIVS C L AMPHIO AVG
SIBI [ET]
C NVMISIO Q F STEL LEG VI PATRONO
NVMISIAE C L SECVNDAE CONCVBIN
C NVMISIO C L PRIMO C NVMISIO C AVCTO
NVMISIAE C L PEREGRINAE

AE 1968, 127

52. SEX AEQVANIVS SEX F
STEL LEG XXX

IX 2167 (*ager Caudinus*)

53. P MANLIO P F STEL
    LEGIONIS $\overline{\text{XXX}}$

    IX 2217 (Telesia)

54. L CAIENO Q F
    VEL LEG VI
    EXS TESTAME

    Quarta miscellanea greca e romana
    (Roma, 1975), 245, no. 11
    (*ager Telesinus*)

55. C VALERIVS C F AEM ARSACES
    LEGIONE V ALAVDAE
        SIBI ET
    VALERIAE C L VRBANAE
    CONCVBINAE SVAE EX
    TESTAMENTO FIERI IVSSIT

    IX 1460 (Ligures Baebiani)

Bergomum
56. ...SEMPRONIO
    C F LEG XI[X?]

    V 5126a

(*Bovianum*)
57.
M PAPIVS SEX F VOL SEX PAPIVS N F C PAPIVS SEX F L PAPIVS SEX F VO[L]
....[PR]IMVS PRINCEPS TERTIVS
....L $\overline{\text{XXXIII}}$
....COERARVNT

    IX 2770 = *ILS* 2234 = *ILLRP* 499

Brixia
58. M MVTELLIVS
    M F FAB
    LEG $\overline{\text{X}}$ T F I

    V 4987

Cales

59. M   AEMILI   M   F   POB
        SOTERIAE EQVITIS DOMO
     OSCENSIS TORQVIBVS ARMILL
        PHALERIS AB IMPERATORE
        DONATVS MILITIS MISSICI
     VETERANI LEG VIIII HISPANIES
     HIC   OSSA   SITA   SVNT

     EE VIII 530 = *ILS* 2321

Capua

60. M BRITIVS M L   M   BRITI[VS]
     PHILAROS PATER   SPVRI   F   MILES
     FECIT   BRITIA M L   DE LE VII P OHSS
                           LAIS MATER
                              VIVIT

     X 3884

61. C   C A N V L E I V S
     Q   F   LEG   VII   EVO
     CAT MORT EST ANN NAT
     XXXV DONAT TORQ ARMIL
        PALER   CORON
     Q   C A N V L E I V S Q F
        LEG VII OCCEIS IN GALL
        ANNOR NAT XVIII
              DVO   FRATR
     IEIS   MONVM   PAT   FEC

     X 3886 = *ILS* 2225 = *ILLRP* 497; Pl. IA

62. P FELSINIVS L F FAL
     Q FELSINIVS L F FAL
        LEG   X
           SIGNIFER

     X 3887

63. L MAGIO M F FAL
     VETERANO LEG X
     FRETENSIS
        MARCIO L
     PATRO[NO ET] SIBI

     X 3890

64. C   SERTORI
    C F LABEON
CLASS OSSA HIC
   SITA   SVNT

   X 3894

65. Fragments of a large slab commemorating L. Antistius Campanus,
deductus a[b hoc in coloniam] nostram. Full text at X 3903 = *EJ*[2] 329.

Cremona

66. C   LANIVS
C F ANI DE
LEG X VENER
L LANIVS C L
EROS   FILIVS
   DE SVO

   V 4191 = *ILS* 2241

67. C DOMITIVS C [F]
LEGIONE II SIB[I]
[ET D]OMITIAE SOR[ORI]
       F

Boll. Stor. Crem. xx (1955–57), 175

68. .....IVS NAE[VI]
VS TER F LEG X[V]
APOLLIN ....

Pontiroli, *Catalogo* no. 252

69. ..ARRVNTIVS   ARRVNTIA C L   ARRVNTIA   ARRVNTIA
MAXVMVS   CALLINICI   C F   C F
..N LEG IIX   MATRI V F   TERTIA   [QVARTA]
               TESTA[MENTO]

Pontiroli, *Catalogo* no. 249

70. T APONIVS P   F
A N I S I G N I F E R
LEG IX HISPANIEN
VETERA DONA TORQ
ARMILLIS PHALERIS
L   APONIVS P   F
FRATRI   FECIT

Pontiroli, *Catalogo* no. 257

Fanum

71. ....RIVS C F
    POL   MILES   LEG
    VIII   VETERAN
    ORIVNDVS   TVDER
    HIC   SITVS   EST

    XI 6351

Firmum

72.   C VETTI L F
      VEL   TVSCI
      LEGIONIS IIII
      MACEDONICAE
      AQVILIFEREI

    IX 5527 = *ILS* 2340

Hadria

73.   ......ARIVS
      ....MAE PIVS
      .....LEG XXIX
      HIC SEPVLTVS EST
          IN SVO

    (above, p. 180)

Hispellum

74.   CN DECIMIVS CN F LEM
            BIBVLVS
      EVOCATVS   LEG XIII
            VI VIR

    XI 5275 = *ILS* 6619a

75.   C ALLIO L F
          LEM
      CENTVRIONI
        LEG XIII

    XI 1933 (Perusia)

Locri

76.   ATICIVS   T   F   POL
      MVTINA   >   L   XXX
          CLASSICAE

    X 18 = *ILS* 2232

Luceria

77.   L ANICIVS L F CLA LEC ...
            SITVS

    IX 794

78.   Q   HELVI[VS]
      BASSVS CEN[T]
      OPPIA   V...
      ......

    IX 796

79.   Q NONIVS Q F
            CLA
      LEG VI SITVS

    IX 797

80.   L LICIN....
          L F
      CENT....

    IX 863

81.

M VECILIVS M F L N CAMPVS PRAEF FABR TR MIL II V[IR IVR]DIC
PONTIFEX/AMPHITHEATRVM LOCO PRIVATO SVO ET MACERIAM
CIRCVM IT SVA PEC IN HONOR IMP CAESARIS AVGVST[I]/
COLONIAEQVE LVCERIAE F C

    AE 1938, 110

82.   Q CVRIVS L F   L CVR[IVS]   L CVRIVS L F
        LEG I   PAT[ER]   LEG I

      AE 1969/1970, 158

83.   Q LE[.]GENIVS STA F
      CLA LE[G] P[RIMA]
        SITVS EST

      AE 1976, 168

84.   .L]OLLIVS L F CLA LIBO
        BVCINATOR   LEG I

      AE 1976, 169

Minturnae
85.   Q ANCHARI
           C F POL
      NARBONES EQVES
      EVOCATVS ANNOR
      NAT XXIII ALA
           SCAEVAE

      X 6011 = *ILS* 2490 = *ILLRP* 498

Nuceria
86.   M   VIRTIO   L   F
        MEN PATRI
      VETERANO LEGIONIS
           XĪX

      AE 1974, 283

Parentium
87.   L   VINVSIVS
           L F VETER
          LEG   VIIII
          TRIVMPH
          SEPTVMIAE
        P   F   SABINAE
            VXORI
      VINVSIAE TERTV
      LLAE   F   ANNO
              X

      V 397 = *ILS* 2240 = *IIt* X. 2. 242

Parma

88. ....TERTIA   L   VETTIDIVS   C   F
        [VXO]R   VETERANVS LEG XII
                                   PATERNAE SEX VIR AED

        XI 1058 = *ILS* 2242

Pisae

89. [SE]X ANQVRINNIO L F
        GALERIA LEG XIX
        Q T ANQVRINNI EX
        TESTAMENTO POSVERV

        XI 1524 = *IIt* VII. 1. 114

Pola

90.

L SERGIVS C F   SALVIA POSTVMA SERGI   L SERGIVS L F   CN SERGIVS C F
  AED II VIR   LEPIDVS AED   AED II VIR QVINÇ
                                                     TR MIL LEG XXIX

        SALVIA POSTVMA SERGI DE SVA PECVNIA

V 50 = *ILS* 2229 = *IIt* X. 1. 72

Sora

91. L   FIRMIO   L   F
        PRIM PIL TR MIL
        IIII   VIR   I   D
        COLONIA DEDVCTA
          PRIM PONTIFICI
        LEGIO IIII SORANA
        HONORIS ET VIRTVTIS
               CAVSSA

        X 5713 = *ILS* 2226

Teanum

92.   C CABILENVS C F FAL
        GALLVS LEG VIII MVTINENSIS

        X 4786 = *ILS* 2239

Tuder

93. [Q] CAECILIO   Q   F
          ATTICO TRI MIL
        [C]OLONI LEG XXXXI

        XI 4650 (cf. 4651–53) = *ILS* 2230

94. C EDVSIVS SEX F CLV
     N A T V S   M E V A N I A E
     CENTVRIO LEGION XXXXI
     A V G V S T I C A E S A R I S
     ET CENTVRIO CLASSICVS
     E X   T E S T A M E N T O

     XI 4654 = *ILS* 2231

95. C ALLIENVS T F VOL
        CENTVRIO

     XI 4649

Venafrum
96. C   ACLVTIVS L F   TER GALLVS
        DVOVIR VRBIS MOENIVNDAE BIS
        PRAEFECTVS IVRE DEICVNDO BIS
        DVOVIR IVRE DEICVNDO TR MIL
        LEGIONIS [PR]IMAE TR MILITVM
        LEGIONIS SECVNDAE SABINAE

     X 4876 = *ILS* 2227

Venusia
97. C OPPIO T F
          HOR
     LEG XII CHORT
     PRIM   OPTION
      PHILARGYRVS
           L

     IX 435

INDEX

abalienatio, 95
Abellinum, 19 n.
Acci, 64 n., 174 n.
Acerrae, 79 n., 120
Acilius, L. (Sylloge 29), 160, 214
Aclutius Gallus, C. (Sylloge 96), 107, 109, 119, 121, 139, 223
Actiaci, 33, 44, 111 f., 196
Actium, settlement after battle at, 69 ff.
adscriptio colonorum, 81
adsignatio, 96
Aebutius Rufus, C. (Sylloge 3), 200, 212
aedes Augusti, 133, 184
Aemilius Lepidus, M. (*cos.* 46, 42), 17 n., 24 f., 29, 34 f., 57, 61, 66 f., 70, 73 ff., 80 f., 142, 155, 191, 194 n.
Aemilius Soterias, M. (Sylloge 59), 85, 218
Aequanius, Sex. (Sylloge 52), 157, 161, 216
Aequum, 209 n.
aerarium militare, 208
Aesernia, 9, 55 n., 79 n., 85
Aesis, 100
Africani (milites), 111 n.
ager Campanus, 89, 92, 95, 98, 114, 138, 143 ff., 148, 150
ager Falernus, 144
ager publicus, 48 f., 54, 87 f., 95, 99, 145
ager scamnatus, 100
ager Semurius, 106
ager Stellas, 144
ager strigatus, 100
agriculture, 100 f., 122 ff., 130
Agrigentum, 103
Aiedius, C. (Sylloge 1), 137, 212, pl. VIII
ala Scaevae, 142, 221
Alba Fucens, 43
Albius, M. (Sylloge 30), 157, 160, 214
Alexandria, 41, 43, 127 n.
Alexandria Troas, 80, 83, 121 n.
Alfaterni, 151
Alfenus Varus, P. (*cos.* 39), 59, 191
Allienus, C. (Sylloge 95), 177, 223
Allifae, 62 n.
Allius, C. (Sylloge 4), 200, 212
Allius, C. (Sylloge 75), 179, 220
allotments, 91 ff., 106, 122 ff., 207
Altinum, 85, 118 n.
Amatius, 113 n.
amphitheatres, 116 ff., 133, 137 n., 145, 148, 150 ff., 163 n., 164 f., 169, 171, 175 n., 177, 181, 204
Anagnia, 5 n., 9 n.

Ancharius, L., 107 n.
Ancharius, Q. (Sylloge 85), 142, 221
Ancona, 6 f., 20, 32, 54, 55 n., 63 f., 66 ff., 79 n., 100, 109 n., 119, 133, 176, 184
Anicius, L. (Sylloge 77), 164, 220
Anqurinnius, Sex. (Sylloge 89), 173 f., 222
Antiochia Pisidiae, 46, 64 n., 91, 120 n., 126 n.
Antistius Campanus, L. (Sylloge 65), 108 f., 145 n., 146, 219
Antium, 6 ff., 135, 210 f.
Antonius, C. (*pr.* 44), 23 n.
Antonius, L. (*cos.* 41), 23, 29, 43, 53 n., 59 f., 62, 67, 69, 106 n., 127, 140, 170, 178, 189, 203 n.
Antonius, M. (*cos.* 44), 16 f., 41, 50, 52 ff., 60 ff., 73, 81, 91, 96, 105, 110 n., 114, 127, 136, 155 f., 185, 189, 196, pl. VIIB; his legions, 24 ff., 74 ff., 79 ff; his colonies, 17, 66, 114, 187 f., 191; his agrarian legislation, 87, 105 f., 108
Aosta, *see* Augusta Praetoria
Aponius, T. (Sylloge 70), 192, 219
Appuleius Saturninus, L. (*tr. pl.* 103, 100), 39, 92
Aprum, 209 n.
aqueducts, 115 ff., 120 ff., 133, 137 f., 141, 145, 169, 192, 204
Aquileia, 6 ff., 91, 110 n., 111, 130, 135, 196
Aquinum, 6, 20, 63 f., 67, 93, 119 f., 133, 137 f., 212
Arausio, 73, 83, 94, 99 n., 149 n., 167 n.
arches, 115 ff., 169, 173 n., 185
Arelate, 24 n., 32 n., 58, 64, 66, 73, 83, 142, 155
Ariovistus, 30
Ariminum, 6, 15 ff., 20, 61, 63, 67 f., 86, 91, 115 f., 119, 133, 184, 187
army
   age of recruits, 38; booty, 36; conscription, 37; donatives, 38 ff., 74, 126; length of service, 35 ff., 210 f; of Roman Empire, 37, 130, 208 ff., 210 f; pay, 35 ff., 38 ff; rewards of service, 38 ff., 208; *vacatio militiae*, 36 n; see also centurions, *cohortes praetoriae, cohortes urbanae, evocati*, legions, *speculatores*, tribunes
Arna, 179
Arretium, 54 f., 57 f., 79 n., 102 f., 131 n., 163, 167, 187
Arruntius, L. (*cos.* 22), 116 n.
Arruntius Maxumus (Sylloge 69), 192, 219
Asetium, 5 n., 62 n.
Asculum, 6 f., 13, 20, 29 n., 63, 67, 90, 119 f., 133, 180 f.
Asinius Pollio, C. (*cos.* 40), 25, 29, 59, 61, 66 f., 156

PLATE I

Photo: Museo Campano (Capua)

A: Stone commemorating the brothers
Canuleius, a soldier and a veteran of legion
VII (Capua). Sylloge 61

*Photo: L. J. F. Keppie (Museo Civico,
Vicenza)*

B: Stone commemorating M. Billienus, veteran
of legion XI (Ateste). Sylloge 6

Photos: Museo Nazionale Atestino (Este)

C: Stone commemorating the centurion L. Blattius Vetus (Ateste); front and side views. Sylloge 24

Photo: Museo Nazionale Atestino (Este)
A: Stone commemorating C. Talponius, veteran of
legion XI (Ateste). Sylloge 14

Photo: Museum of Fine Arts (Boston)
B: Stone commemorating P. Gessius and *familia* (Viterbo)

PLATE II

PLATE III

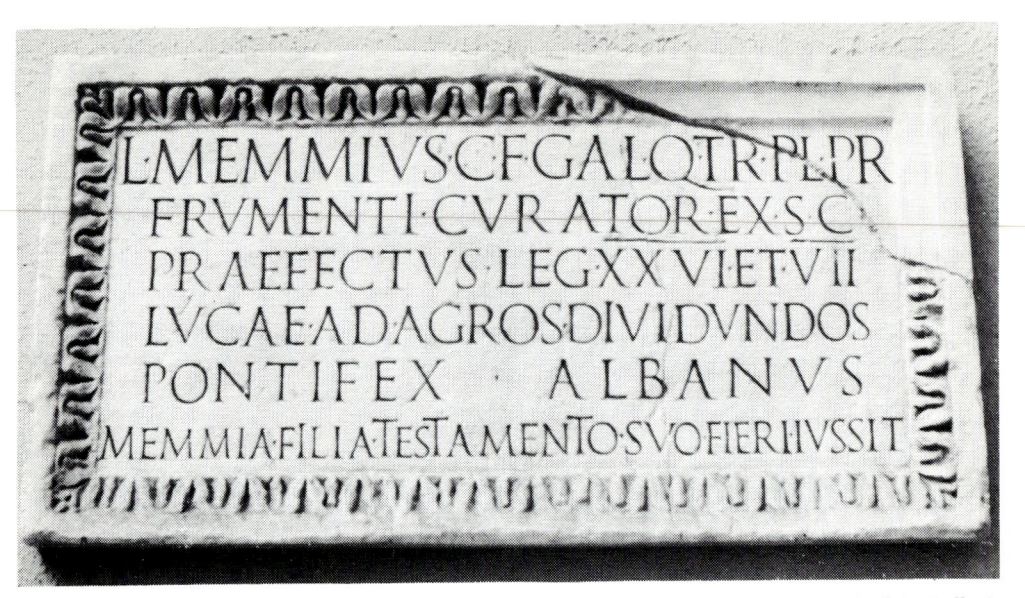

Photo: L. J. F. Keppie, of copy in Museo della Civiltà Romana, Rome; original in Galleria Lapidaria, Vatican

A: Stone honouring L. Memmius, *praefectus* of legions XXVI and VII at Luca

Photo: L. J. F. Keppie

B: Hispellum, the west gate ('Porta Venere'), with a view of the Pianura Umbra

PLATE IV

Photo: Ministry of Defence, Crown Copyright reserved. Reproduced from J. P. Bradford,
Ancient Landscapes (London, 1957), with the permission of Bell & Hyman Ltd.
Aerial photograph of countryside near Pola (Pula, Yugoslavia), showing square *centuriae* of
200 *iugera,* and some evidence of subdivision into plots of 50 *iugera*

PLATE V

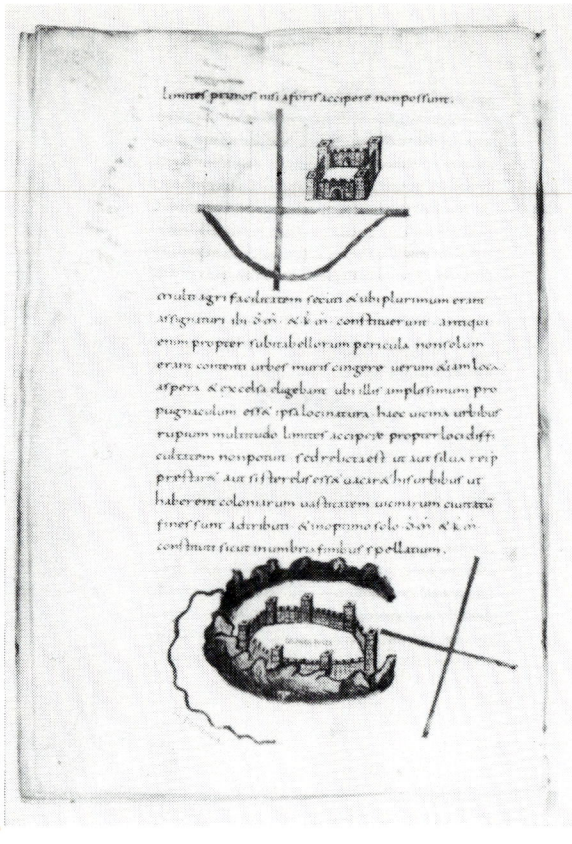

Photos: Biblioteca Apostolica Vaticana
Illustration in the Palatine manuscript of Hyginus Gromaticus, *De Limitibus Constituendis,* showing colony at Hispellum

PLATE VI

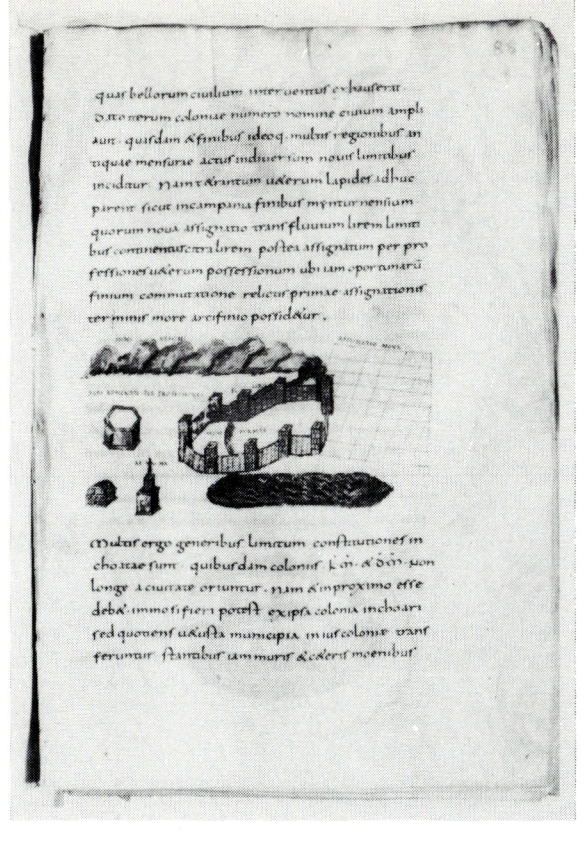

Illustration in the Palatine manuscript of Hyginus Gromaticus, *De Limitibus Constituendis*, showing colony at Minturnae

PLATE VII

Photos: Hunter Coin Cabinet, University of Glasgow
A: *Denarius* of Octavian, 29-27 B.C.

Obv.: head of Apollo

Rev.: Octavian in priestly garb, ploughing the sacred furrow; legend IMP(*erator*) CAESAR

Photos: Hunter Coin Cabinet, University of Glasgow
B: *Denarius* of Antony, 32-31 B.C.

Obv.: galley with standard at prow; legend: ANT(*onius*) AVG(*ur*) IIIVIR R(*ei*) P(*ublicae*) C(*onstituendae*)

Rev.: Legionary *aquila* between two standards; legend: LEG(*ionis*) XII ANTIQVAE

PLATE VIII

Photo: L. J. F. Keppie
Stone commemorating C. Aiedius, veteran of legion III (Aquinum). Sylloge 1